WILLIAM
STILL

Frontispiece. William Still (1821–1902), chairman of the Vigilance Committee of the Pennsylvania Anti-Slavery Society and coordinator of the Underground Railroad's Eastern Line. (Wood engraving, ca. 1865. William Still, *The Underground Railroad* [Philadelphia: Porter and Coates, 1872].)

WILLIAM STILL

THE UNDERGROUND RAILROAD

AND THE ANGEL AT PHILADELPHIA

WILLIAM C. KASHATUS

University of Notre Dame Press

Notre Dame, Indiana

Published by the University of Notre Dame Press
Notre Dame, Indiana 46556
undpress.nd.edu

Library of Congress Control Number: 2020950362

ISBN: 978-0-268-20036-7 (Hardback)
ISBN: 978-0-268-20037-4 (WebPDF)
ISBN: 978-0-268-20038-1 (Epub)

This book was selected as the 2021 Giles Family Fund Recipient. The University of Notre Dame Press and the author thank the Giles family for their generous support.

Giles Family Fund Recipients

2019   *The Glory and the Burden: The American Presidency from FDR to Trump*, Robert Schmuhl

2020   *Ars Vitae: The Fate of Inwardness and the Return of the Ancient Arts of Living*, Elisabeth Lasch-Quinn

2021   *William Still: The Underground Railroad and the Angel at Philadelphia*, William C. Kashatus

The Giles Family Fund supports the work and mission of the University of Notre Dame Press to publish books that engage the most enduring questions of our time. Each year the endowment helps underwrite the publication and promotion of a book that sparks intellectual exploration and expands the reach and impact of the university.

To the memory of

JAMES McGOWAN,

who inspired me, and to my colleagues

at the Chester County Historical Society,

who sustained me.

To the angel of the church in Philadelphia write: These are the words of the One who is holy and true, who holds the key of David. What He opens, no one will shut; and what He shuts, no one will open. I know your deeds. I have placed before you an open door, which no one can shut.

—Revelation 3:7–8

CONTENTS

FIGURES

TABLES

ACKNOWLEDGMENTS

This book would not have come to fruition without the inspiration, guidance, and encouragement of many individuals. At the top of the list is the late James McGowan, an African American historian and dear friend who inspired my initial interest in the Underground Railroad. His work on Quaker stationmaster Thomas Garrett brought us together when I was a high school student. Over the years, Garrett and Jim's interest in Harriet Tubman continued to provide many hours of fruitful conversation on our travels to history conferences in Pennsylvania, Delaware, and New Jersey. In 2005, Jim began working on a database of the 995 fugitive slaves who came under the care of William Still. When he became ill and it was clear that he would not be able to complete the database or the study, he asked that I complete the project and find a publisher. Sadly, Jim died in 2008. I will always be grateful for his friendship and collegiality.

I am also grateful to my colleagues at the Chester County Historical Society, where I worked from 1998 to 2003, specifically Roland Woodward, Barbara Jobe, Susanne Halstead, Michael Dolan, Sarah Wesley, Pam Powell, Ellen Endslow, Rob Lukens, Diane and Laurie Rofini, and Sanderson Caesar. Without their constant support and guidance, I would not have been able to pursue my dream of curating *Just over the Line: Chester County and the Underground Railroad*. Despite my constant pestering, complaining, and cajoling, these folks created the first multimedia exhibition in the nation. Not only was the exhibit recognized by the *Journal of American History* as a "first rate exhibit and model of outreach to the local community," but it also won the American Association of Local Historical Societies and Museums 2005 Award of Merit. Pam, Diane, and Laurie also encouraged my work on William Still and helped me find material for it.

I hope my colleagues at CCHS will accept this book dedication as a small token of my appreciation for all they did to inspire and sustain my interest in—

which later became my passion for—the Underground Railroad. I am grateful to others as well.

When I left CCHS in 2003, I was compelled to abandon my plans for writing a biography of William Still for many years. Family responsibilities, a job change that took me out of the Philadelphia area, and life itself intervened until the spring of 2016, when I was able to take a sabbatical and focus entirely on this project. I am grateful to Janis Wilson Seeley, chair of the Social Sciences / History Department at Luzerne County Community College, as well as Dana Clark, dean of faculty, and President Tom Leary, as well as the Board of Trustees for granting me that opportunity.

Special thanks are also due to Spencer Crew of George Washington University, Lois Horton of George Mason University, Phil Lapsansky of the Library Company of Philadelphia, Tom Hamm of the Quaker Archives at Earlham College, and Christopher Densmore of Friends Historical Library at Swarthmore College for reviewing and commenting on earlier drafts of the manuscript; Doug Uhlmann of the William Penn Charter School for reviewing and offering suggestions on the statistical data; Aslaku Berhanu of the Charles L. Blockson Afro-American Collection at Temple University; Krystal Appiah of the Library Company of Philadelphia; the entire staff of the Historical Society of Pennsylvania for their assistance in making available to me various editions of Still's *The Underground Railroad*, Journal C, and other manuscripts, images, and secondary sources pertaining to his personal and professional life; and Eli Bortz, editor-in-chief at the University of Notre Dame Press, and his production team, especially Elisabeth Magnus, who strengthened the original manuscript with her personal insight and editorial expertise.

Finally, I am grateful to my parents, William and Balbina, and to my spouse, Jackie, and our three sons, Tim, Peter, and Ben. Few men admit to having heroes. I am fortunate to have been raised by, to be married to, and to have fathered mine. The love I have for them is eternal.

Introduction

On August 6, 1850, Peter Freedman, an ex-slave who had recently purchased his freedom, arrived at the office of the Pennsylvania Anti-Slavery Society (PASS) in Philadelphia. The City of Brotherly Love was a nerve center of abolitionist activity because of its large Quaker and free black populations. There he met William Still, a free black abolitionist and mail clerk at the PASS. Freedman, worn down by years of hard labor, looked much older than his fifty years. For more than an hour, the former slave recounted his life's story, explaining that he was searching for his mother, from whom he had been separated some forty years earlier. Still sat and listened, transfixed by the tragic tale.

According to Freedman, he and his younger brother Levin had been "kidnapped" from their mother, whom he referred to as "Sidney." "Carried south," Levin had died a slave in Alabama, but Peter had earned the $500 necessary to purchase his own "ransom" from his owner, a Jewish merchant named Joseph Friedman. With no knowledge of the last names of his mother and father, or where he was born, Peter set out to find his mother. His search took him to Philadelphia, where he planned to have notices read in the African American churches of the city in the hope that some of the older members might recall his mother's circumstances.

As Still listened to the stranger's story, he was struck by the similarities to his own mother's past. Charity Still had been born, raised, and wed in slavery on Maryland's Eastern Shore. She and her husband, Levin, were the young parents of four small children, two boys and two girls. Levin purchased his own freedom, resettled in Burlington County, New Jersey, and became a farmer, hoping to save enough money to secure the manumission of his wife and their children, who remained in bondage. Charity and her two daughters rejoined Levin after a successful escape but were forced to leave behind her two sons, eight-year-old Levin and six-year-old Peter. But the similarities ended there.[1]

Could "Sidney" actually be Charity Still?

Though William was the youngest of the fourteen children Charity had borne in freedom, he was the one most curious about his mother's bondage. That curiosity and, according to family lore, the knowledge that he had two older brothers who remained in slavery, inspired him to take the job as clerk at the Pennsylvania Anti-Slavery Society in 1847.

Indeed, Charity Still had reason to be secretive about her early life. After she escaped, she changed her name from "Sidney" in order to protect her safety and that of her rescued daughters. At the same time, she remained heartbroken over the two sons she had left behind.

Listening to Peter's tale, William couldn't help but notice the facial resemblance between Freedman and his mother. "I could see in the face of my new-found brother the likeness of my mother," he wrote of the moment he realized that Peter was the older brother he had never met. "My feelings were unutterable."[2]

"I think I can tell you all about your kinfolk, because you are my own brother," confessed Still, after regaining his composure. He went on to assure Peter by offering a detailed account of their mother's history, her escape, and how she had been forced to leave her two young sons in bondage.

The next day, the two brothers traveled to Burlington, New Jersey, just across the Delaware River from Philadelphia, where Peter was reunited with his eighty-year-old mother. Four years later, Peter, with William's help, freed his wife and three children whom he had left behind in slavery. They settled on a ten-acre farm in Burlington, where Peter lived until he died in 1868.[3]

The reunion with his long-lost brother Peter reinforced Still's commitment to assist fugitives who also longed to be reunited with their families. To that end, he and his wife, Letitia George, often hid runaways in their own home at 832 South Street. He also communicated with dozens of stationmasters and conductors. With their assistance, Still coordinated the movements of hundreds of fugitives along the Eastern Line of the Underground Railroad from Northern Virginia to Canada. Although his activities were in direct violation of the federal Fugitive Slave Act of 1850, Still assisted nearly one thousand slaves to freedom between 1853 and 1861. In the process, he earned the endearing moniker "Angel at Philadelphia." Fortunately for historians, Still interviewed every freedom seeker who came into his care, eventually compiling the information into a 780-page book titled *The Underground Railroad*, published in 1872. The work is considered to be the most authentic source on the secret route to freedom.[4]

"Underground Railroad" (UGRR) was a code name for the clandestine movement of African American slaves escaping out of the South to a loosely organized network of abolitionists who assisted them to freedom in the North. While the enterprise began sometime after 1780 with the Gradual Abolition Act in Pennsylvania, the UGRR was most active between 1835 and 1865.[5] Traffic along the illegal route increased significantly after the passage of the Fugitive Slave Act in 1850, which greatly strengthened a similar 1793 law. The 1850 measure not only gave slaveholders the right to organize a posse anywhere in the United States to assist in recapturing a runaway but obligated courts, federal marshals, and bystanders to assist in the recapture.[6]

Abolitionists adopted the vocabulary of the railroad to speak in code about their illegal activity. *Underground* suggested a secret, and *railroad* a method of transportation. Abolitionists who opened their homes to runaways were referred to as stationmasters, and their homes as stations. Other abolitionists who guided fugitives between stations were called conductors. "Stockholders" played a less dangerous—and less conspicuous role, but one that was extremely important. They provided the finances needed for bribes, transportation, food, and clothing.[7]

William Still served in all three capacities: stationmaster, conductor, and stockholder. As chairman of the PASS's General Vigilance Committee, he raised funds, corresponded with stationmasters and conductors, and coordinated the movements of fugitives along the Eastern Line of the UGRR, which originated in Virginia, extended through the border states of Maryland and Delaware into Pennsylvania, went on into New York or New England, and ended in Canada. He stocked a storehouse of food and clothing for runaways at his office at 31 North Fifth Street and aided in many daring escapes.[8]

Vigilance committees, which existed in many northern cities, were the most structured vehicles of the UGRR. In Philadelphia, Quakers established and supported the PASS, but working-class blacks served as the backbone of its vigilance committee. Free blacks sheltered and transported fugitives and gathered and relayed crucial information to Still. Others kept watch for suspicious whites they observed in the hotels or boardinghouses or on the streets of the city. Many of the Vigilance Committee members belonged to Mother Bethel, the city's oldest and largest African Methodist Episcopal (AME) church, organized in 1794 by the Reverend Richard Allen, a former Delaware slave.[9]

Acting from a sense of personal obligation to their enslaved brethren, Philadelphia's free black community raised the bulk of the Vigilance Committee's operating funds from African American benevolent societies and AME Church–affiliated auxiliaries.[10] Their success is reflected in the number of runaways they assisted, which has been estimated at 495 between December 1852 and February 1857.[11] Without Still's intellect and energy to coordinate such an extensive network, however, the Vigilance Committee would not have been very effective. Deservedly, William Still, at his death in 1902, was known as "Father of the Underground Railroad" throughout the nation.[12]

Until the late twentieth century, historians ignored William Still's antislavery activities. Instead, the white abolitionists who wrote early accounts of the Underground Railroad tended to emphasize their own heroics, omitting the contributions of others, most notably the free black community and the fugitives themselves. Often these accounts gave rise to a mythology embellished and replicated in subsequent novels, plays, and, in some cases, historical monographs.[13] The result was an overemphasis on white abolitionist involvement, particularly among Quakers, while fugitives were depicted as helpless, frightened passengers who took advantage of a well-organized national network. It was an oversimplification of a complex historical phenomenon that involved many religious groups as well as free blacks and fugitives themselves.

Further complicating matters was the failure to distinguish between the *mythology*, based on tradition, fiction, or convenience rather than fact, and *folklore*, based on the oral testimonies of African Americans. Folklore consists of customs, pastimes, songs, stories, and material culture that are grounded in fact and are often presented in tangible objects, such as arts and crafts. Quilts, for example, were believed to be used as a covert method of communication to aid runaways in their escape, though no primary source documentation exists to support this popular belief.[14] According to folklore, spirituals and popular slave songs also contained codes. "Follow the Drinking Gourd" directed slaves to follow a particular route of escape by way of the North Star. Similarly, "Go Down,

Moses" announced the arrival of conductor Harriet Tubman, the so-called "Moses" of her people, and an impending escape.[15] While folklore and oral testimonies are controversial because they lack corroboration in written documentation, these sources are central to the African American experience and must be addressed in any examination of the UGRR. Because most slaves could not read or write, they were dependent on oral testimonies to tell their history. Additionally, storytelling was fundamentally important to most African cultures as a method of transmitting their history across generations.[16]

Not until the 1960s were the mythology and the folklore addressed by historians. Larry Gara was the first to identify the important roles of the fugitives and the free black community. He argued that the post–Civil War reminiscences by fame-hungry abolitionists and oral tradition exaggerated the history and operation of the UGRR. In *Liberty Line: The Legend of the Underground Railroad* (1961), Gara argued that free blacks like William Still were indispensable to the success of the UGRR and that the fugitive slaves themselves took an active role in their own escapes, receiving aid only after they had reached the border states.[17] Horatio Strother provided a test case for Gara's argument with his examination of fugitives who escaped to Connecticut.[18] Benjamin Quarles added another important corrective with the publication of *Black Abolitionists* (1969). Quarles proved that free blacks played the most significant role in the northern vigilance committees, established to protect fugitives from the slave hunters who pursued them across the Mason-Dixon Line.[19]

In 1977, James A. McGowan offered a more balanced treatment of the UGRR by emphasizing the interracial nature of the enterprise in his biography of Thomas Garrett, a white Quaker stationmaster. McGowan documented the partnership between Garrett and the free black community on the Eastern Line. He also gave long overdue credit to William Still and other African American agents, showing that the success of the movement was largely due to interracial cooperation.[20]

During the 1980s, Charles L. Blockson renewed interest in the UGRR, particularly among African Americans. Blockson, in a series of works, stressed the larger—and more aggressive—role played by African Americans and their churches as most critical to the success of the UGRR. He based his research on family oral history and local records that had previously been ignored by scholars.[21]

Public fascination with the UGRR grew in the 1990s when President Bill Clinton initiated a national dialogue on race. Both black and white Americans looked to the UGRR as a historical model of interracial cooperation and were aided by the works of a new generation of historians. James and Lois Horton quickly established themselves as the most knowledgeable scholars of the topic. Although their research focused on the free black communities of the antebellum North, the Hortons showed that those communities were able to transcend internal differences to cooperate with whites in such areas as abolitionism and involvement on the UGRR.[22] Other works examined the interracial nature and operation of the UGRR as well as the folklore in a regional context.[23] But only one of the histories offered a detailed statistical analysis of runaways themselves—*Runaway Slaves: Rebels on the Plantation*, written by John Hope Franklin and Loren Schweninger in 1999.

Investigating the "slave flight" of more than two thousand runaways between 1790 and 1860, Franklin and Schweninger conclude that the "great majority of these runaways" were "young men in their teens and twenties." They were described as having "dark [skinned] complexion" and as having "travelled alone" instead of in a group. The authors found no discernible patterns in the method of travel or in the moment in time a slave chose to escape; rather, these decisions were "determined by individual circumstances."[24] These conclusions have been accepted by others who have written about the UGRR in the early twenty-first century.[25] However, *Runaway Slaves* also differs significantly from this examination of the fugitives assisted by William Still. The difference can be attributed to the nature of primary source documentation that Franklin and Schweninger use. They rely on newspaper notices of runaway slaves and petitions to southern legislatures and county courts. These records come from five states: Virginia, North and South Carolina, Tennessee, and Louisiana. Such a geographical distribution offers a representative cross section of southern states: two in the Upper South, one between the Upper and Lower South, and two in the Lower South, three in the East, and two in the West.[26] But their data are incomplete. In addition, Franklin and Schweninger often rely on vaguely defined terms in their discussion of the legal implications of the Fugitive Slave Act of 1850. This problem has resulted in a series of misunderstandings about the actual success of the draconian measure in limiting the number of escapes that occurred in the decade of the 1850s.

While Franklin and Schweninger's random sample concentrates on runaways from the South, this study focuses on a self-contained body of documentary evidence from the border states, providing an in-depth look at one of the most important regions of UGRR activity. Other, lesser-known works have relied on William Still's book in their interpretation of the UGRR's Eastern Line, but none offer a careful statistical analysis of the nearly one thousand slaves he assisted.[27]

Between 1853 and 1861, Still personally interviewed and ascertained the needs of 995 runaway slaves. Most of the fugitives traveled the Eastern Line of the UGRR, which began in the states of Delaware and Maryland.[28] Still recorded their names as well as their age, skin color, and gender and paid careful attention to family information, such as number of siblings and names of parents, spouses, and children. He also recorded details about their bondage, including the owner's name, how they were treated, and their reason for running away. Just as important to Still were the details of their escape: point of origin, date of departure, mode of travel, reward for capture, whether they were armed, or if there was any physical violence along the route to freedom.

Still compiled the information in a series of journals and kept them in his possession until 1859, when the papers of the radical abolitionist John Brown were seized by federal authorities after his unsuccessful attempt to lead a slave insurrection. Still, fearing that his own records might be "captured by a pro-slavery mob," hid them in a Philadelphia cemetery and kept subsequent notes of his interviews "on loose slips of paper."[29] In 1872, Still published the records of 846 runaways in a 780-page book titled *The Underground Railroad*. Another 149 cases are contained in a separate "Journal C" that was never published.[30]

Still's book was reprinted in 1873, after he regained exclusive right to the publishing and distribution from Porter and Coates, the white-owned Philadelphia publishing house that produced the first edition of ten thousand copies. A second edition was published in 1883 titled *Still's Underground Railroad: With a Life of the Author* and contained James Boyd's thirty-two-page biography of the former Underground Railroad agent. In 1886, Still self-published a third and final edition with an additional twenty pages of revisions.[31] This work is based on the 1872 edition reprinted in 1970 by Johnson Publishing Company of Chicago.

William Still: The Underground Railroad and the Angel at Philadelphia is a scholarly biography of the free black Philadelphia abolitionist and the most important UGRR agent in the city. Although Still later became a fervent civil rights reformer who fought for the integration of public transportation, his story is inextricably tied to the UGRR and his published account of the clandestine route to freedom. Accordingly, this book offers a detailed statistical analysis of the 995 runaway slaves who were assisted by Still in their passage to freedom. It is important to note however, that there are inconsistencies between Still's published account and the unpublished "Journal C," which contains information on many of the same slaves whose details are given in his 1872 book. These inconsistencies occurred because of the need to hide the records from proslavery elements in the late 1850s. In some cases, Still was forced to recall the details of a conversation that might have taken place months earlier. In other cases, he simply speculated on the age or skin color of a runaway on the basis of his own observation. In this book, every effort has been made to reconcile the inconsistencies between the two sources. If a runaway is mentioned in both, the information contained in the published source is given priority in the database, while any additional information from Journal C is also integrated into the database.

William Still goes beyond the historiography on the Underground Railroad in several important ways. First, the work is the only scholarly biography of William Still, one of the most prominent figures of the UGRR and the most influential agent on the Eastern Line.[32] Second, the biography analyzes Still's own writing, which offers a self-contained body of work widely recognized by scholars as the most authentic record of the UGRR. Most of what we know about the operation of the secret network and the fugitives who traveled it came via word of mouth, slave narratives, or contemporary newspaper advertisements for runaways' capture. While some agents claimed to have assisted hundreds of runaways, none saved records as detailed as those of William Still.[33] As a result, Still's 1872 book is considered by historians, writers, and researchers as the most valuable source on the UGRR, containing primary source information about runaway slaves.

Third, the book contains an accessible and detailed database of the 995 fugitives Still assisted. The data are categorized by some twenty different fields, including name, age, gender, skin color, date of escape, place of origin, mode of transportation, and literacy. The database serves as a valuable aid for other scholars by offering the opportunity to find new information and therefore a new perspective on runaway slaves who escaped along the Eastern Line of the UGRR.

Fourth, a descriptive statistical analysis of the database is given in the context of the existing literature on slavery, abolitionism, and the UGRR. The analysis provides an important corrective to the existing historiography regarding age, skin complexion, literacy, and method of escape used by fugitives.

Finally, the Appendix to this study identifies not only the names of most fugitives who came under William Still's care during the period from 1853 to 1861 but in some cases their owners and the agents who assisted them. The names are cross-referenced with the pages on which they appear in the 1970 reprint of Still's book or in Journal C. These references are especially useful, since Still's book does not contain an index of the runaways he assisted. These contributions make *William Still* an extremely valuable work for scholars and general readers interested in the history and operation of the Underground Railroad as well as those tracing African American ancestors.

O N E

The Price of Freedom

Maryland's Eastern Shore lies on a peninsula situated between the Atlantic Coastal Plain and the Chesapeake Bay. Because the states of Delaware, Maryland, and Virginia hold shared title to the area, it is known as the Delmarva Peninsula. But Maryland is more closely identified with the land mass because of the state's central location on it. Eight counties were carved out of the region in the seventeenth and eighteenth centuries: Caroline, Cecil, Dorchester, Kent, Queen Anne's, Somerset, Talbot, and Worcester. To the north lies Pennsylvania across the Mason-Dixon Line, with Delaware to the east and north, the Atlantic Ocean to the east, and Virginia's own Eastern Shore to the south.

Deer, Canada geese, black ducks, and mallards are plentiful in the region's wetlands, and the forests are rich in oak, hickory, pine, walnut, and sweet gum. The Eastern Shore is also blessed with an extensive network of rivers and creeks offering access to trade and preferable sites for shipbuilding. A mild but humid climate, producing hot summers and cool winters, is ideal for growing tobacco, the earliest cash crop of Maryland's economy. At the same time, tobacco growing is labor intensive. It demands rich, fertile soil and constant attention. And, to be most profitable, tobacco farming must be done by slave labor.

The first African slaves arrived in Maryland in 1642, just eight years after Lord Baltimore established the colony. Since most of the early settlers owned

relatively small parcels of land, slaves were not in great demand. Those planters who became affluent relied on other, more profitable enterprises such as
land speculation, moneylending, trade, manufacturing, and commerce. During
the eighteenth century, slaves were imported to the Eastern Shore in large numbers by a small elite of white merchant planters and a growing class of yeoman
farmers. By the beginning of the nineteenth century there were more than thirty-
eight thousand slaves living on Maryland's Eastern Shore, who accounted for
36 percent of the total population of the region.[1] Nearly all the white inhabitants were advocates of slavery, regardless of their economic circumstances. For
planters, slaves, though expensive to maintain, were profitable because of their
cheap labor. For yeoman farmers and landless whites, the existence of slavery ensured their social status, since there was a class of people below them. It also
fed their ambitions to own slaves, become wealthy, and perhaps even join the
planter class.

At the same time, Maryland's Eastern Shore represented a middle ground
between slave and free labor. The idiosyncratic nature of the region could be
explained, in part, by the presence of a large antislavery population dominated
by the Religious Society of Friends (Quakers) and free blacks. Local Friends
wrestled with the issue of slavery during the eighteenth century. Although
Quaker theology emphasized the spiritual equality of all human beings, regardless of race, there were Friends who owned slaves because their personal wealth
depended on slave labor. Other Quakers adopted the practice of slaveholding as
they increased their property. After 1787, when Baltimore Yearly Meeting, the
governing body of Quakers in Maryland, officially condemned slavery and dis-
owned members who owned slaves, many proslavery Friends joined the Methodist Church, which was less rigid in its discipline against slaveholding. Others
remained visibly active in the antislavery movement.[2] In fact, many Quaker abolitionists were instrumental in founding the Maryland Abolitionist Society in
Baltimore in 1789. The Society's suits against slavery created a hard dilemma for
Maryland slaveholders, many of whom found themselves in court ensnared in a
freedom case. Many of the cases were lengthy and challenging affairs. To defend
himself, the slaveholder was forced to hire legal counsel and relinquish custody
of the alleged slave for the duration of the trial. Even if the court ruled in favor of
the owner, the trial cost him money as well as the loss of his slave's labor during
the legal proceedings.[3]

Ironically, free blacks were in a more precarious position on the Eastern
Shore than their enslaved brethren. Many of the region's free blacks had been

FIGURE 1.1.
Sidney Still (ca. 1775–1857), who later took the name "Charity," escaped bondage from Maryland's Eastern Shore to be reunited with her husband, Levin, in New Jersey. The couple had eighteen children, of whom William was the youngest. (William Still, *The Underground Railroad* [Philadelphia: Porter and Coates, 1872].)

manumitted by local farmers at the beginning of the nineteenth century when they abandoned tobacco farming for the growing of cereal grains, such as wheat, which required far less labor and was still highly profitable. But free blacks lived with the constant fear of being returned to bondage because of the presence of slave catchers like the infamous Patty Cannon, who would readily kidnap a free black person for a bounty. In addition, there were more than eighty slave traders operating on the Eastern Shore who were willing to conspire with Cannon if the price was right. These fears as well as a strong sense of personal obligation to their enslaved brethren motivated the local free black community to dedicate themselves to the abolition of slavery. Together the Quakers and free blacks formed an active Underground Railroad network that wove through Dorchester and neighboring Caroline and Talbot Counties. As a result, more slaves escaped from the Eastern Shore than any other area of Maryland. Some secured passage to the north as stowaways on vessels sailing from the ports of Annapolis and Baltimore. Others found passage in small boats on the Chesapeake Bay, which fed into the Susquehanna River, delivering the fugitives to expectant Underground Railroad agents in Pennsylvania.[4] It was here, on this middle ground between slavery and freedom, that William Still's story begins.

Sidney Steel, William's mother, was a proud woman. Unlike the other slaves on Maryland's Eastern Shore, she refused to cast her eyes to the ground whenever she was reprimanded by her owner, Saunders Griffin. Instead, the comely young woman stared insolently into his eyes, a subtle but powerful way of resisting his authority. In so doing she also hoped to serve as an example to her four small children, teaching them that a slave master might own their bodies but not their souls.

Griffin, on the other hand, considered himself a benevolent master compared to his slaveholding neighbors who routinely whipped their chattel into submission. Rarely did he strike his slaves, and he never laid a hand on Sidney. He treated her with sympathy, knowing that she had seen her father shot dead by a drunken owner when she was just a child. In the 1790s, Griffin even allowed Sidney to take a husband, Levin Steel. Once the couple had children, the Maryland planter kept the family together rather than sell each member to a different bidder at the auction block. Truth be told, the slave owner had a special fondness for Sidney, who kept his house and prepared his meals. Although he had ample opportunity to take advantage of her, Griffin restrained himself, more from fear of her husband than respect for the couple's marriage.[5]

Levin Steel was a well-built, muscular field hand who resented slavery. At age twenty-one, he told Griffin that he would rather "die before submitting to the yoke" of slavery for the rest of his life. Levin was also prouder than Sidney and carried himself with an "uppity air," according to the overseer, who cautioned Griffin to be "careful with him."[6] The Maryland planter faced a difficult dilemma. If he sold Levin, he would alienate himself from Sidney, which he could not bear. If he tried to break the "uppity slave's" will, Levin might strike back or flee from the plantation, depriving Griffin of his labor. Instead, the slave owner allowed the disgruntled slave to hire himself out for pay after he completed his chores on the plantation. He could then save the money he earned to purchase his freedom. Levin made the deal, hiring himself out during evenings and at week's end. By 1800 he had earned the several hundred dollars he needed to secure freedom papers from Griffin.[7] Levin realized that Griffin would never allow him to purchase Sidney's freedom or that of the couple's four children—Levin Junior, Peter, Mahalah, and Kitturah. Even if the slaveholder agreed, it would take Levin many more years to accumulate the funds. Thus, before he left the plantation, Levin conspired with his wife to wait a few weeks and then flee with their children to Philadelphia, where he would be waiting for them.[8]

Sidney grew anxious as the day of her departure neared. She wondered whether she would be forced to rely on her own intelligence and resources to survive the flight to freedom. She knew that the Eastern Shore was home to many Quakers who were active Underground Railroad agents despite danger to themselves and to their families. But how would she be able to identify them? Could she rely on the region's free black population if they lived in fear of being kidnapped and sold into bondage by the many slave catchers who patrolled the Eastern Shore? Sidney also feared that if she were caught the punishment would be severe, possibly resulting in the sale of her children to another master. Despite her many reservations, Sidney strengthened her resolve and late one evening, in the spring of 1805, set out for freedom with her four children.

Guided by the North Star, they traveled at night in darkness through swamps, forests, and fields. Levin Junior and Peter were given the responsibility of helping Sidney with the two younger girls. It was a difficult journey, entailing many hard miles of travel. During the day they foraged for food, finding sustenance in orchards, gardens, and farmlands. They found shelter in forests or in abandoned barns or cabins. After a few weeks Sidney and her children crossed the Mason-Dixon Line separating the free and slave states. They had covered more than one hundred miles before they were finally reunited with Levin, who had found employment at a small sawmill in Greenwich, New Jersey. But the reunion was short-lived.

Griffin hired a posse of slave catchers, who recaptured Sidney and her children and returned them to the Eastern Shore. This time he showed no mercy. Separating Sidney from her children, the angry slave owner locked her in an attic room at night, releasing her in the morning to do her chores. Her confinement lasted for many months and probably would have lasted longer had she not softened the master's heart by catering to his every whim and singing the Methodist hymns he loved to hear.

Months passed, and Sidney grew desperate. Only her love for the children and the hope of being reunited with Levin kept her from taking her life. But she knew how difficult the journey would be if she tried to take all four of her children again. Thus she was forced to make a decision that no parent should ever have to make. To escape bondage this time she would have to choose between her children. It was the price she would pay for her liberty. Since the two girls were "mere infants," Sidney decided to take them with her. If they remained in slavery they would be physically abused and, when older, sexually molested. But the two boys were older and could fend for themselves.

On the evening of her departure, Sidney crept quietly down the stairs of the owner's house and went to the slave quarters, where her children were staying with her mother. Kneeling alongside the bed where eight-year-old Levin and six-year-old Peter slept, Sidney prayed to God that he would protect and sustain them in an uncertain future. With tears streaming down her face, she kissed her mother and, taking her two daughters by the hand, embarked on the hard journey to freedom.[9]

According to Billy G. Smith and Richard Wojtowicz's research of newspaper advertisements for runaways, Sidney was an exception to the majority of slaves who escaped from the tobacco plantations on Maryland's Eastern Shore. Most of those fugitives were unwed males in their twenties who traveled alone. They were accustomed to the rigors of planting and harvesting, and many bore scars from the whiplash, or their owner's brand, which indicated their high financial value and made them easily identifiable if they escaped. Male fugitives had the physical strength and determination to endure the many obstacles they would experience en route to freedom in the North, especially in the winter, which was the most common time to escape.[10] Sidney, on the other hand, was a female house servant with less arduous tasks, including such domestic chores as cleaning, cooking, and washing clothes. She had closer contact with her master, allowing her to manipulate him as well as enabling her to establish loving relationships with her children and mother, whom he also owned. At the same time, those advantages only served to make her bondage as well as her desire for freedom that much more unbearable. "Family" mattered most to Sidney, but to rejoin her husband in the free North meant that she would have to leave her two sons in bondage. It was a painful price to pay for freedom, and one that would haunt her for the remainder of her life.

Sidney escaped sometime during the winter of 1806. The food she stole from her master quickly ran out, and with no fruit or vegetables to be found she was forced to pilfer eggs or cow's milk. Finding shelter was just as difficult. Even when Sidney found refuge in a barn or an abandoned cabin, the bitter cold pierced through their aching bodies. Nevertheless, the fugitives pressed into the night, guided by the North Star. One day, Kitturah became ill and Sidney was forced to leave her behind with a farmer and his wife who gave them shelter. Resuming the journey with Mahala, Sidney eventually crossed into the free state of New Jersey, where she was reunited with her husband. Shortly after, Levin retrieved his daughter Kitturah. To ensure that slave hunters would not find them, Sidney changed her first name to "Charity," and the family adapted the surname to "Still." Levin also relocated the family from Greenwich to Indian Mills, "deep in the pinelands of Burlington County, about seven miles east of Medford."[11]

Life became much more difficult for the two sons Sidney left behind in bondage. Whether Griffin sold them or they were kidnapped by a slave trader is unclear. What is certain is that Levin Junior and his younger brother Peter were either stolen or purchased by John Fisher, the proprietor of a large brickyard in Lexington, Kentucky, for about $150 each. The brothers were put to work in Fisher's brickyard hauling recently molded blocks by wheelbarrow and loading them onto wagons to be transported to market. The physical labor made Levin and Peter strong, and because they were "well fed and endured few sufferings" their value as chattel increased dramatically. When the brothers were sold again as teens they commanded a price of $450 each.[12]

Their new master was Nat Gist, the owner of some twenty slaves who toiled in his brickyard. Gist was not as tolerant as Fisher. A fifty-six-year-old bachelor, he "swore hard, drank to intoxication every day," and "believed that there was nothing so good for a nigger as frequent floggings." Gist exploited his slaves, "feeding them sparingly, working them hard and hiring them out in the winter when they could not make brick."[13] Levin remained with Gist until 1817, when the slaveholder gifted him to his favorite nephew, Levi, the owner of a 480-acre cotton plantation in Bainbridge, Alabama. Four years later, after his uncle's death, Levi Gist inherited Peter and the brothers were reunited. While Levin worked in the cotton fields, Peter served as their master's cook and waiter.[14] Levi was kinder to his slaves than his rough-hewn uncle and allowed the brothers to marry female slaves from nearby plantations and to visit them regularly. But his overseer was less sympathetic to the field slaves. Worn down by hard labor, Levin died in 1831 at the age of twenty-nine. After his brother's death, Peter vowed that he would one day be a free man and find his mother.[15]

The Steel brothers' experience reflects the fact that antebellum slavery was a heterogeneous institution. Slaveholdings varied according to size, location, and crops produced. Masters exhibited varying temperaments and used different methods to run their farms and plantations. Slaves toiled in a variety of capacities, including as skilled craftsmen, nurses, drivers, mill workers, house servants, and field hands. Some lived on large cotton plantations in the Deep South like that of Levi Gist and toiled with other slaves in gangs under the scrutiny of overseers and drivers. Others lived on small tobacco farms on Maryland's Eastern Shore where the resident master worked alongside his slaves and had frequent contact with them, as was the case with Saunders Griffin. Both types of bondage were far removed from the slavery experienced by blacks in cities like Lexington, Kentucky, where owners like John Fisher and Nat Gist put their slaves to work in brickyards and hired them out to others in the winter months for additional income.[16]

Despite these variations, antebellum slavery displayed some distinctive features. First, slavery and commercial agriculture were inextricably related. Eli Whitney's invention of the cotton gin in 1793 made it much easier and more profitable to produce a variety of short-staple cotton that would enable one slave to do the work of fifty removing seeds from the fiber by hand. The invention not only increased the potential for cotton profits dramatically but made cotton the dominant crop of the Deep South, where the soil and climate were ideal for its cultivation.[17] Annual cotton production increased from about 3,000 bales in 1790 to 178,000 bales in 1810.[18] By 1830, cotton exports alone constituted more than 50 percent of the value of the nation's total exports as annual cotton production exploded, with the southern states producing 5,387,000 bales in 1860 on the eve of the Civil War.[19] Cotton not only constituted the United States' leading export but exceeded all other US exports combined. It also made slave labor more valuable.

Between 1790 and 1860, the slave population of the United States grew from slightly fewer than seven hundred thousand to nearly four million, representing an estimated investment of $3 billion. Although the value of slaves fluctuated on an annual basis, young men between the ages of eighteen and thirty sold for $500 to $700 in the Upper South during the 1820s. A healthy female slave, in her childbearing years, was worth almost twice as much.[20] By the 1850s, prime field hands (i.e., male slaves between the ages of eighteen and thirty years old) sold for $700 to $1,000 in the Upper South but commanded as much as $1,800 in the Deep South.[21] According to James Horton, "By 1860 the dollar value of American slaves was greater than the total dollar value of American banking, railroads, and manufacturing combined." In fact, chattel slavery stimulated the nation's early industrialization. It was certainly not "some sideshow in American history," said Horton, "but the main event."[22]

Second, southern slavery, unlike slavery in Central and South America, which depended upon imports from Africa, was self-sustaining. In the half century after 1808, which marked the end of legal importation in the United States, the slave population more than tripled. Such natural population growth resulted in an equal ratio of males to females, allowing southern slaves to form strong familial ties as well as a distinctive culture.[23] Slaves often chose their own partners, lived under the same roof, raised children together, and protected each other by inventing passive strategies of resistance and teaching them to the young.[24]

According to John Blassingame, the family was "the most important survival mechanism for the slave" because it offered "companionship, love, sexual gratification and sympathetic understanding of his sufferings." The family also taught slaves "how to avoid punishment, cooperate with other blacks, and maintain self-esteem."[25]

Third, the profitability of cotton as well as slaves led many owners in the Deep South to maximize production by extracting as much work as possible from their chattel, often by physical violence. Slaves toiled in a cruel system of forced labor. Diets were meager and lacking in nutrition. Punishment was swift and severe even for minor infractions. Field hands could expect to be suspended by their hands, to be lashed with a leather whip, and to have salt rubbed into their wounds. Enslaved women were raped by owners and overseers. Those who tried to escape were sometimes forced to wear bells on their arms, neck, or head. Some were muzzled. Owners occasionally branded their slaves like cattle to show proof of their ownership. Others resorted to the practice of family separation by sale if one member proved to be especially resistant to other types of discipline.[26] No wonder William Wells Brown, a self-emancipated abolitionist, described slavery as "a system that tears the husband from his wife, and the wife from her husband; that tears the child from the mother, and the sister from the brother . . . using almost every instrument of cruelty."[27] In addition to extracting more work, such cruel treatment instilled humility in the slave as well as submission to the master. Even where conditions were less extreme, the slave was still the property of his white master, who exercised complete control of his fate.

Finally, antebellum slaves exercised many forms of resistance in order to escape hard labor or punishment. Sabotage was a popular ploy on both large plantations and small farms. Slaves constantly broke farming tools, destroyed fields, and set forests, barns, and even homes on fire. Other forms of resistance included stealing food or clothing, feigning illness, or, in the case of women, pretending to be pregnant. More desperate slaves deprived the master of their labor by practicing self-mutilation and even committing suicide. These slaves cut off their toes, fingers, and hands in order to render themselves ineffective. Suicide was rare and usually occurred en route to or upon arrival in the United States from Africa, or when a slave mother took her own life and those of her children to prevent them from being sold to the Deep South. But the most overt form of slave resistance was running away.

There were many reasons for running away. Among the most common was the death of a master, which caused great fear and apprehension among slaves

FIGURE 1.2.
Illustrations of runaway
slaves like this one appeared in
nineteenth-century newspaper ads
offering monetary rewards from slaveholders for the capture and return
of their chattel. (William Still,
The Underground Railroad [Philadel-
phia: Porter and Coates, 1872].)

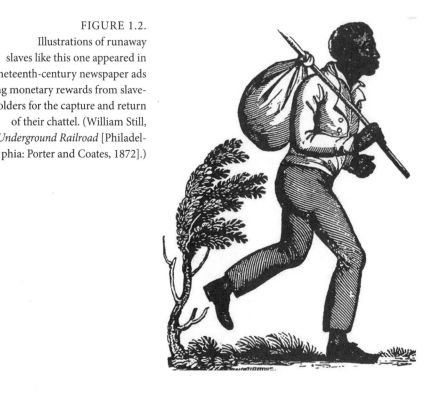

about their own future, as well as the future of their family. Slaves were left at the mercy of heirs who might easily sell them for the profit they could make. Others ran away to escape cruel punishment designed to instill humility and submission in the slave as well as to extract the most work from him. Young women ran away to escape the sexual advances of white masters, their sons, or any white male with authority. Few slave parents could protect their daughters from the sexual conquest of the owner. In fact, many slave men married a woman from another plantation because they did not want to be forced to watch as she was beaten, insulted, raped, or starved without being able to protect her. Still other slaves were habitual runaways, especially if they were spared the whip after recapture. Of all the reasons for running away, however, the desire to be reunited with family was the most persuasive. When families were separated by sale, slaves ran away to find children, parents, and spouses. Separation of slave families was common after 1820, as whites and their slaves migrated to the Tennessee and Mississippi River Valleys. Such forced separation, according to John Hope Franklin, "probably destroyed one out of every three slave marriages and one out of every three slave children under age fifteen was probably separated from one or both parents." Fear of being sold away from loved ones caused almost constant worry. Slaves pleaded with masters not to separate them. Often, their appeals were ignored.[28]

Despite the passage of a federal fugitive slave law in 1793, running away became so widespread by 1850 that Congress passed a stronger measure to enforce the constitutional provision protecting slave property. Nevertheless, the human desire to be reunited with one's family was so deep-seated that slaves continued to flee in increasingly greater numbers after 1850 than before, and the Underground Railroad played a critical role in their escape.[29]

While Levin Junior and Peter Steel grew to manhood among the four million slaves in the antebellum South, their mother began a new life in freedom. After Charity and her two daughters were reunited with Levin Senior, they relocated to Burlington County, New Jersey. It was an ideal place for fugitives to settle.

African slaves arrived at Burlington Island sometime between 1659 and 1664, when it was part of the Dutch colony of New Netherland. Not until 1676 was Burlington County established by the English, who had seized the colony from the Dutch a decade earlier. By 1790, the county had the largest African American population of New Jersey's five southern counties and the largest free black population in the state.[30] Since the region was home to a sizable Quaker population, the first organized group of Americans to speak out against slavery, Burlington was the first of all New Jersey's counties where slaves were given their freedom in large numbers. In 1804, Quaker residents successfully lobbied the state legislature to pass a gradual abolition act emancipating the children of slaves born after July 4 of that year. Although a statute for the elimination of slavery was not passed until 1846, the impact of both provisions reduced New Jersey's slave population to just 236 by 1850.[31]

Burlington's free black community established a strong support network that included Timbuctoo, an all-black settlement. Located along Rancocas Creek about a mile from Mount Holly, "Bucktown," as it was more commonly known, was established about 1820 and served as a refuge for runaway slaves. By 1850, the town had more than 125 residents, a school, and an AME church. There were other black churches as well, including Jacob's Chapel AME Church, originally known as the Coleman Meeting House, established in 1813 at Mount Laurel; Bethlehem AME Church (est. 1830), at Burlington City; and the Wesley AME Zion Church (est. 1844), also at Burlington City.[32]

The county's black community, as well as fugitives who settled in the region, could also rely on their Quaker neighbors for support. William J. Allinson of Burlington City, Thomas Evans of Evesham, Dr. George Haines of Medford, and William Roberts of Moorestown were active agents on the Eastern Line of the Underground Railroad, receiving fugitives from Virginia, Maryland, and Delaware. Together with a growing free black population, these Quaker agents formed a vigilance committee to protect the fugitives that came under their care.[33]

Levin hired himself out to other farmers to provide for his small family. In the spring he planted crops, and in the fall he harvested them. In the winter he cut timber and hauled it to a sawmill in a mule-team wagon. By 1815, he had saved enough money to purchase a forty-acre farm of his own and build a two-room log cabin for his family, which now included an additional three sons: Samuel (born 1807), James (1812), and John (1814). Another four children followed—Mary, Charles, Joseph, and William, who was born on October 7, 1821.[34]

When they grew older, Levin put all of his children to work on the farm, where the family raised corn, rye, potatoes, and other vegetables. William and his brothers were often sent with a yoke of oxen to the cedar swamp, where they cut timber, or to the nearby meadows to pick cranberries. Together with the produce raised on the farm, the timber and cranberries were sold at market in Medford, seven miles away. By adolescence, William enjoyed a reputation as an industrious worker and was often hired out as a harvest hand by the family's "thrifty Quaker neighbors" for "good wages." One of those Quaker neighbors was Samuel Finemore of nearby Lumberton, who hired the teenager to cut a cord of wood. William completed the task before noon and hauled it off to market, a feat the Quaker had "never seen before by a boy under the age of sixteen."[35]

The busy work schedule prevented the Still children from acquiring much formal education, though they occasionally attended a one-room schoolhouse when their father permitted it. There was at least one prolonged absence after the teacher, for some actual or imaginary offense seated William in front of the class to be ridiculed. When Levin learned of the embarrassment, he confronted the schoolmarm, who failed to offer any reasonable explanation for the action. As a result, Levin did not allow his sons to return to school until the teacher left three years later.[36] With such sporadic attendance, it's doubtful that young William was able to read or write, or at least with much competence, though this is a point of contention among his early biographers.

According to James P. Boyd, who wrote a brief biography for the 1886 edition of *The Underground Railroad*, Still "never enjoyed enough schooling to become literate." Not until he relocated to Philadelphia in 1844 did he learn how to read and write, being "encouraged by a wealthy widow" who hired him as an errand runner. Only then did he become "a great reader of books, especially history and geography."[37] But Still's relatives dispute the claim. His daughter Frances, who wrote a brief family history for the reprinting of the 1886 edition of her father's book, insists that Still taught himself to read and write as a youngster. "*The Young Man's Own Book* had a great influence on him as he read it so many times he could quote entire passages by memory," she wrote. "He later purchased a grammar book and studied it daily during his leisure moments."[38] Similarly, Lurey Khan, a Still family descendant, contends that young William was self-taught. She writes that "in his free time, William studied English, history and geography and worked diligently at learning every subject as thoroughly as he could." She adds that he also "subscribed to *The Colored American*, the anti-slavery newspaper in this country owned and published by black men."[39]

Regardless of his ability to read or write, young William Still developed a keen interest in the antislavery cause, probably because of his mother's guilt and suffering over leaving her two eldest sons in bondage. His curiosity became even greater one rainy autumn night when slave hunters arrived at the neighboring farm to recapture a runaway. The fugitive had been hired as a farmhand by the neighbor, a Quaker bachelor by the name of Thomas Wilkins. When one of the slave catchers began beating the runaway, Wilkins seized a shovel from a nearby fireplace, ran it into the hot coals, and flung the embers on the assailants. The ensuing panic allowed the fugitive to escape. Alarmed by the commotion, William and his brother-in-law, Gabriel Thompson, ran to the rescue and piloted the bloody slave through the thick pine forest some twenty miles into the vicinity of Egg Harbor, New Jersey, where he was given refuge by another Quaker family. According to Still biographer James Boyd, the incident "fixed indelibly on William's youthful mind the atrocious character of slavery."[40] During adolescence, William worked a variety of jobs in Burlington County. He cut timber and prepared it for market, burned charcoal, and picked cranberries. But in the spring of 1842 he found steady employment as a farmhand for Joshua Borton, a farmer and carriage maker who lived at Evesham Mount, New Jersey. Still's duties on the hundred-acre farm were extensive and included overseeing the other laborers, preparing the soil for planting, sowing and harvesting in the autumn, and selling the crops at market. He left the Borton farm after the harvest season, intending to relocate to Philadelphia, where there were greater opportunities.[41] But his plans were scuttled by his father's death on Christmas Eve. By the time

Levin's estate was settled there was very little money left for his children. As a result, William was forced to remain in Burlington and resume his search for employment.[42]

Boyd wrote that the loss of Levin had a profound effect on young William Still, leading him to question his relationship with God. Years later Still admitted: "I found myself painfully conscious of the fact that I had, up to that time, turned a deaf ear to the 'still small voice' which had so often admonished me to 'seek first the Kingdom of God and His righteousness.' That I had walked after the imagination of my old sinful heart, contrary to the counsel of the Light of the world, Christ, and that in my blindness and unbelief, I had rejected the preferred salvation of Christ, preferring to follow the voice of the stranger who was seducing me from God."[43]

The quotation, reminiscent of a classical evangelical conversion narrative, suggests that William was a religiously sensitive young man who was "painfully conscious" of his spiritual shortcomings and sought to commit himself more assiduously to his Christian faith in order to achieve the "salvation of Christ." In so doing, he probably hoped to reap the financial security and fame that tend to motivate most ambitious young men who were about to embark on their life's journey. But if Still's words are considered in the context of the 1880s when they were written, a telling revelation emerges.

Still was sixty-five years old when he contributed this personal insight to Boyd's biographical sketch. Self-taught, hardworking, and excessively ambitious, he operated a hugely successful coal and iron business and owned considerable real estate, all of which made him one of the wealthiest African Americans in the city of Philadelphia. Unwittingly, Still had forged a life that was characteristic of the Protestant bourgeoisie, much like his Quaker associates who were so instrumental in the success of the Underground Railroad. In fact, Still's relationship with the Religious Society of Friends was so close that he seems to have embraced their vocabulary, if not some of their religious beliefs. Although his reference to Christ as the "Light of the world" was commonly used by non-Quaker evangelicals, the phrase is strikingly reminiscent of the Quakers' fundamental "Doctrine of the Inner Light," or an indwelling light of Jesus Christ in each person that allowed one to communicate directly with God. This so-called Inner Light was not as much a theological concept as a personal religious experience based on a mystical connection to the divine. Similarly, Still refers to a "still small voice" that admonished him to seek God's kingdom. So, too, did Quakers speak of the Inner Light as a "still small voice within" each person that inspired the person to "walk over the earth answering that of God in others" or to engage in humanitarian activities.[44]

To be sure, Philadelphia Quakers played an important role in William Still's abolitionist career. Friends not only established the Pennsylvania Anti-Slavery Society, which hired Still as clerk after he relocated to the City of Brotherly Love, but also served as important agents on the Eastern Line of the Underground Railroad, which Still coordinated in the 1850s. Without Quaker assistance, Still would not have been as successful in channeling nearly one thousand fugitive slaves to freedom. Thus Still's abolitionist activities cannot be properly understood without first examining the historical context of Quaker Philadelphia where he conducted them.

T W O

Quaker Philadelphia

William Still arrived in Philadelphia during the spring of 1844 with a meager bag of clothing and three dollars to his name. He rented a rickety old frame shanty on Fifth Street above Poplar and began looking for employment.[1] During the next three years the twenty-two-year-old worked at a series of odd jobs to support himself. He waited tables, sold oysters, hauled wood, worked in a brickyard, and served as an errand runner for a wealthy widow.[2] But Still's fortunes began to change in 1847 when he met and married Letitia George, a free black dressmaker. The young couple "set up housekeeping in a humble, two-room house" on Washington Street. Letitia added greater stability to Still's personal life and would eventually provide him with a family of four children.[3] That same September he applied for a position as clerk of the Pennsylvania Anti-Slavery Society.

Eager for professional advancement, Still visited the Anti-Slavery Office at 31 North Fifth Street, where he met James Miller McKim, the corresponding secretary and editor of the *Pennsylvania Freeman*, an abolitionist newspaper. McKim was exceptionally intelligent. A graduate of Dickinson College, he entered the Presbyterian ministry in the early 1830s and founded the Carlisle Anti-Slavery Society despite the unpopularity of abolitionism in his hometown. In 1840, McKim relocated to Philadelphia and began working for the PASS. About

FIGURE 2.1.
Abolitionist J. Miller McKim
(1810–74) lectured extensively,
worked with the Underground
Railroad, cofounded the American
Anti-Slavery Society, and frequently
testified in court on behalf of freed
slaves snared by the Fugitive Slave Act.
(William Still, *The Underground
Railroad* [Philadelphia:
Porter and Coates, 1872].)

the same time, he married Sarah Speakman, a Quaker, and abandoned his Presbyterian faith largely because of its ambivalence over slavery. Although he did not join his wife's church, McKim's personal disposition, strong commitment to abolitionism, and sympathy for Friends ideals led others to believe that he was Quaker.[4]

Still was impressed with the reserved, businesslike McKim, who suggested that he write a letter to the PASS's executive committee applying for the position. He also directed Still to address the letter to his attention, probably to determine the young black man's literacy and penmanship.[5] Although the letter was awkwardly worded, it did demonstrate Still's literacy and considerable vocabulary:

21 September 1847

Dear Sir:

I have duly considered your proposal to me, and I have come to the conclusion of availing myself of the privilege, esteeming it no small honor, to be placed in a position where I shall be considered an intelligent being, notwithstanding the salary may be small.

Therefore, if you think proper to condescend to confer the favor upon me, I am at your service, sir.

I have viewed the matter in various ways, but have only come to the one conclusion at last, and that is this: if I am not directly rewarded, perhaps it may be the means of more than rewarding me in some future days. I go for liberty and improvement.

Yours respectfully.

Wm. Still[6]

Still was hired later that month. While his salary of $3.75 per week was less than he expected, the ambitious young man realized that he would be joining a sympathetic cause and one that exercised a profound influence on his family's history.[7] In addition, Still was now assured of professional advancement by associating himself with Philadelphia's leading abolitionists, most of whom were Quaker.

The Religious Society of Friends pioneered the antislavery movement. Inspired by a theological belief in a divine presence in each person, Friends reasoned that if God made his presence available to each person, then, in his eyes, all human beings were of equal value regardless of race, sex, or creed. This so-called Inner Light doctrine and a concomitant testimony on human equality placed Friends well ahead of other American churches in acknowledging the evils of slavery.[8] As early as 1688, a small group of Friends in Germantown, near Philadelphia, challenged the institution by urging Quaker slaveholders to "stand against" the practice of "bring[ing] men [to this country], or to rob and sell them against their will."[9] However, Philadelphia Yearly Meeting (PYM), the body that set policy for the Quaker meetings of Pennsylvania, New Jersey, and Delaware, could not bring itself to a complete realization of the testimony, especially when many of its own leaders owned slaves or participated in the slave trade. Most of these Friends were large merchants whose commercial interests and personal wealth were closely entwined with the slave labor economy of the South.[10] Consequently, individual Quakers served to plant the seed for abolitionism within the Society of Friends.

There was Benjamin Lay (1682–1759), an eccentric hunchbacked dwarf whose sensationalist behavior confronted Friends with the inconsistency between slaveholding and the Society's testimony on equality. In one of his most shocking demonstrations, Lay, in 1738, went before PYM and plunged a sword into a hollowed-out Bible containing a bladder of red pokeberry juice. Splattering those seated nearby with "blood," Lay accused the slaveholding Quakers of hypocrisy.[11] Lay represented the most radical impulse of Quaker abolitionism, one that placed a single-minded commitment to eradicating slavery at any cost above the practical necessity of achieving that cause through society's established institutions.

FIGURE 2.2.
Benjamin Lay (1682–1759)
was an English Quaker and
radical abolitionist who
engaged in dramatic protests
to convince Philadelphia
Yearly Meeting of the evils of
slaveholding.
(Library of Congress.)

There were other less impassioned but every bit as passionate Quaker abolitionists. John Woolman (1720–72), a Quaker merchant and itinerant minister from Mount Holly, New Jersey, near Philadelphia, refused to draw up wills that bequeathed ownership of slaves to heirs. When he traveled on his ministry he often accepted hospitality from a Quaker slaveholder but insisted on paying the slaves for their work in attending to him. Similarly, Woolman refused to use or eat any products procured by slave labor. His work *Some Considerations on the Keeping of Negroes* (1754) aroused the moral conscience of PYM. Appealing to the Christian sympathies of his readers, Woolman reminded Quakers that slavery was a "contradiction to true religion itself" but that one should "exercise loving-kindness towards all men," including the slaveholder, in order to enjoy the "blessing of God."[12] By focusing on the temporal as well as spiritual welfare of the slaveholder rather than the demoralization of the slave, Woolman encouraged Quakers to reconsider their involvement in the slave trade as well as the practice of slaveholding.

Similarly, Anthony Benezet (1713–84), a French-born abolitionist and educator, founded one of the world's first antislavery societies, the Society for the Relief of Free Negroes Unlawfully Held in Bondage, in Philadelphia on April 14,

1775. He devoted his life to the abolition of the slave trade and the emancipation and education of African Americans. He published many antislavery tracts, including *A Caution to Great Britain and her Colonies, in a Short Representation of the Calamitous State of the Enslaved Negroes in the British Dominion* (1767) and *Some Historical Account of Guinea, with an Inquiry into the Rise and Progress of the Slave Trade* (1772). After many years of teaching at the Friends Public School and tutoring free blacks and slaves in the evening at his home on Chestnut Street, Benezet, in 1770, raised the money, built a structure, hired a teacher, and opened an African School specifically for this purpose. At a time when blacks were considered ignorant and incapable of formal training, Benezet's success in teaching them how to read, write, and do simple arithmetic challenged the deeply rooted belief in black inferiority.[13]

Both Woolman and Benezet made abolitionism the catalyst of a spiritual reformation among Friends. That reformation emphasized the need of PYM to distance itself from worldly practices and to purify the church by requiring all members to return to a primitive simplicity in behavior and lifestyle. Thus Friends became more insistent that their children not mix with non-Quakers at school, preferring a more guarded education. Marriage outside the Society of Friends was discouraged and often resulted in disownment. Members were strenuously urged to rid themselves of "vain customs of the world" such as wearing ostentatious clothing and participating in music, theater, and art. Quakers also placed a greater emphasis on their historic Peace Testimony. Unable to reconcile their pacifist convictions with their public responsibility to defend the frontier during the French-Indian War, Friends resigned en masse from Pennsylvania government. Swift and sometimes severe disciplinary action was taken against wayward members who deviated from Quaker practice.[14] Abolitionism was a fundamental objective of this spiritual reformation, but one that was not easily achieved.

In 1754, PYM declared its "uneasiness and disunity with the importation and purchasing of Negro and other slaves," stating that these practices were "not consistent with both Christianity and common justice." Rather than disown those Friends who engaged in the slave trade, the Yearly Meeting urged them to "make the case of the Africans [their] own, and consider what [they] should think . . . and feel, were [they] in their circumstances."[15] Four years later, PYM directed its constituent monthly meetings to "eliminate from membership all those who continued to buy or sell slaves" and, through visiting committees, "to persuade owners to free their black slaves."[16] However, enforcement of the 1758 discipline varied widely among the Quaker monthly meetings of southeastern Pennsylvania, ranging the spectrum from disownment to lenient treatment for those who claimed ignorance of the change in discipline and promised to treat their slaves well in the future.[17]

The antislavery example pioneered in PYM quickly spread to other yearly meetings in Colonial America. But the final step of disowning from membership those Friends who refused to free their slaves did not come to fruition until the American Revolution. That decision was closely tied to the Quaker refusal to support a war-born government and the persecution that Friends suffered at the hands of American patriots. Suspected of loyalty to the British government, Friends, who refused to fight, swear oaths of allegiance to the American government, or pay war taxes, experienced the confiscation or destruction of their property by patriot neighbors and the forcible requisition of supplies from their households by the Continental Army.[18] To prove their allegiance to and influence events in the fledgling United States, Quakers expanded their involvement in humanitarian reform, and no reform held more importance than abolitionism.[19]

On April 14, 1775, Anthony Benezet met with nine other Philadelphians at the Rising Sun Tavern on Second Street to organize the "Society for the Relief of Free Negroes Unlawfully Held in Bondage," the first antislavery society in America. At least four of the ten attendees were Quaker: Benezet, James Pemberton, Jonathan Penrose, and William Rawle. Over the next few years the group increased to twenty-four members, mostly Quaker artisans and merchants. They focused on intervention in the cases of African and Native Americans who claimed to have been illegally enslaved. Reorganized in February 1784 as the "Pennsylvania Society for Promoting the Abolition of Slavery and for the Relief of Free Negroes Unlawfully Held in Bondage" (commonly referred to as the "Pennsylvania Abolition Society"), the PAS remained a largely Quaker organization. Although they were still occupied with litigation on behalf of blacks who were illegally enslaved under existing laws, the group began to place a stronger emphasis on the abolition of slavery itself. Within two years, the body had grown to eighty-two members and inspired the funding of antislavery societies in other cities.[20]

In 1776, PYM adopted a policy of disownment for slaveholding among members, setting a precedent for all the other yearly meetings in the United States.[21] What had begun a century earlier as a moral protest by a small group of Quakers within PYM had become a matter of spiritual integrity for the Society of Friends itself. Once this decisive step was taken, however, abolitionism was not as pressing a concern for the Society of Friends as it had been earlier. It was clear that PYM viewed slavery as a moral and spiritual evil that had now been purged from the church. Having achieved that goal, Quakers, as a religious body, did not feel compelled to accept blacks into church membership or to involve themselves in a larger campaign to abolish slavery. In fact, a strong fear of miscegenation resulted in subtle forms of discrimination among Friends well into the mid-nineteenth century. While Philadelphia Quakers welcomed African Americans to attend their worship services, they were required to sit in special sections reserved for them, and only a tiny number were received into formal membership. Some monthly meetings even urged members to withdraw from all antislavery work.[22]

However, individual Friends assumed the responsibility of shifting the antislavery crusade to the larger, non-Quaker society. Warner Mifflin (1745–98) was the primary figure connecting Quaker abolitionism before and after the American Revolution.[23] In fact, Mifflin expanded the abolition campaign beyond what even most Quakers were likely to support, to include reparations, or cash payments to former slaves. He also championed the free produce movement and organized groups of former slaves to visit southern plantations to advertise the successes of free blacks and to discredit the proslavery argument that freed people would not work.

After the Revolutionary War, Mifflin pressured state legislatures to eliminate the African and domestic slave trades as well as the kidnapping of free blacks who would be sold into slavery. As a member of the Pennsylvania Abolition Society, Mifflin went before Congress in 1790 to present an antislavery petition, which caused a prolonged and bitter debate. When Congress returned the memorial with contempt, Mifflin responded by publishing "A Serious Expostulation with the Members of the House of Representatives of the United States" (1793), challenging the moral conscience of the federal legislators. In so doing, Mifflin inspired those who believed that the United States had betrayed its founding principles of natural and inalienable rights by allowing the institution of slavery to continue. But Mifflin was not alone.

Gary Nash and Jean Soderlund have shown that Quaker moralism was partly responsible for the abolition of slavery in Pennsylvania itself, since antislavery Friends joined the Pennsylvania Abolition Society to lobby the state legislature for their cause. Those efforts—and the declining economic viability of slavery in Pennsylvania—resulted in the passage of the Gradual Abolition

Act of 1780.[24] According to the measure, "All slaves were to be registered" and "Every Negro and Mulatto child born within the state [of] [Pennsylvania] after the passage of the act on March 1, 1780 [would] be freed upon reaching the age of twenty-eight." When released, those slaves would "receive the same freedom dues and other privileges as an indentured servant." In addition, the act stipulated that Pennsylvanians were prohibited from importing slaves, though they could purchase and sell slaves who had been registered under the measure. At the same time, the law condemned those slaves born prior to March 1, 1780, to a lifetime of slavery.[25] As a result, the total abolition of slavery in Pennsylvania did not come until 1847. The reason for this gradual, two-generation process was to avoid an abrupt halt to slavery in order to limit the financial loss to the state's slaveholders.[26] Nevertheless, the act achieved its desired effect.

After 1780, slavery declined in Pennsylvania. In addition to those slaves freed under the act upon turning twenty-eight years old, there were those owners who provided for the manumission of slaves in their wills, and others during their lifetimes. Still other slaves escaped bondage by running away.[27] Thus, between 1790 and 1800, the number of slaves in Pennsylvania declined from 3,737 to 1,706, and by 1810 to 795. In 1840 there were just 64 slaves remaining in the state, and by 1850 there were none. Philadelphia witnessed a similar decline in the slave population, but it coincided with an increase in a free black population consisting of native-born slaves as well as runaways. Between 1790 and 1800, for example, the city's slave population decreased from 387 to 85, as the number of free blacks grew from almost 2,500 to 7,000 in the same period. In 1810 there were just 8 slaves remaining in Philadelphia, and that number dropped to 2 in 1840 while the free black population almost doubled during that same span from 10,514 in 1810 to 19,831 in 1840.[28]

Quaker involvement in the antislavery crusade was instrumental in the growth of Philadelphia's free black community. Even after the Society of Friends experienced a series of theological schisms in the first half of the nineteenth century, individual Quakers, regardless of dogma, continued to participate in the antislavery crusade.[29] However, there *were* significant differences in approach. Some Quaker abolitionists refused to work with non-Quaker abolitionists, preferring to appeal to the moral conscience of slaveholders by refusing to purchase goods procured by slave labor. Other Friends joined non-Quakers in establishing antislavery organizations, which raised funds for the cause and elevated public awareness through the publication of newspapers and pamphlets. Still others lobbied state and federal governments to adopt antislavery legislation. And there were even those Friends who violated federal law by assisting fugitive slaves to escape to freedom on the Underground Railroad.[30]

There were also differences in the timetable for emancipation. Some Friends advocated a gradual approach followed by the relocation, or colonization, of former slaves in Africa. These Quakers were called gradualists. Others demanded immediate emancipation and the amalgamation, or complete integration, of former slaves into white mainstream society. These more radical Friends were called "immediatists." Still other Quaker abolitionists held positions that ran the gamut between these two extremes.[31] The important point here is that *not all Quakers were abolitionists*—only a minority—and those who were abolitionists did not always agree on the same approach and timetable to end slavery.

The division among Philadelphia's antislavery Friends intensified in the 1830s because of William Lloyd Garrison, the editor of the *Liberator*, a Boston abolitionist newspaper. Although Garrison was a Baptist, his Christian faith led him to view all human beings as children of God and to hate slavery and racism, much like the Quaker abolitionists he courted. According to Henry Mayer, his biographer, Garrison's "religious views had steadily evolved in a Quaker-like direction" that was based on a "generalized respect for the inner light" as well as the Friends' belief that the "ideals of justice and character could not be tailored to formal creeds, but flowed from the inward, God-inspired promptings of the soul." As a youngster, Garrison had embraced the "New Light" evangelicalism of his mother, Fanny. He was strongly influenced by the Baptist revivals and Protestant perfectionism that gripped his native Newburyport, Massachusetts, in the early nineteenth century. Thus Garrison saw himself as a "prophet of the millennium to come," a soldier of the Lord who would lead a moral crusade to free the slaves.[32] Inevitably, his bold agitation for both immediate emancipation and equal rights for blacks served only to create conflict within the antislavery movement.

"The immediate abolition of slavery is the only morally acceptable course for the nation," wrote Garrison in the very first issue of the *Liberator* on January 1, 1831. "And the only way for the enslaved to learn how to be free is by being free."[33] While the gradualists sought to work through Congress and the courts to achieve emancipation, Garrison viewed the political system as "corrupt." He considered the federal constitution to be "null and void," since it was a product of an "unholy alliance" between the North and southern slaveholders and recognized slaves as the property of their masters.[34] Garrison also criticized the churches for showing "great indifference" to ending the peculiar institution.

FIGURE 2.3.
William Lloyd Garrison (1805–79),
editor of the antislavery newspaper the
Liberator, had a reputation for being
the most radical of abolitionists. In
1833, he founded the American Anti-
Slavery Society to promote immediate
emancipation. (Photographic print ca.
1870. Library of Congress.)

Although individual members of the Baptist, Methodist, Presbyterian, and Quaker denominations opposed slavery, their congregations, as a whole, remained "conspicuously silent" on the subject, refusing to permit abolitionist meetings to be held in their churches or to allow antislavery notices to be read from the pulpit. Garrison was furious about their apathy. Drawing a firm line between religious and political dissent, the abolitionist newspaper editor believed in a "Higher Law" doctrine that emphasized a moral obligation to oppose civil laws like slavery.[35] He encouraged women, who did considerable antislavery work, to speak publicly about the issue, even though according to the moral conventions of the period women who assumed the role and tone of male reformers were "unnatural" or even "promiscuous."[36]

These issues became so contentious among Quaker abolitionists that radical Friends distanced themselves from their more moderate antislavery brethren and joined Garrison in founding the American Anti-Slavery Society (AASS) on December 4–6, 1833, at Philadelphia's Adelphi Hall. In fact, Quakers accounted for one-third of the sixty-three delegates at the organizational meeting. Among them were some of the most radical Quakers in the Society of Friends, including Evan Lewis, John Greenleaf Whittier, Thomas Shipley, Bartholomew Fussell, and

FIGURE 2.4.
Lucretia Mott (1793–1880) was one
of the founders of the Philadelphia
Female Anti-Slavery Society in 1833.
Her being prohibited from speaking
at the World Anti-Slavery Convention
in London in 1840 led to her
involvement in women's rights.
(Library of Congress.)

James and Lucretia Mott.[37] Lewis, originally a member of the Pennsylvania Abolition Society, had grown weary of that group's ineffectiveness in advancing the antislavery cause. A lawyer by profession, Lewis became president of the AASS and perfected the organization's legal and political lobbying.[38]

Whittier, a Massachusetts Quaker, was initially interested in politics. But after losing a congressional election at age twenty-five, he suffered a nervous breakdown. After his recovery, Whittier turned to journalism, editing newspapers in Boston and Hartford, Connecticut, and eventually publishing the antislavery pamphlet *Justice and Expediency*. He would go on to become an internationally famous poet and dedicate his life to the abolitionist cause.[39] Shipley, a wealthy Philadelphia merchant, was a member of the free produce movement aimed at undercutting slavery's economic standing in northern households. He served as manager of the AASS during its first two years of operation.[40] Fussell, a physician, operated an Underground Railroad station on his farm in rural Chester County, where he employed fugitive slaves.[41] James Mott, a merchant, was one of Garrison's earliest friends and served as vice president of the American Anti-Slavery Society. He was also a cofounder of the Pennsylvania Anti-Slavery Society and an active member of the Free Produce Society of Pennsylvania.[42] His wife, Lucretia, was a leading women's rights supporter and a prominent member of the Free Produce Society. She also operated an Underground Railroad station and organized the Philadelphia Female Anti-Slavery Society.[43]

Less conspicuous in the founding of the AASS were African American delegates. Only three blacks attended the convention, two of whom were from Philadelphia: James Forten Sr. and Robert Purvis.[44] Forten was a sailmaker, a community leader, and an abolitionist. Born free, he served as a gunpowder boy during the American Revolution under US naval commander Stephen Decatur. He later established a very successful sailmaking business, which allowed him to amass a fortune exceeding $100,000, an enormous sum for any man to accumulate in the nineteenth century. Forten was a key African American abolitionist. Not only was he one of the founders of the Free African Society in 1787, but he was also instrumental in the organization of the first Negro Convention in Philadelphia in 1830 and acted as chairman. When Garrison began the *Liberator* in 1831, Forten solicited many of the 1,700 black subscribers of the abolitionist newspaper.[45] Purvis was the independently wealthy son of an English cotton broker and a free black mother from South Carolina. Brought to the North in 1819, Purvis became an early laborer in the antislavery cause and went on to play instrumental roles in several antislavery organizations, including the AASS, the Philadelphia Female Anti-Slavery Society, and the Pennsylvania Anti-Slavery Society.[46]

After founding the AASS, Garrison spent most of his time raising funds and increasing and cultivating the organization's national membership. He recruited, hired, and trained seventy agents as traveling lecturers to spread the antislavery message. Within two years after its founding, the AASS was raising $25,000 a year. By the end of the decade the AASS boasted 350 affiliated abolitionist societies nationwide, with six hundred thousand antislavery pamphlets in circulation and thousands more copies of a weekly newspaper, the *Emancipator*. The US Congress had received four hundred thousand petitions from the AASS with nearly a million signatures protesting the gag rule on Capitol Hill prohibiting discussion of the slavery issue, as well as the continuation of slavery and the slave trade in Washington, D.C.[47] Unfortunately, the presence of African Americans on the AASS board would become "little more than symbolic," according to Julie Winch. Fewer than twelve blacks were among the one hundred board members by 1838, and later, when the AASS reduced the number of board members, there were even fewer.[48] Still, Garrison continued to cultivate the black community by ingratiating himself with the propertied class, boarding with free black families when he visited Philadelphia, and speaking in their churches whenever he was given the opportunity to do so.[49]

To be sure, Garrison found a receptive audience among Philadelphia's radical Quakers. Women, in particular, flocked to his immediatist movement led by Lucretia Mott, who along with twenty-nine other women founded the Philadelphia Female Anti-Slavery Society in 1833. The PFAS was arguably the most inclusive antislavery society in America, being open to both blacks and whites, men and women, Quakers and non-Quakers. Among the free black members were Robert Purvis, Elizabeth Bustill, and Sarah Mapps Douglas, who was hired as a teacher when the PFAS established a school for black children in 1834. By 1836, the PFAS boasted a membership of eighty women, most of whom were Quaker.[50] But the fullest expression of Garrisonian principles among Quakers occurred when the Pennsylvania Anti-Slavery Society was formed in 1837.

The PASS was a natural outgrowth of Garrison's American Anti-Slavery Society. The founding of the PASS was, in part, a rejection of the older Pennsylvania Abolition Society, which had become a small embattled group with little public support. The PASS distinguished itself from the more conservative PAS by insisting on the immediate abolition of slavery and the inclusion of female speakers at antislavery conventions. Radical Quaker abolitionists like James and Lucretia Mott and J. Miller McKim were instrumental in founding the PASS and attracting a devoted core of stalwarts who had the ability to raise funds, lobby state and federal legislatures, and communicate their antislavery message in both oral and written form.[51] Denied the use of church or public buildings for their meetings, the PASS raised $40,000 to build a handsome, classical building named Pennsylvania Hall. The structure consisted of an auditorium for meetings and office space for the society's work. But on May 17, 1838, three days after it opened, Pennsylvania Hall was ransacked and torched by a racist mob.[52] As a result, the PASS rented space at 31 North Fifth Street for a bookstore, a reading room, and editorial offices for a weekly newspaper, the *Pennsylvania Freeman*. McKim, one of Garrison's traveling lecturers and a lapsed Presbyterian minister who had married into the Quaker faith, was hired to operate the bookstore at an annual salary of $600.[53]

When the AASS suffered a schism in 1840 over the role of women in the antislavery movement and women's rights, the PASS remained loyal to Garrison's original principles: to work outside political parties, to give women a prominent role in the antislavery cause, and to promote other reforms such as temperance, pacifism, and prison reform along with abolitionism.[54] As a result, PASS membership, which averaged about 1,500, consisted largely of radical Quaker abolitionists. Some of the most radical Friends were Underground Railroad agents who broke with Philadelphia Yearly Meeting in the 1840s and established their own "Pennsylvania Yearly Meeting of Progressive Friends" at Longwood in rural Chester County in 1853.[55] Progressive Friends, alternatively called "Congregational Friends," had revolted from their rural monthly meetings, which were more conservative on matters of religious doctrine, humanitarian reform, and especially involvement with non-Quakers in benevolent activities. In fact, Progressive Friends appeared to be more concerned about reform than religion. Accordingly, all people were invited to join the Longwood Progressive Friends Meeting, without regard to sex, race, or religious denomination, and their reform involvements ran the gamut from abolitionism to prison reform, and from temperance to common schooling.[56] But no reform was as important as the abolition of slavery.

Believing that God's law superseded civil law, many members rejected the federal Fugitive Slave Act of 1850 requiring every citizen to aid in the recapture of runaway slaves or face a fine and/or imprisonment.[57] Thomas Whitson stated the group's philosophy when he declared that the "popular notion that government must be obeyed, whatever its requirements, was all wrong." "Divine Law," Whitson insisted, was "superior to acts of Congress," especially if it meant "destroying unjust measures."[58] "Reformers ought to be satisfied to be destructives," echoed Lucretia Mott. ". . . If they are to be 'sharp threshing instruments having teeth' they should have some other name than '*re*-formers.'"[59] Accordingly, Progressive Friends operated a network of safe houses for fugitives and channeled them to conductors along the Underground Railroad's Eastern Line, which ran from Maryland and Delaware through southeastern Pennsylvania and ultimately to Canada. One member, Thomas Garrett of Wilmington, Delaware, assisted more than 2,300 runaways—including Harriet Tubman—in his three decades as an Underground Railroad Agent.[60] Yet the group never *officially* sponsored the Underground Railroad, realizing that to do so would imperil their own lives as well as those they were attempting to aid.[61]

Each year from their beginnings in 1853, the Progressive Friends issued forceful testimonies against the peculiar institution and listened to impassioned denunciations of slavery by such prominent reformers as Garrison, Lucretia Mott, Charles Burleigh, and Sojourner Truth. In fact, by 1856, most of the Progressive Friends subscribed to Garrison's call for the immediate emancipation of slaves. "In dealing with such a sin as slavery," they stated in a testimony encouraged by Garrison himself, "we can adopt no half-way measures. The whole truth must be proclaimed, without concealment, without compromise. No church, no

FIGURE 2.5. Built in 1854, the Progressive Friends Meeting House at Longwood, Chester County, Pennsylvania, was a popular venue for abolitionists and hosted such famous speakers as John Greenleaf Whittier, Susan B. Anthony, Sojourner Truth, and William Lloyd Garrison, who is pictured at the center of this photograph holding a bouquet of flowers. (Chester County Historical Society, West Chester, Pennsylvania.)

government, no constitution, no union which requires us to support or sanction such a crime, can have any binding force upon our consciences. We seek not alone to prevent the extension of slavery, but to exterminate it from every part of the land."[62]

The Longwood Meeting House was often a gathering site for prominent abolitionists, who traveled from all over the country to speak there. Consistent with the Progressive Friends' insistence on a free exchange of ideas, no abolitionist was denied the opportunity to speak. Both Garrison and the famed black orator Frederick Douglass, for example, were frequent speakers at Longwood, in spite of their celebrated conflict.[63] Douglass had, as early as 1841, gained a reputation for his firsthand account of slavery. Hired by the Massachusetts Anti-Slavery Society to give his own account at abolitionist gatherings throughout New England, Douglass was a remarkably powerful speaker because he humanized slavery. When the audience saw the scars on his back, it left a stronger impression than reading about the overseer who put them there with his whip. Douglass also served as living proof that those who argued the intellectual inferiority of blacks were incorrect. By the mid-1840s, however, Douglass began to go further and to analyze, with much insight, the appropriate policies for abolitionism.

Garrison, believing that the philosophy of immediatism was sacrosanct and should be left to those white abolitionists who had first articulated the policy, reprimanded the black orator for straying from his true purpose of simply describing life as a slave. Douglass responded by endorsing greater black initiative and even slave rebellion, in direct contradiction to Garrison's views. When he began his own abolitionist journal, the *North Star*, in 1847, Douglass expressed his appreciation to Garrison and others for their antislavery commitment but declared that it was time for those "who suffered the wrong" to lead the way in advocating liberty. Calling the Negro orator "ungrateful" and "malevolent in spirit," Garrison distanced himself from Douglass, reinforcing the distrust that already existed between black and white abolitionists.[64]

Adding to the Progressive Friends' radical reputation was a common belief among them that African Americans, once freed, should enjoy the same liberties as whites. In one testimony after another, Progressive Friends decried the "cruel spirit of caste" that made the "complexion of even free Negroes a badge of social inferiority, exposing them to insult in the steamboat and railcar, and in all places of public resort, not even excepting the church."[65] "Ability" and "effort," they insisted, should supersede racial considerations.[66] Accordingly, Progressive Friends demanded equal educational opportunities and the full rights of citizenship, including the ability to vote and hold public office.[67]

There was no greater an advocate for this cause than Robert Purvis, a well-educated mulatto who was among the founding members of the Longwood group. At a meeting of the PASS held at Kennett Square in 1858, Purvis lashed out at the sanctimonious statements of one white attender who insisted that he had "never known prejudice against color" and claimed that the fact that he had "eaten and slept in the same bed with black men" was the "severest test of a man's anti-slavery faith." "I utterly repudiate the idea that social intimacy with colored men is a test of anti-slavery character," said Purvis, as he began his heated rebuttal. "Sir, what has eating, or sleeping with a man to do with the question of human rights? This, sir, is a novel anti-slavery doctrine." Purvis went on to argue that blacks asked no favors of any man or class and that the issue was a matter not so much of color as of principle. "Social intercourse is regulated by irreversible social laws," he insisted. "Every man will find his level. Gentlemen will associate with gentlemen; vulgarity will find its natural place, and true refinement will be respected without regard of color. This is what the glorious anti-slavery enterprise should be teaching the people of this country."[68] Realizing that free blacks in the North had long labored for the franchise with no success, Purvis still continued to argue for black citizenship at abolitionist meetings in the future.[69]

As virtuous as their efforts were, Progressive Friends realized that what was needed to effect the immediate abolition of slavery in the country was a much larger movement than they themselves could provide. Consequently, many of their members belonged to other abolitionist organizations, including the PASS. In fact, PASS membership was largely composed of radical Quakers, or those who were in sympathy with their antislavery convictions. Proceedings were dominated by a dozen individuals who routinely served as officers, including Lucretia and James Mott, who served alternatively as president or vice president for fourteen years; Miller McKim, who served as corresponding secretary as well as the first coordinator of the Underground Railroad's Philadelphia network; Sarah Pugh, who was treasurer for twenty years; Robert Purvis, an African American who alternated with James Mott as president for more than a decade; and William Still.[70]

Initially, Still's duties for the PASS were limited to mail clerk and janitor. He supplemented his meager income by six dollars per month after accepting early morning custodial work at the Apprentices' Library on the southwest corner of Fifth and Arch Streets. His wife, Letitia, added to their income as a dressmaker. Still also began investing in real estate. At the suggestion of McKim, he purchased in installments a small lot in West Philadelphia. It would be the first of many properties he would buy over the next two decades.

When the PASS Executive Committee raised Still's salary to seven dollars per week in 1849, he was assigned greater responsibilities.[71] In addition to his custodial and mailing duties, Still, who had earned the trust of the committee, was assigned the additional duty of helping McKim gather intelligence on the movement of fugitive slaves in the city and advancing the information to local stationmasters and conductors. He also opened his new home at 832 South Street as a station on the Underground Railroad's Eastern Line.[72]

THREE

The Underground Railroad

One early morning in the spring of 1849, William Still was opening the doors of the Pennsylvania Anti-Slavery Society (PASS) office at 31 North Fifth Street when a wooden packing crate bound with five hickory hoops was delivered by the Adams' Express office. Measuring nearly three feet deep, two feet wide, and three feet long, the box, lined with baize, was sent by railroad from Richmond, Virginia, addressed to "Wm. H. Johnson, Arch Street, Philadelphia," and marked "This side up with care."

Still closed and locked the doors and shuttered the windows. He quickly summoned the members of the PASS's executive committee: J. Miller McKim, Professor C. D. Cleveland, and Lewis Thompson. All was quiet until McKim, rapping on the side of the wooden crate, inquired: "All right in there?"

Instantly an answer came from within: "All right, sir!"

Still cut the hoops with a saw and hatchet and removed the lid. Rising up inside the box was Henry Brown, a five-foot-eight, two-hundred-pound slave who, with the aid of abolitionists, had had himself freighted from bondage in Richmond, Virginia, to freedom in Philadelphia.[1]

"How do you do, gentlemen?" asked the weary traveler, extending his hand. But when the exhausted fugitive tried to stand, he became disoriented and promptly fainted. Still and the others removed Brown from the crate and gently placed him on the floor. After a few minutes, he came to, telling his rescuers that he felt as if he had been "resurrected from the grave of slavery," and bursting spontaneously into song:

> I waited patiently, I waited patiently for the Lord;
> And he inclined unto me, and heard my calling.
> I waited patiently, I waited patiently for the Lord.[2]

The abolitionists stood in awe of the runaway's presence. They hardly knew what to say or do. Instead, Brown did the talking. He told them that he had worked in his master's tobacco factory along with 150 other slaves and free blacks. After Nat Turner's 1831 failed slave revolt in neighboring Southampton County, Virginia, Brown's master, as well as Richmond's other slaveholders, retaliated in order to discourage ideas of insurrection. Brown saw bondsmen whipped, hanged, and beaten in the streets. He himself was forced to endure the arbitrary abuses of a series of overseers and experienced firsthand that there was "no law by which the master may be punished for his cruelty."

Brown's only salvation was his wife, Nancy, and their three young children. The family joined the First Baptist Church and sang in the choir. But even they were stolen from him in 1848 when they were purchased and relocated to North Carolina. Brown, helpless, watched his wife, his children, and other slaves pass by on their way out of town and resolved to escape their fate. Not long after, he came up with the idea of "shutting myself up in a box, and getting myself conveyed as dry goods to a free state."[3]

Brown enlisted the aid of James C. A. Smith, a free black baker, and Samuel Smith, a white shoemaker, to plan his escape. He paid the white shoemaker eighty-six dollars that he managed to squirrel away to travel to Philadelphia. There Smith met with McKim, Still, and some other members of the PASS to inform them of Brown's impending escape.[4] According to the plan, Brown would be sealed in a crate and shipped to Philadelphia from Richmond aboard a rail car. The desperate slave offered to pay $100 to anyone in Philadelphia who would agree to receive the box. McKim was skeptical that such a plan would work, but he reluctantly agreed to be the addressee, without any financial compensation. The crate was to be shipped on March 13, 1849.[5]

It was an extremely dangerous scheme. With little air in the crate and even less sustenance, as well as the ever-present chance of an accident, Brown was

FIGURE 3.1. Resurrection of Henry "Box" Brown. On March 30, 1849, William Still, Passmore Williamson, Miller McKim, and other members of the Pennsylvania Anti-Slavery Society unpacked runaway slave Henry Brown, who had had himself shipped in a wooden crate to Philadelphia from Richmond, Virginia. (Library of Congress.)

risking his life. Even if he wasn't seriously injured or killed, the Richmond slave might be discovered and returned to the South, where he would face severe punishment. Under those circumstances, McKim and the other PASS coconspirators would be arrested and prosecuted. As a result, McKim backed out of the deal, and another PASS member, William H. Johnson, agreed to receive the shipment.[6]

After many delays, Brown, on March 29, 1849, squeezed himself into a hickory crate and was sealed for shipment to Philadelphia. "I laid me down in my darkened home of three feet by two. And like one about to be guillotined, resigned myself to my fate," Brown would later recall.[7] The journey would nearly kill him.

For the next thirty-six hours, the crate traveled by wagon, railroad baggage car, steamboat, wagon, another railroad car, ferry, a third railroad car, and a final delivery wagon to the PASS office. At times the heat and the airlessness were unbearable and the hunger pains excruciating. Brown's only sustenance was an animal bladder of water, a few biscuits, a hat to fan himself, and a gimlet to carve small holes in the crate for fresh air. Despite the instructions printed on the lid, the crate was hardly handled with care. Brown was often jostled about violently and spent more than half the trip on his head. "My eyes were almost swollen out of their sockets. . . . A cold sweat covered me from head to foot, and every moment I expected to feel the blood flowing over me, which had burst from my veins," he said.[8] Amazingly, Brown emerged from the grueling trip with only a headache.

Nursed back to health by Lucretia and James Mott at their home on Ninth Street, Brown returned to the PASS office to meet with Still, who recorded the details of his escape. Afterward, the fugitive was passed on safely to Providence, Rhode Island, where the PASS made arrangements for him to find work as an antislavery lecturer. Rechristened Henry "Box" Brown, he regaled audiences with the miraculous story of his escape. Appearing before the New England Anti-Slavery Society Convention in Boston, Brown attracted the attention of publisher Charles Sterns, who recorded and printed a version of his story. *Narrative of the Life of Henry Box Brown* would become one of the best-known slave narratives in American history.[9]

Within weeks of the passage of the 1850 Fugitive Slave Act, however, Brown was attacked by two white men attempting to kidnap him. Although his assailants were arrested, he chose to leave the United States for England, where he resumed his antislavery speaking circuit. Brown remained in that country for the next quarter century, marrying and fathering a daughter despite criticism that he should purchase the freedom of his first wife and four children. In 1875, he returned to the United States with his English wife and child and performed as a magician to make a living. As part of his stage act, Brown emerged from the original box in which he had traveled to freedom.[10]

Henry "Box" Brown's escape was unique in the means he chose to deliver himself to freedom but not in its execution. It was common for runaways to be active participants in acquiring their freedom. While Underground Railroad agents provided critical assistance to the fugitives after they fled, the runaways themselves often planned and carried out the escape on their own or with the assistance of family and friends in the South. In fact, McKim had "supposed that [Samuel Smith,] who had made the arrangements with [him]" to have Brown shipped to Philadelphia, was "the principal in devising and executing the project." But he was surprised to learn that the "whole plan was conceived and nearly the whole of it carried out by the slave."[11] Brown's daring flight to freedom also suggests that the Underground Railroad was formally organized with regular agents like McKim, Still, and the Motts, who were eager to assist fugitives on their journeys to freedom.

While the origins of the Underground Railroad are controversial, historians have provided a good understanding of its organization and operation. The enterprise consisted of a loose network of abolitionists who lived in the border and northern states and assisted runaway slaves escaping bondage in the South for freedom in the North. There is evidence that some type of organized assistance existed as early as 1786, when George Washington, in a letter to a friend, referred to a slave "whom a society of [Philadelphia] Quakers attempted to liberate."[12] Washington may have been referring to the Pennsylvania Abolition Society, but virtually all of their work at that time was limited to the relief of free blacks, not slaves. The following year, Isaac T. Hopper, a Philadelphia Quaker, developed a systematic plan for helping slaves escape bondage in the South. Within the next few years, fugitives were receiving assistance from many towns in Pennsylvania, which apparently served as an example for antislavery activists in other towns just over the free state border.[13]

One legend maintains that the term *Underground Railroad* was coined in 1831, shortly after the new technology of the steam railroad was introduced in the United States. According to the story, a runaway by the name of Tice Davids escaped from a Kentucky plantation and made his way across the Ohio River. Refusing to be deprived of his property, the owner followed in swift pursuit. But when he crossed the Ohio he lost all trace of his slave. Confounded, he supposedly remarked that Davids must have "gone off on an underground railroad."[14] Accordingly, the abolitionists who organized the network adopted the vocabulary of the railroad to hide their illegal activities. For example, agents who gave shelter to runaways referred to themselves as "stationmasters" and their homes as "stations." Other agents who guided fugitives between stations were "conductors." Less common but every bit as critical to the success of the enterprise were "stockholders," who contributed the funds needed to feed, clothe, and transport fugitives. Unlike the majority of abolitionists, UGRR agents were the most radical minority of the antislavery movement because they actively violated a 1793 law prohibiting any US citizens from assisting fugitive slaves. Instead, they operated on a "Higher Law" doctrine that placed God's law above civil statutes. The agents were a socially and economically diverse group, hailing from a variety of religious denominations and classes. They were both black and white, male and female, young and old.[15]

These agents formed a national Underground Railroad network that consisted of three major geographical routes by which fugitives escaped to Canada. A "Western Line" began in the Mississippi River Valley, weaving through

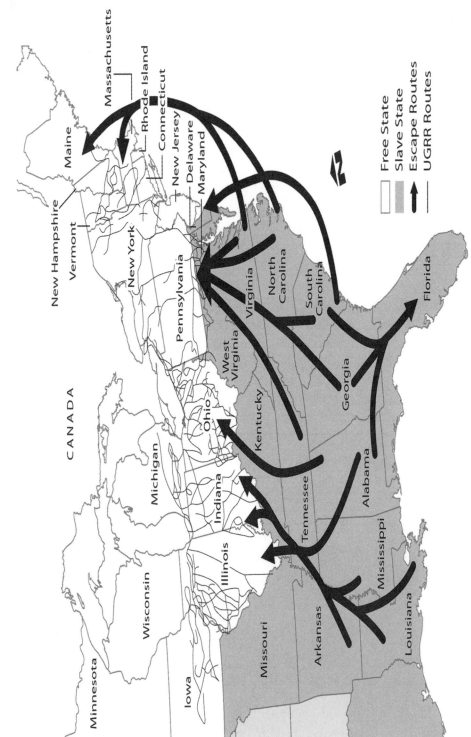

FIGURE 3.2. National Underground Railroad routes and runaway slave escape routes. (Author.)

Kansas Territory and Missouri to Iowa and Illinois. Chicago was the destination point on this route. From there, fugitives were conducted to Canada by way of Michigan. A second, "Central Line" channeled fugitives from states across the South through Kentucky, Virginia, and western Maryland to Indiana, Ohio, and western Pennsylvania. The most popular destination was Cincinnati, where runaways would be funneled to Detroit, Cleveland, or Sandusky, Ohio, or to Erie, Pennsylvania, before crossing over to Canada. Finally, there was an "Eastern Line," which was the oldest of the three routes, dating to the 1780s. On this line, fugitives traveled overland from Maryland, or by water along the coast from Baltimore or one of many ports in Virginia, across the Mason-Dixon Line into the free state of Pennsylvania. Lancaster, Columbia, and Philadelphia were the main entry points. From those locations, freedom seekers would be moved to New Jersey, to New York City, then to New England or to upstate New York, and ultimately to Canada.[16]

Runaway slaves who traveled to freedom on the UGRR were mostly young single men in their twenties and late teens. They had either been separated from their family because of a sale, like Henry "Box" Brown, or did not have any family, making it easier to escape. These male runaways also had the physical strength and endurance to make a long, difficult journey to the North. John Hope Franklin and Loren Schweninger have shown that male predominance among runaways continued well into the nineteenth century. During the period 1790 to 1816, for example, Franklin and Schweninger found a total of 424 male fugitive escapes listed in major newspapers in Virginia, North Carolina, Tennessee, South Carolina, and Louisiana. Of those 424 male fugitives, 227 were in their twenties and 102 in their teens. Conversely, only 81 notices for female fugitives appear during that same twenty-six-year period. Between 1838 and 1860, the number of female escapes more than doubled, but male predominance continued with 835 male and 212 female runaways seeking freedom in the North.[17] Women were often less willing to set out for freedom. It was common for a female slave to give birth to her first child in her late teens. Those with children generally remained in bondage to look after them, praying that they would not be separated by a sale. Those female slaves who did flee often traveled in the company of family or male fugitives. The escape of William and Ellen Craft from the Deep South illustrates this point.

The Crafts were fugitives from Macon, Georgia. Ellen, a quadroon, was the daughter of an enslaved mulatto and her white owner. Often mistaken for a member of her master's family, Ellen, as a child, so annoyed the plantation mistress

FIGURES 3.3 and 3.4. Ellen Craft (1826–91) and William Craft (1824–1900) were slaves from Macon, Georgia, who escaped to the North in December 1848 by traveling openly by train and steamboat. Ellen, who had a light-skinned complexion, was disguised as a young plantation master accompanied by "his" slave, William. The couple arrived in Philadelphia on Christmas Day. (William Still, *The Underground Railroad* [Philadelphia: Porter and Coates, 1872].)

that she sent the eleven-year-old to her daughter in Macon as a wedding gift in 1837. Ellen, who was so light-skinned she could pass for white, was made a house slave. Her husband, William, was a skilled carpenter and lived on another plantation. Although they did not endure the brutal treatment of many slaves, the couple were still the chattel of their respective masters and longed for their freedom. Taking advantage of Ellen's light complexion, the Crafts conspired a daring escape during Christmastime 1848, when their absence would not be recognized for some days.

Ellen pretended to be a young white slave master traveling to the North for medical attention. She cut her hair to neck length and dressed in fashionable men's clothing. To prevent the suspicions of others who would expect a young master to sign a hotel registry or other papers, Ellen's right arm was placed in a sling to ease the supposed rheumatism she suffered, and she wore a pair of green-lens glasses to indicate that she could not see very well. In addition, her face was bandaged to soften an alleged toothache, giving her a reason to limit conversation with strangers. William, who had a much darker hue, posed as the enslaved valet of the young master and doted on his every whim.[18] Disguised in this manner, the couple, on December 21, 1848, set out on a perilous, four-day journey to Philadelphia.

According to William, the couple realized that Ellen's light complexion would only get them so far because "slavery [was] not at all confined to persons of any particular complexion." "There [were] a very large number of slaves as white as anyone," he explained in an 1860 narrative of their courageous escape. "But as the evidence of a slave is not admitted in court against a free white person, it is almost impossible for a white [person], after having been kidnapped and sold into slavery . . . ever to recover his freedom."[19]

The Crafts' ingenious plan was fraught with danger that could easily have led to their discovery and recapture. But their courage, quick thinking, and good fortune enabled them to succeed. The couple was vigilant from the very start of the journey, when Ellen purchased train tickets to Savannah, two hundred miles away. William, who boarded the train's "negro car," spotted his owner on the platform. Turning his face from the window and shrinking in his seat to avoid detection, William was spared at the last moment when the bell rang and the train pulled out of the Macon station. Meanwhile, Ellen, who took a seat in first class, discovered that the person seated beside her was a close friend of her master's. When the seatmate attempted to initiate a conversation, she pretended deafness, remaining on edge for the next several hours.[20]

At Savannah, the Crafts boarded a steamer bound for Charleston, South Carolina. Seated at breakfast the next morning, Ellen was greeted by the captain, who complimented her on William, her "very attentive [slave] boy." When he learned that the "young gentleman" was heading North, the captain warned her of "cut-throat abolitionists" who would encourage him to run away. On another occasion, a slave trader on board offered to purchase William and auction him off in the Deep South. After docking in Charleston, the couple ran into trouble again. When Ellen tried to purchase steamer tickets to Philadelphia, the ticket seller demanded proof of ownership for William and refused to sign their names to the register until she produced it. Fortunately, the captain interceded. Vouching for the "young planter" and "his" slave, he signed their names for them.[21]

One more hurdle remained on the final leg of the journey. On Christmas Eve, the Crafts arrived at Baltimore and were confronted by an especially vigilant border officer who detained them until the "young owner" could prove ownership of "his" slave. "We felt as though we had come into deep waters and were about to be overwhelmed . . . into the horrible pit of misery from which we were trying to escape," wrote William. Providence prevailed and the bell rang for the train to leave. Agitated by the situation and not knowing what to do, the officer allowed the desperate couple to board the train to Philadelphia.[22]

On Christmas Day, the Crafts arrived in Philadelphia, where they were welcomed by William Still at the PASS office. "Scarcely had they arrived on free soil," wrote Still, "when the rheumatism departed (the right arm unslung), the toothache was gone (the beardless face unmuffled) and the blind saw again!"[23] Three weeks later, the Crafts relocated to Boston, where William found work as a cabinetmaker and Ellen as a seamstress. But after the passage of the Fugitive Slave Act in 1850, slave hunters tracked them down and the couple fled to England, where they retold the story of their daring escape in *Running a Thousand Miles for Freedom* (1860). Returning to the United States after the Civil War, the Crafts, in the 1870s, established a school in Georgia for newly freed blacks.[24]

William Still was so inspired by both the Brown and Craft escapes that he interviewed each one of the fugitives and recorded their stories on paper.[25] He would later record the escapes of every runaway that came under his care. Although Still had been employed by the PASS for only a few years, he had already gained the trust of the Executive Committee and was beginning to take greater initiative in the clandestine—and illegal—activities of the UGRR's Eastern Line, which ran through southeastern Pennsylvania.

Pennsylvania, in general, was a hotbed of UGRR activity because of its geographic location above the Mason-Dixon Line dividing the free states of the North from the slave states of the South. There were also three principal UGRR routes in the Keystone State: "Western," "Central," and "Eastern." The Western Route was used primarily by fugitives from western Virginia and Maryland. In West Virginia at least three routes led into Pennsylvania. The first originated in the Blue Ridge Mountains and passed through Morgantown en route to Uniontown, Pennsylvania. A second route paralleled the Ohio River through Point Pleasant, Parkersburg, Moundville, Wheeling, and Wellsburg, then turned east toward West Middletown and into Washington, Pennsylvania. A third route began at Harpers Ferry, cut across eastern West Virginia into Baltimore, and entered Pennsylvania in Adams County.[26]

Those fugitives escaping Maryland on the Western Route came from Frederick, Hagerstown, and Cumberland and entered Pennsylvania at Bedford. Located just twenty-six miles from Cumberland, Bedford was at the head of many secondary routes leading northward. The area was also home to several UGRR stations as well as three black agents who served as conductors: Reverend John

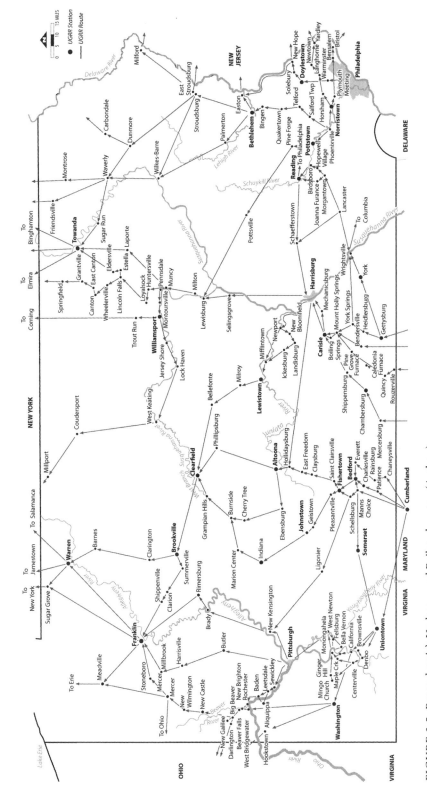

FIGURE 3.5. Pennsylvania's Underground Railroad routes. (Author.)

Fiddler, Elias Rouse, and Joseph Crawley. Because a flourishing free black community already existed in the Bedford area, many runaways chose to remain there and assimilate into that community. Others who decided to continue on the UGRR could choose one of many escape routes. The most popular pathways were due west to Uniontown and then north to Indiana County, or northwest to Pittsburgh, which had its own extensive UGRR network. The other popular route proceeded northward from Bedford to Clearfield and then Altoona. Regardless of the route, every major pathway in western Pennsylvania led to Crawford and Erie Counties in the northwest corner of the state. The proximity of these counties to Canada, located just across Lake Erie, made them a natural destination for most freedom seekers before they completed the final leg of their journey across the Canadian border.[27]

Fugitives traveling on the "Central Route" from Maryland to New York cut through the heart of the Keystone State. This route was bounded on the east by the Tuscarora Ridge of the Appalachian Mountains and on the west by York County and the Susquehanna River. Several passageways existed in this narrow geographic corridor. One route entered Pennsylvania at Mercersburg and passed through Chambersburg, Shippensburg, and Carlisle and into Harrisburg. From there, fugitives continued to Hollidaysburg, Bellefonte, Reading, or Elmira, New York.

Those runaways who chose to go to Hollidaysburg or Bellefonte continued their journeys on the Western Route. Others, who chose to go to Reading, continued on the Eastern Route. Another passageway entered Pennsylvania at Rouzerville and proceeded through Quincy, Caledonia, Pine Grove, Mechanicsburg, and then Harrisburg. Still another passageway entered Pennsylvania at Gettysburg and proceeded to York, and then into Columbia County. From there, the fugitives would be shuttled to either New Jersey or New York and then to Canada.[28]

The Eastern Route was the third and most active of Pennsylvania's major UGRR routes, largely because of William Still's considerable efforts. Without Still's organizational abilities, intelligence gathering, and contacts, the Eastern Route would not have been successful. Most of the fugitives who traveled this route began their journey on Maryland's Eastern Shore, to the west in Baltimore, or further north in Delaware. Those freedom seekers traveling from Baltimore usually entered Pennsylvania in York or Lancaster Counties, while those who started their trek along the Eastern Shore entered at Chester County or the state of Delaware. Each of these counties had complex UGRR networks and many active agents. Although several overland trails emanated from the Eastern Shore, a significant number of runaways chose to escape across the Chesapeake Bay in some type of watercraft to Havre de Grace.[29] Regardless of entry point, Philadelphia was the destination for fugitives traveling the Eastern Route. Not only did the city boast the largest free black population in the country, but it also witnessed a constant traffic of immigrants, both white and black, making it easier for runaways to hide than in many other cities of comparable size. Philadelphia also served as a dispersal center from which freedom seekers were sent northward to New York City and New England.[30] Some freedom seekers continued their journey northward via watercraft because Philadelphia, a major trade port, was a natural place to dock for ships sailing from South to North. Other fugitives traveled over land using a network of stations that ran through northeastern Pennsylvania into upstate New York and into Canada, or another abolitionist network that ran through New Jersey, New York City, and New England and into Canada.[31]

While the Eastern, Central, and Western Routes represented the major avenues of escape on Pennsylvania's UGRR, there also existed a network of secondary routes that were used whenever a slave catcher arrived in the area and a freedom seeker had to be diverted to another station for safety.[32] This was a frequent problem.

Since Philadelphia was a hotbed of Quaker abolitionism and attracted dozens of fugitives, slave catchers often came to the city searching for runaways. If a slave catcher could not locate the freedom seeker, it was not uncommon for him to kidnap a free black resident as a replacement. Anyone with dark skin— free or slave—was suspected of being a runaway. Even when free persons of color carried a certificate indicating their free status, they could be kidnapped by a slave catcher. Despite the repeated petitions of black leaders to Congress and the Pennsylvania legislature, kidnappings became so common that by 1830 slave catchers were stealing upward of fifty black youths each year.[33] Thus the constant presence of this proslavery element required a much higher degree of intelligence than existed in other cities. The Vigilant Association of Philadelphia, as early as August 1837, established a vehicle for intelligence gathering called the Vigilant Committee. Robert Purvis was the driving force behind its establishment.

Purvis was the independently wealthy son of an English cotton broker and a free black mother from South Carolina. After attending Amherst College, he returned to Philadelphia, where he married Harriet Forten, the daughter of

FIGURE 3.6.
Robert Purvis (1810–98)
helped abolitionist
William Lloyd Garrison
establish the American Anti-Slavery
Society Philadelphia in 1833
and later served as president of the
Pennsylvania Anti-Slavery Society.
(Boston Public Library.)

James Forten, one of the city's most prominent free black residents. Well educated and gentlemanly, Purvis was tall, graceful, and extremely handsome. He had dark, wavy hair and sideburns that framed a very light-skinned face distinguished by high cheekbones and a well-formed mouth and chin. Purvis was an active abolitionist and a women's rights advocate who helped organize the American Anti-Slavery Society in 1833. In the summer of 1836, Purvis harbored and later defended four fugitive slave brothers who escaped from Frederick County, Maryland, in an ongoing confrontation with the courts. This experience convinced him of the necessity to organize the Vigilant Committee of Philadelphia in August 1837.[34]

The mission of the committee was "to create a fund to aid colored persons in distress."[35] James McCrummell, a black dentist, was appointed president. James Needham, an officer of the Philadelphia Library for Colored Persons, was made treasurer, and Jacob C. White Sr., a barber and ruling elder at the First African Presbyterian Church, was hired as a secretary and paid agent. White was primarily responsible for taking minutes of the committee meetings, gathering intelligence, and raising revenue for food, clothing, shelter, transportation, and medical attention for runaways. The other officers assisted in gathering intelligence from vigilance committees in other cities as well as from Philadelphia's free black community, distributed supplies to needy fugitives, and, when necessary, hired lawyers to defend fugitives captured in the city.[36]

The committee had an additional fifteen members whose sole responsibility was to gather intelligence on the streets, at the docks, and in the business establishments of the city. At least six of the members were black residents: James J. G. Bias, a dentist; Stephen H. Gloucester, editor of the *Colored American*; Walter Proctor, pastor of the Bethel AME Church; Shepherd Shay, a clothing dealer; and Daniel Colly and James Gibbons, members of the Colored Convention movement. The Vigilant Association met initially at the African Zoar Church on Broom Street and published its proceedings in the city's abolitionist newspaper, the *Pennsylvania Freeman*.[37] In 1838, the "Female Vigilant Association" was formed and joined forces with the men to assist freedom seekers.[38]

Despite these new vehicles for gathering intelligence, the kidnapping of free blacks continued, and on May 31, 1839, the Vigilant Committee decided to reorganize. Purvis was elected as the new president. Edwin H. Coates, a white Quaker tailor, was named vice president. While Needham was retained as treasurer, Robert B. Ayres was elected secretary to relieve Jacob White of taking minutes. White was paid an annual salary of $250 to complete his other duties and to keep records of all fugitive slave cases handled by the PASS. In addition to the officers, the committee streamlined the activities of its members by reducing their numbers from fifteen to twelve.[39]

Purvis was an excellent administrator. He transformed the Vigilant Committee into an effective operation that in six months' time (June to December 1839) dealt with more than fifty cases and sent forty-six fugitives, mostly from Virginia and Maryland, on to Canada by way of New York. Fugitives were screened to weed out imposters. They were lodged in private homes, or "stations," in the city and the surrounding countryside. Those who needed clothing, medical attention, or legal counsel received it before being shuttled further north on the UGRR. Even a financial committee was established to raise funds for supplies and legal assistance. As a result, the vigilance committee was able to increase its assistance of fugitives from an average of two cases a week in the spring of 1841, to an average of three and a half cases by the fall. Accordingly, a total of forty-nine cases were handled between June 23 and October 11 of that year. The following year, the numbers more than tripled. Between January 20 and September 8, 1842, the committee assisted 163 runaways.[40] Then a devastating race riot forced the committee to disband.

Philadelphia had been plagued by race riots throughout the 1830s and 1840s. Nativist tensions in the city increased apace with the growing black population because of the uncertainty of employment in an industrializing society. Steam-powered industry had displaced many artisans, both black and white, just at the time when European immigration was increasing. Competition for jobs was great. Whites resented competing against African Americans in the labor market, especially Irish immigrants who were vying for the same unskilled jobs as laborers and stevedores.[41] According to a September 27, 1834, report in the *Pennsylvania Register*, "Certain portions of [Philadelphia's] business community prefer to employ colored people whenever they can be had," and, as a result, "Many whites who are able and willing to work are kept idle and indigent."[42]

At the same time, the size of the black community was swelling with fugitive slaves relocating from the Chesapeake, aided by Quaker abolitionists who promised to secure their freedom. Although well intended, the Friends' growing antislavery activity worsened the circumstances of the black community. Quaker abolitionists infuriated white mobs, who charged that they aimed to mix the races socially and would cause miscegenation. The inflammatory rhetoric achieved its desired purpose, which was to heighten racial tensions between white and black city dwellers.[43]

During two separate periods (1834–39, 1842–46), Philadelphia's African Americans suffered physical violence repeatedly at the hands of racist white mobs. Black houses, churches, and schools were destroyed by fire, and several people were injured or killed.[44] Mob participants were identified as "young men of the lowest social classes, mostly laborers."[45] The worst riot occurred on May 17, 1838, when the unpopular abolitionists held a convention at the handsome, three-story "Pennsylvania Hall," recently built to serve as a venue for reformers of all causes. The sight of abolitionists, both white and black, promenading arm in arm outside the structure inflamed the white mob beyond control. Disrupting the proceedings, the mob drove out the delegates, torched the building, and burnt it to the ground.[46]

The hostilities dissipated until August 1, 1842, when another white mob attacked a group of African Americans celebrating Emancipation Day in the West Indies. When the marchers retaliated, the assailants, enraged by the attack, laid waste to the black residential section. For two days, the mob vandalized stores and assaulted innocent victims. Robert Purvis's house was a popular target. Not only did the Vigilant Committee meet there, but Purvis's antislavery activities, even his involvement on the UGRR, were well known. During the first day of the riot, Purvis sat inside his house armed with guns waiting to shoot the first intruder. He was spared by two raging fires in the neighborhood that attracted the attention of the mob as they were about to attack his house. Instead, they vented their anger on a nearby black church. Purvis barely escaped the following day too. He was saved when Father Patrick Moriarity, a Catholic priest, discouraged the Irish Catholic mob from committing additional violence. When the Philadelphia sheriff, Lewis Morris, informed Purvis that he could not guarantee his safety, the black abolitionist was forced to flee the city. Not only did Philadelphia's magistrates do little to stop the violence, they later blamed the riot on black residents.[47]

Shaken to the core, Purvis, within a few months, purchased a house in Byberry, to the northeast of the city, and relocated there. "The apathy and inhumanity of the whole [white] community, demonstrated an utter and complete nothingness in its estimation of [blacks]," he wrote, making it impossible for him to reside there anymore.[48]

With Purvis's departure, the Vigilant Committee lost its most dynamic leader. The remaining members realized that they could ill afford to continue their activities lest they inflame the hostilities of white, working-class residents. A feeble attempt to revive the committee was made by the Reverend Charles W. Gardiner of the First Presbyterian Church in December 1843. But the effort was discouraged by many black improvement and fraternal organizations, which feared further retribution by the mob. Nor did the PASS lend much support to the idea, although it had praised the work of the committee at its previous annual meetings. By the early 1850s, the Vigilant Committee ceased to operate altogether and the work of gathering intelligence was assumed by individuals.[49]

F O U R

The Fugitive Slave Act

The Vigilant Committee of Philadelphia ceased operations at the very time freedom seekers needed it most. To placate slaveholders who complained about the increasing number of escapes, Congress, in 1850, passed a stronger fugitive slave law than the earlier 1793 act.[1] The infamous measure placed the freedom of every northern black in jeopardy. Slave catchers became ruthless in their quest. The kidnapping of free blacks increased dramatically. Some blacks armed themselves, intending to fight to the death for their freedom.

"The new law strips us of all manner of protection," editorialized the *Liberator*, William Lloyd Garrison's antislavery newspaper. "It throws us back upon the natural and inalienable right of self-defense."[2] By November, fugitives who had fled to Pennsylvania as well as the free black population of the state were "arming themselves with pistols, bowie knives and rifles to prevent kidnapping."[3] Other blacks sought protection elsewhere. Within three months of the bill's passage, an estimated three thousand fugitive slaves crossed the US border into Canada.[4] "It is hardly too much to say that Pennsylvania is considered wholly unsafe to nine-tenths of her colored population," wrote William Still. "They believe it far better to head for Canada than to remain here."[5]

The Fugitive Slave Act of 1850 brought political tensions between the North and the South to a boiling point. At issue was the future of the United

FIGURE 4.1.
Known as the "Great Compromiser,"
Senator Henry Clay (1777–1852) of
Kentucky promoted the Compromise
of 1850, which was designed to solve
the problem of admitting new
western states while maintaining a
delicate balance between the free states
of the North and the slave states of the
South. (Daguerreotype ca. 1848.
Public domain, Wikimedia.)

States, specifically whether it would become a modern country with an industrial economy based on free labor or remain dependent on an agricultural economy fueled by slave labor. The conflict had been building since the beginning of the nineteenth century as the nation expanded westward. With the purchase of the Louisiana Territory from France in 1803, the federal government acquired some 828,000 square miles, almost doubling the geographical size of the country. In time, thirteen new states would be carved out of the new territory, and the admission of these states to the Union would stir bitter debates in Congress over the expansion of slavery. The first test came in 1819 when Missouri applied for statehood.

Missouri was located along the same latitude as several free states. Its entry into the Union as a slave state would expand the peculiar institution in a northerly direction and upset the congressional balance of eleven slave states and eleven free states. While northerners intended to limit slavery to the South, southerners sought to expand cotton production into the new states, which required slave labor. Heated, sometimes vicious, debates broke out on the floor of Congress until Senator Henry Clay of Kentucky brokered a compromise. Missouri would gain admission as a slave state if Maine, formerly part of Massachusetts, could enter as a free state. In addition, Clay suggested that a boundary line be established at the latitude of 36° 30'. Territories north of that line would remain free, and those to the south could maintain slavery. The so-called Missouri Compromise was passed by Congress in 1820 and determined the extension of slavery for the next thirty years.[6]

During the thirty years that the Missouri Compromise remained in force, Pennsylvania's politicians tended to accommodate southern interests, fearing that slavery would divide both the Democrat and Whig Parties into northern and southern factions. Whenever possible, political leadership in Washington and in the state capitol at Harrisburg ignored the growing sectional dispute. In 1826, for example, Maryland requested that the Pennsylvania legislature pass a bill to assist slave owners in retrieving their runaways. Such a bill was debated, passed both houses, and was immediately signed into law by the governor. The measure strengthened the 1793 fugitive slave law, which had been haphazardly enforced, by permitting the slaveholder to place his alleged runaway in jail pending his trial. However, the new measure placed the burden of proof on the slaveholder by requiring him to secure a warrant for the arrest and produce evidence together with an affidavit subscribed before a justice of the locality from which the fugitive had escaped. While the legislature passed the act partly to appease Maryland's slaveholders, its primary objective was to "prevent the kidnapping of free people of color," which it did by imposing heavy penalties on those slave catchers who attempted to do so.[7]

Almost immediately, the PASS used every legal technicality possible to circumvent the law and secure emancipation for runaways. Realizing that the strength of popular sentiment could be turned to their advantage, the PASS as well as Philadelphia Yearly Meeting besieged the legislature with petitions asking that fugitives be permitted trial by jury. Since the sympathies of the state's courts were almost entirely with the fugitives, these abolitionists believed they could prevent a return to slavery no matter how clear an owner's title.[8] But their proposition was voted down by a decisive majority who believed that to allow a jury trial for a black person would nullify the US Constitution.[9] Despite the setback, the 1826 measure largely accomplished the abolitionists' purpose, as evidenced by *Prigg v. Pennsylvania.*

In 1842, Mary Morgan, a Maryland fugitive, was seized in Pennsylvania by Edward Prigg, an agent of her owner. Prigg did not have a warrant for her arrest, believing himself within rights conferred by the fugitive slave law. But local abolitionists had him arrested under the state's law against kidnapping. Prigg appealed to the US Supreme Court, which ruled that the master need not be restrained by state laws from seizing his slave but also that the state was not required to assist in the recapture. Consequently, the Court upheld Prigg's conviction under Pennsylvania's kidnapping law.[10] The PASS attempted to avoid similar incidents in the future by lobbying for a law to grant the fugitive the right of trial on the same basis as a white man.

In 1846, Philadelphia Yearly Meeting appointed a committee to call the attention of the state legislature to the "unprotected condition of our colored population under the United States Supreme Court's decision in *Prigg v. Pennsylvania*" and to ask that body to "repeal the 1793 law charging state authorities with the responsibility of recapturing fugitives."[11] As a member of this committee, Enoch Lewis, a Quaker stationmaster, successfully petitioned the legislature to pass a new bill that "afforded sufficient protection to free Negroes."[12] With the passage of this new act in 1847, it became virtually impossible for an owner to recover his slave in Pennsylvania. According to the so-called Personal Liberty Law, no judge or state official could take any case arising under the federal law of 1793 or could issue a warrant for removal. If an owner or his agent attempted to kidnap any black person—free or slave—on Pennsylvania soil, he would be charged with a misdemeanor and be subject to fine and imprisonment in the county jail. In other words, even if a slaveholder was clearly within his rights, he could expect no assistance from the state. If caught kidnapping, he would serve time in jail.[13]

Southerners, in general, and Marylanders, in particular, resented Pennsylvania's circumvention of the fugitive slave law as well as the lax federal enforcement of it. They witnessed a steady flow of slaves from the Upper South into Pennsylvania, whose free black population jumped from 32,153 in 1820 to 53,626 in 1850, partly because of successful escapes.[14] Desperate to stop the exodus, state legislatures in the South demanded a stronger fugitive slave act to end the protection that radical abolitionists gave runaways as they fled along the Underground Railroad to Canada. The hostilities reached a climax in 1850 when California applied for statehood. President Zachary Taylor tried to settle the crisis by granting immediate statehood to California and New Mexico, territories acquired after the Mexican War, without specifying if they would be free or slave states. But southern members of Congress blocked the action, fearing it would set a dangerous precedent that could lead to the eventual abolition of slavery altogether.

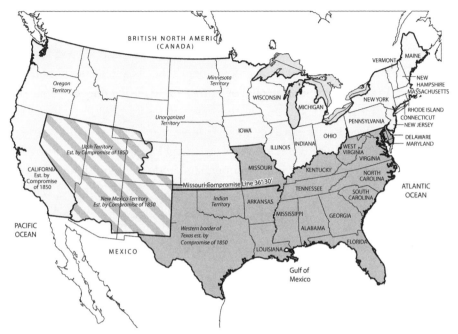

FIGURE 4.2. Map showing the changes in the geopolitical situation under the Compromise of 1850. California and Oregon were added to the free states where slavery was not allowed. The territories of Utah and New Mexico were organized and opened to slavery by popular sovereignty. (Author.)

Again, Senator Henry Clay resolved the problem by forwarding a five-part proposal: (1) California would be admitted to the Union as a free state; (2) the remaining land acquired by the Mexican War would be organized into two territories—New Mexico and Utah—and would remain open to slavery until they joined the Union, at which time the state legislatures could vote on the issue; (3) Texas, whose borders had not been clearly defined since the war with Mexico, would be prohibited from further interference with New Mexico, where it had hoped to extend slavery, and, in return, would receive $10 million in compensation; (4) to appease antislavery northerners, slave auctions—but not slavery itself—would be banned in the nation's capital; and (5) to mollify proslavery southerners, the federal government would create and enforce a new, more rigorous fugitive slave law.[15]

Of all the measures, the Fugitive Slave Act of 1850 was the most controversial. The law dramatically increased the power of the slave owners to capture freedom seekers by strengthening the earlier 1793 law, which had not provided any government support for the retrieval of a slave. According to the provisions, federal magistrates could now be appointed by circuit courts throughout the United States, where they could issue warrants and certificates of removal and could hold hearings. A federal marshal who did not arrest an alleged runaway was liable to a fine of $1,000. Law enforcement officials across the nation now had a duty to arrest anyone suspected of being a fugitive. The only evidence they needed was the sworn testimony of the slave owner. In addition, all citizens, whether they lived in the North or the South, were required to assist in the recovery of an alleged fugitive. If a person was caught assisting a freedom seeker, he was subject to six months' imprisonment and a $1,000 fine. Although the fugitive was entitled to a hearing before a federal magistrate, he was not permitted to testify on his own behalf. There was no jury, and if no attorney volunteered to represent the suspected slave only the slaveholder and the magistrate could speak during the trial. If the magistrate ruled in favor of the slaveholder, he was paid ten dollars; if he acquitted the defendant he was paid only five dollars.[16] In other words, the Fugitive Slave Act assumed the guilt of the accused rather than his innocence.

Essentially, the Fugitive Slave Act of 1850 nullified the personal liberty laws of Pennsylvania, New York, and New Jersey as well as those of the New England states. The full force of the federal government now overrode the rights of the state in favor of slaveholders. The law endangered not only fugitives but also free blacks, who could be kidnapped and sold into bondage. Abolitionists argued in vain that the law was unconstitutional since it denied the alleged slave an impartial trial by jury and thus gave unbridled authority to slave owners to retrieve a runaway.[17] At least that was the intention of the measure. But Matthew Pinsker points out that the Fugitive Slave Act "never really functioned as its framers intended" if the "process of fugitive slave rendition and the common-law doctrine of recaption" are considered.[18]

According to Pinsker, the "preferred solution to the fugitive crisis for the majority of slaveholders was *recaption*, or taking back one's mobile property when it got lost or wandered away," much as in recovery of farm animals. Slaveholders considered recaption to be "an essential element of their right to human property."[19] But abolitionists saw recaption as *kidnapping*. Accordingly, northern antislavery lawyers and politicians worked assiduously in the courts and in Congress to expose the paradox, specifically that "American federalism included a presumption of personal liberty to free black residents on free soil." Acting on this understanding as well as on high-profile cases of federal rendition, Underground Railroad agents and other abolitionists "mobilized over the 1850s to frustrate all types of fugitive recapture." Their efforts, according to Pinsker, were, "to a surprising degree, successful."[20]

Quaker abolitionists, in particular, were incensed by the Fugitive Slave Act, considering it a serious violation of personal liberties and constitutional guarantees by allowing the evils of chattel slavery to expand onto free soil. Those Friends who participated on the Underground Railroad went even further. Inspired by the scriptural passage from Deuteronomy (12:15)—"Thou shalt not deliver unto his master the servant which hath escaped from his master unto thee"—these radical Quaker abolitionists viewed the violation of the Fugitive Slave Act as a sacred duty.[21] In other words, they embraced a "Higher Law" that obliged them to follow God's dictates whenever it conflicted with civil law. It would be a fierce challenge.

The Fugitive Slave Act of 1850 enabled slaveholders to become ruthless in their pursuit of freedom seekers. They hired unscrupulous slave catchers, who, if unable to locate a particular fugitive, often kidnapped free blacks living in the North and sold them into bondage. Young blacks were particularly vulnerable to seizure, not only because they commanded a good price, but because they were a better risk than adults.[22] Kidnapping was not limited to white southerners either. George Walls, a free black landholder from Oxford, Chester County, Pennsylvania, collaborated with slave catchers by "decoying fugitives fresh from bondage to his house on various pretexts." By feigning friendship, Walls learned the "name of their master, his residence, and other necessary particulars." He would then communicate with the master, "telling him what time the fugitive would be at his house." When the slave owner arrived, the "poor refugee would fall into the merciless clutches of his master." Eventually, Walls's activities were discovered and the local black community "forced him to quit the nefarious business."[23] Kidnapping had become so common that within a year after the passage of the new fugitive slave law, increasing numbers of free blacks and runaways emigrated to Canada. The 1851 census for Canada West, for example, reported a population of 4,669 blacks, a number that would swell to near 40,000 by the eve of the Civil War.[24]

Indeed, Canada had much to offer blacks, both free and slave. The Imperial Emancipation Act of 1833 ended slavery in that country, allowing blacks to enjoy full equality under the law. Although African Americans remained on the lower rungs of Canadian society, they suffered little of the kind of racism or legal oppression experienced by blacks in the United States. Viewing Canada as a symbol of black determination, abolitionists organized and funded black communities there, providing former slaves with an opportunity to thrive as emancipated citizens. Settlements such as Dawn and Elgin near Chatham in Canada West effectively challenged proslavery claims of racial inferiority as they were guided by the principles of self-help and improvement. Manual labor schools were established to develop the skills and knowledge blacks needed to prosper in their adopted homeland. Blacks learned various trades and became self-employed citizens.[25] Mary Ann Shadd, an educated mulatto from West Chester, Pennsylvania, felt a powerful attraction to this free and open society when she attended an antislavery society meeting at Toronto in 1851.

"I have been here more than a week, and like Canada," she wrote to her brother back in Chester County. "I do not feel prejudice and if you were to come here or go west of this where shoemaking pays well and work at it and buy lands as fast as you made any money, you would do well."[26] At the age of twenty-eight, Shadd relocated to Canada, where she opened a school for the children of fugitive slaves, founded a newspaper—the *Provincial Freeman*—and aided escaping slaves after they arrived in her new country.[27] But there were also blacks who were determined to remain in the United States on free soil, and they appealed to the Quakers for their protection against the new Fugitive Slave Act.[28]

David Evans, a Quaker farmer and stationmaster at Willistown, Pennsylvania, noted in his journal on December 1, 1850, that the members of Goshen Friends Meeting "received a communication from some colored Methodists desiring the assistance of Friends since the passage of the late fugitive slave law." While some Friends expressed the feeling that "the danger was not much increased by the recent law," many others "gave evidence of their deep regard for the sufferings of a people whose complexion seemed the only reason for their persecution" and expressed a desire "to provide for their relief."[29] Quaker support would be sorely needed a year later when Rachel and Elizabeth Parker, two free black sisters living in West Nottingham, Pennsylvania, were kidnapped and taken to Baltimore to be sold at a slave market.

On December 30, 1851, Rachel, only fifteen years old, was kidnapped from the farm of Joseph C. Miller. Miller set out after the kidnapper and a few days later was found dead, hanging from a tree outside of Baltimore. Two weeks earlier, Rachel's ten-year-old sister, Elizabeth, had also been abducted from Mathew Donnely's farm in neighboring East Nottingham Township. Both of the Parker sisters were taken to Baltimore, where they were deposited in a slave pen to await their sale. While Elizabeth was sold to a New Orleans plantation owner for $1,900, Rachel remained in jail awaiting trial, thanks to West Chester Quakers who tracked her down and filed a petition of freedom on her behalf.

The kidnappings made news throughout Pennsylvania. The governor appointed the attorney general, along with Judge Thomas Bell of West Chester, as counsel. West Chester Quakers raised $300 in legal fees for Rachel's defense, and more than seventy people, many of them Quakers from the Chester County Anti-Slavery Society, were on hand to testify for her, though only forty-nine were called to the witness stand. The counsel for the kidnapper, Thomas McCreary, who was also suspected of murdering Miller, admitted defeat. Indicted by a grand jury in West Chester for the kidnappings, McCreary was sent to Annapolis for extradition, which was promptly denied by Maryland's governor. Shortly after Rachel was released, a party of West Chester Friends rescued her sister Elizabeth by paying her New Orleans master $1,500 to free her.[30]

While the abduction of the Parker sisters served notice to Pennsylvania's abolitionists that antebellum slavery now transcended state boundaries, the Christiana Resistance proved that free blacks and the fugitives they harbored would resort to physical violence to preserve their freedom. This event occurred on the Lancaster County farm of William Parker.[31] Parker, a prominent free black stationmaster, was regarded by his African American neighbors as "their leader, their protector, their Moses, and their lawgiver all at once."[32] He had been born a slave in Anne Arundel County, Maryland, in 1822, but he ran away at age seventeen and eventually settled in Christiana on the farm of Levi Pownell, where he found work at a threshing mill.[33] "Now free, I felt like a bird on a pleasant morning," he wrote. "Instead of the darkness of slavery, my eyes were almost blinded by the light of freedom. When the work was done, the money was mine. I could go out on Saturdays and Sundays, and home when I pleased without being whipped."[34] He also used his intellect and imposing presence to assist other runaways. But as a fugitive himself, Parker understood the limits of his freedom. "I found, by bitter experience, that to preserve my stolen liberty I must pay, unremittingly, an almost sleepless vigilance."[35]

Lancaster County was an especially dangerous area because of the notorious "Gap Gang," a ruthless band that invaded free black homes at night and kidnapped their victims for the bounty.[36] Realizing that he could be seized at any time, Parker, in 1841, formed "an organization for mutual protection against slaveholders and kidnappers at the risk of our own lives."[37] This self-defense organization disdained any law that jeopardized their freedom. They practiced guerrilla warfare and gained confidence in their ability to fight anyone—whether southern slave catchers, northern white racists, or even fellow blacks who regularly betrayed runaways for the bounty money. When a gang of slave catchers tried to kidnap a black girl, Parker's group freed the girl and badly beat the kidnappers. "We learned afterwards that they were all wounded badly, and that two of them died in Lancaster, and the other did not get home for some time," Parker related. The group also beat a black man who had betrayed a fugitive to slave catchers, burned the barn of a white proslavery tavern owner, and chased off a local informer.[38]

Parker's group had established a reputation for looking after and protecting the local free black community and any fugitives who came into the region at any cost. Four of the runaways who sought protection escaped from Retreat Farm in Baltimore, Maryland, in 1849. When George and Joshua Hammond, Noah Buley, and Nelson Ford reached Lancaster County, they naturally sought assistance from Parker, and he readily obliged. He gave each of the fugitives aliases, helped them settle into the community, and kept a watchful eye out for anyone who might come after them.[39] He did not have to wait long. Their owner, Edward Gorsuch, came looking for his slaves in September 1851.

Gorsuch considered himself a "good" slave owner, a benevolent "father" to his twelve slaves. A devout member of the liberal Methodist Church, he did not beat his slaves, and he preferred to run his household with a balance of compassion and firmness. In fact, Gorsuch intended to free his slaves once they turned twenty-eight years old. Thus he could not understand when, in November 1849, his four slaves fled north to Pennsylvania.[40]

During the next two years, Gorsuch seized on every clue that would lead him to the four escapees. Finally, in early September 1851, an informant living near Christiana named William Padgett wrote the Baltimore slave owner a letter informing him that the fugitives were living in Lancaster County, Pennsylvania. Gorsuch immediately prepared for a trip north. First he recruited several friends and relatives: his son Dickinson, his nephew Thomas Pearce, his cousin Joshua Gorsuch, and two neighbors, Nathan Nelson and Nicholas Hutchings. Gorsuch then departed for Philadelphia, where he secured warrants for the capture of the fugitives and enlisted the support of Henry Kline, a US deputy marshal.

Gorsuch's plans began to unravel in the City of Brotherly Love when William Still learned that warrants were being prepared for the arrest of Gorsuch's slaves by a local magistrate. Still immediately contacted tavern owner Samuel Williams, an Underground Railroad agent who had once lived at Christiana, and asked him to contact Parker. Williams's warning "spread through the vicinity like a fire in the prairies." Messengers crossed the countryside, alerting others to arm themselves.[41]

When Parker returned home from work on Wednesday evening, September 10, he found one of Gorsuch's fugitives, Nelson Ford, waiting for him. The two men, along with Samuel Thompson, Parker's wife, Eliza, her sister, Hannah, Hannah's husband, Alexander Pinckney, and another fugitive, Abraham Johnson, had "sat up late in apprehension of an attack." Gorsuch had lost the element of surprise.

Just before dawn on September 11, 1851, Gorsuch and his posse lay in ambush outside of Parker's house. Nelson Ford, one of the fugitives, crept out of the house and spotted the group. He immediately ran back inside to warn the others. The five men and two women in the house gathered up weapons and scurried upstairs so that the slave catchers could not get a clear line of fire from the ground.

Outside, four members of the posse staked out the corners of the two-story house to prevent the fugitives from sneaking through a back window. Gorsuch and Kline approached the front door and called for the owner of the house.

"Who are you?" demanded Parker from the second-floor landing.

"I am the United States marshal," replied Kline.

"If you take another step," Parker warned, "I'll break your neck!"

Kline explained that he was there to arrest Gorsuch's slaves and began reading the warrants. Gorsuch shouted up to Ford that he had seen him take refuge in the house and that resistance would do no good. He came with the proper authority to claim him and would not leave without him.

Kline hesitated about ascending the stairs, to Gorsuch's irritation. "I'll go up and get my property," the slave owner said. "What's in the way? The law's in my favor, and the people are in my favor." He started up the stairs.

"See here, old man," Parker warned, "you can come up but you can't go down again. Once up here, you are mine." One of the blacks pointed a rifle at Gorsuch, who hastily retreated. Shots were fired, although accounts differ as to who fired first. Riots by their very nature are confusing events, and the sometimes contradictory nature of subsequent accounts make it difficult to ascertain exactly what happened next.

At some point Parker's wife, Eliza, blew a horn to summon help. Kline fired his pistol at her, but she crouched below a window and continued to sound the alarm. Within forty minutes between seventy-five and one hundred black neighbors responded to the call, armed with guns, pistols, corn cutters, staves shod with sharp iron, and whatever other weapons they could find. A few whites came as well, attracted by the piercing sound of the horn and the commotion of the impending melee. Among them was a local miller, Castner Hanway. He arrived unarmed and hoped to mediate the dispute. Elijah Lewis, a Quaker shopkeeper, also came, presumably for the same reason. The two white neighbors asked the slave hunters to leave peacefully. When Kline tried to deputize them, Hanway and Lewis refused, again pleading with the slave hunters to leave.

The situation appeared to be a standoff and at one point even turned into a shouting debate about the Bible's stand on slavery. When Gorsuch attempted to climb the stairs again, the defenders leveled their weapons and Dickinson Gorsuch implored his father to come back down.

The adversaries exchanged more threats. A metal projectile flew out of an upstairs window and caught Thomas Pearce above the right eye. Pearce shot back. Someone tossed a shard of wood from the second-floor window, and it struck Joshua Gorsuch on the shoulder.

As the morning advanced, Kline and Dickinson Gorsuch urged the posse to withdraw and return another day under more favorable conditions. But the Baltimore slave owner refused to budge. "My property I will have, or I'll break-fast in hell," he declared. Members of the local self-defense organization continued arriving from every quarter, some on horseback, others on foot, but all armed with whatever weapons they could muster. The deputy marshal finally accepted the wisdom of Hanway's advice and called for the posse to retire. He would not press any further in the arrest, the marshal said, but he would hold Parker responsible for the fugitives.

By this point Parker and the people in the house had come downstairs to the doorway. As Kline and two of his group readied to leave, the elder Gorsuch confronted Nelson Ford. "Old man, you better go home to Maryland," said the runaway.

"You had better give up and come home with me," Gorsuch retorted. Ford responded by pistol-whipping the slaveholder. When Gorsuch tried to regain his feet, the fugitive hit him again. Suddenly all the pent-up tension exploded into violence. Other blacks who had gathered set upon Gorsuch with corn cutters and rifles. Bullets poured into his body. When Dickinson Gorsuch rushed to the aid of his already-dead father, Parker's brother-in-law, Alexander Pinckney, shot him as well. Dickinson staggered off and one of the blacks saved his life by throwing himself on top of the younger Gorsuch while other infuriated resisters were hacking away at his father's corpse with corn cutters and scythes.

When the smoke cleared, the fugitives had escaped, Gorsuch was dead, Dickinson lay near death from a shotgun blast, and the others had run off in

FIGURE 4.3. On September 11, 1851, the free blacks of Christiana, Pennsylvania, defended a group of escaped slaves against their owner and a federal marshal in violation of the Fugitive Slave Act, which had been passed by Congress the year before. (William Still, *The Underground Railroad* [Philadelphia: Porter and Coates, 1872].)

fear. Parker knew his life in Christiana was over. He took refuge at a friend's house and that night left with Pinckney and Johnson for Canada on the Underground Railroad. His wife and children would have to join him later. On the way to Canada, the three men stopped at Rochester, New York, at the home of his good friend Frederick Douglass, where they rested before continuing north to freedom.[42]

Federal troops were called in to investigate the affair. With a posse of fifty citizens, forty-five US Marines searched and terrorized the black and white citizens of Christiana. As a result of the investigation, thirty-seven men were arrested, charged with treason for violating the Fugitive Slave Act, and jailed at Moyamensing Prison in Philadelphia. Hanway, suspected of having incited the mob, was, surprisingly, charged not with violating the fugitive slave law but with "wickedly intending to levy war against the United States."[43]

On November 24, 1851, the defendants were tried in federal court at Philadelphia. Heading the defense team was Thaddeus Stevens, a Lancaster resident and a US congressman. As a young lawyer in Gettysburg, Stevens had once taken a case to keep a Maryland slave from claiming her freedom in Pennsylvania. The experience had apparently left a bad taste in his mouth, for Stevens became a committed abolitionist known for defending fugitive slaves. Once elected to the House of Representatives in 1848, Stevens had a national forum for his anti-slavery views.

Stevens's genius for courtroom drama dominated the proceedings. When the black defendants were led into the courtroom, each was wearing a red, white, and blue scarf around his neck as a show of support for Hanway. Lucretia Mott sat nearby in her plain Quaker garb, waiting for the right moment to express her views if necessary. On December 11, Judge Robert C. Grier instructed the jury and advised them that the charges against Hanway and the others did not constitute treason. The events at Christiana were an outrage, he said. "That the persons engaged in it are guilty of aggravated riot and murder cannot be denied. But riot and murder are offenses against the State Government. It would be a dangerous precedent for the Court and jury in this case to extend the crime of treason by construction to doubtful cases." The jury returned a "not guilty" verdict within fifteen minutes.[44] The verdict sent a signal to the South that the Fugitive Slave Act would not be enforced in the North. According to William Still, the ruling also made clear that "slave hunters, in the future, would be no safer than Gorsuch" by "utterly demolishing proslavery theories of treason."[45]

The Christiana Resistance was one of the most significant incidents in the escalating national confrontation over slavery. It emboldened abolitionists, both black and white, to challenge by any means possible the Fugitive Slave Act. Free blacks organized armed groups to protect themselves and their families from kidnappers. "Should any wretch enter my dwelling to execute this fugitive slave law on me or mine," declared Robert Purvis at the Pennsylvania Anti-Slavery Society's annual meeting on October 17, 1850, "I'll seek the life of that pale-faced specter, I'll shed his blood!"[46] Similarly, Frederick Douglass went so far as to argue the "rightfulness of forcible resistance." Urging free blacks to arm themselves in an 1853 address, the famous black orator insisted that "the only way to make the Fugitive Slave Law a dead letter is to make a half dozen or more dead kidnappers."[47] Such pronouncements of redemptive violence were more than rhetoric. African Americans, frustrated by the alienation they felt in a country that was unwilling to protect them, would no longer hesitate to use force in order to gain the fundamental rights of citizenship.

FIVE

Vigilance

Within a year of the passage of the Fugitive Slave Act, the Pennsylvania Anti-Slavery Society reported that free black citizens as well as fugitives who had sought sanctuary in Pennsylvania were "flying from pursuers as a panic pervaded the [state's] entire colored population." According to PASS records, in 1851 there were "26 cases of alleged slaves delivered up from this state under the Fugitive Law," in addition to "numerous cases of kidnapping and attempts to kidnap."[1] To address the emergency, J. Miller McKim called for the formation of a new vigilance committee. "We have been embarrassed for the want of a properly constructed, active organization," McKim declared at December 2, 1852, meeting of the PASS. "With the old [Vigilant] Committee disorganized and scattered, aid to the fugitive has been extended by individuals in a very irregular manner."[2]

Members agreed that the new Vigilance Committee would consist of nineteen members and that a four-man acting committee would "keep a record of all their doings and especially of the money received and expended on every case requiring interposition."[3] The primary responsibility for these duties would fall to William Still, McKim's thirty-one-year-old assistant, who was made the chairman of the Acting Committee. Joining Still were Nathaniel W. Depee, Jacob C. White Sr., and Passmore Williamson.[4]

The new Vigilance Committee represented a broad cross section of Philadelphia's reform network and a wide variety of institutional affiliations. White was a veteran of the original Vigilant Committee and one of the city's most respected black entrepreneurs. He was active in several reforms, being the superintendent of the First Colored Presbyterian Church's Sabbath School; proprietor of Mount Lebanon Cemetery, a black-owned burial ground; and founder of Snow Hill / Free Haven, a refuge for fugitive slaves in southern New Jersey. White was also active in the free produce movement and the Moral Reform Society.[5] Depee, another founder of Snow Hill / Free Haven, had been active in city's black politics since the 1830s and had championed the anticolonization crusade.[6] Passmore Williamson, a white Quaker conveyancer of deeds and leases, was a seasoned abolitionist who had once belonged to the Pennsylvania Abolition Society.[7] Among the other nineteen members were McKim, a former Presbyterian minister, newspaper editor, and confidant of William Lloyd Garrison; Robert Purvis, the chairman of the original Vigilant Committee and a powerful abolitionist orator; John P. Burr, a board member of the *Colored American* antislavery newspaper and founder of the Demosthenian Institute, a black literary society; Jeremiah Asher, pastor of the Shiloh Colored Baptist Church; Henry Gordon, an active congregant of the Bethel AME Church; Morris Hall, another congregant of Bethel AME and founder of its Sabbath school; Isaiah C. Wears, a feisty debater, skilled public speaker, and frequent delegate to the Negro Suffrage Conventions held in northern cities in the 1840s and 1850s; and Charles H. Bustill, another founder of the Snow Hill / Free Haven refuge.[8]

Still relied on the efforts of these members to gather intelligence on freedom seekers as well as on the federal marshals and slave catchers who pursued them. He coordinated escapes with other Underground Railroad agents at least as far away as Norfolk, Virginia, and Washington, D.C. His office at 31 North Fifth Street served at various times as a reception hall, a social service agency for needy fugitives, and a clearinghouse for intelligence.[9] Still embraced these new responsibilities with a daunting passion. To rally support for the committee, he used the PASS's antislavery newspaper, *Pennsylvania Freeman*, to embarrass Philadelphians into action. Decrying their "shameful indifference to the plight of the fugitive," Still berated readers about "betraying the city's anti-slavery legacy." He also warned all Pennsylvanians that if they "did not rally together to support the [immediatist] cause," the state would be "rendered especially infamous by the new Fugitive Slave law."[10] When some Philadelphians criticized the PASS for "disrespecting" the Fugitive Slave Act and demanded that the measure be

FIGURE 5.1. In 1852, the Pennsylvania Abolition Society organized a new interracial vigilance committee chaired by William Still, then thirty-one. The committee included James Miller McKim (*top left*), N. W. Depee (*top center*), Charles Wise (*top right*), Thomas Garrett (*center left*), Robert Purvis (*center right*), Jacob C. White (*bottom left*), Passmore Williamson (*bottom center*), and William Still (*bottom right*). (Boston Public Library.)

enforced, Still responded by holding a mass meeting to oppose the infamous law. "When those who [are] without crime are outlawed by any government, they can owe no allegiance to [that government's] enactments," he told the gathering. "Let all the colored people of the free states declare, once and for all, we will not ingloriously retreat from the land in which our fathers' bones lie buried, but will, if need be, die, though we die struggling for freedom."[11]

Still's hard-line approach was not appreciated by some of the city's free black activists, though. William Henry Johnson, for example, wrote that Still "could be sneering and self-important" and that he possessed "a puritanical streak"[12]—not uncommon traits for an individual with an all-consuming passion, and ones that would get him into trouble with a younger generation of civil rights reformers in his later years. It would be difficult to deny, however, that Still's words in the local newspapers carried considerable weight. According to Jacob White Jr., who supplemented his salary for teaching at the Institute for Colored Youth by selling copies of the weekly newspaper the *Anglo-African*, he could hawk fifty extra copies if the edition included a letter from the Vigilance Committee chairman.[13] Nevertheless, Still would have to be careful not to alienate the free black community, whose support would be essential for his success.

By 1850, Philadelphia had the largest free black community in the nation, numbering almost twenty thousand members in a total population that was over a quarter-million people.[14] The majority of black residents were poor and lived in wards on the outskirts of the city proper, including Kensington, Spring Garden, and Northern Liberties.[15] There did exist a small propertied class that included James Forten, a businessman, sailmaker, community leader, and abolitionist; the Reverend William Catto, minister of the Wesley AME Church; Robert Purvis, an independently wealthy abolitionist who served as president of the PASS from 1845 to 1850 and was the moving force behind the original Vigilant Committee; Josiah C. Wears, a real estate agent, barber, and member of the original Vigilant Committee and superintendent of the Union AME Sabbath School; and Jacob C. White Sr. These were the leaders of the city's free black community, having descended from an earlier generation that had been born into slavery. They established roots in Philadelphia, worked hard to earn material success, and became active civic leaders.[16]

According to David Brion Davis, this propertied class "provided the key to emancipation" because they "attained material success and, in many cases, education, which refuted the long-held belief that blacks were subhuman."[17] Frederick Douglass, who circulated among Philadelphia's black elite, acknowledged the point, declaring that the "most telling refutation of slavery is the presentation of an industrious, enterprising, thrifty and intelligent free black population."[18] But he also understood and lamented that "every step the colored man takes towards moral or social improvement is repulsed by the cold indifference or the active mob of the whites," so that he "is compelled to live as an outcast from society."[19]

The younger generation of Philadelphia's abolitionist leaders would not tolerate social alienation. Born into freedom, the new leaders were more aggressive, demanding the immediate abolition of slavery, and they found white allies to further their cause. William Still, Isaiah C. Wears, and Charles H. Bustill represented this young generation of abolitionist leaders who resented the limitations imposed upon them by a racist legal system: the inability to vote, hold public office, or testify in a court of law against a white defendant. Viewing themselves as the heirs of earlier antislavery leaders like John Woolman, Anthony Benezet, Richard Allen, and James Forten, they believed that they and other like-minded abolitionists, both black and white, could purge the United States of slavery. Nor did they have any reservation about working together with female opponents of slavery to achieve that momentous reform. Still and his contemporaries on the Vigilance Committee combined efforts with an active network of female abolitionists, including Quaker UGRR agents Graceanna Lewis and Abigail Goodwin; officers of the Philadelphia Female Anti-Slavery Society Mary Grew and Sara Pugh, who raised funds and submitted petitions; and the antislavery lecturer and popular poet Frances Ellen Watkins Harper, who joined the PASS and opened her home as an UGRR station.[20]

This new generation of black abolitionist leaders also felt a moral obligation to uplift their less fortunate brethren in the city's free black community: those who labored in crafts like shoemaking, carpentry, and cabinetmaking, as well as those who dominated the food and service trades, including baking, oyster shops, dressmaking, and haircutting. Some of these tradesmen had been educated at the Quaker-sponsored Institute for Colored Youth, which prepared black students for gainful employment. But they still could not break the racial barriers that prevented them from achieving greater financial success and social mobility.[21]

Despite alienation from the white mainstream—or perhaps because of it—all of Philadelphia's African Americans founded their own self-help institutions. Chief among these were the churches, most notably Mother Bethel AME Church and the Zoar Methodist Church. There urban blacks found spiritual succor and social kinship as well as a vehicle to assist their enslaved brethren to escape on the Underground Railroad. Next to the church, mutual aid societies were of importance because they provided financial aid and emotional support to members. The Free Africa Society, founded in 1787, was the first black self-help association, but by the 1850s the number of such associations had grown to more than one hundred. These included insurance, cemetery, building, and loan associations as well as fraternal societies and the Philadelphia Library of Colored Persons.[22] Together with the Vigilant Committee, these institutions enabled the free black community to assist fugitives to freedom.

According to James Horton, the "fight against slavery was every black person's fight" because "no African American was free from the peculiar institution."[23] Since nine of every ten African Americans were slaves, nearly every free black person either had been enslaved or had family members or friends in bondage.[24] Accordingly, free blacks were involved on the UGRR because they had a personal connection to their enslaved brethren, but also because they realized how fragile their own freedom was. At a time when slave catchers made little or no distinction between free and enslaved blacks, any African American could be captured and sold into bondage. As a result, a clandestine communication network existed between Philadelphia's black community and the wider free black community of the North and the slaves of the South.[25] William Still and the Vigilance Committee relied heavily on that underground communication system and the African Americans who belonged to it.

Phil Lapsansky, curator of African American history at the Library Company of Philadelphia, identified many of these black agents. Using references in Still's book, contemporary maps, and city directories, Lapsansky was able to identify many of the stationmasters on Philadelphia's underground railroad (table 5.1).[26]

Without the assistance of these black agents, Still would not have been able to shepherd the 995 freedom seekers who came through Philadelphia. This fact does not lessen Still's significance but rather reflects his organizational skills and underscores the range of his abilities. He was not only an active participant on the Eastern Line but a historian of the clandestine movement itself, and it is this legacy that is most enduring.

While Still's 1872 history of the Underground Railroad is not as refined as the work of a scholar, the compilation of data he provides for the reader offers insight into the operation of the UGRR as well as valuable information on the fugitives themselves. Beginning in 1853, shortly after he was appointed chairman

TABLE 5.1 Philadelphia's Underground Railroad network, identifying station-master, occupation (if known), and residence. Based on Still's 1872 book as well as contemporary maps and city directories.

Stationmaster	Occupation	Residence
Rachel Ash		418 South Seventh Street
Henry Child		Fifth and Arch Streets
George Custis		Anita Street (between Ellsworth and Federal Streets)
Nathaniel Depee	Tailor	742 South Street
Basil Goines		Carter's Alley (between Second and Third Streets, below Chestnut)
John Griscom		Tenth and Arch Streets
Rachel Myers		412 South Seventh Street
Samuel Nickless	Clothier	826 Bainbridge Street
Jacob White Jr.	Teacher	718 Lombard Street
Jacob White Sr.		
Charles Wise		455 North Fourth Street

of the Vigilance Committee, until 1861, when he resigned from the PASS, Still personally interviewed the 995 runaway slaves who came through Philadelphia. He recorded their names as well as their age, skin color, and gender and paid careful attention to family information, such as number of siblings and names of parents, spouses, and children. He also recorded details about their bondage, including the owner's name, how they were treated, and their reason for running away. These details were critical to achieving Still's fundamental purpose: "reuniting and comforting fugitives with their families" after the passage of the Thirteenth Amendment in 1865 abolishing slavery in the United States.[27] Just as important to Still were the details of surrounding each fugitive's escape, especially date of departure and means of travel. This information was critical not only for reuniting the freedom seeker with his family in the future but also for tracking his movement as he progressed from one station to the next.

The total number of escapes for which a year is known is 954. Of those 954 cases, the most runaways (205) escaped in 1857. Table 5.2 illustrates that the number of runaways jumped from 69 in 1853 to 128 in 1854 and steadily increased each year for the next three years.

TABLE 5.2 Year of escape, 1853–61, based on 953 known cases.

Year	No. of Runaways
1853	69
1854	128
1855	165
1856	179
1857	205
1858	102
1859	62
1860	43
1861	1

This steady increase of runaways between 1853 and 1857 can be explained by a series of events that brought into question the issue of expanding slavery onto free soil. The events included *Maxwell v. Righter et al.* (1853), a US Supreme Court case that rejected Pennsylvania's claim that state sovereignty transcended federal law in the execution of the Fugitive Slave Act, and Stephen Douglas's introduction of the Kansas-Nebraska Act on May 30, 1854, which incorporated the principle of popular sovereignty and permitted the admission of new states with or without slavery. By implication, Douglas's bill repealed the Missouri Compromise and formally established the doctrine of congressional nonintervention in the territories. Thus, when the inhabitants of Kansas applied for statehood the following year, differences between proslavery and antislavery settlers resulted in armed conflict. In retaliation for proslavery depredations, John Brown and six other radical abolitionists executed five proslavery settlers at Pottawatomie Creek in late May 1856. The incident widened the already significant divide between North and South, anticipating the arrival of a bloody civil war.

The final event was the *Dred Scott* decision of March 6, 1857, when the Supreme Court declared that African Americans, slave or free, were not US citizens (or entitled to the rights of citizenship) and that the federal government could not interfere with the free movement of property in the North. Since slaves were legally defined as the property of their white owners, they would remain slaves no matter where they resided in the United States.[28]

With each of these events, a slave's opportunity for freedom was diminishing. Thus those slaves who most desired freedom in Canada seized the opportunity increasingly after 1853, with the greatest number of escapes taking place

TABLE 5.3 Month/season of escape, 1853–61, based on 659 known cases.

No. Escaped by Month	No. Escaped by Season
89 November	211 Autumn: September, October, November
74 October	162 Spring: March, April, May
62 March	159 Summer: June, July, August
60 June	127 Winter: December, January, February
60 December	
57 July	
51 May	
49 April	
48 September	
43 January	
42 August	
24 February	

in 1857 after the *Dred Scott* ruling. In addition, Harriet Tubman's most active period as a conductor occurred between 1853 and 1857, a time period that also coincided with more active and larger vigilance committees in the North as well as highly publicized fugitive slave rescues in the abolitionist newspapers of the time.[29]

Unlike the years of escape, the specific date of the escape is not always reliable. Generally, the day listed in the database is the day the runaway arrived at Still's Philadelphia office. There are occasions, however, when the day represents the day the owner reported the slave missing in a newspaper advertisement. The latter cases are indicated by an asterisk (*) in the database. The month of escape is a more reliable indicator. The month of escape listed in the database is either the month when the fugitive claims having escaped or the month Still claims the fugitive arrived in Philadelphia. Occasionally, the owner's newspaper advertisement differs from Still's account. In this case, the owner's date is used.

The database reveals that November was the most popular month of escape. Of the 659 cases for which month of escape is known, 89 (14 percent) occurred in November, just after harvest. October was the next most popular month, with 74 (11 percent) escapes. Thus autumn, with a total of 211 escapes or 32 percent of the total, was the season when most runaways struck out for freedom (table 5.3).

These findings are consistent with the historiography, which identifies the autumn as the most common season of escape and the month of November in

TABLE 5.4 Instances of using a means of escape, 1853–61; 350 instances based on 343 known cases.

Means of Escape	Instances of Using a Means of Escape (350 instances, used by 343 individuals)
Watercraft	152
Foot	146
Horse and carriage/wagon	32
Horseback	10
Railroad	9
Chest, crate, or box	1

particular. One of the most significant findings of this study, however, is the means of escape used by Still's fugitives.

The most common means of escape for the fugitives on the Eastern Line was watercraft (i.e., boat, schooner, skiff, or steamer). This finding offers a corrective to the historiography, which stresses that the majority of slaves escaped over land and minimizes water transportation.[30] Of the 350 known instances of means used, 152 (43 percent) were via watercraft (table 5.4). (The total number of instances in the table, 350, is seven more than the total number of escaping individuals. The discrepancy is due to the fact that some of the slaves used two means of transportation such as foot and carriage, or foot and boat.)

Escape by water was especially attractive on the Eastern Line, since Virginia and Maryland are directly linked to Philadelphia by water. William Peel, for example, escaped from Baltimore in April 1859 by having himself wrapped in straw, secreted in a wooden crate, and shipped by steamer to abolitionists in Philadelphia.[31] Five years earlier, Susan Brooks escaped bondage in Norfolk, Virginia, by convincing the officer of a steamship that she was simply a laundress delivering some freshly pressed shirts. Once aboard, she hid below decks until the vessel reached Philadelphia.[32]

However, a water escape could be just as perilous as an overland journey. For example, Thomas Sipple and his wife Mary Ann were among a group of six slaves who, in 1860, escaped from Kunkletown, Maryland, across the Delaware Bay in an old wooden boat. Since they believed that a land route "presented greater dangers, they decided to escape by water." Shortly after the party had embarked on their journey, they were attacked by five white men in a small boat. The conflict lasted several minutes, but the slaves fought valiantly, forcing their assailants to retreat.[33] Another dangerous escape was made by Edward Davis in March 1854. Hiding in a tiny space in the bow of the steamship *Keystone State*, Davis endured the repeated splashing of the waves from the moment the vessel left Georgia until it reached the mouth of the Delaware River three days later. He was found near dead from the constant buffeting of the waves and exposure to the icy water. But he managed to survive, earning the moniker "Saltwater Fugitive."[34]

Other fugitives who stowed away in the various holes and crannies of steamships and schooners were able to escape detection with the aid of sympathetic ship officers or free blacks who served as sailors. For example, John W. Dungy, a twenty-seven-year-old slave from Richmond, Virginia, escaped by steamer in February 1860. He stowed away in a storeroom containing furniture, kettles, and pots, a space that "had often been used for Underground Railroad purposes." However, Dungy was almost discovered when a family of Irish immigrants boarded and were directed to take up quarters in the same place. The captain, an Underground Railroad agent, quickly intervened and ensured Dungy's safe passage to Philadelphia.[35] Another captain carried a party of fifteen runaways from Norfolk, Virginia, in July 1856. He stowed them in a small compartment below deck specifically made for fugitives and covered the hiding place with a well-fitting oilcloth and heavy table. The quarters were so cramped that the fugitives nearly suffocated in the summer heat. Twice the schooner was searched by federal officers. Each time the officers abandoned their search because the hatchways were "so shockingly perfumed with foul air," leading them to conclude that "nobody could live in such a place."[36] However, William Still points out that the majority of the ship captains were not acting out of sympathy for the runaways; they demanded compensation for bringing fugitives to the North. One of these captains "would bring any kind of freight that would pay the most" and required at least three runaway passengers paying a hundred dollars each before he would make a trip from Richmond to Philadelphia.[37]

Though a water passage did present such dangers and might have been more difficult to arrange, it was much less physically demanding than walking over a land route and was taken when runaways had the geographical opportunity. Escape on foot was of course the second most common means employed by Still's runaways, while being sealed in a crate was rare and arguably the most dangerous means of escape.

Still mentions two crate escapes from the period 1853–61 (only one of whom he assisted and interviewed). Most likely these slaves had learned of

Henry "Box" Brown's success in 1849. The one Still assisted was Lear Green, an eighteen-year-old female slave of James Noble, a Baltimore butter dealer. Green secreted herself in a chest with "a large pillow, a small quantity of food, and a bottle of water." Strong ropes were fastened around the crate and it was safely stowed among the freight on a steamship bound for Philadelphia. Lear enlisted the help of William Adams, another slave who had proposed marriage to her. His mother, who was a free woman, agreed to sail on the steamer as a passenger in order to keep watch over her. After passing eighteen hours in the chest, Lear arrived safely in the City of Brotherly Love. Adams later escaped as well, and the couple was married, settling in Elmira, New York.[38] In addition, Still mentioned that in the winter of 1857 another young female fugitive from Baltimore arrived in Philadelphia "nearer to death than any other box or chest cases that came under notice of the vigilance committee."[39] This mode of escape was the most unusual among fugitives and illustrates the desperation as well as ingenuity of the runaways.

The choice of autumn as the time of escape held for all means of escape employed by a fugitive (table 5.5). Of the 152 instances of a slave escaping by water, 38 (25 percent) took place in the autumn, the majority of those escapes occurring in November (30). Of the 146 instances of a slave escaping on foot, 52 (36 percent) occurred in the autumn, the majority of these taking place in October (42). Of the 32 instances involving a horse and carriage or wagon, 11 (34 percent) took place in the autumn, with the majority occurring in November (11).

Both the means and the date of escape selected by a runaway slave were largely due to the opportunities available to him. Since water passage to Philadelphia and other northern destinations was more readily available along the Underground Railroad's Eastern Line than it was on the Central or Western Lines, fugitives from slave states like Virginia, Maryland, and Delaware were more likely to escape on boats, schooners, or steamships than to risk a more physically demanding journey over land. Similarly, autumn—the month of November in particular—was the most popular time to escape because the absence of a slave was less noticeable after the autumn harvest than in the spring or summer, when the demands of farming were greater, and the fugitive could get a head start before his master realized he was missing. In addition, the autumn afforded better travel conditions than the winter, when the weather grew significantly colder and snow became a major obstacle.

The means and date of escape also reflect the efficiency of the underground communication established by the Vigilance Committee and by the slave com-

TABLE 5.5 Means of escape by season, 1853–61; 350 instances based on 277 known cases.

Instances of Using a Means of Escape	Season	No. of Instances
Watercraft	Summer	42
(152 instances; month unknown for 20)	Autumn	38
	Spring	32
	Winter	20
Foot	Autumn	52
(146 instances; month unknown for 41)	Spring	25
	Winter	19
	Summer	9
Horse and carriage/wagon	Autumn	11
(32 instances; month unknown for 1)	Spring	11
	Winter	6
	Summer	3
Horseback	Summer	6
(10 instances)	Winter	4
Railroad	Spring	4
(9 instances; month unknown for 3)		
Chest, crate, or box		
(1 instance; month unknown)	Winter	2

munity. Intelligence on runaways as well as information about pro- and antislavery activities found its way back to family members still in bondage. Conductors like Harriet Tubman or black sailors and boatmen carried messages to slave parents from adult children living in freedom.[40] In this manner, slaves communicated imminent dangers to family members and friends as well as opportunities for escape. At the same time, Still made sure to balance secrecy and publicity regarding the activities of the Vigilance Committee.

According to Elizabeth Varon, Still "aimed to win new converts and secure financial contributions by assuring potential supporters of the Committee's unmitigated success." This was a "marked departure from the original Vigilant Committee," which was extremely careful to "cloak its operations in secrecy."[41]

By December 1853, just a year after its organization, Still had become so brazen that he published an advertisement in the *Pennsylvania Freeman* inviting "any of our friends who may be interested in the cause to visit the [PASS's] Office and inspect the [Vigilance Committee's] record books containing accurate accounts of the number of escapes and the amount of expenditures and receipts." Those who accepted the invitation would be "afforded the most abundant satisfaction."[42] Throughout the 1850s, Still continued to boast of the Vigilance Committee's success to secure both human and financial resources. His essays appeared in antislavery newspapers in the United States as well as in Canada, though he kept secret the names of the fugitives and the details of their escapes.[43] In a November 4, 1854, issue of the *National Anti-Slavery Standard*, Still wrote: "The Underground Railroad through Philadelphia has been doing such a smashing business that it is found difficult to keep up with expenses."[44]

Still also continued to provoke Pennsylvania's abolitionists into supporting the Vigilance Committee, though not with the same biting criticism he had employed earlier. "Pennsylvania is peculiarly situated, geographically, commercially and politically—being under the immediate eye and domination of the South," he wrote in the *Provincial Freeman*, published in Windsor, Canada. "Hence, with two exceptions, Illinois and Indiana, Pennsylvania is notoriously the most pro-slavery state this side of the Mason-Dixon Line."[45] Later, in the *National Anti-Slavery Standard*, he wrote that because of Philadelphia's geographical "proximity to slavery" the city's abolitionists "could, by wise and determined effort, do what the freed colored people of no other state could possibly do to weaken slavery." He ends the commentary by encouraging the city's abolitionists "to strike the most effective blows against oppression."[46]

As Varon points out, Still was engaging in double-speak. On one hand, he embarrassed Pennsylvanians in general, and Philadelphians, in particular, into supporting immediate abolitionism by calling the state "pro-slavery based on temperament and geographic location." On the other hand, Still was attempting to rally his readers by identifying the unique position they enjoyed to end slavery. By publicizing Philadelphia and its Vigilance Committee as the heart of the Eastern Line while simultaneously keeping secret the names of the fugitives who passed through the city as well as the details of their escape, Still not only promoted the antislavery cause but piqued public curiosity about the success of the Underground Railroad.[47] The case of Jane Johnson illustrates the effectiveness of Still's approach.

S I X

The Bondswoman's Escape

In July 1855, Jane Johnson, a house servant of US minister to Nicaragua John Hill Wheeler, planned to escape with her two young sons, Daniel and Isaiah. Wheeler had returned briefly to Washington to fulfill a diplomatic duty and to pick up Jane and her two sons before sailing to New York and then on to the Caribbean. Stopping in Philadelphia, Wheeler checked his party into Bloodgood's Hotel and locked his three slaves in their room while he took dinner. Jane had planned to escape when she reached New York, until a free black hotel worker who was also a member of the Philadelphia Vigilance Committee offered his assistance.

Desperate for help, she accepted the offer. The hotel worker sent for William Still and Passmore Williamson. But the two agents arrived at Bloodgood's only to discover that the Wheeler party had already left for the steamship.

Still and Williamson hurried to the wharf, accompanied by five free black members of the Vigilance Committee: William Curtis, James P. Braddock, John Ballard, James Martin, and Isaiah Moore. When the contingent caught up with Jane and her sons on the second deck of the steamer, Still asked: "Are you traveling?"

"Yes," she replied promptly.

FIGURE 6.1.
Jane Johnson (ca. 1820–72) was the slave of Col. John H. Wheeler of North Carolina, who was also the US minister to Nicaragua. (William Still, *The Underground Railroad* [Philadelphia: Porter and Coates, 1872].)

"With whom?"

Johnson nodded in the direction of her owner.

Williamson turned to Wheeler and asked: "Do they belong to you, sir?"

"Yes," he replied, "they are in my charge."

Redirecting his attention to Jane, Still informed her of her rights.

"You are entitled to your freedom according to the laws of Pennsylvania, having been brought into the state by your owner. If you prefer freedom to slavery, as we suppose everybody does, you have the chance to accept it now." By "the laws of Pennsylvania," Still was referring to Pennsylvania's personal liberty laws, which were in direct contradiction to the 1850 Fugitive Slave Act.

Frightened that Wheeler would attack her with his walking stick, Jane, noticeably distraught, hesitated.

"Act calmly," Still advised. "Don't be frightened by your master. You are as much entitled to your freedom as he is."

Infuriated by the challenge to his authority, Wheeler exclaimed: "She understands the law, and she has the right to leave if she so desires. But she does not want to leave her three other children who live in the South."

Ignoring Wheeler's protest, Still continued.

"Judges have time and again decided cases in this city and State similar to yours in favor of freedom," he said. "Of course, if you want to remain a slave with your master, we cannot force you to leave; we only want to make you sensible of your rights. Remember, if you lose this chance you may never get another." Emboldened by Still's words, Jane regained her confidence.

"I am not free," she said firmly. "I want my freedom, but he holds me!" "She belongs to me!" cried Wheeler. "I intend to free her in time. But until then, she is my property!"

"I've *always* wanted my freedom," said Jane sternly, taking hold of Still's arm with one hand and beckoning her sons to her side with the other.

A crowd had gathered. Many onlookers appeared to sympathize with Johnson, while only one man, presumably a slaveholder, supported Wheeler.

When Still began to escort the Johnsons toward the stairway leading to the deck below, Wheeler rushed them. Williamson, with the assistance of the two Vigilance Committee members, restrained the slaveholder.

Still guided Jane and her sons down Delaware Avenue to Dock Street and then onto Front Street, where they procured a carriage, which would take them to one of the city's safe houses before their journey to Canada. Jane could not have been happier. For the first time in her life she felt free.[1]

Johnson's escape illustrates the complexity of the Underground Railroad. Escapes were both well-planned and spontaneous events and were both organized and individual actions. Escapes not only placed the lives of the runaways in danger but also jeopardized those of the members of vigilance committees who assisted fugitives to freedom. Incensed by Jane's escape, Wheeler charged Williamson with assault and sued him, insisting that his slaves had been taken against their will and demanding that they be returned. He also charged Still and the five black agents with highway robbery, inciting to riot, and assault and battery.[2] Wheeler then approached his friend Judge John Kintzing Kane, a proslavery Democrat who served in the Federal District Court and had presided over the Christiana Resistance case four years earlier.

On July 27, 1855, Judge Kane ordered Williamson to appear and present Jane Johnson and her sons in court. The Quaker abolitionist insisted that he could not do so because he had never had custody of Johnson and did not know where she was. Rejecting the excuse, Kane ordered Williamson to Philadelphia's Moyamensing Prison, where he spent the next three months.[3]

During his incarceration, Williamson kept a visitors' register, which contains the signatures or names of the more than five hundred people that came

FIGURE 6.2. On the evening of July 18, 1855, William Still rescued Jane Johnson and her two sons from slavery as five black dockworkers restrained her owner, Col. John H. Wheeler. (William Still, *The Underground Railroad* [Philadelphia: Porter and Coates, 1872].)

to see him, including Frederick Douglass, Harriet Tubman, and Mary Ann Shadd.[4] The PASS publicized the unjust imprisonment by printing and selling a lithograph of Williamson in his cell.[5] In addition, William Still made sure that both the Johnson escape and Williamson's imprisonment were widely covered in the antislavery press. Still portrayed the Quaker abolitionist as the "victim of a tyrannical judge," and Colonel Wheeler and Judge Kane as part of a "slave power conspiracy," reflecting the marriage between southern slaveholders and northern Democrats that had long influenced the federal government. When Philadelphia's Democratic press attacked Johnson as a "worthless and degraded pawn," and the abolitionists who rescued her as a "lawless mob," Still fought back in the abolitionist press. Jane Johnson was a "woman of uncommon good sense and genteel manners," he wrote, and the abolitionist Passmore Williamson was "a devoted Friend of Freedom."[6] As a result, Still and the Vigilance Committee gained greater public support and Williamson the sympathy of dozens who sent him letters, including Senator Charles Sumner, poet John Greenleaf Whittier, the Philadelphia Yearly Meeting of Progressive Friends, and the British and Foreign Anti-Slavery Society.[7] In fact, Williamson's imprisonment was so beneficial

FIGURE 6.3.
Passmore Williamson (1822–95)
served one hundred days between
July 27 and November 3, 1855, in
Philadelphia's Moyamensing Prison for
his involvement in helping Jane Johnson
and her sons escape slavery.
(Chester County Historical Society,
West Chester, Pennsylvania.)

to the antislavery cause that, according to Lucretia Mott, his father, Thomas, expressed the concern that his son "will come out of Prison too soon."[8]

On August 30, Williamson appeared again before Judge Kane, along with William Still and the black dockworkers, who were put on trial for riot and assault and battery. While Williamson continued to insist that he never knew what happened to Jane Johnson, Wheeler was just as adamant that he did know and that Still had forcibly abducted her. Wheeler's lie was exposed when Johnson herself made a daring court appearance, testifying that she was "not kidnapped" but rather "went away on her own free will" and that she would rather "die than go back" to Wheeler. William Still was found not guilty, and the dockworkers were either acquitted or found guilty of lesser charges. But Williamson remained in jail until November 3, 1855, when Judge Kane, relenting to public pressure, released him.[9]

Although the court's verdict was mixed, abolitionists viewed it as an enormous victory. It served to raise the consciousness of the general public by illustrating that slaves, both male and female, were willing to die for their freedom. The high drama of the confrontation between Johnson and Wheeler captured the attention of country and, according to the *Philadelphia Daily Sun*, "made more 'abolitionists' and excited a more rancorous feeling against slavery than all the debates, feuds and broken promises of the past."[10]

While Jane Johnson's case garnered national attention, she was just one of the 237 female runaways assisted by William Still.[11] The sheer number of female fugitives assisted by Still between 1853 and 1861 offers an important corrective to the traditional interpretation of the Underground Railroad, which holds that single men between the ages of eighteen and thirty-two composed the overwhelming majority of runaways and that when women began to escape in greater numbers, after the passage of the 1850 Fugitive Slave Act, they did so in groups headed by male slaves.[12] This interpretation is not completely accurate when compared to the database of Still's 995 runaways.

Of the 967 runaways whose gender is known, 730 (75 percent) were male. Of the 334 runaways known to have escaped alone, 270 (81 percent) were male. While these statistics agree with the historiography, a significant number of women escaped on the Underground Railroad as well. Of the 967 runaways whose gender is known, 237 (25 percent) were female. Of the 334 runaways known to have escaped alone, 63 (19 percent) were female. Thus, while it was rare for women to run away independently, this did happen.

Women were especially daring as well as ingenious in their escapes. Maria Weems, for example, was a fifteen-year-old slave girl from Washington, D.C., who disguised herself in men's clothing. Posing as a coachman to an abolitionist, Weems journeyed to Philadelphia by carriage in November 1855. The case of Lear Green, an eighteen-year-old slave who had herself secreted in a wooden chest and shipped to freedom on a steamer, has already been mentioned.[13] Even older women traveled the Eastern Line alone. Jane Davis, estimated to be "between sixty and seventy years old," escaped from Maryland's Eastern Shore in 1857 on foot. She spent "three weeks in the woods, almost wholly without nourishment," before reaching Philadelphia.[14]

While many more women escaped in male-led groups, it was not uncommon for women to strike out in all-female groups. This study found that eight female fugitives escaped in female-led groups. Two of these women escaped with several children: Anna Maria Jackson (seven children) and Harriet Shephard (five).[15] Another two women—Elizabeth Young and Sarah Bell—escaped with a single child. Four other women—Susan Stewart and Josephine Smith escaped together and Mary and Sarah Redden escaped together—relied on each other's help in making the trek to freedom.[16] The total number of female fugitives, escaping alone or in male- or female-led groups, is given by year in table 6.1.

TABLE 6.1 Female escapes: individual versus group, 1853–60, based on 237 known cases.

Year	Individual Escapes	Group Escapes	Total Escaped
1853	6	13	19
1854	15	20	35
1855	15	26	41
1856	6	44	50
1857	7	35	42
1858	8	15	23
1859	3	4	7
1860	1	10	11
Unknown	2	7	9
TOTALS	63	174	237

The table shows a steady increase in the number of female group escapes and the total number of female escapes between 1853 and 1856. This was part of a pattern of increasing escapes among slaves generally that can be explained by a series of events limiting congressional power to curtail the expansion of slavery, including the Wilkes-Barre, Pennsylvania, fugitive slave case of 1853; the Kansas-Nebraska Act of 1854; and the *Dred Scott* decision of 1857.

The category of "age" is not as reliable a statistic as gender because slaves generally did not know the date of their birth. As a result, Still, as well as many of the slaveholders whose advertisements are reprinted in his book, was forced to estimate the age of the runaways. In some cases the two estimates conflict with each other. For example, Jane Johnson was at a loss when asked her age during her court testimony in the case of Passmore Williamson. Instead, she estimated that she was born sometime between 1820 and 1830, which would have made her somewhere in the age range of thirty-five to forty-five during her escape in July of 1855.[17] Similarly, Bill Cole, a runaway from Howard County, Maryland, was reported to be thirty-seven years old in the newspaper advertisement written by his owners, William and Hammond Dorsey. Cole, however, insisted that he was ten years older and accounted for the discrepancy by explaining that his master could "sell him for much more at thirty-seven than at forty-seven."[18] These two cases represent the most extreme discrepancy, though. Most of the

TABLE 6.2 Age and gender of runaways, 1853–61, based on 602 cases where Still identified a runaway's age (121 female / 481 male).

Age Range	Female	Male	Total Escaped
1 month to 9 years	12	12	24
10 to 19 years	25	49	74
20 to 29 years	53	288	341
30 to 39 years	18	94	112
40 to 49 years	9	29	38
50 to 59 years	3	8	11
60 to 69 years	1	1	2
TOTALS	121	481	602

others involve a difference of just a year or two. Still's estimate is given preference in the database.

Of the 602 runaways whose age is known, 341 (57 percent) were in their twenties (table 6.2), and 510 (85 percent) were between the ages of seventeen and thirty-two. The majority of these fugitives (481; 80 percent) were male. These statistics confirm the assertion of the existing literature that male slaves in the prime years of their life made up the majority of fugitives.

Similar patterns exist for both men and women when the category of gender is examined. Of the 121 female slaves whose age is known, 53 (44 percent) were in their twenties when they escaped, and 75 (62 percent) were between the ages of seventeen and thirty-two. Of the 481 male slaves whose age is known, 288 (60 percent) were in their twenties when they escaped, and 384 (80 percent) were between the ages of seventeen and thirty-two. The average age for female runaways was twenty-four, and the average for male runaways, twenty-six.

The youngest fugitive was the one-month-old daughter of Daniel and Martha Bennett, who escaped from Leesburg, Virginia, in June 1855.[19] The oldest fugitive was either Jerry Mills, age sixty-five, or Jane Davis, who Still estimates was "either 60 or 70 years old." The escapes of these elderly slaves suggest that the desire for freedom did not dissipate with the passing of years. Mills escaped from Maryland in 1860 with his fifty-seven-year-old wife, Diana, and their three adult children, Cornelius, Margaret, and Susan. William Still noted that Mills was "smart for his years, but bore evidence that much hard labor had been wrung out of him by slavery." David Snively, the family's owner, had been a fierce taskmaster. Though he had been dead for several years before their escape, his widow treated them worse.[20] Jane Davis fled from Roger McZant of the New Market District on the Eastern Shore of Maryland in 1857. Many years earlier, her four children had been sold at auction. When she learned that McZant was about to sell her, she struck out on her own. She traveled "three weeks in the woods, almost wholly without nourishment," before reaching Philadelphia. "Jane, doubtless, represents thousands of old slave mothers," wrote William Still. "After having been worn out under the yoke of slavery, they are frequently offered for sale for a trifle, turned off to die, or compelled to eke out their existence on the most stinted allowance."[21]

Essentially, this study reveals that 85 percent of the runaways were in the seventeen-to-thirty-two age range and that the average age was twenty-five, which is consistent with the historiography. However, the significant number of women among Still's fugitives—as well as the identification of independent female runaways—offers a corrective to the historiography, which maintains that female escapes were rare and that those women who did escape traveled in the company of men. Women who traveled the Eastern Line of the Underground Railroad were not only courageous but highly creative in their escapes.

The Jane Johnson case also raises the issues of skin complexion and literacy. According to the historiography, mulatto, or lighter-skinned, slaves enjoyed many advantages over those of a darker hue. Owners often gave lighter-complexioned slaves positions as house servants, maids, cooks, tailors, waiters, and barbers. Some masters allowed them to be educated as well. Because of their privileged position, mulatto slaves often adopted the manners and general demeanor of whites. These advantages were especially helpful to light-complexioned runaways. Since the proportion of mulattos in the free black population was much higher than in the slave population, a light-skinned runaway, who was twice as likely to be literate than a black runaway, could more easily pass as a free person of color or assimilate into the free black population of a large northern city. On the other hand, the darker-complexioned field slaves composed the majority of runaways and were presumed to be illiterate.[22] But Jane Johnson was a house slave who could not sign her own name and was described as "chestnut colored" by William Still.[23] That description alone would contradict the historiographical profile of a "literate slave."

But the level of Johnson's literacy captured the public imagination in 2002 when Henry Louis Gates, chair of the Afro-American Studies Department at

Harvard University, discovered a manuscript titled the "Bondswoman's Narrative," written sometime between 1853 and 1860.[24] Hannah Crafts, the author of the manuscript, was a marginally educated black woman. Crafts was owned by John Hill Wheeler, a North Carolina politician who was living in Washington, D.C. Wheeler's ownership of Crafts and Jane Johnson, as well as other historical similarities, led Gates to surmise that the two women might be the same person. Among those similarities was a "hesitant penmanship" characterized by many strike-throughs, erratic capitalization, eccentric punctuation, and a vocabulary equivalent to the eleventh grade by modern standards, all of which suggest someone "who struggled to be educated."[25] Gates also pointed out that Johnson had to "affix her mark" to her affidavits in the wake of her escape from Wheeler but that she did acquire some degree of literacy between 1855 and 1860, probably when she settled in Boston and received a rudimentary education through the city's vigilance committee.[26] It is important to note, however, that Gates also identified many differences between Johnson and Crafts that suggest the similarities were mere coincidences. Other scholars contend that Johnson and Crafts were, in fact, the same woman, in part because of their demonstrable literacy.[27]

Regardless, the Jane Johnson case raises many interesting questions about skin complexion and literacy among freedom seekers. First, what exactly were the respective definitions of *black* and *mulatto*? Second, how were these definitions established, and were they accepted by both antebellum African Americans and whites? Finally, is there a direct correlation between literacy and the lighter-complexioned runaways assisted by William Still?

Defining the terms *black* and *mulatto* is complicated. Some social scientists consider the terms to describe "racial" traits, others "cultural" traits, and still others "ethnic" traits. Sociologist F. James Davis, in his work *Who Is Black? One Nation's Definition*, makes some important distinctions between these categories. He defines *race* as a "category of human beings being based on average differences in physical traits that are transmitted by the genes, not by blood." The term *culture*, on the other hand, is a "shared pattern of behavior and beliefs that are learned and transmitted through social communication." *Ethnicity* refers to a "group with a sense of cultural identity, such as Czech or Jewish Americans, but it may also be a racially distinctive group." Davis adds the caveat that a group that is "racially distinctive in society may be an ethnic group as well, but not necessarily." He concludes that most American blacks, though racially mixed, are "physically distinguishable from whites, but they are also an ethnic group because of the distinctive culture they have developed within the general American framework." Such an inclusive definition suggests that the terms *black* and *mulatto* should be viewed as describing "racial," "cultural," and "ethnic" traits.[28]

Davis also contends that historically the term *black* has been used in the United States to refer to "any person with any known African black ancestry" and reflects the "long experience with slavery." *Mulatto*, on the other hand, was originally used to mean the offspring of a "pure African Negro" and a "pure white." In the antebellum South, however, whites blurred the distinction by adopting the so-called one-drop rule, meaning that a single drop of "black blood" made a person black.[29] Naturally, this revision was made as miscegenation increased between owners and their female slaves and was done in order to increase the human chattel of the master as well as to maximize his financial income, which was based on slave labor. In fact, William Still notes that many of the slaves he assisted were "half brothers, and sisters, cousins, nephews, and nieces to their owners," and if there was any doubt, "blood would tell."[30] However, the above definitions of *black* and *mulatto* appear to have been established by the federal government. US census takers, for example, were extremely careful in distinguishing between all of the following terms:[31]

> Blacks: "those having three-fourths or more of African blood."
> Mulattos: "those having three-eighths to five eighths African blood."
> Quadroons: "those having one-fourth African blood."
> Octoroons: "those having one-eighth or any trace of African blood."

Among antebellum blacks there existed a caste system based on skin color. Although "whiteness" was denied to anyone with African blood, those African Americans with lighter skin generally commanded a higher position in the slave community as well as in the free black community. Blacks with biracial ancestry justified their social status by reversing the federal government's definitions and citing the amount of *white* blood they possessed. An octoroon had seven-eighths or more white blood, a quadroon three-fourths white blood, and a mulatto, five eighths to three-eighths white blood. Accordingly, an octoroon believed himself to be superior to a quadroon; a quadroon felt superior to a mulatto; and a mulatto felt superior to all who were less than mulattos, though all mixed bloods were called mulattos.[32]

This caste system was so entrenched in the slave community that, according to some accounts, there were slave women in the Deep South who did not resist the sexual advances of their white masters because of the "the prestige

T A B L E 6 . 3 Still's descriptors for skin color of runaways, 1853–61, based on 390 cases where he mentioned skin color. In this study, Still's several descriptors have been reduced to two: "black" and "mulatto."

Black

Bright Brown	Bright Orange	Light Chestnut	Full Black
Brown Skin	Ginger Bread	Jet Black	Superb Black Complexion
Chestnut Color	Light Brown	Dark Complexion	Unmixed Blood
Dark Orange	Dark Chestnut	Dark Hue	Very Dark Hue

Mulatto

Yellow Man	Mixed Race	Anglo Saxon Blood
Dark Mulatto	Light Mulatto	Mixed Blood
Near White	His Master's Blood	

that such a relationship would bring for them" and the "social acceptability" their mulatto offspring would gain. In fact, miscegenation was so common in the antebellum South that by 1850 there were 246,000 mulatto slaves out of a total slave population of 3.2 million.[33] Ten years later, in 1860, there were a total of 411,000 mulatto slaves out of a total slave population of 3.9 million. Thus the caste system that emerged from the arbitrary distinctions between "black" and "mulatto" appears to have been accepted by both African Americans and whites in antebellum society.

William Still went to great lengths to acknowledge these distinctions. He, and the slaveholders in the newspaper advertisements contained in his book, identify two dozen different skin complexions in their description of runaways (table 6.3). They range from "very dark hue" to "near white." In this study, the various descriptions have been reduced to two categories: "black" and "mulatto."

While these are subjective descriptions, the fact that Still and the slaveholders listed them underscores the importance of skin color among blacks and whites in antebellum America. If we reduce the various descriptions Still assigned to the skin color of the fugitives to two—"black" and "mulatto"—one discovers that the majority of runaways were "black." Specifically, of the 390 fugitives whose complexion is known, the majority (288; 74 percent) can be considered "black" according to the above-mentioned categories, while just 102 (26 percent) can be considered "mulatto." This finding is consistent with the historiography.[34]

While skin complexion was an important means of identifying runaway slaves, it was also an indicator of social status among slaves and their white owners, as previously noted. But there were exceptions. Lewis Lee was a twenty-five-year-old field slave of William Watkins, who lived near Fairfax, Virginia. According to Still, Lee, a mulatto, was "entirely too white for practical purposes." When Watkins refused to let him earn his own money, Lee "struck out on his own hook." He had saved a little money for himself, and because of his "near white color" he believed that he could "pass for white." Instead of stowing away on a steamer, or traveling through the woods under the cover of darkness, Lee "boldly approached a hotel and called for accommodations, as any other southern gentleman." His deception worked so well that Lee was "treated first rate in Washington and Baltimore" and arrived in Philadelphia without incident. However, Still noted that Lee had no intention of "disowning his [African American] origin." Once he arrived in Canada and felt safe, he intended to "assume his true status."[35]

Lee's case is instructive. Unlike other mulattos who took special pride in their mixed-race ancestry, Lee exploited his whiteness for the practical purpose of escaping. He had every intention of assuming his African American identity once he achieved his freedom. "Passing for white," in other words, was simply the means to a desired end. Lewis Lee saw himself as a *black* man by *choice* and by his *personal experience* in slavery. His example adds yet another dimension to the racial, cultural, and ethnic categories that have already been identified as composing the criteria for definitions of *black* and *mulatto*. Nor should the aspect of "choice" be marginalized with regard to racial identity.

Some male runaways assisted by Still chose to begin a new life in freedom with a white woman. For these couples, racial considerations were secondary to the love and intimacy they shared with each other. John Hall and Mary Weaver serve as an example. Hall was a thirty-five-year-old fugitive who escaped from James Dunlap of Richmond, Virginia, in April 1855. According to Still, Hall was "light complexioned, intelligent, rather handsome-looking, and of good manners." Though Dunlap valued him at just $1,000, Still surmises that if John had been "a few shades darker and only about half as intelligent he would have been worth at least $500 more," since the "idea of having had a white father depreciated the pecuniary value of male slaves."

While in slavery, John met and fell in love with Mary Weaver, a white Irish domestic. She helped earn the money that paid for his passage on the Underground Railroad to Philadelphia, where he came under the care of William Still.

Shortly after John's escape, Mary left Richmond for Hamilton, Canada, where the couple wed in September 1856.[36] According to Still, Mary Weaver was "certainly not annoyed by the kinks in John's hair," nor was she "overly fastidious about the small percentage of colored blood visible in John's complexion." Yet he was at a loss to explain why a white woman should want to marry a black man, noting that it was "a strange occurrence."[37] Interestingly, a year later in 1857, Still observed that a "great number of male fugitives in Canada" had found themselves "very acceptable to Irish girls, and frequently legal alliances are the result." It is clear that he did not condone these "alliances," believing that many of the male runaways had left wives and children in slavery. Still speculated that there were "many white women in Canada today who are married to some poor slave woman's fugitive husband."[38]

Such "alliances" between male fugitives—single or married—and Irish women were not made only by choice: they also reflected the common experience of servitude shared by both parties. Irish women who immigrated to the United States after the Potato Famine of the 1840s were often forced into indentured servitude to pay for their passage or to take low-paying jobs as domestics to wealthy white families. Among the European immigrants, the Irish were most discriminated against because of their lack of skills as well as for their Catholicism, which was greatly distrusted by white, Anglo-Saxon Protestant Americans.[39] In addition, poverty relegated various social groups to the same residential areas, and that proximity led to familiarity, sometimes even marriage. This tendency, as well as their common experience with discrimination, might explain why a runaway slave like John Hall and a white Irish immigrant like Mary Weaver were drawn to each other.

This study reveals that there was no significant difference in literacy rates between dark- and light-complexioned fugitives. Most slaves, regardless of skin complexion, never had the opportunity to learn to read and write. Both law and custom conspired to keep them illiterate or to prevent them from achieving positions closer to equality with whites. Of the sixty-nine cases where literacy is known, twenty-six (38 percent) of the mulatto runaways were literate and twenty (30 percent) of the black runaways were—not an appreciable difference. Skin color was not known for the remaining twenty-three runaways who were identified by Still as literate. However, the 8 percent difference in literacy rates between black and mulatto fugitives challenges the notion that light-complexioned slaves held a major educational advantage over those with a darker hue. In fact, there were varying degrees of literacy among the fugitives who were assisted by William Still, and not all of the mulattos were as refined in their writing skill as some of the blacks.

John Thompson, for example, was a nineteen-year-old mulatto who escaped bondage in Huntsville, Alabama. He was born in Farquhar County, Virginia, but was sold several times. Once he achieved freedom Thompson settled in Syracuse, New York, and sent the following letter via William Still, to his mother, Matilda, who was still a slave in Virginia:[40]

> Mr. Still: You will oblige me much If you will Direct this Letter to Vergenia for me to my Mother & iff it well sute you Beg her in my Letter to Direct hers to you & you Can send it to me iff it sute your Convenience I am one of your Chattle.
>
> JOHN THOMPSON

> My Dear Mother: I have imbrace an opportunity of writing you these few lines wanting that they may fine you as they Leave me quite well I will now inform you how I am getting. I am now a free man Living By the sweet of my own Brow not serving another man & giving him all I Earn But what I make is mine and iff one Plase do nit sute me I am at Liberty to Leave and go some where elce & can ashore you I think highly of Freedom and would not exchange it for nothing that is offered me for it I am waiting in a Hotel I suppose you remember when I was in Jail I told you the time would Be Better and you see that the time has come when I Leave you my heart ws so full & yours But I knew their was a better Day a head, & I have Live to see it I hird when I was on the Underground R. Road that the Hounds was on my Track but it was no go I new I was too far out of their Reach where they would never smell my track when I Leave you I was carried to Richmond & sold & From their I was taken to North Carolina and sold & I ran away & went back to Vergenia Between Richmond & home & their I was caught & Put in Jail & their I Remain till the oner come for me then I was taken & carried Back to Richmond than I was sold to the man I now Leave he is nothing But a But of a Feller Remember me to your Husband and all in quirin Friends & say to Miss Rosa that I am as Free as she is & more happier I no I am getting $12 per month for what Little work I am Doing I hope to here from you a gain I your son & ever By
>
> JOHN THOMPSON

Thompson's letter is rife with misspellings and little to no punctuation. Although he expresses himself in writing much in the same manner as an educated person would speak, his poor grammar reveals a limited writing ability. On the other hand, Mary Epps, a forty-five-year-old black runaway from Petersburg, Virginia, is much more refined in her writing. In the following letter she informs William Still of her safe arrival in Canada:[41]

Toronto, March 14th, 1855

Dear Mr. Still: I take this opportunity of addressing you with these few lines to inform you that I arrived here today, and hope that this may find yourself and Mrs. Still well. I will also say to you that I had no difficulty in getting along. The two young men who were with me left me at Suspension Bridge and went another way.

I cannot say much about the place as I have been here but a short time. But so far as I have seen, I like it very well. Please give my respect to your lady, and to Mr. and Mrs. Brown.

If you have not written to Petersburg you will please write as soon as you can.

Respectfully,

EMMA BROWN (old name MARY EPPS)

These two letters, along with the 8 percent difference in literacy rates between black and mulatto runaways, challenge the popular notion that there was a correlation between literacy and lighter-complexioned slaves. At the same time, literacy may be considered just one indicator of intelligence. John Thompson, for example, may not have been well-read, but his letter does indicate that he possessed the practical intelligence to escape and find gainful employment. On the other hand, there is no certainty that Emma Brown was as literate as her letter suggests. She might have had the letter written for her by another highly literate person, although Still suggests that she did her own letter writing.

Just as interesting is the fact that the literacy rates for both black and mulatto fugitives in this study are slightly higher than the estimates provided by other historians. Of the 996 runaways in this study, 69 (7 percent) were able to read and write compared to the more common estimate that only 5 percent of the slave population was literate.[42] The slightly higher literacy rate among William Still's fugitives may be attributed to the fact that the overwhelming majority were enslaved in the Upper South. They worked in closer proximity to their owners, often adopting their behaviors and speech.

In some cases, a literate slave was advantageous to a master. Sam Nixon is an example. Nixon was owned by a prominent Norfolk, Virginia, dentist, Dr. C. F. Martin. Martin taught Sam dentistry so he could "fulfill professional engagements, both at home and at a distance, when it did not suit his convenience." In fact, Sam was fully responsible for one-third of the annual income of $3,000 that Martin enjoyed from his dental practice. Though he had "never received an hour's schooling in his life," Sam was also Martin's "book-keeper," having learned to read and write on his own. Once he escaped, Sam assumed the alias Dr. Thomas Bayne and earned a living as a dentist.[43]

The escape of Jane Johnson is only one of dozens of escapes that were engineered by William Still on the Eastern Line. Philadelphia's free black community was critical to the success of that escape as it was to many others. While most free blacks served as conductors, others were stationmasters, and still others gathered intelligence that was essential to avoiding recapture by a slave hunter or a federal marshal. Just as significant was the assistance of white abolitionists who were motivated by the "Higher Law" doctrine, or the belief that whenever civil law and God's law conflicted, they had an obligation to follow the Almighty.[44] Many of these white abolitionists belonged to the Religious Society of Friends and formed a network that began in Philadelphia and extended in every conceivable geographic direction. Among the most influential of those Quakers was Thomas Garrett, who quickly became a dear friend to William Still.

S E V E N

"Dear Friends"

William Still worked with dozens of stationmasters and conductors during his tenure as chairman of Philadelphia's Vigilance Committee. But his closest ally was Thomas Garrett, a white Quaker merchant from Wilmington, Delaware. The two men made an unlikely pair, differing in temperament, background, and age, yet their fierce opposition to the moral evil of slavery bound them together as coconspirators on the Underground Railroad. Their relationship grew from one of mutual respect to affection as they routinely corresponded with each other to provide food, clothing, shelter, and funds for fugitive slaves. Both agents considered each other "personal friends," as evidenced by Still's remarks in his 1872 book and by Garrett's letters to the free black abolitionist, many of which began with the warm salutation, "Dear Friend."[1]

Like most Quakers, Garrett favored a broad-brimmed hat and long, dark waistcoat, and he projected a genial disposition—that is, unless he was defending his abolitionist beliefs. Then he could be outspoken, if not abrasive. Because Garrett was less circumspect in his activities than Still, he found himself embroiled in a legal dispute of his own making in 1848. Found guilty of harboring a family of fugitive slaves, the defiant Quaker was ordered to pay $5,400 and was warned by the court "not to meddle with slaves again."[2] Infuriated by the

FIGURE 7.1.
Thomas Garrett (1789–1871),
a Wilmington, Delaware,
hardware merchant, served as
a stationmaster for more than
four decades. He collaborated
with William Still in assisting
some hundreds of enslaved
people on their journey to
freedom. (Ambrotype ca. 1850.
Boston Public Library.)

sentence, Garrett quipped: "I have assisted over 1,400 runaways in 25 years on their way to the North, and I now consider the penalty imposed upon me as a license for the remainder of my life!"

Judge Roger B. Taney, who presided over the trial, was noticeably shocked by the Quaker stationmaster's belligerence. Taney believed that it was both a legal and a moral obligation to defend the constitutional right of slaveholders to reclaim their property—a conviction he would uphold nine years later as a Supreme Court justice in the *Dred Scott* decision. Just in case Taney doubted the Quaker agent's resolve, though, Garrett turned to the spectators and added: "If any of you know of any slave who needs assistance, send him to me, as I now publicly pledge myself to double my diligence and never neglect an opportunity to assist a slave in obtaining his freedom."[3]

Thomas Garrett's open defiance of civil authority was an inherited trait, part of a Quaker birthright. Born on August 21, 1789, at Upper Darby, Pennsylvania, Garrett was the son of Thomas and Sarah Price Garrett, Quakers whose farmhouse was an active station on the Underground Railroad. Although young Thomas assisted his parents in their abolitionist activities, he did not experience a personal conversion to the cause until 1813. Returning home after a hard day of farming, Garrett found his family in "sorrow and indignation" at the kidnapping of a free black woman in their employ. He immediately set out to rescue the woman before she could be sold into bondage. During his pursuit, the young Quaker had a spiritual revelation of the "utter sinfulness of slavery." Recovering the woman, he made an unconditional vow to assist slaves in their flight to freedom. Shortly after, Garrett joined the Pennsylvania Anti-Slavery Society and committed himself, wholeheartedly, to the Underground Railroad.[4]

In 1822, Garrett moved to Wilmington, Delaware, where he became a wealthy merchant and made no secret of his antislavery views and activities. Wilmington, which had a population of more than five thousand and was growing rapidly, was a popular destination for many industrious Quakers who wanted to take advantage of the town's agricultural trade and industry. It was also a hotbed of Underground Railroad activity, being the northernmost town in a slaveholding state. Fugitives from southern Delaware, Maryland, and Virginia flocked there in hope of being channeled to freedom.[5] Joining the Delaware Anti-Slavery Society, Garrett and his wife, Rachel Mendenhall, opened their home at 227 Shipley Street as a station on the Underground Railroad.[6] From there he would conduct fugitives across the Mason-Dixon Line into Chester County, Pennsylvania, where he had established contacts with other like-minded Quakers.

Between 1822 and 1863, Garrett assisted more than 2,320 fugitives on their flight to freedom.[7] His station was the starting point of the most active routes on the Eastern Line, and his activities were so prominent that neighbors considered him "dangerous to their community and destructive to the Union." Garrett's success in assisting runaways was so impressive that his example served as the inspiration for "Friend Phineas," a character in Harriet Beecher Stowe's famous work *Uncle Tom's Cabin*, published in 1852. Nevertheless, Garrett relied heavily on more than 120 stationmasters and conductors, and most of these agents were radical members of the Society of Friends that he met through his membership at the Progressive Friends Meeting at nearby Kennett Square, Pennsylvania.[8]

Robert C. Smedley, one of the earliest historians of the Underground Railroad, identified two of the major routes that originated at Garrett's Wilming-

FIGURES 7.2 and 7.3. Quaker abolitionists Isaac (1806–82) and Dinah Mendenhall (1807–89) harbored fugitive slaves on Chester County, Pennsylvania's Underground Railroad. The couple helped found Longwood Progressive Meeting in 1853, and Dinah met with President Abraham Lincoln in 1862 to urge him to enact the Emancipation Proclamation. (William Still, *The Underground Railroad* [Philadelphia: Porter and Coates, 1872).

ton station and extended through Chester County. Smedley's work not only is invaluable to understanding the operation of those routes but also offers insight into the backgrounds and activities of those agents who assisted Garrett in channeling fugitives to William Still in Philadelphia. One of the routes that originated at Garrett's station entered Chester County in Kennett and passed through East Marlborough, Newlin, Downingtown, Lionville, Kimberton, and Phoenixville to Philadelphia. The other route that began at Garrett's station in Wilmington extended through Kennett, East Bradford, West Chester, and Willistown to Philadelphia.[9] Regardless of the route, Garrett often sent runaways directly to "Oakdale," the Kennett home of Isaac and Dinah Mendenhall. Distinguished by two stone gateposts, this large, square brick house, along with the adjoining barn and springhouse, sheltered many fugitive slaves until nightfall, when they would be guided on northward. Garrett placed special trust in the Mendenhalls not only because they were Quakers but because they were also family members, being related to his wife Rachel.[10] But Oakdale was just one of many Kennett area stations.

To avoid predictability, Garrett also sent fugitives to the "Pines," the home of Dr. Bartholomew Fussell, one mile east of Kennett. Fussell was a very re-

FIGURES 7.4 and 7.5. John (1786–1880) and Hannah Cox (1797–1876) were also founding members of Longwood Progressive Meeting and harbored freedom seekers in their Chester County, Pennsylvania, home located less than twenty miles from the Mason-Dixon Line. (William Still, *The Underground Railroad* [Philadelphia: Porter and Coates, 1872].)

spected Quaker physician who had developed a commitment to abolitionism while living in Maryland and observing firsthand the evils of slavery. There he taught school during the week and studied medicine at night. Once, when asked to deliver an address before the Medical Society of Baltimore, many of whose members were slaveholders, Fussell denounced the peculiar institution as "the most preposterous and cruel practice" and expressed his hope that one day the "arrogant master and his menial slave will make a truce of friendship and be guided by the same light of Truth."[11] When he moved to Kennett he became involved in a number of reforms, including abolitionism, common schooling, temperance, and women's rights.[12] He also opened his house as a station on the Underground Railroad and established a boarding school for girls, "irrespective of color."[13] "A quiet, discreet, conservative Friend in religious matters," Fussell, according to one fellow abolitionist, was a "radical of the first order in political ones," being a fierce supporter of the Free Soil Party.[14] Predictably, he hired fugitives to work on his own farm. According to one legend, a former slave by the name of Eliza was paid to keep house while another fugitive, James Washington, was a hired laborer in the fields. Both of them were, after a time, married in a Quaker wedding ceremony at the good doctor's home.[15]

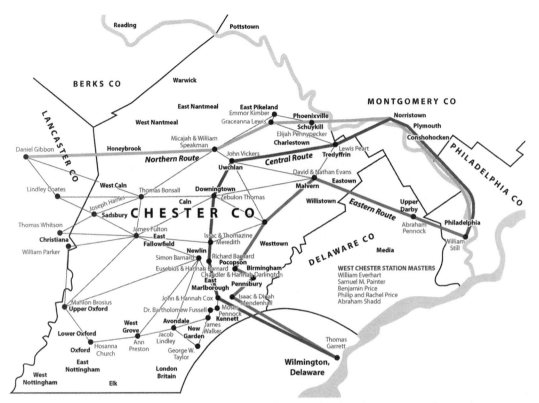

FIGURE 7.6. Chester County, Pennsylvania, Underground Railroad routes. Located in southeastern Pennsylvania just over the Mason-Dixon Line dividing free and slave states, Chester County had three major Underground Railroad routes and several secondary routes where fugitives could be diverted when being pursued by a federal marshal and/or slave catcher. (Chester County Historical Society, West Chester, Pennsylvania.)

John and Hannah Cox, who also lived near Kennett, provided yet another alternative station. Their home, "Longwood," was on the main road to Philadelphia from points south and west, and they eagerly opened it to fugitives, providing food, shelter, and clothing before transporting them on to the next station.[16] Inspired by the writings of William Lloyd Garrison, editor of the *Liberator*, and the poetry of Quaker abolitionist John Greenleaf Whittier, the Coxes joined a host of reform movements, including temperance, peace, women's rights, and prison reform.[17]

Once a fugitive reached Kennett, the particular route he or she took depended largely on circumstance. Since Kennett was like the hub of a wagon wheel with spokes leading in all directions, the fugitives had many choices open to them. Roads led east to Philadelphia and New Jersey; north to West Chester, Downingtown, Phoenixville, Lionville, and Kimberton; northwest to Ercildoun and Coatesville; and west to Avondale, West Grove, and Christiana in Lancaster County. To the south were the villages of New Garden, Landenberg, and Hockessin, Delaware. Consequently, if there was no space available at a station in West Chester, for example, the route could easily be altered to accommodate that problem. Similarly, alternative stations were often used when a fugitive was being pursued, if only to avoid predictability.

Kennett was not the only center of Quaker Underground Railroad activity either. New Garden, to the west, also took an active part on the clandestine route to freedom. Members of the New Garden Friends Meeting were instrumental in the success of the Eastern Line. Among the most dedicated abolitionists was Enoch Lewis, a distinguished teacher at Westtown, a local Quaker boarding school. Born on January 29, 1776, in Radnor Township, Lewis was introduced to the Underground Railroad in 1798 while teaching at a Friends' school in Philadelphia. There he met and married Alice Jackson, the daughter of a prominent Quaker abolitionist.[18] In 1827 he became the editor of a monthly abolitionist magazine, the *African Observer*. Devoted to the peaceable extinction of slavery, Lewis avoided provoking slaveholders; instead he appealed to their reason as well as moral conscience, attempting to convince them that slavery not only was "economically wasteful" but contradicted Christian principles.

"The slave is not the only object that demands our consideration," he wrote. "The introduction of negro slavery into the United States was not the work of the present generation. The system was entailed upon them by their ancestors and justice demands the admission that evils—both moral and political—are more easily discovered than removed." Those who are "subjected by the circumstances of their birth" are, then, "objects of sympathy with the Christian mind."[19] Such sympathy for the slaveholder was rare among even the most compassionate abolitionists. But that did not lessen the ardor of Lewis's struggle for emancipation, particularly when it came to protecting the human rights of those blacks who had made it to the North.

Jacob Lindley was another New Garden Quaker and the most respected minister in the meeting. A physically huge man with a booming voice, he was known to intimidate slave catchers. In fact, he was a man of true compassion for the poor and oppressed. His home on Indian Run Road, west of Avondale, was a popular station on the Underground Railroad and contained some ingenious hiding places. Carefully concealed beneath the closet floor was a small trapdoor that appeared to be part of the floor but led to a small, brick-enclosed hiding place below. He also had a secret staircase on the second floor that led to a small third-story attic, another hiding place for runaways.[20]

George W. Taylor was yet another New Garden Friend who was an intimate of both Lindley's and Lewis's. Born on March 14, 1803, he moved with his parents to New Garden in 1812 and studied there under Enoch Lewis. Like his mentor, he taught school at Westtown before opening a free produce store in Philadelphia, where he also published an abolitionist magazine, the *Non-Slaveholder*.[21] In 1834, Taylor established and served as secretary of the Free Produce Association of Friends, for the purpose of "free labor and placing those goods in stores where other, non-free labor goods are kept." With the assistance of Levi Coffin, a well-known abolitionist in Newport (present-day "Fountain City"), Indiana, he attempted to supply the entire market with cotton cloth made by free labor. His home in the village of Kaolin was another station on the Underground Railroad and contained an elaborate tunnel leading from the basement root cellar to a nearby barn that could aid in a quick escape if a slave hunter came calling. Taylor was also known to transport fugitives to the next station in a false-bottom wagon, designed so runaways could hide beneath a false floor that, in turn, could be piled high with bales of hay or other farm produce.[22]

After the passage of the Fugitive Slave Act in 1850, Eusebius and Sarah P. Barnard of Pocopson opened their home in northern Chester County as a station in order to accommodate the growing traffic of runaways. Eusebius, who descended from a long line of Quaker abolitionists, was one of the most respected ministers in the Society of Friends and along with his first wife, Sarah Painter, became involved in many religious and reform activities.[23] After being widowed and left to raise eight children, he remarried the daughter of another prominent abolitionist family, Sarah Marsh of Caln Township. Together, they and the children continued to receive fugitives from Garrett, the Mendenhalls, and Fussell.[24]

Eusebius sent most of the fugitives who came to his station to Dr. Eshelman of Downingtown, the most reliable of his numerous contacts. Many stories have been handed down through the generations about the close association between these two stationmasters. In March 1861, for example, two women with four children were brought to Eusebius's home late in the evening. Though he had already gone to bed in order to be fresh for a lecture he was to deliver at the Fairville Seminary the next day, Eusebius assumed his responsibility. After feeding the fugitives and bedding them down for a few hours' sleep, he awakened

FIGURE 7.7.
Quaker potter John Vickers
(1780–1860) transported
runaways in his wagon concealed
in the hay among pottery. When
forwarding freedom seekers to the
next Underground Railroad station
he often signed a letter of introduction as "Thy friend, Pot."
(William Still, *The Underground
Railroad* [Philadelphia: Porter
and Coates, 1872].)

them at 2:00 a.m. and started out on the journey to the next closest station. Three times he approached local stationmasters and three times he was turned away for one reason or another. Disappointed at every turn, Eusebius went to Eshelman, who gladly accepted the slaves.[25]

Of all Chester County's Quaker stationmasters, John Vickers, a potter, appears to have been the most colorful. Parties of six, seven, or more slaves were often brought to his Lionville home near midnight from stations across the county. After a good meal, they were secreted in the cellar, which was accessible through a carefully hidden closet off one of three dining rooms. Vickers himself frequently conducted slaves in his pottery wagons, with children being concealed in some of the larger jardinares. According to one tale, Vickers set out on a thirty-mile trip to Philadelphia one night with two female runaways concealed in the rear box of his dearborn. Midway through the journey a storm began, and Vickers, traveling too close to the edge of the turnpike, overturned. No one was hurt, but the carriage was badly damaged. Vickers instructed the two runaways to hide in the woods and to remain there quietly until he returned and gave them a special signal. Riding his horse into the nearest town, Vickers borrowed a wagon from the local innkeeper, who insisted on repairing his broken dearborn.

FIGURE 7.8.
In 1831 Elijah Pennypacker (1802–88) was elected to the US House of Representatives, but eight years later he resigned to focus on the antislavery cause. He became active in various antislavery societies, opened his home as a stop on the Underground Railroad, and spoke widely against slavery. (William Still, *The Underground Railroad* [Philadelphia: Porter and Coates, 1872].)

When the two men arrived at the scene of the accident, not a sound was made until the innkeeper left with the damaged carriage. Only then did Vickers give the whistle he had promised, and the two women reappeared to continue their journey to the next station.[26] Nor was it unusual for Vickers to forward a slave to the next station with a letter of introduction bearing the signature "Thy friend, Pot."[27] It is said that one frustrated slave owner, after a fruitless search at the Vickers house, remarked, "You may as well look for a needle in a haystack as for a nigger among Quakers!"[28]

Among Chester County's other prominent Quaker stationmasters were Emmor Kimber of Kimberton and Elijah Pennypacker of Phoenixville. Kimber took an early and active part in the abolition of slavery. In 1787 he established a boarding school for girls, which he conducted for nearly twenty years. Together with his own home, the school was an important station on the Underground Railroad, and tunnels that ran beneath the building and its grounds were used as hiding places for runaways. His abolitionist involvements were well known among neighbors and largely unappreciated. Not surprisingly, when a fugitive slave who had been given work on the school's grounds attacked Kimber with a pitchfork, the local community viewed it as fitting retribution for his illegal activities.[29]

Elijah Pennypacker was one of the more unusual UGRR agents because of his active involvement in politics, something the majority of agents distrusted.

A state representative of the Anti-Mason Party, Pennypacker served in the legislature from 1831 to 1835. He was subsequently elected secretary of the Board of Canal Commissioners, which at that time was the most responsible political position in the Commonwealth aside from governor, as it controlled all internal improvements. When he returned to private life in the 1840s, he became one of the more radical abolitionists in the country as well as a stationmaster on the Underground Railroad.[30] He served, at various times, as president of the Phoenixville Anti-Slavery Society, the Chester County Anti-Slavery Society, and the Pennsylvania Anti-Slavery Society. Despite his controversial reputation and his close personal friendship with Rep. Thaddeus Stevens, who would later lead the Radical Republican Congress during the Reconstruction era, Pennypacker was, by all accounts, a gentle, modest, and courteous gentleman who combined "in a remarkable degree, strength and tenderness, courage and sympathy." His home, near Phoenixville, was considered by the free black community as "an important station since the majority of fugitives proceeding through the southern and rural districts of eastern Pennsylvania, passed through his hands."[31]

Garrett, Fussell, Lewis, Taylor, Lindley, Vickers, Kimber, Pennypacker, the Coxes, and the Mendenhalls, among others, were all prominent Chester County Quakers engaged in the Underground Railroad. They constituted part of a highly influential and fairly well-organized network of abolitionists, related through patterns of religion, kinship, and reform activity. It was also an intimate network, founded upon the conviction common among Friends that they were a "peculiar people," called to be different from the "world's people." Their social testimonies on equality, simplicity, pacifism, and community, as well as the personal etiquette and dress by which they publicly displayed these testimonies, distinguished Friends from their non-Quaker neighbors.[32]

Of the 127 agents known to have been involved in Chester County's Underground Railroad, 87 of them belonged to the Religious Society of Friends. Although these Quakers ranged in age from young adults to people in their eighties and varied in occupation, their Quaker faith and the peculiar culture it bred allowed them to be highly successful stationmasters and conductors on Chester County's Underground Railroad.[33] Of the 27 Quaker agents whose wealth is known, the average estate was valued at $5,258, fixing this group solidly in the middle class. Forty of the 87 agents were related by blood or marriage, including 11 husband-wife couples: Eusebius and Sarah Barnard; Mahlon and Mary Brosius; John and Hannah Cox; Joseph and Ruth Dugdale; Bartholomew and Lydia Fussell; Benjamin and Hannah Kent; Robert and Rachel Lamborn; Isaac and Dinah Mendenhall; Isaac and Thomazine Meridith; Moses and Mary Pennock;

and Benjamin and Jane Price. Of the eleven couples, four—the Barnards, Brosiuses, Pennocks, and Prices—made their Underground Railroad activity a family affair, involving at least one child. The families of Cox, Garrett, Lewis, Meredith, and Preston were in turn connected by blood and intermarriage with those of Lamborn, Mendenhall, Fussell, and Pennock. Additionally, at least ten Quaker abolitionists had been associated prior to their abolitionist activities. George Taylor was a student of Enoch Lewis's at Westtown, for example, and Emmor Kimber and Lewis taught for a brief time at the Friends Public School in Philadelphia. Similarly, Sumner Stebbins was apprenticed to Dr. Bartholomew Fussell to learn the practice of medicine, and Elijah Pennypacker and William Everhart were active members of Chester County's Republican Party.

Another outstanding characteristic of this Quaker network was its involvement in reforms outside of abolitionism. Of the eighty-four Friends, thirty were involved in at least one other reform activity, sixteen in women's rights alone. Women's rights was probably the second most popular reform activity outside of abolitionism because of the special empathy women felt for the slave and his lack of basic human rights. Women such as Hannah Darlington, Graceanna Lewis, Lucretia Mott, and Ann Preston garnered from abolitionism not only valuable experience in organizational tactics but a growing awareness of the striking similarities between the oppression of women and that of slaves as they continually faced denials of their right to speak or act politically.[34] "When once it is admitted that women have souls, and they are accountable to God for the uses of the powers which he has given them," wrote Preston, who campaigned for the right of women to enter the field of medicine, "then men will come to understand that the study and practice of medicine are proper, womanly, and adapted to our mental, moral and physical condition."[35] But the more active they became in antislavery activities, the more hostility they encountered. For the Lewis sisters, the attacks only strengthened their resolve as stationmasters.

Left fatherless at an early age, the sisters quickly became attached to their uncle, Dr. Bartholomew Fussell, who made sure that they grew up with an abolitionist influence. One of their earliest experiences was seeing a "colored man, Henry, bound in chains and carried off into slavery." It so shocked them that the sisters began collecting and reading antislavery poetry. By 1836, they had joined the American Anti-Slavery Society and were instrumental in forming a local abolitionist society.[36] Their home at Kimberton was an important station, receiving passengers from Wilmington, York, and the southern parts of Chester and Lancaster Counties. During one especially busy week, the Lewis sisters passed about forty fugitives through their house and were later amused to hear one neighbor remark: "There used to be a pretty brisk trade of running off niggers at the Lewis house, but there's not much of it done there now."[37] In fact, the Lewises' neighbors were bitter opponents of abolitionism, especially toward the three sisters because of their involvements in temperance and women's rights as well as the Underground Railroad.

Male abolitionists were divided about women's rights. Denied permission to speak at the World Anti-Slavery Convention in 1840, Lucretia Mott resolved to increase her women's rights activities. By 1848, her efforts resulted in the convening of a women's rights convention at Seneca Falls, New York, to protest the inferior treatment of women by creating a list of their grievances. Modeling the language of their Declaration of Sentiments on the Declaration of Independence, the women at Seneca Falls declared that it was a self-evident truth that "all men and women are created equal" and that men had usurped women's freedom and dignity. "Man has endeavored in every way he could to destroy woman's confidence in her own powers," the Declaration charged, "to lessen her self-respect, and to make her willing to lead a dependent and abject life." The document concluded with eleven resolutions calling for equal opportunities in education and work, equality before the law, and the right to appear on public platforms. The most controversial resolution, however, called for a woman's "sacred right to the elective franchise."[38]

Hannah Darlington was so inspired by the Seneca Falls convention that she organized a similar meeting at West Chester's Horticultural Hall on June 2, 1852. Lucretia Mott delivered the major address at that conference. Darlington, Preston, and the Lewis sisters, along with other female stationmasters such as Hannah Cox, Dinah Mendenhall, and Sarah Barnard, were all in attendance, as were many other middle-class women. Men also answered the call to discuss the role of women in society and ways to improve women's legal and political status. Among them were John Cox, Joseph Dugdale, Isaac Mendenhall, Simon Barnard, and Thomas Garrett. Despite their participation, the convention explicitly blamed men for the injustices suffered by the female sex. A series of resolutions, similar to those proposed at Seneca Falls, were approved, including one that asserted women's "natural right to equal participation with men in the political institutions."[39]

Local press coverage was relatively benign, simply reprinting the text of the major speeches and the resolutions. Only the *Pennsylvania Freeman*, an abolitionist newspaper, applauded the meeting as a "formidable assault upon old ideas and institutions."[40] The conservative *Jeffersonian*, on the other hand, attacked the women who attended the conference as "old maids, amazons, and infidels," and the male participants as "old women in pantaloons."[41]

Despite the criticism—or perhaps because of it—many of these same female reformers were responsible for joining black and white abolitionists together in their work on the Underground Railroad. Among the first to do so was Lucretia Mott, who established the Philadelphia Female Anti-Slavery Society in 1833. This organization was composed of both black and white women, including Chester County Quakers Ann Preston and Graceanna Lewis and black female abolitionists such as Sarah Douglass, Mary Ellen Shadd Cary, and Charlotte Forten.[42]

To be sure, Quakers earned an early and well-deserved reputation as friends to fugitive slaves and dominated the abolitionist ranks of southeastern Pennsylvania. However, they were not the only stationmasters or conductors to assist Garrett.[43] Unlike other reform movements, where Quakers tended to divide along theological lines between interdenominational and sectarian involvement, in the cause of abolition radical Quakers worked together with non-Quakers on the Underground Railroad.[44] Stationmasters and conductors were able to transcend denominational differences for the success of their common cause. The Eastern Line, like the Underground Railroad itself, was a truly ecumenical movement. Agents belonged to several religious denominations, most notably the African Methodist Episcopal, Presbyterian, and Episcopal Churches.

One of those from the AME Church with whom Garrett worked most closely was Harriet Tubman. Born into slavery in Dorchester County, Maryland, Tubman escaped in 1849 and vowed to help her family and others flee from bondage. Having escorted more than one hundred slaves to freedom, Tubman was called the "Moses of her people."[45] Between 1845 and 1860, Garrett estimated that she "passed through my hands 60 to 80 persons from Maryland."[46] On her trips north, he provided Tubman with sanctuary, shoes, and funding. If he didn't hear from Tubman for an extended period of time, he would write to William Still, "anxious to learn of [his] heroine's whereabouts."[47]

Speaking with great admiration for Tubman's dangerous journeys to the North and inspired by her deep and abiding Christian faith, Garrett once claimed that "Harriet has a good deal of the old-fashioned Quaker about her" and described her as a "firm believer in a spiritual manifestation." He spoke of her having the "Lord's hand to guide her"; she had once confided to him that "God will preserve me from harm in all my journeys, 'cause I never go anywhere

FIGURE 7.9. Born into slavery on Maryland's Eastern Shore, Harriet Tubman (ca. 1822–1913) escaped to freedom in the North in 1849. She became the most famous "conductor" on the Underground Railroad, risking her life to lead dozens of family members and other slaves to freedom. (Library of Congress.)

without His consent."[48] To be sure, Tubman believed that Garrett's assistance was the result of the divine will as well.

Whenever she approached Garrett for funding, she would greet the Wilmington Quaker with the phrase "God has sent me to you for money and a new pair of shoes." On one occasion though, Garrett, playing devil's advocate, responded: "Harriet, art thou sure thou art not deceived? I cannot find money enough to supply all God's poor. I had five here last week and had to pay 8 dollars to clothe and forward them."

"God never fools me," she insisted. "Now I'm sure you've got enough money to pay for a pair of shoes and to pay for my own and a friend's passage to Philadelphia." Impressed by her determination, Garrett gave her twenty dollars.[49]

While Tubman's deep spiritual connection to God and profound religious devotion endeared her to Garrett, William Still was not as impressed by her. She did not fit Still's idea of a proper woman in appearance or behavior. Tubman, who had jet-black skin, a homely face, and the physical strength of a man, reminded Still of an "unfortunate farm hand of the South." He was embarrassed by her illiteracy and rough-hewn behavior. In the only two pages devoted to her in his 1872 book, Still noted that Tubman carried a revolver when conducting fugitives and threatened to shoot any runaway who tried to turn back on the journey, declaring that "a live runaway could do great harm" to the safety of the others but that a "dead one could tell no secrets." Still may have been put off by Tubman because he felt himself above her in social status and etiquette. His rising stature among Philadelphia's white middle class reinforced his elite self-perception and the belief that he belonged to a "better sort" than Tubman. Nevertheless, Still conceded that "in point of courage, shrewdness and disinterested exertions to rescue her fellow men" by repeatedly returning to the South, Tubman "was without equal."[50]

Among the Presbyterian agents who assisted Garrett were William Everhart and Joseph Fulton. Everhart, a general store owner–turned–lawyer, purchased land in West Chester, which he subdivided and sold as building lots. He built his own home at Market Street and Church Street in 1831 and converted it into the Mansion House Hotel.[51] Garrett, John and Hannah Cox, and other Quaker stationmasters would direct fugitives to the hotel, where they remained until dark before being transported on to the next station.[52] Everhart's legal experience was valuable in protecting other Underground Railroad operators like the Quaker physician Dr. Bartholomew Fussell when he was charged with harboring slaves in violation of the Fugitive Slave Act of 1850. It also allowed him to become a national advocate for abolitionism when he was elected to the US Congress as a Whig in 1852.[53]

Fulton, a farmer from Sadsbury, not only opened his home as a station but after working in the fields all day stayed up late into the night writing letters to congressmen on behalf of the abolitionist cause. According to the *Village Record*, he died at the young age of thirty-eight from "typhoid fever, attended by congestion of the brain." His illness was attributed by friends to "excessive activity, bodily and mental induced by the slave question before Congress."[54]

Episcopalians Benjamin Pyle and John T. Worthington were also active on the Eastern Line. Both men were West Chester lawyers and stationmasters, though much less is known about their activities.[55] These non-Friends joined with Garrett and his Quaker network in channeling fugitive slaves through Chester County and on to freedom. Aside from the Society of Friends, only the Free Will Baptists and Wesleyans viewed slavery as sinful and wanted to see it abolished. Not even the African Methodist Episcopal Church would publicly condemn slavery, though its members gave unconditional support to emancipation, never questioning the evils of the peculiar institution, the need to abolish it, or the moral obligation to assist runaways.

Conversely, the white mainstream churches of the North disagreed on the nature and extent of their antislavery positions. Like the Society of Friends, some churches favored a gradual and peaceful end to slavery by appealing to individual slaveholders to emancipate their chattel instead of violating the federal law by actively assisting fugitives. Others advocated immediate emancipation, also within the scope of federal laws. For any denomination to identify itself publicly with the Underground Railroad would incriminate all its members, subjecting ministers and congregants to incarceration and/or stiff fines for violating the Fugitive Slave Act. As a result, the success of the Underground Railroad was largely due to the efforts of individuals of many different churches who viewed their activities as consistent with the principles of Christianity as set forth in the Bible.[56] Together with Philadelphia's free black community, William Still relied on these radical abolitionists for their support in gathering intelligence, housing fugitives, and conducting them to freedom.

Still, in his 1872 book, identified several of the agents who assisted him. Like those who assisted Garrett, this group transcended the boundaries of race, gender, religion, and age. What is important to note is that while Still identified at least two dozen agents, he purposely omitted the names of others or referred to them as a group when he recorded the interviews of runaways in the 1850s,

TABLE 7.1 Underground Railroad agents, 1853–61, with the number of fugitives they helped, based on 172 cases where a runaway identified a stationmaster and/or conductor.

Captain Alfred Fountain (55)	Frank Wanzer (3)	William Bagnell (1)
Thomas Garrett (53)	Elijah Pennypacker (2)	James Jefferson (1)
"Captain B" (27)	English sailors (2)	Emily Ann Mah (1)
Harriet Tubman (21)	Abraham Shadd (2)	James Massey (1)
Captain Robert Lee (6)	Samuel Williams (2)	Robert A. Parrett (1)
Mrs. Buchanan (5)	Rev. Hiram Wilson (2)	Jacob Parsons (1)
Henry Franklin (5)	"Colored Boatman" (1)	E. L. Stevens (1)
"Friends" / Quakers (3)	"Doctor H" (1)	

fearing that he might incriminate his assistants if his writings were ever discovered by federal authorities.[57] As a result, of the 995 runaways in the database, there are only 172 cases where the assistance of a stationmaster or conductor is known. For those 172 cases, Still identifies a total of twenty-three different agents, many of whom assisted multiple runaways. The most frequently identified agent is Captain Alfred Fountain, who assisted fugitives in 55 (31 percent) of the cases. Garrett served as a stationmaster in another 53 (30 percent) cases, sometimes aided by the most prominent black conductor Harriet Tubman, who was involved in a total of 21 (12 percent) of the 172 cases. Table 7.1 lists all the Underground Railroad agents with the number of fugitives they assisted.

Note that the table gives the total number of fugitives assisted as 197. The discrepancy between this number and the 172 cases for whom the assisting agent is known is due to the involvement of two agents in multiple cases. For example, Thomas Garrett and Harriet Tubman worked together in fifteen cases, and Garrett joined with Captain Alfred Fountain in another eight cases.

The most compelling pattern that exists among this group of agents is that it was composed of both black and white abolitionists, reflecting the interracial nature of the Underground Railroad network. Although the majority of agents were white, there were also many African Americans. Some were former slaves like Harriet Tubman, James Massey, Frank Wanzer, and Samuel Williams.[58] Other agents were free blacks, such as the "colored boatman" from Richmond, Virginia, who helped runaways make their escape via steamer, and Abraham Shadd, a West Chester, Pennsylvania, shoemaker who was a prominent member of the American Anti-Slavery Society.[59] These black agents worked *directly* with white agents.

For example, Tubman was a frequent visitor to the home of Thomas Garrett, who relied heavily on other free black conductors such as Severen Johnson, Comegeys Munson, James Walker, and Joseph Hamilton.[60]

William Still recognized the importance of interracial cooperation and credited white abolitionists, free blacks, and the fugitives themselves with the success of the Underground Railroad. He acknowledged the "Christ-like exhibition of love and humanity" extended by white and free black abolitionists working together to "serve the anti-slavery cause in its darkest days." No less important were the freedom seekers, who, "as a general rule," were "physically and intellectually above the average order of slaves and were determined to have liberty even at the cost of life."[61] Whether they were runaways themselves or former slaves who returned to the South as conductors, these African Americans were not helpless individuals but very capable, self-reliant people who took matters into their own hands.[62]

Another group of agents were the captains of steamers and schooners who stowed away fugitives in the holds of their ships. Ship captains made a business of shuttling fugitives from southern ports to freedom in the North. While the risks were great, the possibilities of profit were even greater. According to Still, the majority of the captains "would bring any kind of freight that would pay the most," some charging as much as $100 per fugitive.[63] Of the 175 agents identified by Still, there were three ship captains: Captain "B," Captain Alfred Fountain, and Captain Robert Lee. Of the three seafaring agents, Fountain assisted the most fugitives. His schooner sailed out of the port cities of Richmond and Norfolk, Virginia, conducting a regular packet service to New York City. Fountain often stopped at Wilmington, Delaware, to drop off or pick up Garrett's fugitives, and at Philadelphia, where Still arranged to have his "cargo" shuttled to his office.[64]

Between 1855 and 1859, the crafty sea captain made at least six trips to the North shuttling fifty-five fugitives safely to freedom. Still considered the seafarer "a true friend of the slave" and one of the most daring and heroic captains ever connected with the Underground Railroad." Fountain's intimidating physical appearance and crude manner suggested that he was a formidable challenge to any slave hunter. He possessed brute strength, and his rugged features were highlighted by "a large head, wide eyes and bushy eyebrows." According to Still, Fountain lived in two worlds, that of the abolitionists as well as that of the slave hunters, and, "with the faith of a martyr" he could "deliberately enter the enemy's domain with his Bowie knives and revolvers for humanities sake." He was more than willing to sacrifice his life for the cause and had "no fear of death however it might come." Fountain's resoluteness was tested on several occasions, but none more severe than in November 1855, when the mayor and police of Norfolk, Virginia, boarded his schooner in search of runaways.

Hidden in the hold were twenty-one fugitives—sixteen men and five women. Demanding to inspect the ship, the mayor and the police officers, equipped with long spears and axes, were granted permission by Fountain, who had a "natural gift for concealing the inner workings of his mind and feelings." No sooner did the policemen begin axing the decks than the crafty sea captain outwitted them. Seizing one of the axes, Fountain offered to break open any spot the mayor desired and began attacking the decks with a ferocity that bordered on insanity. The outrageous display convinced the mayor that he had seen enough and—after accepting the five-dollar search fee required of every vessel leaving Virginia—allowed Captain Fountain to set sail for the North.[65]

While Fountain was more committed to fugitives out of benevolent feelings, he was "not averse to receiving compensation for his services."[66] But Captain William Baylis, who conducted another twenty-seven runaways to freedom on his schooner, *Keziah*, considered his services a business. According to Still, who referred to Baylis as simply "Captain B," Baylis required at least three passengers, each paying a hundred dollars, before he would sail his schooner from Richmond to Philadelphia. Captain "B" believed that the fee was justified by the risk he was taking in breaking smuggling laws. On at least one occasion, however, the enterprising captain refused to earn a substantial profit offered by a slaveholder. The owner happened to receive a boastful letter from his former slave who had escaped to Canada. Infuriated by the insult, he offered Captain "B" $2,000 if he would locate the runaway and return him. Whether the captain was compelled by feelings of benevolence is not known, but he refused the offer.[67]

In 1858, Baylis's luck ran out. Caught in the act of transporting a group of fugitives at Petersburg, Virginia, Captain "B" was excoriated in the local newspapers as a "medley of Avarice and larceny." When the freedom seekers were interrogated by the authorities, they told how the captain had approached them at a marketplace in a Virginia coastal town and extorted a hefty payment to transport them North. Sentenced to forty years in the state penitentiary, Baylis, after just six years, was pardoned by Confederate president Jefferson Davis and released. He returned to his native Delaware, where William Still arranged to set him up as a grocery merchant.[68]

Quakers and non-Quakers, blacks and whites, men and women, young and elderly, free blacks and slaves, farmers, merchants, and even ship captains composed William Still's extensive network of agents. Their collective effort indicates that involvement on the Eastern Line of the Underground Railroad was an *individual* decision based on moral choice and had little to do with religious denomination, race, gender, age, or occupation—just like Still's relationship with his dear friend Thomas Garrett.

E I G H T

Canada West

William Still and his colleagues on the Philadelphia Vigilance Committee hoped that the hundreds of fugitives they assisted would remain in the United States and carve out a new life of freedom in large northern cities, where they could assimilate into the free black population, or in the small black communities that dotted the rural North. But the growing number of freedom seekers choosing to relocate to Canada indicated that they believed otherwise.

Between 1840 and 1860, the Underground Railroad transported thousands of fugitives to freedom in Canada from Nova Scotia to British Columbia.[1] The Act Against Slavery, passed in 1793, made Upper Canada (Ontario) the first British colony to prohibit slavery. In the 1820s Canada stopped the extradition of fugitives to the United States, and by 1833 the entire country had abolished slavery.[2] Most runaways settled in Canada West, present-day southwestern Ontario, where black men had the right to own property and purchase land at reduced rates. Educational subsidies were available, and those who met the property requirements could even vote.[3]

Although there had been a steady trickle of fugitives to Canada for decades, the passage of the Fugitive Slave Act in 1850 triggered an exodus of former slaves from every US city with a sizable black population. According to the

British and Foreign Anti-Slavery Society, within a year of the bill's passage, some five thousand African Americans emigrated to Canada, three thousand within three months after the enactment of the new law.[4] Because blacks were not guaranteed liberty, even in the "free states" of the North, entire church congregations and neighborhoods from such cities as Buffalo, Boston, and Pittsburgh picked up stakes and relocated across the border to take advantage of the legal protection Canada afforded.[5] During the next decade, some fifteen thousand to twenty thousand runaways fled to Canada West, settling in such cities as Toronto, Chatham, London, and Windsor as well as in rural areas along Lake Erie and Lake Ontario and in the all-black communities of Dawn, Wilberforce, Dresden, and Buxton.[6] There they became productive citizens, clearing and cultivating the land, building homes, and raising families. They founded churches, schools, benevolent societies, fraternal organizations, and two newspapers. Some became businessmen, operating grocery stores, barbershops, livery stables, pharmacies, and even a taxi company. Others were teachers, farmers, waiters, carpenters, carters, rope makers, blacksmiths, coopers, and dockside workers. Still others became ministers, physicians, and lawyers. Regardless of wealth or occupation, these former slaves fought for racial equality, and their communities were centers for abolitionist activities.[7]

The African American fugitives were also ardent supporters of the most conservative Tories, believing that if Canada remained under British rule, their freedom, and hence their future, were secure. Runaways who settled in Canada West did not want to be viewed as objects of charity. They made a strong effort to contribute to the region and to serve in the colonial militia. There was a special sense of pride in bearing arms to defend a country that ensured freedom for all its citizens. For a people who had spent a lifetime in bondage, who were prohibited from carrying firearms, and who faced the severest punishment for protecting a family member, the opportunity to defend themselves the most liberating experience of all.[8]

William Still was updated on the progress of freedom seekers who resettled north of the US border in a correspondence he conducted with John Henry Hill, a fugitive from Petersburg, Virginia, whom he assisted in January 1853. After settling in Canada West, Hill wrote Still several letters describing the "better quality of life" blacks enjoyed there and repeatedly requested that Still arrange for the escapes of his family members and friends who remained in bondage. According to one letter, the fugitives assisted by Still were so content with their new life in Canada that "they will not go back" to the United States. One of these runaways even wrote his former master and dared him to "come after me" because if he did "the [Canadian] [black] people here will kill him."[9]

Realizing that Canada had become the desired destination for runaway slaves after the passage of the 1850 law, southern planters painted a bleak picture of that country to discourage their slaves from escaping. Some of the tales emphasized widespread famine due to the ten-month-long winters that limited agricultural production. Other rumors maintained that the Canadians were operating their own illegal slave trade by kidnapping runaways and returning them to slavery in the United States. There were even reports that bounty hunters, after recapturing a fugitive, would cut off their hair and sell it to Canadian haberdashers, who would use it to make collars for winter coats. Although the horrendous tales were intended to convince slaves that they enjoyed a better life in bondage, they only seemed to increase the number of escapes.[10]

On the other hand, emigration to Canada was encouraged by many black abolitionists, but none was more passionate than Mary Ann Shadd, the editor of the antislavery newspaper *Provincial Freeman*.[11] Having been born in Delaware and raised in Pennsylvania, she possessed the life experience, education, and writing skills to best articulate the differences between the two countries. Shadd, a mulatto, was the daughter of free black abolitionist Abraham Shadd, an Underground Railroad agent in Pennsylvania who relocated to Canada in 1851 and became the only black man elected to public office in that country before the Civil War.[12]

Educated at a Quaker boarding school, Mary Ann Shadd, in 1840, established a school for black children in Wilmington, and later others at Norristown, Pennsylvania, and Trenton, New Jersey. By the age of twenty-one, she was a seasoned teacher with strong opinions. Although Shadd was a mulatto, she identified herself as African American. Yet she benefited from advantages that most blacks, free or enslaved, did not enjoy, including a secondary education and a strong influence among both white and free black abolitionists. In January 1849, she wrote a long letter to Frederick Douglass, editor of the abolitionist newspaper *North Star*, on how to improve the "wretched conditions" for free blacks in the North.[13] Criticizing the ineffectiveness of the many conventions held by the Pennsylvania Anti-Slavery Society and the inability of free blacks to implement any of the programs they devised, Shadd insisted that "we should do more and talk less." She went on to promote agricultural investment so that blacks could become producers and not just consumers; greater educational opportunity; and interracial political organization. She also criticized the AME Church

FIGURE 8.1.
Mary Ann Shadd Cary (1823–93)
was an active abolitionist and the
first black female newspaper editor in
North America when she founded the
Canadian antislavery newspaper, the
Provincial Freeman. Cary earned a law
degree in 1883 from Howard University,
becoming the second black woman in
the United States to do so.
(Public Domain, Wikimedia.)

to which she belonged, bemoaning the influence black clergy exercised both as community leaders and as teachers. "Their gross ignorance and insolent bearing, together with the sanctimonious garb," she wrote, "is attributable to more of the downright degradation of the free colored people of the North, than from the effect of corrupt public opinion."[14] Douglass published the letter, impressed by her theories on racial uplift. It was the first of many important essays she would write.

In 1851, Shadd, discouraged by the discrimination she faced both as an African American and as a woman in the United States, joined her father in Toronto, where she opened another school for black children. The following year, she wrote *A Plea for Emigration or, Notes of Canada West, in Its Moral, Social and Political Aspect: with Suggestions Respecting Mexico, West Indies, and Vancouver's Island, for the Information of Colored Emigrants,* a forty-four-page pamphlet comparing the quality of black life in Canada West to what she viewed as the "degrading conditions" suffered by African Americans in the northern United States.[15] In 1853, Shadd established her own newspaper, the *Provincial Freeman,* in Chatham. It quickly became an instrument for black emigration to and permanent settlement in Canada as well as for full integration and racial and sexual equality.[16] Shadd's views brought her into sharp conflict with another Canadian newspaper editor, Henry Bibb. Bibb, a fugitive slave who published *Voice of the Fugitive,* argued that blacks were merely temporary residents in Canada and should be preparing for their return to the United States. He also supported black segregation in Canada, stating that "strangers in a foreign land, no matter what country or color they may be, experience a greater degree of happiness in being associated with those who may have come from the same region as themselves."[17] Both of these positions were repugnant to Mary Ann Shadd, who not only rejected the idea that black emigrants to Canada should return to the United States but also opposed racial separatism. Instead she advocated the creation of autonomous, self-sufficient black communities within a larger, integrated society.[18]

Not only did Shadd and Bibb compete for readers, but also their newspapers struggled financially because of a lack of black readership in general. As a result, Shadd was forced to relocate the *Provincial Freeman* to Toronto, where a group of wealthy black businessmen kept the paper afloat. Even then, money remained an issue, and she decided, in 1855, to return to Chatham, which boasted the largest black population in Canada West.[19] For the remainder of the decade, Shadd solicited donations, organized bazaars, and conducted lectures, both in the United States and in Canada, in order to raise funds for her newspaper. As an antislavery and feminist lecturer, Shadd placed herself in great danger when she spoke on these issues in the US. After all, she was a black woman who made her home in Canada and openly urged fugitive slaves to flee the United States.[20] Her efforts were especially challenging after 1856, when she wedded Thomas Cary of Toronto. It was an unconventional marriage with him living in Toronto and her in Chatham. Their circumstances became even more challenging when Mary Ann gave birth to a daughter and had to rely on extended family for child care support.[21] Being a wife and mother did not slow her activism, though.

During her many speaking tours to Philadelphia, Mary Ann Shadd Cary and William Still became close friends and confidants. Still was impressed by her success as the "first colored woman on the American continent to establish and edit a weekly paper." He not only acted as an American agent for the *Provincial Freeman,* selling subscriptions to the antislavery periodical, but also made occasional essay contributions to it.[22] However, Still was not convinced that Cary's support for emigration to Canada was the best course of action, either for free blacks or for runaways. While black emigrants might have enjoyed formal political rights in that country, it was difficult for him to believe that they would not be subject to the "same discrimination and [white] hostility" they experienced in the United States.[23] There were other concerns, too.

Isaiah Wears, stating the position of the Vigilance Committee, placed black emigration to Canada "in the same category as African colonization." For free blacks "to desert the United States would have disastrous consequences," he argued. "The slave in his chains would be forsaken, the fugitive left unprotected and, in short, the humiliating concession would appear, as our enemies have said, that the colored man cannot be elevated in this country." Instead, Wears pointed to the "great progress" African Americans had already made as "proof that their elevation will ultimately be effected."[24]

Shadd, on the other hand, romanticized her life in Canada, praising British rule, the educational opportunities afforded to black children, and the country's integrated churches where "the presence of colored persons, promiscuously seated, elicits no comment whatever."[25] At the same time, Shadd was careful to distinguish between emigration to Canada, which was *voluntary*, and colonization in Africa, where blacks would be "forcibly relocated against their free will."[26]

In the autumn of 1855, Still decided to visit Canada. He secured letters of introduction from J. Miller McKim and James and Lucretia Mott, colleagues at the Pennsylvania Anti-Slavery Society. "Our highly esteemed and well-beloved friend, William Still of Philadelphia," wrote the Motts, "is about to visit Canada to inspect the conditions of the colored people, many of whom are largely indebted to him for their deliverance from the bonds of slavery."[27] McKim described Still's "tour of observation" as being "connected with the duties of his office as the secretary and agent of the Philadelphia Vigilance Committee."[28]

Still's Canadian tour included stops at Toronto, St. Catherine's, Hamilton, Ontario, Kingston, Buxton, and Chatham, which was the most popular destination for freedom seekers. Located at the fork of the Thames River, Chatham was home to more than one thousand African Americans in a total population of nearly four thousand by 1861.[29] Fugitives settled there because it provided navigational access from Detroit, Michigan, it was a safe distance from the US border, and it provided several employment opportunities.

According to Benjamin Drew, a freelance journalist, who also visited Chatham in 1855, he realized "more fully than anywhere else [in Canada] the extent of the [African American] exodus." "At every turn," he wrote, "the traveler meets members of the African race, single or in groups: he sees them building and painting houses, working in mills, engaging in every handicraft employment; here he notices a street occupied by colored shopkeepers and clerks; if he steps into the environs, he finds the blacks in every quarter, busy upon their gardens and farms. The white population of Chatham is reckoned at four thousand; the number of colored persons in the town may be safely estimated at eight-hundred."[30] William Wells Brown, who had escaped from slavery, been recaptured, escaped again, and become an abolitionist, was more specific about the nature of the town's black population, noting that it was "made up entirely from the slave states, but with few exceptions." "Every shade of the southern sons and daughters of oppression" could be found in Chatham, he observed, "from the polite house servant down to the coarsest field-hand."[31]

Chatham's black residents also enjoyed a strong social network with the nearby communities of Wilberforce, Dawn, and Buxton, which were all located within a fifty-mile radius and were home to substantial African American populations. Together with many sympathetic white neighbors, the black community refused to allow racial discrimination to prevent their success in education, business, or religion.[32] Yet Chatham was not the utopia that Mary Ann Shadd Cary portrayed in the *Provincial Freeman*. The town witnessed a fair share of racial discrimination due to the actions of some public officials, especially Edwin Larwill, a town councilor, school commissioner, and editor of the white newspaper, the *Chatham Journal*. Larwill made several efforts to restrict black residents' access to public schools and the polls. Fortunately, Chatham's strong partnership with the surrounding black communities of Wilberforce, Dawn, and Buxton prevented him from succeeding.[33]

Another popular destination for runaways who escaped by way of Philadelphia was the village of St. Catherine's, which boasted its own Underground Railroad agency, the St. Catherine's Refugee Slaves' Friend Society. William Wells Brown, who visited in 1861, estimated the population of the village and its environs to be "eight-hundred colored people, representing every Southern State," of whom "about seven-hundred [were] fugitive slaves."[34] These fugitives had become constructive members of the community, contributing to the economy as carpenters, coopers, shoemakers, and blacksmiths, among other occupations. They took pride in their properties, their church, and especially their minister, the Reverend Hiram Wilson. Not everyone shared their enthusiasm for Rev. Wilson, though. While Mary Ann Shadd applauded the success of the village's black residents, she excoriated Wilson for enriching himself at the expense of his congregants:

> During my stay . . . I had frequent opportunities of examining the general improvement of the place, and was in no way more gratified than when

viewing the snug homesteads of the colored people. . . . Their success is a standing refutation to the falsehood that begging is needed for the fugitives of St. Catherine's. The African Methodist Episcopal Church, too, for which the Rev. Hiram Wilson is now a paid Agent, is a fine building; by the way, Rev. Wilson is erecting a large brick mansion for his own house in the suburbs, which, when completed, must, from its adornments, cost several thousand dollars. Mr. Wilson has long resided in St. Catherine's, and, like other enterprising Americans, has profited by his change of position; having but little of this world's goods on his arrival in Canada, he has, by superior skill, as a missionary to fugitives for many years, and lately as a preacher, and Agent for the African Church, become possessed of some valuable town lots. Mr. Wilson's prosperity only confirms one in the irresistible conclusion, that no missionary field is more profitable than that in which the fugitives of Canada are the victims.[35]

St. Catherine's was also home to the Welland Canal, just ten miles from the American side of the Niagara River. The canal linked Lake Erie to Lake Ontario, creating a water detour around Niagara Falls that enabled runaways to escape to Canada. Sympathetic ferry captains often gave fugitives free passage across the Niagara River. After 1848, runaways could walk across a new suspension bridge over the falls, and it quickly became a major crossing point funneling hundreds from slavery to freedom. Fugitive traffic across the bridge increased dramatically after 1855, when a railway line was added.[36]

Harriet Tubman, St. Catherine's most prominent resident, often led runaways across the suspension bridge on the final leg of her journey to Canada. Many of those fugitives came through William Still's office in Philadelphia and traveled from there to New York City and then to the home of Jermain and Caroline Loguen in Syracuse en route to Canada. The experience of crossing the suspension bridge was extremely emotional for freedom seekers, as the case of Josiah "Joe" Bailey illustrates.

In November 1856, Tubman guided twenty-eight-year-old Joe Bailey, his brother William, Peter Pennington, and Eliza Manokey out of bondage in Maryland. Bailey was an overseer for William Hughlett, who owned thousands of acres of farmland along the Choptank River. Hughlett, a cantankerous master, regularly flogged his slaves simply to assert his authority. Joe Bailey decided that his first flogging would also be his last, and he asked Tubman to help him escape.

When Hughlett discovered that Bailey had disappeared, he offered a $1,500 reward for his return, sending advertisements as far north as New York City. Such a high price captured the attention of determined slave hunters. It took two weeks instead of the usual three days for Tubman to reach Thomas Garrett's station at Wilmington, Delaware. On November 26, they reached William Still's office in Philadelphia. Still sent them to New York City the next day, where Oliver Johnson sent them on to Albany and then Syracuse.

This was only Tubman's second trip to Syracuse, where Reverend Jermain Loguen coordinated the local lines of the Underground Railroad with the help of a well-organized support network. Loguen sent the black conductor and her fugitives on to Maria G. Porter, treasurer of a Ladies' Anti-Slavery Society at Rochester, New York. There Joe Bailey learned that advertisements for his capture had reached as far as New York City and that Tubman still had over three hundred miles to go before the group reached Canada. "From that time Joe was silent," recalled Tubman. "He sang no more, he talked no more; he sat with his head in his hand, and nobody could amuse him or make him take any interest in anything." Even after the group boarded a train and reached the suspension bridge, Joe remained silent. When the train began to cross the bridge, Harriet became anxious to have her companions see the wondrous Niagara Falls. William, Peter, and Eliza eagerly obliged, but Joe remained in his seat, head in hand. Shortly after, the train crossed the Canadian border. Harriet, who knew they had reached freedom by the rise in the center of the bridge and the descent on the other side, sprang across to Joe's seat, shook him with all her might, and exclaimed, "Joe, you've shook the Lion's paw!"

Confused by the remark, he asked what she meant. "You're free, Joe! You're free!" shouted Harriet. As the reality set in, tears began to stream down his face. Then suddenly, Joe got to his feet, raised his hands high, and shouted as loud as he could: "Glory to God and Jesus too!" Unable to contain his excitement, Joe continued to shout the phrase. When the train stopped on the Canadian side. Joe Bailey's feet were the first to touch British soil. "The other passengers gathered round him," recalled Tubman, "till I couldn't see Joe in the crowd. I could only hear him shouting, 'Glory to God and Jesus too!' louder than ever."

Tubman and her freedom seekers made their way to St. Catharine's, where Reverend Hiram Wilson operated a fugitive aid society. Wilson reported that Tubman was "a remarkable colored heroine," "unusually intelligent and fine appearing." He would become a close friend years later when she established a home in St. Catherine's for herself and her family.[37]

Still was extremely impressed with all these African American communities. According to James P. Boyd, his first biographer, Still found the fugitives "in good spirits, well cared for," and "able to care for themselves by industry and frugality." Although they were "new to freedom, they were not disposed to abuse it."[38] His experience in Canada West gave him a better understanding of why freedom seekers relocated there instead of remaining in the United States. Later, when those black settlements were criticized in the mainstream press, Still was quick to defend them. On January 21, 1860, for example, the *Philadelphia Public Ledger* published an account of the "Colored Population in Canada" that argued that blacks were taking over the country. "Canadians are beginning to experience the evil of the encouragement that they have given to fugitives escaping from the United States," read the article. "In some districts they outnumber the white population and, of course, [the blacks] wish to rule by the power of their numbers. Collisions are becoming common between them and the white population, and the laws are obstructed by riot and other outrages." Chatham was singled out as an example of the disquietude. According to the article, the town's "colored people took possession of the [white] schoolhouses" and "refused to let the white teachers and children inside them," in spite of the fact that they already "had schools of their own." Instead, the black residents demanded that "all schools be opened in common to blacks and whites." The essay concluded with the statement that "similar riots and outrages from the same demand" were occurring in other Canadian towns.[39]

Angered by the proslavery article, Still wrote an editorial for the *North American*, insisting that the *Public Ledger* "misrepresented entirely the facts of the case relative to the colored people in Canada." Then, in a methodical fashion, Still refuted each and every accusation on the basis of his own experience five years earlier. First, Still pointed out that the "entire population of Chatham is from seven to eight thousand" and that the "colored inhabitants do not exceed fifteen-hundred." Since the black population of Chatham is the largest anywhere in Canada, he added, "it does not look as though they outnumber the white population."

Second, Still rejected the notion that black Canadians "wish to rule by the power of their numbers." He stated that while blacks, like all Canadians, had the right to vote, they had "never attempted to organize a colored party." Instead, black Canadians had "always been loyal to either the regular Reform Party or the Conservative Party, the same as all other white Canadians." Third, Still refuted the accusation that blacks had "committed riots and other outrages" and had "taken possession of the schools in Chatham." Instead, he insisted that the blacks in Chatham, as well as in other towns, were, "in general, an industrious, peaceable people." In Chatham, they had "their own four churches, three schools, a fire company and a company of soldiers." In the trades, blacks "can be found as masons, plasterers, blacksmiths, cabinetmakers, carpenters, shoemakers, one watchmaker, one gunsmith, two or three wheelwrights and carriage makers and one constable."

Still corroborated his arguments by citing his correspondence with others who visited Canada West as recently as August 1858. Those letters, he said, indicated that the "condition[s] of the colored people in Canada remain the same" as when he visited the country in 1855. Thus, Still concluded, "If the colored citizens of Canada were the 'lawless, lazy wretches' that they are represented to be by the *Public Ledger*, would not the Canadian Parliament, the intelligent press, and the rigidly impartial laws of the land adopt measures to prohibit their emigration?"[40]

Still's experience in Canada West had had a profound effect on his attitude toward black emigration there. To be sure, the towns were not the utopias portrayed by Mary Ann Shadd Cary in the *Provincial Freeman*. Racial discrimination and corrupt politicians, even ministers, could be found. But Still also observed the genuine pride fugitives had in their new country as well as in the material success they had achieved. While he continued to believe that African Americans had a right to remain in their native country and that they could best serve to affect emancipation in it, Still did not discourage black emigration to Canada. In fact, he often directed those fugitives with the largest bounties to go there. If Still hoped to reunite those freedom seekers with their enslaved families, he would have to wait for the federal government to abolish the peculiar institution for all time.

N I N E

Kidnapped and Ransomed

Of the South's four million slaves in 1860, the Underground Railroad allegedly assisted in the escape of one hundred thousand. But we will never know the exact number for certain because of the necessity for secrecy.[1] Nor does history reveal the numbers of freedom seekers who were caught en route to the North and returned to slavery. However, William Still does indicate that not all of the attempts made by his network of agents were successful. The most painful failure involved a rescue mission to free his brother's family.

Shortly after Peter Still was reunited with William in Philadelphia, the two brothers began making plans to rescue his wife and three children, who were still enslaved in Florence, Alabama. To that end, William publicized Peter's story in the *Pennsylvania Freeman*, secretly hoping to generate interest among other abolitionists who might assist them.[2] Meanwhile, Peter headed south to gather as much information as possible about the town of Florence and the McKiernan Plantation where his family lived. He stopped in Cincinnati to ask Joseph Friedman, his former owner, to write a pass for him as if he were still a slave because free blacks were not permitted to enter Alabama. The pass would allow Peter to return to his "master" in Cincinnati. When Peter finally arrived in Florence, he asked Bernard McKiernan how much it would cost to purchase the freedom of

FIGURE 9.1.
Peter Still (1801–68),
a former slave who secured his
freedom in 1850, raised enough
money to purchase the freedom
of his wife and three children in
1854. His efforts were documented
in the book *The Kidnapped and the
Ransomed*, by Kate E. R. Pickard,
published in 1856. (William Still,
The Underground Railroad
[Philadelphia: Porter and Coates,
1872].)

his family. Whether or not Peter or the slave owner realized that Alabama law prohibited masters from freeing their slaves either by sale or by emancipation is uncertain because McKiernan set the price at $5,000. Regardless, Peter knew that he could not raise that kind of money, so he put into motion his plan to steal his family. Vina, Peter's wife, gave him a gingham cape as identification for the Underground Railroad agent who would later be sent to rescue her and the children.[3]

When Peter returned to Philadelphia, William informed him that a Quaker abolitionist by the name of Seth Concklin had volunteered to undertake the dangerous rescue mission. Concklin was so moved by Peter's story after reading about it in the *Pennsylvania Freeman* that all he asked in return was that his expenses be paid. The forty-nine-year-old Quaker was an experienced Underground Railroad conductor in upstate New York. Despite his small physical stature, he was fiercely independent and fearless in promoting the antislavery cause. Once he defended a black man against a racist mob. On another occasion, he attacked a proslavery ruffian who was attempting to lynch a black man. The white terrorist was about to place the noose around his victim's neck when Concklin assaulted him, forcing him run for his life. On several occasions, he ventured into the South to initiate or assist in escapes. But he always acted alone, refusing any assistance from other abolitionists. Although there is no record of his membership in any abolition society, he did read the antislavery press. Since he often traveled between his home at Troy, New York, and Philadelphia, where his two sisters lived, it's not surprising that he learned about Peter's heartbreaking story in the *Pennsylvania Freeman* and volunteered to rescue his family.[4]

Concklin's mission was known only to the Still brothers and J. Miller McKim, the PASS's executive director.[5] Although they were skeptical about the success of the mission, they realized that the price of purchasing the freedom of Peter's family would be far beyond their means and agreed to take their chances with the fearless Quaker. On January 1, 1851, Concklin, furnished with all the necessary information about Florence, Alabama, and the McKiernan Plantation, set out to Cincinnati to confer with Levi Coffin, the principal agent of the Underground Railroad's Central Line. The two agents determined that arranging an escape by steamer would be too risky. Instead, Concklin procured a large, flat-bottomed rowboat, and had it shipped south to Florence. He planned to carry Peter's wife and children by boat up the Tennessee River, which was located near the McKiernan Plantation, to the Ohio River. From there, the small party would travel east, taking the Wabash River north into Indiana, and would disembark at Princeton, where David Stormont, another agent, would guide Peter's family on the remainder of their journey to Canada.[6]

On January 28, Concklin arrived in Florence to meet Peter's family. Handing Vina the gingham cape Peter had provided to identify himself, Concklin described the plan of escape. Although he had hoped to depart on March 1, the mission had to be delayed until the night of March 16. Debarking on the Tennessee River, the party had 250 miles to travel before reaching the mouth of the Ohio River. Fortunately, the journey was all downstream, and Vina's two sons, Peter and Levin, both in their early twenties, were able oarsmen. Those two factors allowed the party to make the trip in just fifty-one hours. But now they had to row upstream on the Ohio and cope with colder temperatures, aggravated by heavy rain. The presence of slave catchers made this the most dangerous part of their journey. Traveling at night in the extreme cold, Concklin and Peter's two sons rowed seventy-five miles up the Ohio and forty-four miles up the Wabash River. Whenever the skiff came within sight of another boat, Concklin pretended to be a slave owner standing over the two young men who were rowing while Vina and her thirteen-year-old daughter, Catherine, hid beneath blankets. On March 23, the small party debarked at New Harmony, Indiana. It was the seventh day of their journey, and they had somehow managed to travel a total of 369 miles without incident.[7]

FIGURE 9.2. Seth Concklin's escape route (indicated by dotted line). (Author.)

At New Harmony, the group was greeted by Charles Grier, a free black agent, who provided them with a change of clothes: jeans and black cloth coats for Peter and Levin, plaid shawls for the Vina and her daughter, and the more formal dress of a prosperous midwestern farmer for Concklin. From there,

Concklin and the fugitives set out for Princeton, where they would rendezvous with David Stormont. Since Vina and her children didn't have passes, Concklin pretended to be their master escorting them to his brother's farm for work. Instead of going to Stormont's as planned, however, Concklin decided to remain with Peter's family, and they continued on to another station at Vincennes.[8]

Sometime along their journey through Indiana, they met Reverend N. R. Johnston, a Cincinnati minister and friend of Levi Coffin's. Johnston would later report on Concklin's progress in letters to William Still. But after they met with the minister, their journey to freedom was aborted. Twenty-three miles north of Vincennes, a group of slave catchers spotted them. One of the slave hunters, John Emison, was suspicious and questioned Concklin. Flustered, the Quaker abolitionist gave contradictory statements, further arousing the slave catcher's suspicions. Emison took Vina and her children into custody and returned to Vincennes, where he placed them in the city jail. Over the next few days, Emison made inquiries over the telegraph about missing slaves who might fit their description. Meanwhile, Concklin visited the fugitives every day, despite Vina's pleas for him to leave town and save himself. Instead, he hired a lawyer and attempted to have Peter's family released on a writ of habeas corpus, claiming that the runaways were his property. But a local judge denied the writ, not on any hard evidence, but on the mere hope that such evidence would eventually arrive.[9]

Shortly after, Bernard McKiernan wired Emison that he was offering a reward of $400 for four runaways and $600 for the capture of the individual who helped them escape. The telegraph also indicated that John S. Gavitt, the federal marshal from Evansville, Indiana, was en route to Vincennes with the necessary documents to detain the suspects. When McKiernan arrived, Vina and the boys confessed that they were his property. Concklin was quickly apprehended and heavily shackled to prevent his escape. All five were transferred to the slave owner without a trial and taken by stagecoach to Evansville to await the arrival of a southbound steamer, the *Paul Anderson*, that would return them to Alabama. Emison also accompanied the slave owners and the fugitives, as he would collect the reward money when the steamer arrived in Alabama.[10]

During the voyage, McKiernan told Concklin that he would see him hang for violating the Fugitive Slave Law. But the crusty abolitionist refused to be intimidated and replied that he was "not at all sorry" for what he had done, "believing it was his Christian duty." Accounts differ as to what happened next. According to McKiernan, Concklin tried to escape when the boat docked at Smithland,

Kentucky, by trying to jump onto a passing barge, but failed and fell into the river, where he drowned.[11] But Levi Coffin believed that McKiernan murdered the Quaker agent and threw his body overboard. Whatever the case, Concklin's corpse was recovered still in chains with his head bashed in. When Levi Coffin learned that the party had been "captured by tyrants in Indiana," he immediately wrote to William Still, expressing his concern that Concklin had "fallen victim to their inhuman thirst for blood" and that Vina and her children had been returned to slavery in Alabama.[12]

When Peter learned of the failure of the mission and the return to slavery of his family, he decided to inquire again about purchasing their freedom. He had his brother write a letter to Mr. L. B. Thornton, an attorney in Tuscumbia, and ask McKiernan at what price he would sell Peter's family. In August 1851, McKiernan replied that it would cost $5,000.[13] To raise the money, Peter embarked on the lecture circuit beginning in May 1852 at Syracuse. From there, he traveled from town to town in New England and upstate New York, speaking at church gatherings, at antislavery meetings, and to benevolent associations. His appeal was simple: he described his experience as a slave, his struggle for freedom, and his effort to bring his family out of slavery. By 1854, Peter had raised the $5,000 needed to purchase his wife and three children. They were reunited in January of that year and settled near his parents' farm in Burlington, New Jersey.[14]

A fictionalized version of Peter's story was written by Kate E. R. Pickard, a teacher at a female seminary at Tuscumbia, Alabama. Titled *The Kidnapped and the Ransomed*, Pickard's work, published in 1856, testifies to the important role that William Still and the Philadelphia Vigilance Committee played on the Underground Railroad. But the book also concealed the fact that Still's mother, Sidney, had been a slave. Instead, Pickard presents her as a free northern woman and Peter as a freeborn son who was kidnapped, taken south, and sold into slavery. Not until 1872, when William Still published his book on the Underground Railroad, were the true facts of his brother's story revealed.[15] Despite Pickard's literary license, her book proved extremely useful to the antislavery cause by emphasizing that compassion and mutual respect between the white and black races were not only possible but necessary if the two races were to live together in harmony in the future. But the failed rescue mission also offers important lessons about the mixed success of the Underground Railroad network.

Failed escapes were almost always related to the high financial stakes involved in chattel slavery. Seth Concklin was destined to failure in his attempt to rescue Peter's family because owners like Bernard McKiernan could not afford to lose the labor of runaway slaves like Peter and Levin Still, who were both in their early twenties. Nor could McKiernan allow them to steal themselves away to freedom because they represented a significant investment, especially in the 1850s, when the average price of a slave in his prime years of life doubled from $900 to $1,800.[16] Similarly, slave catchers like John Emison were always on the lookout for fugitives so they could claim bounty money that was being offered for their capture. McKiernan's reward of $400 for Vina and her three children— or $100 per runaway—was $25 greater than the average reward, which usually did not rise above $75 per slave.[17] What attracted Emison's attention, however, was the $600 that the slave owner was offering for the capture of Concklin. That is why the slave hunter made sure to keep the Quaker agent close by. At the same time, it is important to note that McKiernan, as a large planter from Alabama, was exceptional compared to the overwhelming majority of other owners in this study who lived in the Upper South and border states.

Peter Kolchin points out that very large plantations—those that had two hundred or more slaves and were devoted to raising cotton, sugar, and rice— were a rarity in antebellum America. Those that did exist were located in the Deep South, especially along the banks of the Mississippi River and in the coastal low country of South Carolina and Georgia. By contrast, slaveholdings in the Upper South and the border states were relatively small and "constituted more than nine-tenths of rural slaveholdings in antebellum America." Slaveholders in this region were of "modest means" with "small or medium-sized farms." They were "resident masters" who lived on their holdings, took an active interest in running their own estate, and, in many cases, worked alongside their slaves. Many of these slaveholders were tobacco farmers who owned fewer than ten slaves.[18] But that did not mean the small planters who make up the overwhelming majority of slave owners in this study were less concerned over the financial loss a runaway represented. In fact, the financial income of those small planters was so acutely tied to slave labor that they would feel the loss of income more immediately than a large planter. As a result, these owners were just as dogged in their pursuit of their human chattel as a large planter like Bernard McKiernan.

Most of the slaveholders identified by William Still appear to fit Kolchin's profile of a small farmer with fewer than ten slaves. Of the 780 owners identified in this study, 595 (76 percent) owned just one runaway slave aided by Still. In most cases, little more is known about them than name and residence. The remaining 185 (24 percent) owned two or more fugitive slaves. Of those 185 owners, 13 (12 percent) were widowed women. Table 9.1 indicates the most prominent

TABLE 9.1 Slave owners with three or more runaway slaves, 1853–61, with number of runaways from each in parentheses, based on 780 cases where runaways identified their owner. Names of female slave owners are in bold italics.

Owners with 3 to 5 Runaways		Owners with 6 to 9 Runaways
Baines (3)	March (3)	Joseph Brown (9)
Brodins (3)	Massey (4)	Daniel Coolby (6)
Cain (4)	McLane (5)	William H. Hyson (6)
Carter (3)	Newbold (3)	Kendall Major Llewis (7)
Coley (3)	Pearcy (4)	Reuben E. Phillips (7)
Count (5)	Pendleton (4)	
Davidson (4)	Peterson (4)	
Dellum (4)	Poole (3)	
Dorsey (3)	Royster (4)	
Duvall (4)	Ryebold (3)	
Ennis (3)	Shaffer (4)	
Fiery (3)	Simmons (5)	
Gibson (3)	Snively (5)	
Giddings (5)	Stewart (4)	
Griffiss (3)	*Thompson (3)*	
Hodges (3)	Tom (4)	
Hollan (5)	Wheeler (3)	
Houston (3)	Wiley (3)	
Johnson (3)		

slaveholders identified by Still's fugitives. These forty-two owners lost three or more slaves, all of whom escaped in groups. The fugitives volunteered considerably more information on these owners, revealing not only the character of the master but also their reason for escape.

Of the five owners who lost the greatest number of slaves (six to nine), Joseph Brown was the most unique. An absentee slaveholder who owned land in both Milford, Delaware, and Vicksburg, Mississippi, Brown was described by fugitive Ann Maria Jackson as a "very rich, sly master, who swears very hard and drinks." Jackson explained that Brown had threatened to "take four of her children to Vicksburg with him" and that that was when she had decided to set out for freedom. The nine slaves Brown lost included Jackson, her seven children, and another male runaway. The only one for whom he offered a reward was

TABLE 9.2 Cash values of runaways based on age, 1853–61 (35 known cases).

No. of Runaways	Age (years, average)	Value of Runaway
6	31	$150 to $999
22	26	$1,000 to $1,599
7	25	$1,600 to $2,000
(35 runaways; 31 male, 4 female)		

seventeen-year-old James Jackson, whose labor was evidently worth a bounty of $200 in state and $100 out of state.[19]

Daniel Coolby of Havard, Maryland, Reuben E. Phillips of Cambridge, Maryland, and Kendall Major Llewis also threatened to separate families by selling them at auction. Coolby lost six slaves and Phillips and Llewis lost seven each to the Underground Railroad in group escapes.[20] William H. Hyson, a Maryland farmer, was the owner of William Henry Moody. Moody described him as a "stout-built, ill-natured man" who habitually robbed him of his labor when he hired himself out to other white planters. When Moody learned that Hyson would have to sell some of his slaves to meet the expense of an extensive building enterprise, he set out for freedom with six others.[21]

Still occasionally lists the financial reward for the return of a runaway slave, and sometimes the financial value of a particular slave assigned by his owner. Such a practice underscores the economic foundation of slavery. Slaves were chattel, the human property of their owners. They were held in bondage for the purpose of increasing their master's financial income and thus were assigned a monetary value.

Generally, the value of slaves rose slowly throughout the nineteenth century, with the rate based upon the amount of labor each slave could produce above the cost of maintaining him or her. Slaves in the prime of their lives—between the ages of eighteen and twenty-five—were valued higher than those who were younger or older. Accordingly, an able-bodied male field hand was worth between $1,600 and $1,700 in the 1850s, while female slaves in their childbearing years were priced between $1,325 and $1,400.[22]

Once again, the historiography is consistent with this examination of Still's fugitives. The value of the runaways in this study indicates that the younger the slave, the higher his or her value (table 9.2). Of the thirty-five cases where the value of a runaway is given, twenty-two (63 percent) are valued at $1,000

TABLE 9.3 Cash rewards offered for runaways based on age, 1853–61 (73 known cases).

No. of Runaways	Age (years, average)	Maximum Reward (in or out of state)
7	29	Under $100
53	23	$100–$500
2	25	$501–$999
11	20	$1,000–$3,000

to $1,599 each and the average age is twenty-six years old. In another six cases where the average age is five years older, the value of each runaway is between $150 and $999. In the final seven cases where the average age is the youngest at twenty-five, the value of each runaway ranges from $1,600 to $2,000.

The values of the rewards offered for Still's fugitives are discrepant with those found by John Hope Franklin and Loren Schweninger in their study. Franklin and Schweninger point out that generally owners offered 5 percent or less of the value of the runaway as a reward because the owners could rely on an increasingly sophisticated system for recovering their chattel, especially after the passage of the Fugitive Slave Act in 1850. Therefore, a runaway valued at $1,600 in 1860 would bring a maximum reward of just $80.[23] But this study shows that the average reward for Still's fugitives was much higher, both in and out of state (table 9.3). Of the seventy-three fugitives for whom a reward was posted, fifty-three (73 percent) were valued at $100 to $500. If those estimates are calculated on the basis of Franklin and Schweninger's formula of 5 percent of the total value of the slave, these runaways would be worth between $2,000 and $10,000 each. Such cash values are extremely high, even given the twenty-three-year-old average age of these runaways.

The individual circumstances of the runaway must be taken into account when considering the reward a slaveholder would offer to pay for his recapture. For example, Jim Bow-Legs, alias Bill Paul, was an exceptionally built runaway from Lexington, Georgia. His owner, Dr. Thomas Stephens, offered a $500 reward for his recapture. Still described Jim as a man of "uncommon muscular strength": he weighed 180 pounds and "his entire structure was as solid as a rock." Though no age is recorded, the description of Jim suggests that he was in the prime of his life. In addition, his "mechanical genius was excellent." Jim had the ability to "make shoes" or do "carpenter's work" in addition to field chores. He was also extremely intelligent, as evidenced by his escape. Jim managed to "elude slave hunters and bloodhounds living for several months in the woods, swamps and caves and subsisting mainly on parched corn and berries." He was "always road-ready" and had "an uncommon memory," so it didn't matter if he traveled by day or night. Such an exceptional slave would command a high reward.[24]

Similarly, Josiah Bailey, a twenty-nine-year-old slave who escaped from Easton, Maryland, commanded a reward of $1,500. Josiah served as the overseer of forty slaves on his owner's farm. Still describes him as "well-qualified for the position," since he was strong, polite in his manners, and a man of "good, common sense." His owner, William H. Hughlett, was also a dealer in ship timber. Appreciating Josiah's exceptional abilities, Hughlett also "entrusted him with the management of the ship-timber." Finally, Josiah was regarded as "one of the most valuable hands in that part of the country, being valued at $2,000." Thus Hughlett's financial income was largely dependent on Josiah's labor.[25]

But physical prowess and remarkable intelligence were not the only reasons a slaveholder offered a significant reward. Of the seventy-three cases in which a reward was posted for a fugitive, forty-eight (66 percent) featured rewards that were for "in-state" recapture or were greater for "in-state" than for "out-of-state" recapture. And of those forty-eight cases with strictly or higher in-state rewards, twenty-four (50 percent) were offered by slaveholders residing in Delaware or Maryland. In other words, the closer the slave was to the Mason-Dixon Line, the greater opportunity for his owner to recapture him because of the greater numbers of slave patrols and slave hunters in those states. Thus the financial rewards of slavery to owners are reflected in the price that owners were willing to pay to recapture a runaway. And those rewards are inversely reflected in the high cost of slavery to the slaves themselves, in labor and in deterioration of their physical, emotional, and psychological welfare. Family members became more willing to take the risk to stay together rather than to be separated in slavery, and group escapes consisting of family members became more common as the decade of the 1850s unfolded.

TEN

The Memorable 28

On October 24, 1857, Aaron Cornish decided that the time to secure his free-dom had arrived. Although his owner, William Traverse of Cambridge, Mary-land, had made provision to free him, no will could be found after his death in May. As a result, Cornish was claimed by a nephew, the Reverend Levi Traverse.

Under his former master, Cornish had been allowed to hire out his time and earn his own money. He had also been permitted to live with his wife, Daff-ney, and their children, who were the property of a nearby planter. But when the Methodist minister became his owner, those privileges were revoked.

According to Cornish, the reverend was a "bad young man" and "lacked the good sense to properly manage the great amount of property that he had inherited." Fearing that he would be sold and separated from his family for-ever, Aaron conspired with other slaves from Maryland's Eastern Shore to escape from bondage.

It was a formidable group, totaling twenty-eight fugitives, and included four large families: the Anthonys, Cornishes, Hills, and Vineys. Realizing that fif-teen other slaves had escaped just the week before and that every slave catcher in the vicinity was on alert, the Cambridge party armed themselves with three re-volvers, three double-barreled pistols, three single-barreled pistols, three swords, four butcher knives, and a bowie knife.

TABLE 10.1 Groups of escaping slaves, each identified by a letter (horizontal axis) and number (vertical axis) combination. A "group" is identified as two or more runaways.

	A	B	C	D	E	F	G	H	I	J	K	L	M
1	4	2	3	4	3	3	4	28	14	2	4	3	2
2	6	4	2	4	3	6	3	2	3	2	4	2	6
3	2	2	10	2	2	2	8	14	2	2	6	2	3
4	2	2	3	2	2	3	4	4	2	2	3	3	4
5	3	4	4	3	2	3	4	7	2	4	6	2	2
6	6	5	5	13	2	5	8	4	2	5	4	2	3
7	3	2	2	3	2	2	2	3	2	4	2	2	2
Total	26	21	29	31	16	24	33	62	27	21	29	16	22

	N	O	P	Q	R	S	T	U	V	W	X	Y	Z
1	6	2	4	4	2	8	2	6	2	21	3	6	2
2	2	8	4	6	3	5	4	2	6	3	4	2	2
3	2	2	5	3	3	2	2	4	4	2	2	2	3
4	2	2	6	4	2	4	4	2	6	6	3	9	5
5	3	3	3	2	2	4	2	4	2	2	2	2	2
6	2	2	6	2	2	2	3	2	5	7	2	2	8
7	5	3	2	6									
Total	22	22	30	27	14	25	17	20	25	41	16	23	22

Their limited provisions of parched corn and dry crackers were exhausted within a day's time. Rain showers marred their journey for three straight days, with several of the children becoming sick. But never did they consider turning back, resolving to achieve their freedom or die in the process.

When they arrived in Philadelphia in tattered garments, hungry, sick, and penniless, William Still dubbed them "the Memorable 28," and clothed, fed, and doctored them before sending them on their way to Canada.[1]

"The Memorable 28" was the largest group of runaways assisted by William Still.[2] Like many other groups in this study, it was composed of families

TABLE 10.2 Largest group escapes (identified by letter-number combination from table 10.1), based on number of runaways per group, 1853–61.

Group	No. of Fugitives	Year	Place of Origin	Means of Escape	Families (no. of members)
C-3	10	1856	MD, NC, VA	Schooner	Thompson (2)
D-6	13	1856	Norfolk, VA	Schooner	Gray (6)
H-1	28	1857	Cambridge, MD	Foot	Anthony (5), Cornish (8), Hill (4), Viney (6)
H-3	14	1856	Norfolk, VA	Schooner	Cole (2), Jones (4), Taylor (3)
I-1	14	1857	Cambridge, MD	Foot	Amby (2), Stanly (6)
W-1	21	1855	Norfolk, VA	Schooner	Nixon (2), Wilson (3)

and originated in Maryland. Its uniqueness lies in the group's considerable size and the fact that many of its members were armed. In this study, a "group" is defined as two or more runaways. Table 10.1 identifies which slaves escaped in each group. Each group is assigned a letter and a number. The horizontal axis contains letters from A to Z, the vertical axis numbers 1 to 7. The group "H-1," for example, identifies the Memorable 28, with twenty-eight runaways. At the bottom of each column is the total number of fugitives. Adding the total of each column, we find that of the 995 fugitives in the database, 661 (66 percent) escaped in 173 groups, compared to the 334 (34 percent) who escaped on their own. The larger number of group escapes is consistent with the historiography, which contends that most slaves ran away in groups because it was safer.

Though the average size of a group was four runaways, six groups consisted of ten or more fugitives (table 10.2).[3]

Group C-3 stands out in that all but two of its members were single, young men who escaped from various states and appear to have made their way to Norfolk, Virginia, to escape by schooner. All the other groups contain members who originated from the same county and state and were composed of families, though their means of transportation differed. Groups D-6, H-3, and W-1 originated at Norfolk, Virginia, and traveled by water, while Groups H-1 and I-1 originated at Cambridge, Maryland, and traveled by land.

The existence of kinship in these groups reinforces the significance of family in the slave community as well as a pattern of family escapes, which increased dramatically after the passage of the 1850 Fugitive Slave Act. Convinced that compromises over slavery would not stand, families became determined to escape bondage or die in the process.

The family and the slave community were the twin pillars that helped sustain African Americans in bondage. Slaves often chose their own partners, lived under the same roof, raised children together, and protected each other by using passive strategies of resistance and teaching them to the young. Strong as the slave family was, however, it was not strong enough to prevent separation. Many adolescent sons and daughters were sold off. In the absence of their own family, slave children found comfort in the slave community, which built kinship networks to support them.

Ultimately, the desire to prevent the sale of family members or to be reunited with loved ones compelled many slaves to run away.[4] If a master was angered over the escape of his chattel, he might seek retribution by selling a family member. For example, Caroline Aldridge, a twenty-three-year-old slave in Unionville, Maryland, had watched as three of her older brothers escaped from the clutches of their mean-spirited owner, Thornton Poole. Shortly after, Poole sold one of Caroline's younger brothers and sister to the Deep South as revenge. Informed that Caroline and her remaining sibling "would soon go down the same dreadful road," she struck out for freedom with her youngest brother in tow.[5]

The death of a more benevolent owner often caused great fear and anxiety among slave families because of the uncertainty of their future. If the widow needed money, the sale of slaves was a common method of addressing the need. This was the case for Elizabeth Ann Wright, a thirty-two-year-old slave of Jane Cooper of Laurel, Maryland. Cooper was a widow, whose deceased husband had promised to set all of his slaves free when they reached the age of thirty. But after he died, no will could be found, which caused Elizabeth and the other slaves to distrust her. As time passed, the Widow Cooper began to hire out her slaves more frequently, a sign that she was in need of more money. Since Elizabeth was "getting on in years," she suspected that the widow was "on the eve of selling her." She informed her husband John Wright, a slave on a nearby farm, of the impending need to escape, and they set off together on the Underground Railroad.[6]

Such fears and anxieties made Harrison Cary resolve that he would "not entangle himself with a family until he had obtained his freedom." Cary, a twenty-eight-year-old mulatto, was the slave of Mrs. Jane Ashley of Washington, D.C. His mother had been sold several times. A brother, William, had escaped when he was a youngster and had not been heard from again. Learning that his mis-

TABLE 10.3 Number of runaways by state, based on 943 known cases, 1853–61.

State	No. of Runaways	State	No. of Runaways
Alabama	1	Maryland	476
Delaware	89	North Carolina	31
Georgia	3	South Carolina	2
Kentucky	1	Virginia	297
Louisiana	1	Washington, D.C.	40
Missouri	2		

tress's sister had been trying to persuade Ashley to sell him, Cary escaped, hoping to be reunited with his family.[7] In fact, most of the groups containing four or more fugitives in the database represent *family* escapes. It's important to note, however, that many of the groups were married couples or parents with adult children rather than families with young children.

Of the 995 runaways in the database, 96 (less than 10 percent) have been identified as children, ranging from three to fourteen years of age. The physical demands of an escape made the presence of young children dangerous, especially for families heading to Pennsylvania, where eighty-six fugitives were arrested and many returned to slavery in the decade after the passage of the 1850 Fugitive Slave Act.[8] A crying baby made the group vulnerable to recapture, as did a hungry and exhausted toddler complaining for food and rest. In Group D-6, for example, the young children of Henry and Mary Gray had to be placed "under the influence of liquor to keep them still" while the family was hidden below deck on a schooner being searched for fugitives.[9] There were exceptions, though. In Group H-3, for example, nine-year-old Mary Taylor tended to a fellow fugitive who was "suffering excruciating pain from the wounds he received while escaping." She spent "hours and hours of her own accord" with him, nursing him in "the most devoted and tender manner during the two or three days of their sojourn."[10]

Since family groups composed the majority of escapes in this study, most of the groups originated in the same geographical location. Of the 995 runaways in the database, the state of origin is known for 943. Table 10.3 illustrates the ten states (plus Washington, D.C.) from which Still's fugitives escaped and reveals that the greatest number of runaways came from Maryland (476; 51 percent), followed by Virginia (297; 32 percent) and Delaware (89; 9 percent).

The high incidence of fugitives from these three states can be explained by several factors. First, many of the fugitives were probably owned by urban merchants who hired them out to other employers or were rural slaves with high rates of absenteeism. These slaves were often gone for extended periods of time, so there was no reason for their masters to suspect that they had run away. Because these slaves were so close to the Mason-Dixon Line, they were more likely than bondsmen from the Deep South to have contact with northern abolitionists at farmers' markets or port cities, enabling them to secure information about the Underground Railroad. Under these circumstances, the opportunity to escape to freedom was not only tempting but also very real.[11]

Second, William Still's location at Philadelphia was like a magnet for fugitives, especially from the border states of Delaware and Maryland. Since Philadelphia was home to almost twenty thousand free blacks by 1850, the city afforded runaways the possibility of easily assimilating into its African American community.[12] Finally, several geographical considerations also made Philadelphia a logical destination for runaways from these states.

William Switala, who has researched the Underground Railroad networks of the Middle Atlantic region and the Upper South points out that Maryland's terrain was ideally suited to Underground Railroad travel. The Chesapeake Bay, which separates most of eastern Maryland from the rest of the state, provided an accessible water route north to Philadelphia. Similarly, fugitives from the Eastern Shore could easily cross over into Delaware and connect with the Underground Railroad routes of that state. Many runaways took advantage of these water routes after securing boats, skiffs, and canoes. For those enslaved in the western part of Maryland, the heavily forested ridges and valleys of the region afforded ample cover to elude capture en route to Pennsylvania. Switala has also shown that Delaware's geography was also conducive to Underground Railroad travel. The flat terrain provided fugitives with easier—and shorter—escape routes to Pennsylvania than if the state had been mountainous. The rivers and streams on the eastern coast of the state, which paralleled the lengthy border with Maryland, also provided a navigable, if not enticing, water route for runaways. In addition, Maryland and Delaware had fairly well-organized Underground Railroad networks and abolitionists, both black and white, who were willing to aid fugitives in their bid for freedom. These many advantages made the possibility for escape more feasible for slaves in Maryland and Delaware. On the other hand, Virginia had numerous Indian trails cutting through the Allegheny Mountain range in the state that served as escape routes to the North. Runaways could also fa-

TABLE 10.4 Number of runaways by county, for Maryland, Virginia, and Delaware.

Maryland (476 cases)	Virginia (297 cases)	Delaware (89 cases)
Dorchester 75	Norfolk 66	Sussex 35
Baltimore 39	Henrico 25	New Castle 11
Kent 22	Fairfax 17	

cilitate their escapes by water using the lower Chesapeake Bay and its many tributaries.[13]

If we examine the counties in which most of the runaways lived, one finds that runaways tended to come from two or three specific counties in the two border states. Of the 476 fugitives who escaped from Maryland, 75 (16 percent) came from Dorchester County, another 39 (8 percent) came from Baltimore County, and still another 22 (5 percent) came from Kent County. Of the 89 fugitives who escaped from Delaware, 35 (40 percent) came from Sussex County, and another 11 (12 percent) hailed from New Castle County (table 10.4).

Switala has shown that all of the above-named counties had well-developed road systems that connected their various towns as well as residents with strong antislavery sentiments. For example, Sussex, the southernmost county in Delaware, had interconnecting roadways from its western and southern areas to Lewes on the Delaware Bay. Another land route headed north through Kent and New Castle Counties to Wilmington, near the Pennsylvania border.[14] Along these routes, runaways could find sanctuary among such prominent stationmasters as Quakers Thomas Garrett of Wilmington and John Hunn of Odessa; Methodists Allen McLane and John Thelwell of New Castle County; and the African Methodist Episcopal churches that existed in both Sussex and New Castle Counties.[15]

Maryland, on the other hand, had three general Underground Railroad networks: Eastern, Central, and Southern. Most of the fugitives who were assisted by William Still traveled the Eastern network, which connected Maryland's Eastern Shore to Baltimore, Wilmington, and Philadelphia. Escapes on the Eastern network were mostly by land travel over established roads or the many Indian trails that wove through the mountains and valleys of Maryland into Pennsylvania. Some runaways also used the Chesapeake Bay and its interconnecting rivers. Still others used a combination of both water and land routes.

Entry into Delaware could be made by either the several roads linking the two states or the Choptank and Nanticoke Rivers, both of which flowed from the Delaware, through Dorchester County, and to the Chesapeake Bay.[16] Like Delaware, Maryland was home to significant Quaker, Methodist, and African Methodist Episcopal populations who were active participants on the Underground Railroad. In fact, two of the most prominent African American agents were Harriet Tubman and Frederick Douglass, both of whom were born and escaped bondage on Maryland's Eastern Shore.[17]

The high incidence of fugitives from Virginia was primarily due to the accessibility of water routes to the North. Unlike Maryland and Delaware, Virginia lacked an extensive road system. As a result, most of the fugitives who were assisted by Still resorted to water escapes. Of the 297 Virginia fugitives in this study, 66 (22 percent) began their trek to freedom at Norfolk on a steamer or schooner. Norfolk, located at the southernmost tip of the Chesapeake Bay, was the entry point for these runaways, who were assisted by sympathetic—and, in some cases, entrepreneurial—ship captains. Another 25 (8 percent) made their escape by either waterway or railroad from Henrico County, where Richmond is located. Norfolk and Richmond were port cities located on Virginia's rivers or coast. Those cities served as exit points to the North for the South's agricultural products like cotton and rice. They also offered fugitive slaves their best escape route.

To summarize, the majority of fugitives in this study escaped in groups that consisted of one or more families. The majority of the runaways came from three states: Maryland, Virginia, and Delaware. The high incidence of fugitives from these three states was due to their proximity to Philadelphia and significant antislavery sentiment in the border states of Maryland and Delaware, and to the accessibility of water routes to the North in the case of Virginia.

William Still wanted to increase the numbers of families he assisted: his intention in keeping such meticulous records was to reunite families, either before or after the Civil War. But sometimes he simply could not accommodate the requests because of dangers at the time. For example, Lewis Burrell and his brother Peter (Group S-6) escaped from Fairfax, Virginia, in April 1856. They made their way to Philadelphia, where William Still passed them along the UGRR network to Canada. The brothers left their two parents, another brother, and three sisters behind. Lewis also left a wife, Winna Ann, and two children, Joseph and Mary. "The separation constituted Lewis's daily grief," according to Still. Three years after settling in Canada, Lewis wrote to William, pleading with him to help his wife escape and offering to "pay [him] for his trouble."[18] But Still could do nothing to help since the "way of escape was so completely blocked."[19] Similarly, James Morris, who escaped from North Carolina in July 1856 and was assisted by Still (Group C-3), wrote to the Vigilance Committee director and begged him to help his "dear wife and child" to escape. Morris added that he had recently "received two letters from [her] and the second one said that she was treated awful since I left." Still, while admitting that Morris's "sad letter made a mournful impression," could do nothing to "deliver her from bondage."[20]

While it may have been heartbreaking for Still to deny these requests, he could console himself by the dozens of enslaved family members he did assist in gaining their freedom. What infuriated Still was the recapture of runaway family members when they had crossed the Mason-Dixon Line, especially when the failure was due to the carelessness of an agent. On May 21, 1854, for example, Stephen Pembroke and his teenaged sons, Robert and Jacob (Group M-6), escaped on foot from Sharpsburg, Maryland. When the group reached Chambersburg, Pennsylvania, thirty-three miles away, they boarded a train for Philadelphia, where they arrived the next day. Still immediately contacted the New York Vigilance Committee to inform them that he would be sending the fugitives on to New York City by train. When the Pembrokes arrived, the Vigilance Committee placed them at a station considered to be safe. But slave catchers hired by their owner tracked them down, broke into the "safe" house, and recaptured the father and his two sons. They were taken before the local magistrate, who ordered that they be returned to their owner by train and under police custody. Although abolitionists managed to raise the finances to purchase the freedom of Pembroke and his sons, Still was furious. He complained that the failed escape was due to a "serious weakness" in the New York Vigilance Committee. Defending his own actions, Still insisted that he had "spared no pains to render the [Pembrokes'] success sure" and that he had made certain that the father and sons would arrive in New York City with "sufficient time for the [vigilance] committee to place them beyond the reach of their infernal pursuers." In the future, Still added, he would try "to avoid sending [fugitives] through New York as much as possible."[21]

ELEVEN

Fighting for Freedom

By the late 1850s the United States was on the perilous course to civil war. Despite their common heritage, language, and political tradition, North and South were divided over the issue of slavery. Although northerners were not die-hard abolitionists, they protested the expansion of the peculiar institution into the western territories, favoring the extension of free labor. Most southern whites defended slavery, viewing it as inextricably bound to the American economy and the cotton culture they had developed.[1] The issue created a conundrum for the major political parties. Neither Democrats nor Whigs could afford to alienate either section. Therefore, in 1820 and again in 1850, Congress attempted to reach a compromise solution by limiting the expansion of slavery in the West and allowing the residents of territories to vote on the issue, a concept known as "popular sovereignty."[2] But each time new territories were added to the nation, compromise failed. Three events would force the North and South into an inevitable Civil War: the Dred Scott controversy, John Brown's raid of Harpers Ferry, Virginia, and the election of Abraham Lincoln, an abolitionist and the Republican candidate for president.

The Dred Scott controversy had its roots in the 1840s, when Scott, a Missouri slave, was taken by his owner, army surgeon John Emerson, to live in the

FIGURE 11.1.
Although Judge Roger B. Taney (1777–1864) considered slavery an evil and freed his own slaves before he was appointed to the Supreme Court, his 1857 ruling that a slave was not a citizen and could not sue in a federal court and that Congress had no power to exclude slavery from the territories became a violently divisive issue in national politics and dangerously undermined the prestige of the Supreme Court. (Library of Congress.)

free state of Illinois and, later, to Minnesota Territory, where slavery was also illegal. While in Minnesota, Scott married a female slave, and the couple's two daughters were also born there. Scott and his family eventually returned to Missouri, but in 1846 he sued Emerson for their freedom, insisting that residence on free soil made him and his family free. It took eleven years for the case to reach the Supreme Court.[3] On March 6, 1857, the Court ruled, by a 7-2 decision, that Scott was still a slave despite his residence in the North. Chief Justice Roger B. Taney read the majority opinion in one of the Court's most controversial rulings. Taney explained that Scott had returned to Missouri before making the claim for his freedom and that within Missouri he was a slave and as such could not file a suit in any court. But the chief justice went further in an attempt to prevent slaves from suing for their freedom ever again. Declaring the Missouri Compromise of 1820 unconstitutional, Taney contended that Congress had no authority to interfere with the free movement of property in the territories. In other words, a slaveholder had the right to take his chattel anywhere in the Union, including free states and territories, without losing title to them.[4] The implication was that any attempt to restrict the westward expansion of slavery was prohibited by the nation's highest court. Taney had made slavery the law of the land.

FIGURE 11.2.
Radical abolitionist John Brown (1800–1859) advocated the use of armed insurrection to overthrow slavery in the United States. He first gained national attention when he led small groups of vigilantes during the Bleeding Kansas crisis of 1856. Three years later, he was hailed as a martyr by northern abolitionists when he was hanged for a failed attempt to lead a slave insurrection at Harpers Ferry, Virginia. (Library of Congress.)

Proslavery southerners applauded the *Dred Scott* decision, while Republicans, an exclusively northern party, were outraged by it. For them the decision reinforced their belief that a "slave power conspiracy" existed among the southern legislators on Capitol Hill, and they vowed to reduce their political power. Abolitionists were even more infuriated.

In April 1857, William Still gathered with hundreds of other abolitionists in Israel Church to hear Robert Purvis state that the Court's "atrocious" decision confirmed northern suspicions that the Constitution was, in fact, a "slave owner's document" that supported proslavery notions of black inferiority.[5] Charles L. Redmond of the American Anti-Slavery Society was more blunt: "We owe no allegiance to a country which grinds us under its iron hoof and treats us like dogs," he declared. "The time has gone by for colored people to talk of patriotism."[6] In Philadelphia, as in many northern cities, African Americans mobilized for what they viewed as a war on slavery. They believed that anger among the slaves was so great that a general uprising needed only a spark to be ignited.[7] That "spark" was triggered by John Brown, a radical abolitionist who planned to launch a bloody insurrection against the South.

Brown, a native of New England, was a tanner by trade. He also circulated among the most passionate abolitionists and endeared himself to blacks by living in African American neighborhoods and adopting a black child, raising him along with his own four sons.

Initially, Brown's antislavery activities were limited to conducting runaways on the Underground Railroad, but he eventually adopted the belief that slavery could be ended only when the "land was purged with blood."[8] In 1855, Brown and his five sons relocated to Kansas, a territory that had recently been opened by Congress for the possible expansion of slavery.[9] According to the Kansas-Nebraska Act of 1854, the issue would be decided by popular sovereignty of those who settled there. But when the election was finally held, throngs of proslavery advocates from Missouri crossed the border and stuffed the ballot boxes, stealing the election for proslavery settlers. In retaliation, the antislavery Free Soilers formed their own government. As a result, Kansas had both a proslavery territorial legislature in Lecompton and an antislavery government in Topeka.[10]

The new proslavery government immediately set out to crush its opposition and make Kansas a slave territory. In 1856, when proslavery forces sacked the "free state" town of Lawrence, Brown sought revenge by leading an assault on a proslavery settlement at Pottawatomie Creek, killing five reputed proslavery settlers. The act provoked more vigilantism from both sides.[11] Armed bands roamed the countryside, burning towns and killing innocent victims. In what was dubbed by the newspapers as "Bleeding Kansas," vigilantism became so common that John Brown and his followers were just one of several murderous bands who were never arrested, never brought to trial, and never stopped from committing further violence.[12] Brown justified the murders as "obedience to the will of a just God."[13]

After the *Dred Scott* decision, Brown became more emboldened to eliminate slavery once and for all. He concocted a wild scheme to establish a guerrilla base in the Blue Ridge Mountains of northwestern Virginia from which he would launch raids on the surrounding plantations to free slaves and pass them on to freedom in the North.[14] He traveled east to raise money, recruit soldiers, and inform other abolitionists of this scheme. At the end of January 1858, Brown visited with Frederick Douglass in Rochester, New York, where he spent a week drafting a constitution for a "Provisional Government" for his vision of a colony for freed slaves. According to that constitution, the government would consist of a unicameral legislature, a president and a vice president, a supreme court, and a commander in chief, all of whom would serve without pay. He also told Douglass about his plan for igniting the insurrection. First, he would capture the Virginia town of Harpers Ferry, at the confluence of the Potomac

FIGURE 11.3.
Born into slavery,
Frederick Douglass (1818–95)
became one of the most famous
intellectuals of his time,
advising presidents and lecturing
to thousands on a range of
causes, including abolitionism
and women's rights. (Chester
County Historical Society,
West Chester, Pennsylvania.)

and Shenandoah Rivers; then he would seize the federal arsenal in order to arm the thousands of slaves he expected to join him in raiding nearby plantations. Afterwards, they would retreat into the mountains.[15] Douglass's earlier remarks urging blacks to arm themselves after the Christiana Riot of 1851 might have led Brown to believe that the great orator would participate in his scheme, especially since Douglass had insisted that "the only way to make the Fugitive Slave Law a dead letter [was] to make a half dozen or more dead kidnappers."[16]

Brown's next stop was Peterboro, New York, where he met with one of the state's most prominent abolitionists, Gerrit Smith. Smith agreed to fund the radical's scheme and introduced to him to Franklin Sanborn, a well-connected abolitionist and educator. Sanborn accompanied Brown to Boston, where he secured the financial support of four more prominent—and wealthy—abolitionists who had already financed the Free State cause in Kansas. The group consisted of Samuel Gridley Howe, a journalist and educator; George L. Stearns, a wealthy linseed oil manufacturer who had supplied guns for Kansas; Thomas Wentworth

Higginson, a radical Unitarian minister who would later become the editor of the *Atlantic Monthly*; and Theodore Parker, another Unitarian minister and antislavery orator. Together with Smith and Sanborn, these four abolitionists would become known as the "Secret Six."[17]

In March 1858, Brown traveled to Philadelphia, where he met with William Still. After outlining his plan to "beat up a slave quarter" in northwestern Virginia, Brown presented the constitution he had written, discussed his plan to establish a mountain fortress in the Blue Ridge, and appealed to Still for funds. Still rejected the request outright, realizing the danger not only to himself but to the entire Underground Railroad.[18] If Brown failed, anyone who supported him would be considered an accomplice and would be prosecuted for treason by the federal government. Worse, many of those individuals who were connected to Brown were also active agents on the UGRR. Their execution would inflict a severe blow to the clandestine operation, limiting the number of fugitives that other agents could assist. Discouraged by Still's refusal to fund his plan, Brown returned to upstate New York and met with Jermain Loguen in Syracuse. Loguen's role was to recruit the black volunteers Brown needed to carry out his raid on Harpers Ferry. Brown also hoped that either Loguen or Douglass would agree to serve as president of his provisional government.[19]

Brown's next stop was St. Catherine's in Canada. There, on April 7, 1858, he met with Harriet Tubman, then living in a rented house on North Street. By this time, Tubman was a celebrity within the UGRR network, having guided some fifty fugitives out of bondage to freedom in the North. She also endeared herself to Brown because she shared his belief that abolitionism was not simply a matter of moral uplift but also part of a war in which the combatants must be prepared to die.[20] Further, she could be invaluable to his cause. Tubman was familiar with dozens of former slaves living in Canada who could serve as potential insurgents. In addition, her knowledge of support networks and resources in the border states of Pennsylvania, Maryland, and Delaware could be vital to his success as he refined his plans for an invasion of the South.

At the meeting, Brown told a gathering of Tubman's friends that it was time for "God's wrath to descend" and that he was the divine instrument ordained to deliver it.[21] After informing the group of his plan, Tubman agreed to stump across New England to raise funds for his cause. She also encouraged him to conduct the assault on July 4, 1858, believing that the anniversary of American independence would be ideal to commemorate by freeing the slaves.[22] Brown was pleased with their meeting, as he wrote his son the following day, informing him that "I am succeeding to all appearance beyond my expectations."[23]

On May 8, at a secret convention in Chatham, Brown proclaimed the establishment of the provisional government whose constitution he had written at Douglass's home five months earlier and assured the gathering of his eventual success. Osborne Perry Anderson, a printer for the *Provincial Freeman*, was impressed by Brown's admonition to accept the "Christian duty of every man" and "strike down slavery through the use of arms." Believing the radical abolitionist to be "chosen by God to this great work," Anderson agreed to join in the insurrection.[24]

Of the forty-six men present, thirteen were Brown's white followers from Kansas. Among the more prominent black attendees were Isaac Shadd, Mary Ann Shadd Cary's brother and the publisher of the *Provincial Freeman*; and two leaders of the Detroit underground, William Lambert and Reverend William Monroe, who chaired the convention. Conspicuously absent were Tubman, Douglass, and Loguen. The delegates adopted Brown's constitution and unanimously elected Reverend Monroe as the provisional government's temporary president and Brown as its commander in chief.[25] Brown left Chatham confident that hundreds, perhaps thousands, of Canadian blacks would join his assault. He also believed that he enjoyed the full support of the most prominent abolitionists in both the United States and Canada. But he was woefully mistaken.

Tubman, Douglass, and Loguen may have given their moral support to Brown's scheme, but they had serious reservations about its success and withdrew their direct participation in it. Like William Still, they probably concluded that if the plan failed they would certainly be arrested and executed and that the operations of the Underground Railroad as well as the identities of the agents would be revealed to the authorities. None were willing to take that risk. In fact, after Still learned of Brown's plan in March 1858, he discouraged Douglass from participating in it. According to Still's biographer, James P. Boyd, the Philadelphia Vigilance Committee director told Douglass that he viewed the assault on Harpers Ferry as "a venture sure to end in disaster." Still, who knew that Douglass was "expected to play a leading role in the raid," warned him that Brown's action would be done "more of desperation than valor, more of precipitation than prudence," and that it would be in Douglass's best interests to remove himself from any involvement.[26]

Although Brown wanted to launch his raid in the summer of 1859, repeated postponements and poor communication prevented him from doing so for another year. Finally, on October 16, 1859, Brown and an army of twenty-one raiders that included five blacks launched their fateful assault on Harpers Ferry. The previous night they had established a base camp at a farm just over the Maryland border. Leaving three men behind as guards, Brown and his guer-rillas slipped into town and easily seized the federal arsenal. The vigilantes had hoped to arm themselves and the slaves they freed, adding to their numbers as they invaded plantation after plantation, liberating the bondsmen. To their surprise, however, few of the local slaves joined the revolt. Most were afraid that Brown would be unsuccessful and did not want to risk their lives for a fanatic. Even more incredible, Brown had made no provision for escape. Instead, he and his band of raiders held some local citizens hostage as they tried to stave off a force of US Marines, commanded by Colonel Robert E. Lee. Within three days, the federal troops captured Brown and six of his men. Another twelve guerrillas were killed in the ambush. Charged with treason, conspiracy, and first-degree murder, Brown and six of the survivors would stand trial. Only two of the free black raiders escaped: Francis J. Meriam, age twenty-one, who guarded the group's base camp in Maryland; and Osborne Perry Anderson, age twenty-nine, who somehow survived the fiercest fighting.[27]

Although William Still was discreet about his association with Brown and discouraged others from participating in Harpers Ferry raid, he was not unaffected by the event. Not long after, Meriam and Anderson, the only two of Brown's men to escape, turned up at Still's doorstep "footsore and famished."[28] He felt obligated to take them in because of his close association with other in-fluential abolitionists. Meriam was the grandson of Boston antislavery activist Francis Jackson, and Anderson was a printer for Mary Ann Shadd Cary's *Provincial Freeman*. Still gave Meriam money and passed him on to another agent, Dr. I. Newlin Pierce, who initiated the passage to Canada. During the Civil War, Meriam served in the Third South Carolina Colored Infantry and died of wounds sustained in combat six months after the end of the fratricidal conflict.[29]

Anderson was in worse condition. He arrived at Still's office "literally in rags, [gun]powder-grimed and penniless, with only a revolver in his belt." In addition, the raider was being pursued by several bounty hunters, as Virginia's governor had offered a huge reward for his arrest. Aside from Still and his family, only Miller McKim and Passmore Williamson were aware of Anderson's arrival, and both pressed Still to move him on to another station immediately. Ander-son spent just one day in Philadelphia to recover from his journey and was then "furnished with a new suit of clothing and tickets for Canada." During the Civil

War, he served in the US Colored Troops, contracted tuberculosis, and died in 1872.[30]

Harboring Brown's accomplices placed Still at great risk, but an even greater danger presented itself when a personal memorandum addressed to Still was discovered by the authorities among the possessions of Captain John Henry Kagi, Brown's second in command.[31] Fearing that he might be "attacked by a pro-slavery mob," the Vigilance Committee director packed up all his UGRR records and relocated them to a crypt at Mount Lebanon Cemetery on the outskirts of the city. He made Jacob C. White Sr., the owner of the cemetery, the custodian of those records.[32] In addition, Still suspended his elaborate record keeping for the Vigilance Committee for a time and later was careful to write his letters in code when corresponding with other stationmasters. "God's poor," for example, became a synonym for "fugitives." Similarly, "Moses" was adopted as the pseudonym for the famous conductor Harriet Tubman.[33] Others, like Thomas Garrett, went so far as to destroy all correspondence with other agents in order to eliminate any incriminating evidence. Garrett later wrote of not feeling at liberty to "keep any written word of Harriet's or my own labors, except in numbering those whom I have aided."[34]

Despite the possibility of incriminating himself, Still opened his home to Brown's wife, Mary, while preparations were made for the guerrilla leader's trial at Charlestown, Virginia. Traveling through Philadelphia from her home in upstate New York, she had hoped to attend the proceedings, but Still and his wife, Letitia, discouraged her from making the trip. "Excitement was running too high" in the nation, they explained, "and she would likely be disappointed in the outcome of the trial." The soon-to-be widow eventually yielded to their advice, and the Stills "made her as comfortable as possible under the circumstances."[35] She didn't have to wait long. Her husband was convicted, sentenced to death, and executed in less than a week.

Throughout his trial, John Brown spoke against slavery with an eloquence that moved northerners and horrified southerners. Holding a Bible in his right hand, Brown told the court: "If it is deemed necessary that I should forfeit my life for the furtherance of the ends of justice, and mingle my blood with the blood of millions in this slave country whose rights are disregarded by wicked, cruel and unjust enactments, I say let it be done."[36] Indicted for treason against the state of Virginia and criminal conspiracy to incite a slave insurrection, Brown was sentenced to death by hanging. He accepted the court's ruling with the calm resignation of a martyr. Back in Philadelphia, Still, on the day of the execution, tried to comfort Brown's wife. "As the time of her husband's execution drew near, Mary grew paler," he recalled. "Folding her hands across her breast, she looked straight ahead for nearly an hour as if in reverie." A few weeks later, Mary Brown sent Still a lock of her husband's hair as a reminder of the cause for which he had died.[37]

Brown's dignified behavior at his trial and speedy execution on December 2 unleashed powerful passions, further widening the gap between North and South.[38] Lauded as a martyr by abolitionists, Brown was celebrated in the North with public rites of mourning. Church bells tolled, buildings were draped in black, prayer meetings were conducted, and ministers extolled Brown's virtues in their sermons. In the South, however, Brown's failed insurrection outraged whites because it struck at their greatest fear—slave rebellion. Large planters and yeoman farmers alike labeled Brown a "dangerous fanatic" and believed that his behavior and opinions were typical of most abolitionists.[39] Their fears were confirmed when documents belonging to him were discovered after his capture. Those documents revealed that Brown had secured the financial support of the "Secret Six," some of the wealthiest abolitionists in the North.[40] To be sure, people in both regions questioned Brown's sanity, and even those who admired him questioned his methods. In Philadelphia, for example, the public was divided. While members of the Pennsylvania Anti-Slavery Society considered Brown a martyr and Robert Purvis delivered a stirring address at Independence Hall praising the heroism of the radical abolitionist, more than six thousand Philadelphians attended a public meeting to condemn Brown and applaud Virginia for hanging him.[41] Predictably, when Brown's corpse arrived in Philadelphia where it was to be prepared for burial in upstate New York, it had to be secretly carried from the train station to the undertakers in order to prevent a proslavery riot.[42]

Brown's raid also had a dramatic effect on the outcome of the 1860 presidential election by heightening the inflammatory rhetoric already dividing an increasingly antislavery North and a proslavery South. Brown's raid convinced southerners that all abolitionists were radicals intent on eliminating slavery at any cost. While the Republican Party purposely distanced itself from radical abolitionism by advocating gradualism and the old, discredited solution of colonization, most abolitionists supported Abraham Lincoln, the Republican candidate.[43]

Widely considered a moderate, Lincoln, who emphasized tariff protection, subsidized internal improvements, free labor, and a homestead bill, also opposed the extension of slavery. During the presidential campaign he skillfully staked out a moral position on slavery and race that was not only extremely progressive for the time period but more controversial than that of Stephen Douglas, his Democratic opponent. Lincoln declared that he personally considered slavery a "moral, social and political evil" but that he was barred by the Constitution from doing anything about the institution "where it already exist[ed]." Because the Republicans believed slavery to be wrong, however, he would "deal with it as a wrong" and "place slavery on a course of ultimate extinction."[44] Lincoln's opposition to slavery and his intention to "ultimately extinguish" it struck fear into the hearts of southerners and made secession inevitable.

South Carolina was the first state to secede from the Union on December 20, 1860. Over the next six weeks, six more states from the Deep South followed her lead—Mississippi, Florida, Alabama, Georgia, Louisiana, and Texas. Slave-based plantation farming dominated the economies of these seven states, and the planter class, the driving force of secession, controlled the states politically. The Upper South (Virginia, North Carolina, Arkansas, Kentucky, and Tennessee), by contrast, had a more diversified economy and chose not to secede until April 1861. But after Confederate batteries fired on Fort Sumter, a federal installation in Charleston Harbor, and forced the US troops inside to surrender, those five states joined the Confederacy as well.[45] Lincoln subsequently called for seventy-five thousand volunteers to put down the southern rebellion. Northerners eagerly answered the call.[46] What was destined to become the bloodiest war in American history had begun.

The outbreak of the Civil War coincided with William Still's decision to leave the Pennsylvania Anti-Slavery Society and strike out on his own. On June 1, 1861, he resigned from his position as chairman of the Vigilance Committee. There does not appear to have been any conflict with his supervisor, J. Miller McKim, who expressed the PASS's "lively appreciation" for Still's "integrity, ability and courtesy in the discharge of [his] duties."[47] Instead, Still, according to his biographer James Boyd, left because of "stringency in money matters" and because the PASS was going through yet another "retrenchment."[48] The fact that Charles Wise, the Society's treasurer, assumed Still's responsibilities, including the recording of fugitive interviews, seems to confirm these reasons.[49] In addition, the PASS's reorganization was probably influenced by the fact that fugitive traffic had nearly ceased by 1861. The database indicates that the number of runaways passing through Philadelphia had steadily decreased from 1857, when Still interviewed a total of 205 fugitives, to the spring of 1861, when he interviewed just one in his last five months on the job. With the UGRR falling into disuse, retaining Still as a paid employee was a luxury the PASS could not afford. But there are also indications that Still had tired of the job and its demands and wanted to earn more money than the PASS could afford to pay him.

The year before, Ellen Wells, a fugitive slave, had successfully sued Still for libel. Wells had been traveling across the North raising funds, allegedly for the purpose of purchasing the freedom of enslaved family members. Still, suspecting fraud, wrote a letter to another abolitionist implying that Wells was an imposter and a prostitute. Somehow, Wells gained possession of the letter and filed a suit against the Vigilance Committee director. When he appeared in court, Still admitted that he had written the letter and was sentenced to ten days in jail and a $100 fine.[50] To be sure, Still had a self-righteous streak that would later get him into trouble with a younger generation of civil rights activists. But he could also be mean-spirited and vindictive if crossed by someone. The incident certainly embarrassed him and probably provided the incentive to move on with his career.

Whatever the case, Boyd relates that Still, who maintained good relations with the PASS, rented their office to embark on his own business. He used the first floor as a repair shop for old stoves and the second for a family dwelling. With less than $300 to his name, the only actual wealth he possessed was in real estate, specifically $2,000 worth of property he had purchased during the previous decade. Not wanting to mortgage those properties, Still sold coal on commission to pay the rent. He was taking a huge risk, but he made the business successful through "personal industry, good work, fair prices and strict attention to details."[51]

During his second year in business, coal sales increased dramatically, allowing Still to purchase his own building at 107 North Fifth Street and expand his stove business.[52] He hired competent sheet-iron workers to make gas stoves, boilers, range appliances, and heaters, and he enlarged his stock of sample stove castings.[53] By 1863, Still was attracting both black and white customers and had established himself as one of Philadelphia's most successful African American businessmen.[54] He had also become a respected black community leader.

One of his earliest civic projects was founding the Social, Civil and Statistical Association of the Colored People of Philadelphia. Like the earlier Pennsylvania Anti-Slavery Society, which had performed a census of black Philadelphians in 1838, the aim of the SCSA was to collect statistical data on the city's black community that would refute white charges of inferiority and criminality.

In so doing, Still and the other founders hoped to demonstrate to white Philadelphians the "common humanity" of blacks and to convince them that "God had ordained the black race to the [same] level as whites in the brotherhood of man."[55] The Civil War would give African Americans the opportunity to show that they deserved that fundamental right by fighting—and dying—for the Union cause.

During the first two years of the fratricidal conflict, Lincoln refused to raise a large black army for fear of losing the support of the border states—Delaware, Maryland, Missouri, and Kentucky—who had remained loyal to the Union and were allowed to keep their slaves.[56] Black leaders continued to urge the necessity of enlisting African American troops, realizing that if the black man proved his patriotism and courage on the battlefield, the federal government would be morally obliged to grant him first-class citizenship. Debate continued within the Union command until January 1, 1863, when Lincoln signed the Emancipation Proclamation. Having freed, by executive order, those slaves in the South, the president could no longer deny the black man the opportunity to fight. Now the Civil War was being fought not only for the preservation of the Union but for the freedom of all people, white and black.[57] The success of the Fifty-Fourth Massachusetts Regiment, the first black regiment recruited by the Union, reinforced that position.

On July 16, 1863, Colonel Robert Gould Shaw, the white commander of the Fifty-Fourth Massachusetts, agreed to lead the Union attack on Fort Wagner. The taking of the fort was critical to Union success in the effort to reclaim South Carolina. As the black regiment neared the fort, Confederate riflemen let loose a torrent of fire. Men fell on all sides, but those who were able continued to charge with Shaw in the lead.[58] The assault amounted to a suicide mission. Of the 600 men of the Fifty-Fourth, 272 were killed, wounded, or captured, including Shaw.[59] Subsequent waves of federal troops were unable to capture the fort, sustaining more than one thousand casualties. From a military standpoint, the assault on Fort Wagner was a costly failure, but it did prove to be a turning point for black soldiers. The courage and sacrifice shown by the soldiers of the Fifty-Fourth Massachusetts served to dismiss any lingering doubts about the combat readiness of African Americans.

During the next two years, 178,985 black men, many of them runaway slaves, fought for the Union Army in segregated units called US Colored Troops.[60] William Still, along with Robert Purvis, promoted enlistment by convincing black Philadelphians that the best way to affect emancipation was to

FIGURE 11.4. Some eleven thousand free blacks and escaped slaves were trained for the US Colored Troops at Camp William Penn in Cheltenham Township outside of Philadelphia. This 1864 recruitment poster depicts some of the recruits from Pennsylvania, which provided more black soldiers than any northern state during the Civil War. (Public domain, Wikimedia.)

volunteer and fight for the Union Army. On June 27, 1863, the two men joined with the Institute for Colored Youth to create a recruitment committee that would focus on the city's Seventh Ward, where the largest percentage of blacks made their homes.[61] In addition, a local training camp was established to prepare the recruits for combat.

Located in Cheltenham Township about eight miles northeast of Philadelphia, Camp William Penn was adjacent to "Roadside," the country home of Quaker abolitionist Lucretia Mott.[62] Training lasted just two months, but it was intense. Reveille sounded at 5:00 a.m. Drilling followed and continued throughout the day until taps at 10:00 p.m.[63] Mott's son-in-law, Captain Edward M. Davis, was a member of the supervisory committee to raise black troops and to identify and hire trustworthy civilian help. In January 1864, Davis offered William Still the position of camp sutler. Initially, Still refused, believing that his coal and stove business would suffer. But he later accepted the post, realizing that he was registered for the Union draft and that he preferred Camp Sutler to regular enlistment and combat duty.[64] Camp commander Lieutenant Colonel Louis Wagner immediately approved the appointment, being familiar with Still's reputation for honesty.[65] The camp had, by 1864, become a target of swindlers intent on war profiteering, and two of the culprits were "white men pretending to have authority from the War Department to act as camp sutlers." Among their abuses were the smuggling and sale of alcohol and jewelry. Wagner was ordered to "remove the offenders" and find a replacement.[66] Still was a logical choice to fill the position because of his unimpeachable integrity as well as the fact that he had already been selling coal to the camp.[67]

Still's dedication to the Union cause was reflected by his generosity to the soldiers. Shortly after his arrival, he purchased two subscriptions to William Lloyd Garrison's newspaper, the *Liberator*, and donated the copies to the camp and an urban military hospital.[68] On one occasion, Still even donated $500 to the camp fund for the benefit of the soldiers.[69] At the same time, he did not make many friends among them because of his close scrutiny of the purchases made at the camp store. Some soldiers tried to pay for goods with counterfeit money. When Still refused to accept it, they insisted that he was the one who had given the money to them as change during a previous sale. In fact, the soldiers had been victimized by local shopkeepers who were passing the counterfeit bills. To keep peace, Still refused to give out any change unless it was in approved notes directly from the bank.[70] Unfortunately, soldiers from the Twenty-Fifth US Colored Troops accused him of short-changing them. The accusation was probably due to Still's middle-class status and tendency to act as if he were better than the soldiers who came from the poor and working classes.[71]

While Still may not have been liked by the soldiers, he was generally respected by them. It's even possible that he may have helped some of them escape bondage on the Underground Railroad years earlier. Perhaps the greatest benefit Still enjoyed from his two years as camp sutler was making the acquaintance of Fannie Coppin and Octavius Catto, members of a younger generation of black reformers. Coppin, a former slave, was head of the Institute for Colored Youth in Philadelphia, where many of the camp's recruits had been students. Catto, a highly respected instructor at the ICY, had opened the school at 715-717 Lombard Street as a recruitment headquarters. He was among the first to volunteer for the Union Army, and many of his students followed his example.[72] Still would befriend both of these young activists and, after the war, work with them in the struggle for civil rights.

TWELVE

The Streetcar Protest

William Still tried to redefine himself as a civil rights activist after the Civil War. It wasn't an easy task, however, because a younger generation of black activists was assuming leadership. Still was one of many African American abolitionists who came of age during the antebellum era. They were self-made men who advanced their fortunes through business, journalism, and the ministry to become highly respected members of the Protestant middle class.[1] Like the other abolitionists, Still joined with white Quakers in his antislavery activities and adopted their tactic of moral suasion to further the cause. He also prided himself on his civic involvements.

In 1860, Still was one of the organizers and financiers of the Social, Civil and Statistical Association of the Colored People of Pennsylvania (SCSA), which collected data on free black men and women, as well as advocated for universal suffrage and temperance. After the war, he became an active member of the Freedmen's Aid Commission, founded an orphan asylum for children of black soldiers and sailors, and served as president of the Berean Savings Association, the first black-owned banking institution in Philadelphia. He also assisted in the management of homes for the aged and for destitute black children, and he organized a Sabbath school for the Presbyterian Church as well as one of the first Young Men's Christian Associations for black youth.[2]

Because Still relied on moral suasion in all of his benevolent activities and eschewed the political process, he had difficulty relating to the new generation of black reformers who assumed positions of leadership during the post–Civil War era. They advocated direct action, drafted resolutions, and pressured municipal as well as state and federal officials to legislate change. They also discouraged involvement with white reformers unless these were legislators who could advance their cause. Their segregated approach was at odds with Still, who partnered with like-minded white reformers. Nor did Still's unimpeachable character, driven by the Protestant work ethic, strict temperance, and disinterested benevolence, endear him to the younger generation, who shunned personal austerity. While these young activists worked to end discrimination at the voting polls and on urban streetcars, they also believed in having a good time. They indulged in such popular entertainments as theater, dancing, and sporting events. For Still, such "idle and frivolous activities" reflected the *moral* failure of the younger generation—something he believed weakened the black race as a whole.[3] The best illustration of these conflicting approaches to civil rights can be seen in the city's decade-long streetcar protest.

Antebellum Philadelphia was one of the most segregated cities in the North. Churches, schools, and libraries turned away African Americans unless those institutions were operated by blacks themselves. The mass transit system, which began in 1858 with the introduction of privately owned, horse-drawn streetcars, also discriminated. Although a few of the lines allowed blacks to pay a fare to stand on the narrow, mud-splattered platform at the front of the trolleys, they were banned from riding inside with white passengers. At a time when access to affordable public transportation was vital for urban residents to travel to work, blacks suffered the indignity of having to stand on a trolley platform exposed to the elements.

Still viewed the effort to integrate the city's streetcars as a critical part of a much larger struggle for human equality.[4] He began a campaign to end the racial discrimination in the summer of 1859 with an open letter published in Philadelphia's *North American and United States Gazette*. Still shamed the Quakers, who "prided themselves in their benevolent enterprises to elevate [former] slaves," while ignoring the rights of "[free] colored people who live in the city." "Excluding colored passengers from the railroad cars is unparalleled in any of the other leading [American] cities," Still wrote, pointing out that blacks were able to ride streetcars in Chicago, New York, and Boston. He also challenged the common white perception of Philadelphia's blacks as a "low and degraded class," insisting that the "great majority" of city's twenty thousand African American residents were "industrious colored people," who "attend church," "live in neat houses," and "pay taxes."

"Why then," he asked, "should colored people who are taxed to support highways be rejected from riding streetcars on those very highways?"[5]

Still's letter was widely reprinted in the antislavery press and was hailed by most of the city's African American community. But instead of the mass action he hoped to spur, there were just a few isolated protests.

Determined to be heard, Still, in 1861, urged the SCSA to draft a petition and circulate it among the city's white business leaders, demanding the right of blacks to ride the streetcars.[6] The SCSA appointed Still as chairman of a committee of four, including Stephen Smith, Isaiah C. Wears, and Jonathan C. Gibbs, to draft the petition. Within a year's time, Still, acting alone, secured the signatures of 369 of the city's most prominent white residents, including Bishop Alonzo Potter of the Episcopal Church; Horace Binney, a former state legislator; Morton McMichael, publisher of the *North American*; and Daniel Dougherty, an influential Democratic Party leader. Dozens of Quaker residents also signed the petition and agreed to ride on the front platform of the streetcars to demonstrate their solidarity with the cause.[7]

"The colored citizens of Philadelphia suffer very serious inconvenience and hardship daily by being excluded from riding in the city's passenger cars," wrote Still in the opening sentence of the petition. He pointed out that Philadelphia's African American residents, who labored faithfully in their various callings, "pay more taxes" than blacks "in any other northern city." "The members of the Social, Civil and Statistical Association," he added, "paid annually about $5,000 to the tax collector." So did the city's "twenty colored churches, Sabbath Schools and . . . day schools." Thus "colored people who are taxed to support highways" should be "permitted to ride streetcars in the City of Brotherly Love," especially when that city has a reputation for "benevolence, liberality, love of freedom and Christianity."[8]

Still presented the petition to the presidents of the Board of Railway Company in early June 1862. Despite his eloquent appeal, however, only two of the twenty railway presidents signed the petition, and two or three others said that they favored the petition but did not sign. Most of the presidents rejected the petition, insisting that they would lose business from white passengers if they desegregated. As a result, the request was denied and the city's trolleys remained "white only."[9]

The enlistment of black soldiers into the Union Army accelerated the streetcar protest, though. By 1864, African American soldiers were sacrificing their lives for the Union cause, yet they and their families could not ride the streetcars to travel to Camp William Penn, the nation's first training ground for black troops located in Cheltenham. As a result, black soldiers were often late returning from the city to the camp for their duties. Nor could black women ride the trolleys to visit their wounded husbands convalescing at army hospitals in the city. Still experienced this humiliation in December 1863 when he and a white companion returning to Philadelphia from Camp William Penn boarded a trolley in Germantown and took seats inside the car. When the conductor approached, Still paid the full fare for both himself and his companion but was told to "step out onto the platform."

Infuriated, Still wrote another open letter to the *Philadelphia Press*. This time he detailed several incidents of discrimination against black riders. One case involved an elderly minister who, "on a cold, rainy winter night, was forced to stand outside the trolley on the platform." When the trolley stopped suddenly, he "fell onto the street and was killed." Another incident involved two "elegantly dressed young women returning home from a lecture." After taking a seat inside the car, they were "seized by the conductor and thrust out of the car with physical force." Other, more prominent blacks experienced the same humiliation, including the great orator Frederick Douglass, who was thrown off the city's streetcars on two occasions, and Captain Robert Smalls, a runaway slave who absconded with a Confederate warship by dressing in a stolen uniform. Smalls, who joined the Federal Army and was a hero of the Union siege of Charleston, became an important source of intelligence for the US Navy.[10]

Still's open letters in the newspapers and his encouragement of the city's black residents to oppose the streetcar ban resulted in limited success. He noted that some of the railway lines began to accommodate blacks. For example, the West Philadelphia and Darby Road line "admitted all colored people without distinction." Similarly, the Ridge Avenue Road "made an advanced step by having cars run every half hour [specifically] for the accommodation of colored people," and the Union line "unanimously resolved to [reserve] some cars [for] Colored people."[11] Not until the summer of 1864, however, when the younger generation of black activists became involved, did the city's African Americans mobilize to demand equal rights on all the city's streetcars.

The incident that triggered the mass mobilization occurred in July when Reverend William Alston hailed a streetcar. Alston, rector of the African Episcopal Church of St. Thomas, was a graduate of Oberlin College and a highly respected member of the city's black community. He had been on an outing with his two-year-old son, who suddenly became gravely ill. Desperate to return home, the minister flagged down a trolley. Though there were no other passengers, the conductor refused to allow Alston and his ill son aboard.[12] Although the child eventually recovered, the cleric was furious and wrote a letter that was published in the *Philadelphia Press*. "Is it humane," Alston asked, "to exclude respectable colored citizens from your street cars when so many of our brave and vigorous young men have been and are enlisting to take part in this heavenly ordained slavery extermination?"[13]

Alston's letter struck a painful chord among the young generation of black activists, who seized the opportunity to make the streetcar protest their own crusade. The reformers were graduates of the Institute for Colored Youth, which fostered an atmosphere of political activism. Among them were Octavius V. Catto (class of 1858), Jacob C. White Jr. (1857), John Quincy Allen (1862), and James Fields Needham (1862). Many of them had also joined the US Colored Troops and fought for the Union during the Civil War, only to return home to a segregated city with a history of racism. Determined to affect social change, the young activists founded the Pennsylvania Equal Rights League (PERL), the most influential auxiliary of the National Equal Rights League, established in 1864 to lobby for equal rights and against segregation policies.[14] They were more militant, more segregated, and much less patient than the earlier generation of reformers, though some, like Isaiah C. Wears, Jacob C. White Jr., and William D. Forten, collaborated on similar reforms with the old guard in organizations like the SCSA.[15] Instead of moral suasion, the young reformers used direct action and engaged in the political process to force local and state legislators to desegregate public transportation.

Their leader was Octavius Valentine Catto, a teacher at the Institute for Colored Youth, who used his position to advance the needs and interests of the city's African American community. Born on February 22, 1839, in Charleston, South Carolina, Catto was the son of Reverend William T. Catto and Sarah Isabella Cain. Since they were a prestigious family in Charleston society and wealthier than the city's other black residents, Octavius was born into a free culture. Relocating to Philadelphia in 1848, Reverend Catto became the rector of the Brick Wesley African Methodist Episcopal Church and rented rooms for his family on Kessler Alley in the Spring Garden section of the city. Largely self-educated, the AME minister often traveled across the country on the antislavery

FIGURE 12.1.
Black educator Octavius Catto
(1839–71) led a young generation
of black activists in the struggle for
civil rights. Catto became a martyr
for black suffrage when he was shot
and killed in election-day violence
in Philadelphia on October 10,
1871. (Library of Congress.)

speaking circuit with some of the most prominent black abolitionists, including Charles L. Redmond of Salem, Massachusetts, Martin Delany of Pittsburgh, and Frederick Douglass of Rochester, New York. He also befriended William Still. Within five years after his arrival, Catto earned a reputation as an outspoken advocate for emancipation, black education, and suffrage.[16]

Octavius embraced his father's antislavery legacy. He was an exceptionally gifted student who, in 1858, graduated from the Institute for Colored Youth as class valedictorian. He also met Jacob C. White Jr., who became his closest friend and ally among the young generation of black reformers. The following year Catto was hired as a mathematics and English teacher at the school. Catto went on to become an influential member of the Banneker Institute, an exclusive intellectual society for the city's black elite. Here he learned the art of debating on social justice topics such as emancipation, voting suffrage, and equal wages.[17]

During the Civil War, Catto helped to raise eleven regiments of the US Colored Troops, whose ranks included ICY graduates Lumbard L. Nicken, Henry Boyer Jr., Joseph S. White, Martin M. White, and William T. Jones. Although he never saw combat, Catto served with the Pennsylvania National Guard and as a major and inspector for the Fifth Brigade of the US Colored Troops.[18]

After the war, Catto and White were elected corresponding secretaries of the Republican-founded National Equal Rights League. Catto, whose military experience made him an ardent member of the Republican Party, was also appointed secretary for the League's Pennsylvania auxiliary founded in November of 1864. Together with D. B. Bowser and William Forten, he was part of a three-man committee that lobbied the Pennsylvania State Legislature on a routine basis. In addition, Catto and White acted as liaisons to US congressmen William Kelley and Thaddeus Stevens on behalf of the League.[19] Thus the former Union major was familiar with the legislative process at the state and federal levels. But he also realized that the process was a time-consuming one that did not always result in success. For Catto, direct action was the key to success in the black civil rights movement.

After learning of the insulting way Reverend Alston had been treated by the Railway, Catto and the other young activists who called themselves a "band of brothers" decided to embark on a dual strategy.[20] Catto would work on legislation to end the streetcar ban with Republican state senator Morrow B. Lowry, an abolitionist from Erie who, in 1861, had tried unsuccessfully to pass a bill integrating public transit. At the same time, Catto, with the assistance of his fiancée, Caroline Le Count, organized a movement of black Philadelphians to board streetcars in open defiance of the regulations. Le Count and other African American women, working together through local church organizations, began to protest the ridership ban against blacks. They petitioned local and state governments to overturn the ban, arguing that streetcars were essential to transport black soldiers to hospitals and camps. Soon, men, encouraged by Forten, Wears, and White, also joined the crusade. Anticipating the civil rights demonstrators of the 1960s, the activists refused to engage in physical violence against the conductors and policemen who forced them off the cars. Instead, they let their bodies go limp, making it more difficult for the officials to remove them. Although there were some occasions when conductors were unwilling to challenge large groups of young black male passengers and gave them the ride they had sought, the mass nonviolent protest captured the attention of local officials and state legislators as never before.[21]

Meanwhile, William Still continued to rely on moral suasion by appealing to white public opinion. To embarrass the city's railway presidents, he penned another open letter published by the *North American* on December 8, 1864. Citing Philadelphia's "ten or eleven regiments of colored men" who had volunteered for the Union Army, Still informed his readers that "many of these brave men have already won imperishable honor on the battlefield." But they and their families were "daily compelled to endure the outrageous rules that govern the roads of the city." Then he addressed the hypocrisy of city officials who would take the tax dollars of Philadelphia's African American community but refused to allow blacks to ride inside the streetcars:

> Nobody insults a colored man or woman in the Tax Receiver's Office, no matter how full it may be. Nobody insults a colored man or woman in entering a store, even though it may be the most fashionable in the city. . . . [But] the fifteen-hundred wounded [black] soldiers who lay in pain at the Summit and Satterlee hospitals receive but few visits from their colored brethren simply because the rules enforced on the streetcars will not allow decent colored people to ride, and the $8 or $9 charge for a carriage hire is beyond the means of the masses to pay. Yet, we repeat, by the regulations of the city passenger railways, not one mother, wife, or sister can be omitted even to see a U.S. soldier or relative, although the presence and succor of such mother, wife, or sister might save a life.[22]

On January 13, 1865, Still, with the assistance of J. Miller McKim, conducted a public meeting at Concert Hall. The crowd was integrated and consisted mostly of the old guard of reformers who had worked together in the antislavery crusade, including Cadwalader Biddle, Benjamin Coates, Thomas P. Cope, Robert Corson, Thomas Mott, Edward Parrish, and John Price Wetherill. Reverend Alston and Robert Purvis shared their stories of public humiliation by conductors who had refused to let them take a seat inside their trolley. After the speakers concluded, the following resolutions were adopted at the meeting and were to be presented to the presidents of the railway companies at a later date:

1. That we are opposed to the exclusion of the respectable persons from our passenger railcars on the ground of complexion.

2. That we have heard with shame and sorrow that decent women of color have been forced to walk long distances or accept a standing position on the front platform, exposed to inclement weather, while visiting relations at our military hospitals.

3. That we recognize the enslavement of the Black man in the South and contempt for him in the North are the main causes of our present troubles, and we protest that an un-Christian prejudice or a fastidious taste may any longer be allowed to take precedence over justice and humanity in determining the rights of any class or our citizens to use our public conveyances.

4. That we respectfully request the presidents and directors of our city's Railways to withdraw from their list of regulations this rule of exclusion which deprives our people of color their rights.

5. That in view of their recent decisions, the rights of our colored population, in respect to the cars, are without reserve; and to confine them to the use of special cars bearing aloft the degrading labels of caste, and running long intervals, is a simple substitution of one set of injustice for another, and is as much in violation of their rights as is the rule of total exclusion.

6. That a Committee of 21 be appointed by the Chairman to present, in person, a copy of these resolutions to each one of the Presidents of our City Railroads on or before Wednesday, January 25, 1865.[23]

When the Board of Presidents received the resolutions, they decided to allow their white passengers to determine the issue for themselves by taking a poll. On January 31, 1865, the day the US Congress adopted the Thirteen Amendment abolishing slavery, the railway presidents announced the results of that poll. White riders voted to maintain the "whites only policy" by a huge margin of 4,000 to 200 votes. The decision reflected the widespread racism in the city, especially that of unskilled white immigrants who knew that access to streetcars gave them an advantage in getting to available jobs. Although the Frankford and Southwark Company initially offered to admit blacks inside their cars, it reverted to separate "colored" cars after one month because of a decline in white passengers.[24]

Catto and his band of brothers increased the pressure on state and federal legislators in 1866. Joining with state senator Morrow Lowry and the other members of PERL's "Car Committee," the young civil rights activist solicited the support of Radical Republican state legislators to desegregate the streetcars. He also helped Lowry rewrite the legislation.

Since Congress had recently passed the Civil Rights Act of 1866 guarantee-
ing citizenship without regard to race, color, or creed, Catto sensed that the national mood was now behind the streetcar cause and that one last effort to create
legislation would result in even stronger protections than the last two measures
had proposed. Catto also lobbied national representatives, chief among them the
Radical Republicans Thaddeus Stevens and William D. Kelley. At the same time,
Philadelphia's black residents continued to push the issue by boarding streetcars
in open defiance of the regulations. Often they were forced off, sometimes violently. But there were some successful challenges as well. In June 1866, a group
of thirty young men recently graduated from Lincoln University (the nation's
first black college) rushed onto a city-bound streetcar. The conductor, unwilling
to challenge them, ended up giving them the ride they had sought.[25]

During the protest, John W. Forney, owner of the *Philadelphia Press*,
emerged as the strongest white advocate of the movement. The *Press* was a Republican newspaper, and it gave much greater coverage of the streetcar protests
as well as other black events than any of the city's other white dailies. Forney
even hired an African American correspondent to cover those events. Together
with the efforts of Catto and the young activists, Forney kept the streetcar issue
in the news, much to the dismay of the Board of Railway presidents and other
city officials, who were beginning to buckle.[26]

Finally, on February 5, 1867, as the US Congress was poised to pass the
Fifteenth Amendment, which would grant voting rights to black men, Senator Lowry presented a new streetcar bill to Pennsylvania lawmakers. This time
it passed, probably because the Republican-dominated legislature realized that
their reelection depended upon newly enfranchised black constituents. On
March 22, Governor John Geary signed the bill and Philadelphia's black residents, at least in theory, could at last ride the city's streetcars. Catto's dual strategy
of direct action and political pressure had prevailed.[27]

Just three days later, the new law was tested when Catto's fiancée, Caroline
Le Count, was refused service when she attempted to board a streetcar on Eleventh and Lombard Streets. "We don't allow niggers to ride," shouted the conductor, adding insult to injury. Le Count, a principal at the Institute for Colored
Youth, hailed a policeman and showed him a newspaper clipping proving that
the ban was illegal. The conductor was arrested and fined $100.[28] Although the
battle for the streetcars had been won, more fights lay ahead. Unfortunately, one
of the most painful battles occurred between Still and Catto's young activists and
their political allies in Harrisburg.

After the streetcar victory, Still realized that moral suasion and impassioned newspaper editorials might have inspired an earlier generation of abolitionist-reformers but that the young black reformers led by Catto favored direct action and pressure politics. He was also jealous of the younger generation for their success in the streetcar protest and for establishing a new, more effective civil rights organization, PERL. While Still and his associates on the SCSA had struggled with the streetcar ban for nearly a decade, Catto and PERL managed to achieve desegregation of the cars in under four years. What irked Still was their reform ideology. PERL debated whether they would realize more success in securing their future objectives—equal educational opportunity for black children and black suffrage—as a biracial alliance or as a blacks-only organization. Still, in contrast, had never allowed racial pride or a personal mistrust of potential white allies to interfere with his antislavery or civil rights activities. Instead, Still had dedicated his life to the principle of color blindness and the necessity of coexisting with a racist white majority.[29] In fact, he might never have achieved the success he enjoyed as an Underground Railroad agent had it not been for the constant support of Philadelphia's white Quakers.

Tensions between Still and the young activists escalated when PERL adopted a resolution that any member "who refuses to accommodate and treat colored men under all circumstances in his place of business, as he treats white men, is guilty of the greatest dereliction of duty."[30] The issue gained greater public exposure when the *Christian Recorder*, an African Methodist Episcopal newspaper that served as the unofficial organ of PERL, excoriated those black businessmen who continued to stand "in the way of the elevation of their race by taking the unmanly and degraded position of catering to American prejudice."[31] Still considered the charge a personal affront. As one of the city's most prominent black businessmen, he reserved the right to serve or not serve whomever he pleased. Because many of his customers were white and wealthier than his black customers and because he often refused to serve those who asked for credit, many blacks became suspicious of his influence and jealous of his wealth and prestige. Accordingly, Still's coal yard on Washington Avenue near Twelfth Street was subject to boycotts and threats of arson.[32] Infuriated by the hostile treatment, Still began to defend himself in public speeches, newspaper editorials, and pamphlets. He insisted that he had "for many years" encouraged the "young colored men of Philadelphia to begin their own businesses instead of patronizing those owned and operated by whites": "Surely, such places of business would have great weight upon the prejudices against us and thousands of responsible white people would delight in encouraging such enterprises. If our young men and women would gradually open stores and learn trades and businesses it would greatly increase the incentive amongst our people to establish business places."

Still also praised the city's several black-owned businesses. He maintained that those businesses served as worthy examples because they were "patronized by all classes without respect to color" and because their proprietors were "proving that good workmanship, energy, integrity and professional deportment can and will surmount prejudices." He also identified himself as a role model for the younger generation, insisting that his "hard labor, strict temperance habits, rigid economy and unimpeachable character in business relations" had enabled him to "work [his] way up to a respectable position as a man of business."[33]

Naturally, when Still was attacked for not doing more to help the younger generation, he explained that "few heeded [his] advice" and that his "many labors of both a private and public nature" prevented him from mentoring younger blacks. Perhaps this was simply an excuse to explain why the young activists "steered clear of [him]."[34] Whether Still intended it or not, his remarks reflected a self-righteous attitude and one that suggested that he considered himself better than others. He blamed the younger generation for a lack of ambition. Still's defense of his reputation did not win much support from the city's African American community. Nor did he make many friends among state legislators like Sen. Marrow Lowery and Rep. John S. Mann, who criticized Still as "one of the worst enemies of his people" because he advocated only for ridership for the black elite and not for the rights of the city's entire African American population.[35]

Believing that he was unappreciated for his longtime efforts to overturn the streetcar ban, Still defended himself in a pamphlet titled *A Brief Narrative of the Struggle for the Rights of the Colored People of Philadelphia in the Railway Cars; and a Defense of William Still Relating to His Agency Touching the Passage of the Late Bill*, published in 1867. He argued that he was "misrepresented by some and willfully slandered by others, who for more than a dozen years have been my bittersweet enemies and have spared no pains to destroy my reputation." Chief among his critics were Lowery and Mann, who, while "contending for the rights of the colored people . . . strongly denounced our conduct and branded us as 'base enemies' of our race."[36]

According to Still, a loyal member of the Republican Party, these "duplicitous" state officials and other white citizens of Philadelphia were "going around trying to prevail on colored people not to buy coal from me and boldly declaring that they would prefer getting their coal from [Democratic] Copperheads." While Still insisted that he did "not fear the effect these men might have on his business, he did remind readers that *he* had been responsible for "every word of the several appeals" printed in the newspapers since 1859. Still called attention to the fact that those appeals, "together with the petition" he had drafted three years later, were "prepared by myself" and that "every name to the petition was procured through my individual effort."[37]

Despite Still's efforts to defend his reputation, the pamphlet only served to worsen his relationship with the city's African American community. That community now viewed him as an elitist and questioned whether his intentions were based on a genuine commitment to their welfare or his own self-interest. Still's relationship with young black activists became much worse. An inevitable showdown would occur during the 1870s, when the Fifteenth Amendment was ratified and blacks were given the right to vote.

THIRTEEN

The Politics of Reform

By 1869, William Still was a very bitter man. Although he was not yet fifty years old, Still had been cast aside in the struggle for civil rights by the younger generation of black activists, who took the credit for the success of the streetcar protest, a cause to which he had devoted a decade of his life.

Just as painful was the defection of Jacob C. White Jr., who had worked closely with Still in the antislavery movement and who had once served as a secretary of the now-defunct Social, Civil, and Statistical Association. Once the SCSA disbanded in 1869, White, also an active member of the Pennsylvania Equal Rights League, shifted his complete allegiance to Catto and his "band of brothers." According to Harry Silcox, the death of the SCSA was due in large measure to Still's "sharp and sometimes biting personality." He alienated those who disagreed with him, and White became one of those victims.[1]

Still could not understand why the younger generation of reformers indulged in the game of baseball, for example, when, in his opinion, they should be investing all their energies into the advancement of the black race. On the other hand, White, Catto, and other members of the Equal Rights League believed that the sport was a healthy form of recreation and established the Pythian Base Ball Club in 1865. The team name referred to the Olympic games

FIGURE 13.1. Known for his organizational skills, Jacob C. White Jr. (1837–1902) held leadership positions in numerous African American organizations, including the Institute for Colored Youth and the Pennsylvania Equal Rights League. After Octavius Catto's death in 1871, White became the preeminent statesman for Philadelphia's African American community. (Public Domain, Wikimedia.)

of ancient Greece and reflected the education of the team's members. Many of the players were graduates of the Institute for Colored Youth and were members of the Banneker Institute and other social, political, and intellectual organizations representing Philadelphia's intellectual elite. The players also liked to indulge in material comforts, especially Catto, who earned one of the highest black salaries in Philadelphia at the time.[2] He spent considerable money on the latest fashions in men's clothing, ate well at the many banquets he attended, and basked in the summer parties at the New Jersey shore. The baseball club was just one of many pleasurable diversions for Catto, who was the team's second baseman and captain.[3]

The Pythians quickly became the most outstanding baseball team in Pennsylvania and one of the most successful African American clubs on the East Coast, routinely defeating teams from Baltimore, Brooklyn, and New York.[4] Pythian games became an important event for Philadelphia's black community, especially when the team played Washington, since those games included picnics and the exchange of gifts. Like other social clubs, the Pythians operated with rules, dues, regular meetings, and committees. They relied on the sponsorship of the city's most prominent black businessmen, including William Still.[5] But by 1869, Still's resentment of the younger activists got the better of him.

When White, the secretary of the ball club, wrote to Still to remind him to pay his annual membership dues of one dollar, the elder reformer replied with a snippy letter excoriating the Pythian players for ignoring more worthy causes like the education of the freedmen "who are famished for knowledge."

"So great and pressing are the [freedmen's] needs that I feel bound to give of my means in their direction instead of frivolous amusements like baseball," he added. Refusing to pay his annual dues, Still demanded that his "name be erased from the membership roll without delay."[6]

White replied a month later with a sarcastic letter of his own. He informed Still that "neither the acquisition nor the disposition of [his] means is of interest to us as an organization" and that what he did in his private life and reform involvements was "no one's business but his own." White closed the letter by reminding the former abolitionist that he is "charged on the club's books for $2.00, and upon payment of that sum his resignation will be accepted."[7] While the nasty exchange ended the possibility of collaboration between Still and his former friend, the final break between the forty-nine-year-old reformer and the young activists came in the struggle to restore black voting rights in Pennsylvania.

Since 1860, Still's Social, Civil and Statistical Association had been lobbying the state legislature to restore the franchise blacks lost in 1838 when a new state constitution was adopted. Catto and the Pennsylvania Equal Rights League joined the fray in 1865. But neither organization had much success. Every post–Civil War referendum to extend the franchise to blacks was defeated. During the winter of 1869, however, the national Republican leadership decided to support a constitutional amendment that was acceptable to all factions of the party. Their decision was based more on political than humanitarian interests.[8]

The Republicans hoped to ensure their domination of both houses of Congress by protecting black voters in the South and cultivating other black voters in the North, especially in Pennsylvania, where the Democrats were beginning to challenge Republican hegemony in the state. Since the early 1860s, Simon Cameron, a US senator, had commanded the corrupt Republican machine and willfully used public funds, kickbacks, and corporate donations to finance campaigns as well as to increase his own wealth. With thousands of federal, state, and local patronage jobs in his control, the Cameron machine assembled a virtual army of political faithful, enabling it to manipulate voters in the majority of urban wards in Philadelphia and Pittsburgh as well as the rural areas of the state. In fact, the only Democratic strongholds in Pennsylvania were the Irish wards in Philadelphia, the anthracite region in the northeastern section of the state, and rural communities heavily populated by Catholic immigrants.[9]

The Cameron machine's reach was so extensive that it controlled the Pennsylvania Assembly, where legislators sold their votes to grant corporate privileges. Then they would blackmail those same corporations by threatening to pass strike bills to deprive them of the very same privileges they had granted earlier. Notoriously corrupt, the state legislature also auctioned the offices of US senator and state treasurer to the highest bidder and ensured the reelection of Republican members, as well as the control of the party machine at both the state and municipal levels, by refusing to reform the 1869 Registry Act.[10]

In Philadelphia, the Republican machine was controlled by James Mc-Manes, an Irish immigrant and mill owner, who, beginning in 1865, gained political influence as a trustee of the powerful company that supplied illuminating gas to the city. Within two years, McManes was able to manipulate influential friendships in Washington, Harrisburg, and Philadelphia to become the city's first party boss. "King" McManes and his political machine, aptly called the "Gas Ring," controlled more than five thousand public jobs and exerted control over city businesses, banks, contactors, and street railways through the use of Gas Works funds.[11] McManes also manipulated local elections through the Gas Ring–dominated Philadelphia Board of Aldermen, who determined the appointment of election officials. Those same officials controlled the registration of voters, supervised elections, and eliminated any challenge to the Ring. To be sure, Republican control over state politics was so flagrantly corrupt that by 1870 reform-minded members of the party were joining with Democrats to demand a revision of the state constitution in order to dislodge the Cameron machine.[12]

With support for the Democratic Party growing, Pennsylvania governor John W. Geary and other state Republican leaders decided to pander to black voters and pushed for passage of the Fifteenth Amendment when it was sent to the states for ratification. After a limited discussion, the House, on March 11, 1869, passed the measure by a partisan vote. Two weeks later, the state senate approved the amendment, and Geary immediately signed a resolution ratifying the measure. A year later, on March 30, 1870, the Fifteenth Amendment became law when three-quarters of the states approved the measure.[13]

African Americans in Philadelphia rejoiced. William Nesbitt, president of the Pennsylvania Equal Rights League, declared April 26, 1870, to be a "day for prayer and thanksgiving."[14] Blacks throughout Pennsylvania responded by holding religious services and marching in parades.[15] But the largest celebration was in Philadelphia and showcased the up-and-coming black political leadership, all of whom were members of the Equal Rights League: Isaiah C. Wears led the "Uptown" wards (above Callowhill Street); Octavius Catto, the "Downtown" wards (below South Street); Andrew F. Stevens, William Whipper, and Jacob Purnell, the "Middle" wards (Lombard Street section). After each leader was publicly recognized, Frederick Douglass rose to deliver a speech. Insisting that blacks vote "as they pleased" because "each man must decide what candidate and measures will be best," Douglass identified the major dilemma of the black voter—"Should he vote Republican due to his appreciation for emancipation, or should he use his vote to further the African American race, regardless of party?"[16]

Catto, a staunch Republican, was angered by Douglass's remarks. He was convinced that the black struggle for civil rights depended on getting elected to political office, and that meant courting the Republican Party. Instead of engaging the black orator in a debate, however, Catto ignored him. Wears, on the other hand, refused to let the issue die. During the next month, he and Douglass conducted a public debate in the *Philadelphia Press*. While Wears believed that no black person could vote Democrat because of the party's poor record on race, Douglass continued to insist that blacks could not afford to become a tool of the Republican Party.[17]

Meanwhile, Philadelphia's white residents reacted to the news of black suffrage with hostility. Nearly one hundred petitions flowed into Harrisburg objecting to the new amendment. Some whites resorted to violence. On April 26, for example, as black families were returning home from celebrations, a group of white rowdies stoned them. Incidents like these intimidated the city's black residents. Even during the October elections, when blacks had the opportunity to exercise their vote for the first time, many were scared away from the polls by the prospect of violence. Despite the valiant efforts of Isaiah C. Wears and the Equal Rights League to get out the black vote for those elections, the Republican Party made very little effort to organize the black voters, fearing a white backlash. Yet there was only a minor disturbance at the polls on Fifth and Lombard Streets, and Mayor Daniel Fox immediately called the state militia to the scene to prevent any violence.[18]

White resentment for black voters boiled over the following year during the mayoral election, and this time there were no state or federal troops to protect black voters. Party allegiances were divided along racial lines. William Stokely, the Republican candidate, was the favorite of the city's black voters because of his strong law-and-order platform. Philadelphia police, mostly Irish Democrats, did little to protect blacks when they were attacked on the streets by race haters. Thus a Republican victory appeared to offer the African American community the best chance for protection.[19]

Since the Registry Act of 1869 gave the Ring-dominated Philadelphia Board of Aldermen control over the appointment of election officials, who in turn controlled the registration of voters and supervised elections, Stokely's victory was a fait accompli. Even the few African American election officials who were appointed were selected on the basis of their ignorance of the voting process or their corruptibility. With little to no interference by the courts, the Republicans were free to rig the elections by hiring outsiders and repeat voters to flock to the polls. Democratic pols responded with inflammatory rhetoric to mobilize their immigrant voters. The Irish, in particular, took to the polls to prevent blacks from voting in the city wards they controlled.[20] "As the Irish became the tool of the Democrats, the Negro became the tool of the Republicans," observed W. E. B. Du Bois in his groundbreaking book *The Philadelphia Negro: A Social Study*, published in 1899.[21]

Racial politics boiled over on Election Day, October 10, 1871. Philadelphia witnessed one of the worst race riots in the city's history. Already appalled by black suffrage, the Irish, in particular, were poised to attack. The Democrats exploited white resentment with the rhetoric that "Republicans considered the [white] working man as no better than a negro." Riots began in the Fifth Ward, where black voters accused white Irish police of intimidation. Shortly after, a fight broke out in the Seventh Ward when a black man was turned away at the polls. Violence spread to the Fourth, Sixteenth, and Seventeenth Wards as white mobs attacked black voters with the assistance of the police.[22]

Catto, who had been instrumental in organizing black voters, was teaching at the ICY when he learned of the rioting. He had already voted that morning. Fearing for the safety of his students, he dismissed them shortly after 1:00 p.m. An hour later, James Milliken, an adjutant of the Fifth Brigade, arrived at the institute and informed the thirty-two-year-old teacher that their unit was commandeered to protect the city. Catto, who had been a major and inspector in the brigade during the Civil War, retained his rank in the unit as a reserve officer. He was ordered to arm himself and report to headquarters at Broad and Race Streets at 6:00 p.m. sharp. Although the brigade would provide Catto with a horse and he still had his sword, he no longer owned a sidearm. He planned to purchase one on his way home, where he would dress in his blue uniform and get his sword.[23]

Before leaving, a concerned colleague approached Catto and pleaded with him to take a circuitous route home to avoid the rioting. A pupil had made a similar plea the day before when the rioting started, and Catto had replied, "I will not stultify my manhood by going to my home in a roundabout way."[24] This time, however, he followed the advice.

Stopping at a bank at 919 Lombard Street to withdraw twenty dollars, Catto proceeded north—away from the rioting—to Chestnut Street. Still, he was accosted by a white rioter and narrowly escaped. Hurrying east to Third Street, he found a pawnshop and purchased a revolver. Instead of going directly to South Street where he lived, Catto chose a safer route and walked north up Lombard away from the rioting. Turning south on Ninth, he walked one more block to South Street and doubled back east to return home. Catto was just yards away from his house at 814 South Street when a white man wearing a long dark coat and a Kossuth hat passed him walking west on the same side of the street. His head was bandaged, but not in a manner that covered his eyes, so he could recognize the black civil rights leader.

Suddenly the white man turned, drew a pistol, and fired. The shot hit Catto in the torso just as a horse-drawn streetcar was passing. Crossing his arms and squeezing himself as if to relieve the pain, Catto cried out to his assailant, "What are you doing?"

There was no response. Instead the shooter crouched down preparing to fire another shot. Somehow Catto managed to scurry behind the rear of the streetcar, which had come to a complete halt. The white attacker followed.

Pedestrians and the streetcar passengers, both black and white, were initially stunned by the gunfire but became horrorstruck as they realized what had just occurred. Catto turned to face his assailant one more time before he fired another round of shots at close range. The young black activist staggered and then fell into the arms of a policeman who arrived as the bloody scene unfolded.[25]

Catto was one of three black men who were murdered that day. Another forty black voters were hospitalized. The US Marines were called in after the killings to prevent further violence. Catto's body was guarded by the militia at the Armory at Broad and Race Streets, and he was buried with full military honors in one of the largest funerals ever held in Philadelphia. No one was ever found guilty for his death.[26]

Octavius Catto's murder robbed Philadelphia's African American community of its most promising leader. The young activists he had once led became wedded to the Republican Party in the hope of greater political influence. Some, like Isaiah C. Wears, increased their involvement with the Equal Rights League. Others quit their activity in the organization. But Jacob White Jr., the individual who might have succeeded Catto as the leader of the Pennsylvania auxiliary, gradually drifted away from political reform. Devastated by the death of his close friend, White devoted himself to improving the education of black youth, principally through his involvements at the Institute for Colored Youth and the city's public schools.[27]

In 1873, Pennsylvania's Democratic Party leaders secured the passage of a new state constitution designed to curtail political machines. To prevent fraud at the polls, the new constitution required that all ballots be numbered, provided a clear definition of bribery and its punishment, guaranteed minority representation on election boards, and ensured that contested elections would be decided in the courts. It also nullified Philadelphia's notorious Registry Act by creating statewide registration requirements and made it difficult for political machines to exploit patronage by requiring that all officials of counties with more than a population of 150,000 be salaried. At first glance, the Constitution of 1873, which also restored black suffrage in Pennsylvania, appeared to be an unconditional victory for Democrats and Republican reformers alike.[28] In reality, the new constitution was more of a hollow victory.

That same year, Republican governor John F. Hartranft signed into law a congressional reapportionment act that consolidated populous Democratic counties into large districts and created smaller Republican districts. The new gerrymandering limited Democrats to a maximum of nine of twenty-seven seats in both the Senate and House, leaving the state legislature firmly under the control of the Republican machine.[29]

Because of the Republicans' strong hold on electoral politics, William Still felt compelled to protect the political independence of the black community. Rebuffed by Republican mayor William Stokely in 1872 when he requested the inclusion of blacks on the Philadelphia police force, Still realized that the black vote was being taken for granted by the GOP. As a result, he broke ranks with the party when Stokely ran for reelection in 1874. Instead, Still supported Alexander K. McClure, an independent "People's Party" candidate. McClure, a former Republican state senator, accused Stokely and "King" James McManus, who controlled Republican patronage in the city, of unbridled corruption and promised to clean up municipal government.[30] Like McClure, Still considered the Republican machine a "corrupt ring," and insisted that his "sense of duty would not allow him to vote for either a Republican or a Democratic candidate" because those parties had been involved in "numerous election frauds," among other evils. His decision to support McClure was based on the candidate's "active cooperation with the reformers of the city, and his strong advocacy of a new constitution to restore [black] suffrage."[31]

Isaiah C. Wears, once an ally of Still's, called him a "traitor" and led a wave of protest against him in the black community. Some accused Still of paying off a political debt for his recent appointment to the previously all-white Philadelphia Board of Trade. Others threatened to boycott his coal business or burn it to the ground. Some blacks even threatened to lynch him. At one point, the police intervened to protect Still at his home.[32] But there were also those in the black community who simply wanted an explanation for his decision to break ranks with the Republican Party. They requested that he "deliver a public address" on the matter, which Still agreed to do.[33]

On Tuesday evening, March 10, at Concert Hall, William Still attempted to justify his support for McClure. The hall was "well filled" and the "interest as great as has ever been noticed at any other lecture," reported the *Philadelphia Press*. It was a racially mixed audience that included Still's critics as well as his supporters. Seated on the platform were such "well-known champions of the old anti-slavery movement in this city" as Robert Purvis, Bishop P. Campbell of the AME Church, Passmore Williamson, and Charles Wise. Still was accompanied to the speaker's platform by Reverend W. H. Hunter, publisher of the *Christian Recorder*, and when he took his place behind the lectern there was an "outburst of applause" by his allies.[34]

Still began his speech by addressing the charge that he had "deserted [his] [civil rights] principles by voting for the mayoral candidate of the People's Party." "Politics for me have had no charm since the colored man has been invested with the right of suffrage," he insisted. In fact, Still admitted that he could have "cared less whether . . . Stokley or McClure won the campaign." The important issue for him was the decision of the majority of black voters to give their unconditional loyalty to the Republican Party "simply out of gratitude."[35] Those black voters, according to Still, followed the example of the young activist leaders by "simply voting indiscriminately the entire Republican ticket irrespective of the claims of the candidate being voted for." He also suggested that it was "rather presumptuous" of these "leading colored gentlemen—who do not touch with their delicate fingers the burdens that oppress the colored people—to assume the right to dictate how others will vote." They are the ones who are "getting their pockets lined with Republican stamps." Instead, Still emphasized that a "colored voter should be free to vote an independent or non-partisan, or even Democratic ticket." No longer should he be "compelled to think or act only at the bidding of others, and especially of the dominant race."[36]

Turning to his own defense, Still pointed out that he was not the only black citizen to vote against the Republican machine. Other, "long-tried friends of freedom, voted . . . for McClure." They were abolitionists, the same "friends of freedom of *all* parties who openly espoused the cause of the slave when it was extremely unpopular and even dangerous to do so." "Have all these voters turned traitors, too?" he asked his critics.[37] Finally, Still addressed the charge that his vote for McClure was bought by either the People's Party or the Democratic Party. The "allegations that money was used is wholly false, as the offer of a single farthing was never made to me by anyone, nor was it ever demanded by me from any source." Satisfied, Still ended his speech by stating: "You have now fully and frankly my position [on] politics; what I think about 'gratitude' to the [Republican] ring; and what I think about the duties of colored men generally, under their peculiar and delicate situation as citizens."[38]

Still's break with the Republican Party was the exception, not the rule. Most of the city's blacks continued to blindly support the machine, which blamed the Democratic Party for Catto's murder, the race riots of 1871, and pandering to the Irish and their intemperance.[39] Occasionally, Democrats would launch a reform movement. In the early 1880s, for example, a "Committee of One Hundred" middle-class professionals and educators was created to limit the corrupt practices of ward politicians. Matthew Quay, party boss of the state machine, even supported the committee's recommendation for charter change in Philadelphia that limited the patronage powers of the Gas Ring pols. But he did so specifically to humiliate his chief rival, James McManes, and the Gas Ring succeeded in shutting down civil service reform. Again, in the 1890s, department store mogul John Wanamaker headed a reform movement to cleanse the Republican Party, but state party boss Boies Penrose, a native Philadelphian, easily defeated the campaign. Thus Democrats were never able to sustain their reform efforts to eliminate the corruption. Free to assert its will, Philadelphia's well-oiled Republican machine, which exercised a strong mutual influence with the state machine, controlled elections from the end of the Civil War through 1900.[40]

As the nineteenth century drew to a close, the city's blacks built a political base in the Seventh Ward in South Philadelphia. The center of black political activity was the Citizens Republican Club, founded by Andrew Stevens, a caterer. As the name suggests, the club was yet another tool of the city's Republican machine. Another dozen black political clubs were established by 1900 in the saloons or corner poolrooms of the Thirteenth Ward between South and Christian Streets west of Broad, where the hub of black politics shifted.[41] W. E. B. Du Bois, who belonged to an up-and-coming generation of middle-class black activists, denounced these clubs as "crowds of loafers and idlers and laborers" who indoctrinated younger "newcomers who immigrate from the South to seek their fortunes."

"On election day, the newcomer, who's been treated so well at the club is asked to do a favor," explained Du Bois. "He's given a ticket with the names of [Republican] candidates and told to deposit it in the voting box. Once the favor is done, he's 'an official member of the club,' joining a network of intrigue, influence and bribery."[42]

African Americans, never a large portion of the city's voters, continued their routine support of the Republican ticket, enabling the party to extend its corrupt hegemony into the twentieth century. Of Philadelphia's twenty-five thousand eligible African American voters in 1900, Du Bois estimated that between one-half to two-thirds belonged to the class of "bribed black voters," while the "better class" or minority of educated, middle-class blacks "don't vote because of the corruption involved in the process." It was exactly this "better class" of blacks, insisted Du Bois, who were the ones needed to reform the process. Until then, there would be "no democratic government in Philadelphia," he concluded, echoing the same sentiments as William Still a generation earlier. "There will only be an oligarchy of ward politicians and businessmen using public office for private gain."[43] Predictably, Still quickly soured on the political process, insisting that economic self-improvement was a much better course for black advancement. He also turned his attention to business and philanthropic interests and to the writing, publishing, and marketing of a book that would preserve the unique history of the Underground Railroad.

FOURTEEN

Legacy

Between 1871 and his death in 1902, William Still ensured his historical legacy by devoting himself to black social causes, promoting racial pride among the next generation of African Americans, and writing, publishing, and marketing his book *The Underground Railroad*. These were important contributions to Philadelphia's black community at a time when thousands of freedmen from the South were migrating to the City of Brotherly Love in search of employment and a new life. Their arrival inspired the founding of mutual aid societies, black-sponsored employment agencies, schools, and banking institutions. In addition, an African American newspaper, the *Philadelphia Tribune*, was established to keep black readers informed about the activities and achievements in their community.[1]

Still, whose coal business was flourishing now, enjoyed enough leisure time to become involved in black benevolence. His position as a manager on the city's board of trade allowed him to promote black business ventures. Similarly, his membership on the Freedmen's Aid Commission enabled him to find housing and employment for recently freed slaves who migrated to the city. In 1880, Still founded a YMCA branch for black children. In 1888, he served as president of the Berean Building and Loan Association, an extension of the Berean Presbyterian Church, which helped blacks purchase their own homes. Still also managed homes for aged blacks and destitute black youngsters as well as an orphan asylum for the children of black soldiers and sailors. He even found the time to cultivate promising young African American men and women, including Matthew Anderson, a Presbyterian minister and prominent businessman; Edward Wiley, another talented businessman; and Francis Harper, a poet and prominent women's right advocate.[2]

All of Still's efforts contributed significantly to the social and economic uplift of Philadelphia's black community, which, by 1890, numbered forty thousand residents, about 3.8 percent of the city's total population.[3] The majority of blacks lived in the crowded ghettos of the city, sharing their neighborhoods with other new immigrants of European ancestry. These neighborhoods were ridden with crime, prostitution, and poverty. Blacks were confronted daily with racial discrimination, both by new immigrants and by working-class whites.[4] Even middle-class whites believed that their "great, rich and famous city was going to the dogs because of the crime and venality of its Negro citizens."[5] In fact, the University of Pennsylvania, in 1896, hired W. E. B. Du Bois, a newly minted black PhD in sociology from Harvard University, to conduct an empirical investigation to prove this deeply ingrained notion. For eighteen months, Du Bois lived in and studied the city's Seventh Ward, home to 8,861 African Americans, the city's largest concentration of blacks.[6] The product of his research was *The Philadelphia Negro*, one of the very first studies to integrate urban ethnography, social history, and descriptive statistics. To the dismay of Penn's faculty—and the city's white middle class—Du Bois concluded that the poverty and crime of the Seventh Ward were the result, not of race and biological distinctions that separated blacks and whites, but of environment and the social conditions that confronted blacks, including the legacy of slavery, race prejudice, and competition with white immigrants for jobs.[7]

While Du Bois asked Philadelphia's whites for "greater understanding and tolerance of the Negro's condition," he faulted the city's more successful blacks for their lack of leadership. He called on this "talented tenth" to serve as mentors and role models for the larger black community before they became permanently separated from the mainstream of society.[8] Du Bois also referred to William Still in his book, albeit fleetingly. Still was mentioned along with a small group of black businessmen who, between 1840 and 1870, "wielded great personal influence" and whose "conspicuous success opened opportunities for Negroes in other lines."[9]

Since Still was in his mid- to late seventies when Du Bois conducted his study, it is doubtful that the black sociologist was referring to him when he

FIGURE 14.1.
William Edward Burghardt
Du Bois (1868–1963) was a
sociologist, a historian, an
author, and the best-known
spokesperson for African
American rights during the
first half of the twentieth
century. (Library of Congress.)

faulted the failure of the "talented tenth" to provide leadership for the next generation. Although no documentary evidence exists revealing Still's reaction to
Du Bois's remark, he would certainly agree with the conclusion that other successful black businessmen like himself had a responsibility to mentor the next
generation, just as he tried to do in his professional career and personal life.

If Still's four children are a measure of his success at mentoring the next
generation, he did an outstanding job. Still made sure that all of his children
received a good education as well as a religious upbringing and understood the
importance of service to the black community. They were his greatest personal
legacy. Caroline, the eldest child, was a pioneering female physician, community
activist, and educator. After attending Oberlin College and the Women's Medical
College of Philadelphia, she established a private medical practice in Philadelphia, married Edward Wiley, a successful black businessman, raised a son, and
became an active member of the Presbyterian Church.[10] William Wilberforce

Still graduated from Lincoln University, spent some time in the South "work-ing for [his] race," and later practiced law in Philadelphia.[11] Robert George Still became a journalist and printshop owner in Philadelphia, and Frances Ellen Still became a kindergarten teacher in the city.[12]

Still's most enduring legacy, however, was his book *The Underground Railroad*, published in 1872. It is a compilation of fugitive slave interviews Still recorded during the period 1853 to 1861, as well as the correspondence he con-ducted with other agents, and biographical sketches of abolitionists that were mostly solicited from the subjects themselves. While the uniqueness of the book is based on Still's insights into the operation of the UGRR, the book is also sig-nificant for other reasons.

First, Still, inspired by the "heart-rendering history of [his] own family," af-forded other fugitives an invaluable opportunity to be reunited with their fami-lies after slavery was abolished in 1865. The interviews provide important details that allowed a fugitive's family members to trace his whereabouts. Still recorded not only the names of those runaways he assisted but also their age, skin color, and gender, and he paid careful attention to family information, such as number of siblings and names of parents, spouses, and children. He also recorded details about their bondage, including owners' names, how fugitives were treated, and their reasons for running away. Just as important to Still were the details of their escape, including point of origin, date of departure, and, in some cases, ultimate destination. Such meticulous record keeping suggests that Still had intended to "reunite and comfort" family members separated by slavery. He later admitted that the work "afforded me the greatest satisfaction" for that very same reason.[13]

Second, Still allowed the fugitives to speak for themselves and credited them as active agents in their quest for freedom. While he acknowledged white agents like Thomas Garrett, Seth Concklin, and Samuel Smith for their "Christ-like exhibition of love" toward fugitives, Still placed a greater emphasis on the "physical and intellectual" abilities of the runaways themselves, who emerge as the heroes in his account along with the free black agents who assisted them.[14]

Their "heroism and desperate struggles," wrote Still, as well as "the terrible oppression that they were under, should be kept green in the memory of this and coming generations."[15] Subsequent accounts of the Underground Railroad written by white agents did not acknowledge the significant role played by fugi-tives or the free black community. Instead, those accounts assumed an autobio-graphical nature, promoting the author's UGRR activities, or gave all credit for the success of the enterprise to white agents. In addition, Still understood that it was important to let the runaways to speak for themselves because marketing and book sales would depend largely on the authenticity of the accounts as well as the dramatic retelling of the fugitives' own experiences. According to Stephen Hall, Still reinforced the credibility of the dramatic escapes by writing his own preface in which he shared some of his own experiences with the slave community and assured readers that "the most scrupulous care has been taken to furnish artless stories, simple facts,—to resort to no coloring to make the book seem romantic."[16]

Third, Still wanted to demonstrate that a book written by a black man would disprove the argument that blacks were intellectually inferior. At a time when white America was debating the place of blacks in postbellum society and black leaders, in response to white racism, were promoting the colonization of freedmen to Liberia, Still, in writing and publishing *The Underground Railroad*, hoped to prove that blacks were worthy of US citizenship in every conceivable way. Although calls for colonization had been muted during the 1860s and early 1870s, AME clerics like Henry M. Turner, R. H. Cain, and B. F. Porter actively promoted black emigration to Liberia in the later 1870s as Reconstruction failed.[17] Still saw his book as a way to promote race pride among the younger generation of blacks so that they would remain in the United States and seek their rightful claim to the American Dream of upward social and economic mobility. According to Still, the Underground Railroad, more than any other historical movement, reflected the pride, perseverance, and praiseworthiness of the African American people. Nor should it ever be forgotten: "For the colored man no history can be more instructive than this, of his own making, and written by one of his own race. The generations are growing in light. Not to know of those who were stronger than shackles, who were pioneers in the grand advance towards freedom; not to know of what characters the race could produce when straightened by circumstances, nor of those small beginnings which ended in triumphant emancipation, will, in a short time, be a reproach."[18]

Finally, Still continued to harbor some resentment toward critics who marginalized his contributions to the civil rights struggles of the 1860s and early 1870s and hoped that his eight-hundred-page book would increase his public visibility and restore his once-impeccable reputation.[19] To appear disinterested, he asked James P. Boyd to write his biographical sketch in the preface to the 1886 edition. Encouraged by Still, Boyd portrayed his subject as the "black Benjamin Franklin" by offering a prescription for success to the African American community. "The author does not seek to make himself conspicuous in any way," wrote Boyd, who served as Still's apologist. "He is a modest man and content with the quiet, unrewarded favor of his kind. However, there is an example in his life, and he does seek . . . to set a lesson before the colored people of America [that] may serve to acquaint them with the possibilities within their reach."

Describing Still's personal example of "pluck and perseverance," Boyd praised the author for "overcoming poverty, illiteracy and prejudice to make for himself a large, growing and profitable business" and saluted Still for "becoming a useful and influential member of society." Like Franklin, who shamelessly promoted himself in his own autobiography, Boyd portrayed Still as a role model for the African American community by offering black readers the former abolitionist's own formula for success based on religious devotion, self-sufficiency, and the Protestant work ethic.[20]

Plans for the book came to fruition in May 1871, when the Pennsylvania Anti-Slavery Society held its final meeting and passed the following resolution:

> *Whereas,* The position of William Still in the vigilance committee connected with the "underground railroad," as its corresponding secretary, and chairman of its acting sub-committee, gave him peculiar facilities for collecting interesting facts pertaining to this branch of the antislavery service; therefore
>
> *Resolved,* That the Pennsylvania Anti-Slavery Society request him to compile and publish his personal reminiscences and experiences related to the "Underground Railroad."[21]

To be sure, Still was the ideal candidate to write the first published history of the Underground Railroad. Not only did he have the best understanding of the secret routes to freedom because of his extensive involvement on the Eastern Line, but as a successful businessman he knew how to market his product to ensure high sales. He was also a self-taught journalist. Still took meticulous notes on the fugitives he harbored and diligently recorded them in his journals. This unique position allowed Still to achieve all of his objectives by merging his keen sense of history with a shrewd business acumen. The timing for such a venture was also fortuitous because of a seven-month-long coal strike in the spring and summer of 1871. With the decline in coal sales, Still had the leisure time to work on the project.[22]

For more than a year, Still worked diligently on the preparation of his book. He did not simply copy his earlier notes on the fugitives he interviewed. Instead, he brought their stories to life by communicating them in highly dramatic prose.

He appealed to his readers' emotions and sense of social justice. It was a gift, but one that required diligence. From "five o'clock in the morning until eleven at night," seven days a week, Still churned out at least four pages a day.[23] He corresponded with former agents and abolitionists, asking them to provide recollections. Some contributed, including Thomas Garrett, Passmore Williamson, and Grace Anna Lewis. Others did not, like Mary Ann Shadd Cary, whom Still asked to contribute to a chapter on the Christiana Riot.[24] He gathered together the journals in which he had recorded interviews and rewrote the various accounts of dramatic escapes. He collected other material from newspaper clippings and letters he had saved and integrated them into the work. He labored over biographical sketches of those who had assisted him. Perhaps the most difficult was J. Miller McKim, his supervisor at the PASS. When Still requested information, McKim asked him to outline the material that concerned him for his approval. "It would not be just to confine you to any special department of the work," replied Still tactfully, "but to represent you as a general laborer in the anti-slavery cause."[25] On the other hand, Frederick Douglass, widely considered the greatest abolitionist orator, was conspicuously absent from Still's book, an omission that was probably purposeful. Douglass attributed the snub to an earlier criticism he had made about Still's treatment of fugitives he had assisted.[26] But Still's snub of Douglass was probably motivated by jealousy. He tended to marginalize the UGRR activities of black figures who were admired and celebrated by white abolitionists since he did not enjoy the same reputation.

For engravings, Still hired T. Elwood Zell, a longtime acquaintance and publisher of the *Zell's Illustrated Universal Encyclopedia*, who agreed to produce them "at a reasonable rate." Another friend, Reverend William H. Furness, a Harvard-trained Unitarian minister and former fund-raiser for the Philadelphia Vigilance Committee, read Still's early drafts and helped him get a publishing contract with Porter and Coates, a white-owned Philadelphia publishing house.[27] Founded in 1848 by Robert Porter, the firm specialized in the printing of trade and art books. By the time Henry Coates joined the firm in 1867, it was on the cutting edge of the publishing industry. Using the latest technological advancements, the publishing house used created electro-type plates created by James B. Rogers and Company, setting them on a steam-driven flatbed press to produce books more inexpensively than ever before. This process allowed for flexibility in the size of the initial print run and easy printing of later editions.[28] At the same time, Porter and Coates relied on the author for advance sales via subscription. According to the agreement, the book would be published by subscription only, on good-quality paper and in a variety of bindings, ranging from plain cloth covers with gilt lettering on the spine to elaborate gift bindings pictorially decorated in gilt at prices ranging from $4.50 to $6.50. Porter and Coates agreed to print ten thousand copies of the book, reserved the sole right to publish for one year, and insured the electrotype plates for $2,500. Still would receive a 62 ½ cent royalty for each sale and purchase the plates to continue publication after the one-year contract expired.[29]

When the 780-page book was published in 1872, it was the largest work published by an African American to that date. Still was extremely aggressive in the marketing process. He actively solicited sales from his former associates in the abolitionist community, advertised in the Philadelphia-based AME Church newspaper the *Christian Recorder*, and worked with a national network of book agents. He also sought and secured endorsements from J. Miller McKim; Supreme Court Justice Salmon P. Chase; Horace Greeley, the abolitionist publisher of the *New York Tribune*; US senator Charles Sumner, a prominent Radical Republican from Massachusetts; General Oliver Otis Howard, a Civil War officer and commissioner of the Freedmen's Bureau; and William Lloyd Garrison, publisher of the antislavery newspaper the *Liberator*.[30] Garrison's endorsement, prominently featured in the front matter of the first and subsequent editions, was especially glowing:

> Your book is a most important portion of anti-slavery history which might nearly have been lost to posterity without your industry, research, personal experience and knowledge. The work is not "fiction founded upon fact" and embellished with a lively imagination, but rather fact without particle of fiction, narrated in a simple, ingenious, straightforward manner and needing no coloring whatever.
>
> What a revelation it makes of the barbarities of the slave system, of the formidable obstacles which interposed to prevent a successful exodus from bondage, of the terrible sufferings to which the fugitive slaves were subjected in their attempts to be free, of the daring and heroism required to run the risk of betrayal, recapture, starvation in the swamp and drowning in the river, suffocation in the box, seizure by the two-legged and four-legged blood-hounds in hot pursuit and a thousand other perils . . .
>
> I hope that the sale of your work will be largely extended, not only that the large expense incurred by its preparation and printing may be liberally covered, but for the enlightenment of the rising generation as

to the inherent cruelty of the defunct slave system. It is a book for every household.[31]

Still promoted the book by going on a tour of Washington, D.C., and the border states in the spring of 1872. According to biographer James Boyd, the trip was initially planned to "look into the condition of the freedmen and especially to see what was being done in the way of providing school facilities for them."[32] But the tour was a good marketing strategy as well, since most of the runaways assisted by Still came from this region and it was reasonable to assume that it would be the largest market for book sales. He also made good use of US Supreme Court chief justice Salmon P. Chase's complimentary endorsement by paying for several dozen lithographic facsimiles and distributing them widely throughout the tour.[33]

On February 5, 1873, when Still regained exclusive right to the publishing and distribution of the book, he had a stock of ten thousand copies and advertised in the *Christian Recorder* for agents to market and sell those books. Sales must have been brisk because he ordered an additional one thousand copies to be printed three months later, and another five thousand in August.[34] Stationery was also printed with the following inscription:

WILLIAM STILL
Author & Publisher of "The Underground Railroad"
No. 244 South Twelfth Street
Philadelphia

Above the letterhead were two short phrases: "Good Agents Wanted" and "Liberal Terms Offered."[35]

Suspicious of experienced subscription agents, Still created his own network among his contacts in the AME Church and black schools. His close friendship with Benjamin Tanner, AME bishop and editor of the *Christian Recorder*, allowed Still to market and sell the book in the South, where the AME Church had expanded after the Civil War. Among the booksellers were AME bishop Daniel Payne, president of Wilberforce University; William and Ellen Craft, former fugitives; General Samuel Chapman Armstrong, president of Hampton Institute; William Wells Brown, a former fugitive and abolitionist lecturer and writer; and Edward Wiley, the husband of Still's daughter, Caroline. But most were young agents, both black and white, male and female and college educated. He carefully cultivated them by contracting on a trial basis. Some discovered that they were not suited to book peddling and quit. Others were fired after receiving shipments of books without prior payment, selling them, and keeping the profit. Others proved successful and were assigned a larger territory after months of trial.[36]

Initially, Still's financial compensation was based on 40 percent of the sales, but he quickly raised the rate to 50 percent. In addition, agents were able to purchase copies of the book at a reduced rate of $3.75. These were generous terms, something that enabled Still to increase the number of agents from thirty to more than one hundred in just a few months.[37] But he also made his agents accountable to him.

Since he expected an exclusive commitment to his book, Still discouraged those who asked to sell subscriptions to other literary works. He expected them to secure prepaid orders from customers. If they failed to do so, they were not to deliver the book until full payment had been made. To improve sales in the South, he also urged agents to work with the newly founded Freedmen's Savings Bank to establish layaway accounts for the purchase of the book. To ensure that agents were meeting predetermined sales, he also conducted a regular correspondence with them in addition to the weekly reports they had to file with him.[38] One of the more poignant stories involving the sales of *The Underground Railroad* is revealed in Still's correspondence with his son-in-law, Edward A. Wiley.

Wiley, a partner in many of his father-in-law's business interests, was an articulate individual and an astute businessman who controlled several agencies in Harrisburg and Pittsburgh. But he was also sickly and spent considerable time at the New Jersey shore to restore his health. When Wiley began selling copies of *The Underground Railroad* in July 1872 at Cape May, New Jersey, he was unaware that Cape May was a "Democratic town." To attract potential customers, Wiley, a staunch Republican, would engage them in discussion on a variety of topics, including politics. Predictably, he "got into a number of spates" and learned to keep his politics opinions to himself.[39] During the next two years, Wiley would travel routinely to Newark, Harrisburg, Pittsburgh, and Baltimore to sell books and experienced considerable success.[40] But he also complained to his wife, Caroline, that it was "difficult to provide for their family" on what her father was paying him. In April 1873, Wiley asked Still for 60 percent of the profit he was making from book sales instead of the 50 percent he was being paid.[41] It appears that Still agreed to the increase, for he wrote to his son-in-law on May 22, praising him for his considerable sales in Pittsburgh.[42] In fact, Wiley would sell more than four hundred copies of the book in Pittsburgh over the next few months, earning more than $1,500.[43]

Still, on August 11, began to show concern over his son-in-law's deteriorating health, asking that he "not go to Brooklyn or Hartford, Connecticut, just yet so."[44] The request might have been made at Caroline's behest. She had become increasingly concerned about her husband and directed him to "stop canvassing for [her] father's book" and to "return home" that same month.[45] If Wiley did return to Philadelphia, it was for less than a month, for Still wrote to his son-in-law again on September 27 and congratulated him on selling 90 copies of the book in Baltimore in such a "short time."[46] Wiley's sales increased to 140 by October 3, but his absence from home caused a rift between his wife and her father.[47]

Caroline, desperate to have Edward home on a full-time basis, wrote to him on November 19 and insisted that "canvassing will be too hard during the winter months" and that he must return home. Caroline also informed Edward that their two-year-old son, Willie, was "walking, climbing and trying to speak" and suggested that it was too demanding to raise him alone. Sensing that her husband did not have the courage to tell her father that he wanted to be released of his bookselling responsibilities, Caroline wrote that she had already told her parents of Edward's "desire to enter the ministry."[48] Her pleas appeared to have fallen on deaf ears, though. During the winter, Edward suffered a brain hemorrhage and died while on a sales trip to Baltimore.[49] One family friend could not help but believe that Wiley had "worked himself to death" selling copies of Still's book.[50]

The 1876 Centennial Exhibition provided a considerable market for the book. By that time, Still was promoting the work as a testimony to the "heroic deeds of the brave men and women of [the] [black] race determined to strike out on their own for freedom." Since the international exhibition was held in Philadelphia, Still, along with AME bishop Tanner and other local black leaders, ensured that African Americans would be given a role in the planning process. Thus a massive sculpture of Cleopatra by Edmonia Lewis, a black sculptress, was included, as well as another of Richard Allen, the founding father of the AME Church. In addition, Still was provided with a prominent space to advertise and sell his book.[51]

Although it is impossible to determine the number of books sold during Still's lifetime, Stephen Hall estimated that "between five and ten thousand copies sold by the late 1870s."[52] Thus *The Underground Railroad* enjoyed a much wider circulation than any other eyewitness account of the clandestine route to freedom. In 1879, Still self-published a second edition, and four years later, in 1883, a third edition was released with James Boyd's thirty-two-page biography. Still continued to promote a final edition, published in 1886, for the remainder of his life. When he died of a heart attack on July 14, 1902, William Still, age eighty, was hailed as "Father of the Underground Railroad" and one of the wealthiest African Americans in the country, with an estate estimated at between $750,000 and $1 million.[53] But he also left behind a mixed legacy.

Still's antislavery activities made him one of the nation's most significant African American reformers of the mid-nineteenth century. Not only did he assist nearly one thousand fugitive slaves to freedom, but he wrote and published the most authentic account that exists of the Underground Railroad. As a speaker and editorialist, Still used moral suasion to convince city officials and state legislators to desegregate Philadelphia's streetcars and reinstitute the black franchise. At the same time, Still, in the 1870s, refused to join forces with a younger generation of black activists who were led by the charismatic Octavius Catto and who promoted the strategy of direct action to achieve the same reform goals. Instead, Still became highly critical of Catto and his followers, believing that he was being attacked and that his role as the leader of Philadelphia's black community was being challenged.

Unwittingly, the Still-Catto conflict helped to spawn a fundamental dialectic in African American history itself, one that has since defined distinctly different strategies to achieve civil rights: the constant and inevitable tension between "passive resistance" and "active defiance," "docility" and "aggression," "self-reliance" and "direct action." That dialectic emerged within the civil rights movement in the early twentieth century and manifested itself in the differing philosophies of Booker T. Washington, a former slave who became the founder of the Tuskegee Institute, and W. E. B. Du Bois, the first African American to earn a doctorate at Harvard.

Like William Still, Washington embraced an accommodationist philosophy. He believed that blacks would progress only by winning support from the "better sort" of whites and by working hard, living frugal and moral lives, and developing and supporting black enterprises. These were the very same virtues that enabled Still to succeed in Philadelphia's white mainstream society. Also like Still, Washington believed that "employment" and "economic self-sufficiency" were the twin pillars that supported racial equality.[54] It was a practical philosophy given the realities of race relations in the early twentieth century, since it acknowledged segregation without accepting the inferior status it imposed on African Americans. "In all things that are purely social we can be as separate as the five fingers, yet one as the hand in all things essential to mu-

FIGURE 14.2.
Booker T. Washington
(1856–1915) was an educator,
the first president of Tuskegee
Industrial Institute, and the
most influential spokesman for
African Americans between
1895 and 1915. (Library of
Congress.)

tual progress," Washington said, giving comfort to white audiences. At the same time, he urged blacks to "make friends with the people of all races by entering the mechanics, commerce, domestic service and the professions."[55] Washington encouraged blacks to develop useful economic skills instead of protesting racial discrimination, and he founded the Tuskegee Institute to promote industrial and vocational education.

Although he worked behind the scenes against segregation, disenfranchisement, and lynching, Washington convinced white society that blacks would accept social segregation and disenfranchisement in exchange for educational and economic opportunities.[56] Whites hailed this "compromise" as the solution to the "race problem." Northern industrialist philanthropists such as Andrew Carnegie and John D. Rockefeller contributed millions of dollars to Tuskegee and other southern black schools. President Theodore Roosevelt, impressed by Washington's effort to blend practical education and political conciliation with whites, welcomed his counsel. But as Washington's influence grew, so did opposition to his accommodationist philosophy. Chief among his rivals was William Edward Burghardt Du Bois.

Du Bois, like Catto, emphasized a philosophy of direct action that promoted the integration of the races and full citizenship for blacks. Rejecting Washington's conciliatory stance toward white society as "silent submission to racial inequality," Du Bois accused him of "preaching a gospel of work and money" that "overshadows higher aims" for black people.[57] "If we make money the object of training, we shall develop moneymakers, but not necessarily men," he argued. "If we make technical skill the object of education, we may possess artisans, but not men. Men we shall have only as we make manhood the objective of our schools." For Du Bois, the "object" of black education had to be "intelligence, broad sympathy and knowledge of the world." "These," he insisted, were "the same qualities necessary for full citizenship" for the black man. Nor is it coincidental that Du Bois equated these qualities with "manhood."[58] Unless blacks actively pursued and embraced these virtues, they would never be accorded the respect that came with racial equality. Accordingly, Du Bois believed that blacks were emasculated by Washington accommodationist policies, and in 1905 he organized the Niagara movement to demand an end to racial discrimination in education, public accommodations, voting and employment.

As a result, the African American community was split into two antagonistic camps: the "Bookerites" and the "Niagarites." The two groups closely monitored each other's activities and published essays critical of each other. While Washington's opposition resulted in the demise of the Niagara movement in 1909, Du Bois helped to establish its successor, the National Association of Colored People (NAACP), and became editor of its monthly journal, the *Crisis.*[59]

Unfortunately, William Still did not set a very constructive example for Washington or Du Bois. His legacy was tarnished by a refusal, or perhaps an inability, to understand that both accommodationist and activist strategies were necessary to achieve civil rights. If Still died a bitter man, he had no one but himself to blame. His many positive contributions to abolitionism and the Underground Railroad were marginalized by a new generation of black reformers who viewed him as an obstacle to their own efforts. His reputation was sullied by his refusal to work with those same young reformers who embraced direct action. Had Still done that, he might have been the most effective reformer, black or white, ever to have emerged from the City of Brotherly Love.

APPENDIX

Database of Runaway Slaves Interviewed by William Still, 1853–61

Compiled by James A. McGowan and William C. Kashatus

This database of 995 runaways was compiled from the Johnson Publishing Company's 1970 reprint of William Still's *The Underground Railroad*, originally published in 1872, and from the unpublished "Journal C" manuscript at the Historical Society of Pennsylvania. The data were entered into an Excel spreadsheet to determine the total numbers of runaways for each of the twenty-two variables. The multivariate analysis of the data that appears in chapters 5, 6, 7, 9, and 10 was completed using worksheets of those variables.

KEY TO VARIABLES

Last Name (948 cases): Surname of runaway. For 47 cases a last name is not identified: 37 of these, listed as "unidentified," have no name or alias at all`, and for 10 cases only a first name is identified.

First/Middle Names (914 cases): First/middle names of runaway. For 81 cases first/middle names are not identified: 37 of these, listed as "unidentified," have no name or alias at all, and for 44 cases only a last name is identified.

Alias (173 cases): Alias identified by newspaper advertisement, or by Still.

Gender (967 cases): Sex of runaway. There are 730 males, 237 females, and 28 cases where gender is not identified: of the unidentified, 14 cases are children, 13 cases are listed as "unidentified" runaways, and one case is a thirty-five-year-old runaway named Jenkins.

Age (602 cases): Age is not always reliable because many slaves did not know the date of their birth. In these cases, the ages reported in the database are Still's estimates.

Color (390 cases): Skin complexion of runaway. Still identified two dozen skin hues among runaways. For sake of simplicity, skin color has been reduced to two types: black (i.e., dark complexion) and mulatto (i.e., light complexion). Of the 390 cases where skin complexion is known, 288 are black and 102 are mulatto.

Day (566 cases): Day of escape is not always reliable. In most cases, the day listed in the database is the day the runaway arrived at Still's office in Philadelphia. There are occasions when the day represents the day the owner reported the runaway missing in a newspaper advertisement. The latter cases are indicated by an asterisk (*).

Month (659 cases): Month of escape is either the month the runaway claimed he escaped, or the date Still claimed the runaway arrived at his office in Philadelphia.

Year (954 cases): Year of escape as reported by Still and confirmed by newspaper advertisements for runaways. Earliest year recorded by Still is the case of John Henry Hill, who ran away in 1853, and the final recorded case is that of James Hill in 1861.

City (782 cases): City of runaway's origin, identified by newspaper advertisement and/or reported by Still.

County (713 cases): County of runaway's origin, identified by newspaper advertisement and/or reported by Still.

State (943 cases): State of runaway's origin, identified by newspaper advertisement and/or reported by Still. The database identified 943 runaways who escaped from ten states—Alabama, Delaware, Georgia, Kentucky, Louisiana, Missouri, Maryland, North Carolina, South Carolina, and Virginia—and from Washington, D.C. The greatest number of runaways came from Maryland (476; 51 percent), followed by Virginia (296; 32 percent), and Delaware (89; 9 percent).

Group (661 cases): Group escapes, where a "group" is defined as two or more runaways. The database identifies 661 runaways who escaped in 173 groups with an average size of four runaways. Each group has been assigned a letter and a number that corresponds with Tables 10.1 and 10.2. The largest group consisted of 28 runaways, who escaped in October 1857.

Child (96 cases): Runaway children ranging in age from a female baby named with the last name of Bennett, who was one month old, to Maria Weems, who was fifteen years old.

Literate (69 cases): Ability of runaway to read and/or write as reported by Still.

Stationmaster/Conductor (172 cases): Name of Underground Railroad agent other than William Still who assisted in a runaway's escape. A total of twenty-three different agents are listed in the database. Among the 172 runaways who identified an agent, many agents assisted multiple runaways.

Armed (38 cases): Those runaways who carried a pistol, sword, and/or knife as reported by Still.

Violence (14 cases): Runaways who encountered violence during their escape. Note that in every case the runaway was armed.

Transportation (343 cases; 350 instances of use of a particular means): Means of escape reported by runaways include watercraft (i.e., boat, schooner, skiff, or steamer), foot, carriage or horse and carriage, horse, and railroad train. Some runaways used more than one means.

Owner (780 cases): Name of runaway's owner identified by newspaper advertisement and/or by Still.

$ Reward (73 cases): Financial reward based on the real dollar value in 1855. According to the US Bureau of Labor Statistics consumer price index, $100 in 1855 is equivalent in purchasing power to about $2,966.84 in 2020, a difference of $2,866.84 over 165 years.

$ Value (35 cases): Financial worth of the runaway based on the real dollar value in 1855. Note that the value of a runaway was commensurate with the dollar value of the reward offered for him. The higher the reward, the more valuable, financially, the runaway.

Source: Page number(s) from the Johnson Publishing Company's 1970 reprint of Still's *The Underground Railroad* (1872) or from the unpublished "Journal C" manuscript at the Historical Society of Pennsylvania.

L. Name	First / Middle	Alias	Gender	Age	Color	Day	Month	Year	City	County	State	Group
——	Celia		Female			27	Mar	1854	Norfolk	Norfolk	VA	
——	Charles		Male	22	Black	20*	Sept	1856	Mount Airy	Carroll	MD	A-2
——	David		Male	27		31	May	1856	Leesburg	Loudon	VA	D-2
——	Hannah		Female	23		17	Oct	1857	Marshall Hope	Caroline	MD	I-1
——	Hanson		Male	47	Black	5*	Sept	1857		Howard	MD	J-4
——	Isabella		Female				Oct	1857	Portsmouth	Norfolk	VA	Q-7
——	Isaiah		Male			7	Sept	1855	Tanner's Creek	Norfolk	VA	T-2
——	Perry		Male	25	Black	20*	Sept	1856	Mount Airy	Carroll	MD	A-2
——	Richard		Male	30	Black	22	Mar	1857	New Kent			
——	William		Male	25	Black	17	Oct	1857	Cambridge	Dorchester	MD	I-1
Airs	Peter	Peter Johnson	Male	30		21	Nov	1854	Berlin	Worcester	MD	
Airs	Sarah		Female	25		26	Oct	1854		Worcester	MD	
Albert	James		Male					1853	Eastern Shore		MD	X-1
Aldridge	Bazil		Male	17	Mulatto			1857	Unionville	Frederick	MD	D-7
Aldridge	Caroline		Female	23	Mulatto			1857	Unionville	Frederick	MD	B-4
Alexander	John		Male	44	Black			1857		Kent		M-4
Allen	Andrew		Male	24	Black			1857	Norfolk	Norfolk	VA	R-4
Allen	Henry		Male	18		14	Nov	1854	Wilmington	New Castle	DE	
Allen	William	William Parnet	Male			10	Feb	1853	Perryville	Caroline	MD	
Alligood	George		Male	22				1858		Sussex	DE	G-5
Alligood	James		Male					1858		Sussex	DE	G-5
Allison	Edenezer		Male		Mulatto			1858	Richmond	Henrico	VA	
Amby	Lizzie		Female	28	Black	17	Oct	1857	Cambridge	Dorchester	MD	I-1
Amby	Nat		Male		Black	17	Oct	1857	Cambridge	Dorchester	MD	I-1
Amos	Anna Elizabeth	Anna Elizabeth Johnson	Female	12			May	1854	Baltimore	Baltimore	MD	U-1
Amos	Ann Rebecca	Ann Rebecca Johnson	Female	26		12	May	1854	Baltimore	Baltimore	MD	U-1
Amos	Harriet	Mary Jane Johnson	Female		Mulatto	12	May	1854	Baltimore	Baltimore	MD	U-1
Amos	Mary Ellen	Mary Ellen Johnson	Female			12	May	1854	Baltimore	Baltimore	MD	U-1
Amos	Stephen	Henry Johnson	Male			12	May	1854		Prince Georges	MD	U-1
Amos	William H.	William H. Johnson	Male			12	May	1854	Baltimore	Baltimore	MD	U-1
Anderson	George		Male				July	1856	Elkton	Cecil	MD	C-3
Anderson	George	Henry Jones	Male	19		16	Dec	1854	Herberts Crossroads			
Anderson	Henry	William Anderson	Male	25	Black				Beaufort	Carteret	NC	
Anderson	James		Male	7		17	Jan	1855	Petersburg	Dinwiddie	VA	
Anderson	Jonas		Male			7	Sept	1855	Tanner's Creek	Norfolk	VA	T-2

Child	Literate	Station Master/ Conductor	Armed	Violence	Transportation	Owner	$ Reward	$ Value	Source
						David Baines			Journal C
						Robert Dade	250 in state / 100 out		212-213
					Horse & Carriage	Joshua Pusey			219-221
					Foot	Charles Peters			94-95
						W. Baker & Hammond Dorsey	100 in state / 200 out		436-437
		Captain Robert Lee			Skiff				87-89
									300-301
						Robert Dade	250 in state / 500 out		212-213
					Foot	Captain Tucker	100 in state		116-222
					Foot				94
						Comfort & Betsy Airs			Journal C
						William Purnell			Journal C
					Foot				207
						Thornton Pool		900	407-408
						Thornton Pool			417-418
						George Handy			447
						Mrs Sarah Twyne			455
						Dr. Johnson			Journal C
						Henry Chamberlain			Journal C
			X			George M. Davis			510-511
						William Gray			511
	X					John Tilghman Foster			468
					Foot		300 in state		92
			X		Foot	John Muir			92-93
X						John S. Giddings			Journal C
X						John S. Giddings			Journal C
					Foot	William Giddings			156-157
X						John S. Giddings			Journal C
					Foot	John S. Giddings			156-157
X						John S. Giddings			Journal C
		Captain Alfred Fountain			Schooner				325-329
						Harom Stump	1000 in state		Journal C
					Foot				131
X									Journal C
									300-301

L. Name	First / Middle	Alias	Gender	Age	Color	Day	Month	Year	City	County	State	Group
Anderson	Joshua John		Male	22	Black			1858	Alexandria	Baltimore	MD	
Anderson	Thomas	Jonathan Fisher	Male	19		30	Jan	1856	Sassafras Neck		MD	K-3
Anthony	Adam		Male			24	Oct	1857	Cambridge	Dorchester	MD	H-1
Anthony	Kit		Male	23		24	Oct	1857	Cambridge	Dorchester	MD	H-1
Anthony	Leah		Female	28		24	Oct	1857	Cambridge	Dorchester	MD	H-1
Anthony	Mary		Female			24	Oct	1857	Cambridge	Dorchester	MD	H-1
Anthony	Murray		Male			24	Oct	1857	Cambridge	Dorchester	MD	H-1
Archer	Sam		Male	30				1860	Belleair	Harford	MD	
Armstead	Moses		Male	24	Black			1857	Norfolk	Norfolk	VA	
Atkins	Susan		Female	40	Black			1854	Richmond	Henrico	VA	B-2
Atkins	William Henry		Male	28	Mulatto	23	Apr	1854	Richmond	Henrico	VA	B-2
Atkinson	Anthony		Male	36	Mulatto	1	Aug	1855	Norfolk	Norfolk	VA	O-2
Atkinson	Henry		Male			23	Apr	1854	Norfolk	Norfolk	VA	
Atkinson	John		Male	31	Mulatto	28	Aug	1854	Portsmouth	Norfolk	VA	
Bacon	Abe		Male	22	Black			1857		Cecil	MD	P-4
Baddums	Matthew		Male	23		21	July	1856	Plymouth	Washington	NC	C-3
Bailey	Josiah		Male	29	Black	15*	Nov	1856	Easton	Talbot	MD	P-2
Bailey	William		Male		Black	15*	Nov	1856	Easton	Talbot	MD	P-2
Baker	Henry	Charles Lightfoot	Male			13	Mar	1855	Norfolk	Norfolk	VA	
Ball	Joe		Male	34	Mulatto			1857	Alexandria	Fairfax	VA	Y-4
Ball	Oscar D.	John Delaney	Male	20	Black	13		1857	Alexandria	Fairfax	VA	A-4
Ballard	George Henry		Male	26		2	Feb	1858				V-4
Banks	Elizabeth		Female	25	Black	17	Aug	1855	Easton	Talbot	MD	
Banks	Henry		Male	19		21	Dec	1854		King Georges	VA	R-2
Banks	Jim		Male	29	Mulatto			1858	Georgetown		DC	F-5
Barlow	Archer	Emit Robins	Male	31	Mulatto			1853	Norfolk	Norfolk	VA	
Bayne	Richard		Male	23	Mulatto			1858	Alexandria	Fairfax	VA	A-5
Beesly	Dick		Male		Black				Wheldon		NC	
Bell	Anna		Female			12	June	1856			MD	
Bell	Dianna		Female	30		30	June	1856	Liberty district			
Bell	Garrett		Male	8 mos.						Kent	MD	S-5
Bell	Harriet Ann		Female	14		10	Apr	1854	Norfolk	Norfolk	VA	H-2
Bell	Harrison		Male	40		10	Apr	1854	Norfolk	Norfolk	VA	H-2
Bell	Louisa		Female	28	Black	22	June	1855	Norfolk	Norfolk	VA	M-2
Bell	Susan		Female	4				1858	Washington	Washington	DC	L-7
Bell	Sarah Jane		Female	25	Mulatto					Kent	MD	S-5
Belle	Jim		Male	26	Black			1857	Upper Marlboro	Prince Georges	MD	
Belt	Robert	Charles Williams	Male	29		15	Nov	1854	Baltimore	Baltimore	MD	

Child	Literate	Station Master/ Conductor	Armed	Violence	Transportation	Owner	$ Reward	$ Value	Source
						Skelton Price			492-493
						Anthony Ryebold			349, 350
X					Foot				87
	X		X		Foot				87
			X		Foot				87
X					Foot				87
X					Foot				87
									549
						John Halters			448
					Steamer	Thomas Eckels, Esq			213-214
	X				Steamer				215-217
						Josiah Wells			277
						Jesse Hendrian			Journal C
	X				Steamer	James Ray			308-309
						Hon. L. McLane			450-451
		Captain Alfred Fountain			Schooner	Samuel Simmons			Journal C
		Harriet Tubman				W.R. Hughlett	1500 in state	2000	279-280
						John C. Henry	300 in state		279-281
									Journal C
	X					Miss Elizabeth Gordon			488
	X					Elizabeth Gordon	100 in state / 200 out		414-417
	X					William Jackson			466-467
						James Tomlinson			299-300
					Foot	Dr. James			292-294
						John J. Richards			509
					Steamer	Dr. George Wilson			205-206
			X			Rudolph Massey			499-500
						Richard Smallwood			493
									Journal C
						Walker Simpson			Journal C
X						Massey			530
X					Boat	John G. Hodgson			232
					Boat	James Snyder			232
		Captain "B"			Schooner	L. Stasson			270-271
X						Henry Harding (Mrs)			483-484
						Massey			530
						Zachariah Berry	100 in/ out state		438
									Journal C

L. Name	First / Middle	Alias	Gender	Age	Color	Day	Month	Year	City	County	State	Group
Benjamin	Dickinson		Male	28	Black	23	Mar	1856				H-3
Bennett	Daniel	Henry Washington	Male	32		1	June	1855	Leesburg	Loudon	VA	K-2
Bennett	George		Male	1		1	June	1855	Aldie. P.O.	Loudon	VA	K-2
Bennett	——		Female	1 mo.		1	June	1855	Aldie. P.O.	Loudon	VA	K-2
Bennett	John	Joseph Pant	Male	27		22	Feb	1857	St. Michaels		MD	
Bennett	Martha	Martha Washington	Female	27		1	June	1855	Leesburg	Loudon	VA	K-2
Benton	Samuel		Male	26	Black			1857		Kent		M-4
Bird	Charles		Male	24	Black	3	June	1856	Hagerstown	Washington	MD	F-2
Bird	Mary		Female			4	July	1856	Norfolk	Norfolk	VA	D-6
Bishop	Elijah		Male	28	Black			1858	Baltimore	Baltimore	MD	U-4
Bivans	——		Female					1857				W-6
Bivans	——		Female					1857				W-6
Bivans	Belinda		Female	30	Black			1857				W-6
Blackson	James Henry		Male	25		26	May	1854				
Blockson	Jacob		Male	27				1858		Sussex	DE	G-5
Blow	Anthony	Henry Levison	Male		Black	1	Nov	1854	Norfolk	Norfolk	VA	
Bodams	Matthew		Male	23	Black		July	1856	Plymouth	Washington	NC	C-3
Boggs	Alexander	Johnson Henson	Male	50	Black	3	Apr	1854	Baltimore	Baltimore	MD	
Bohm	Henry		Male	25		30	July	1855	Norfolk	Norfolk	VA	
Boice	Henry		Male				Jan	1858	Lewes	Sussex	DE	C-5
Boile	Susan		Female					1857	Georgetown		MD	
Bolden	Andrew		Male	18					Newark		DE	
Booce	Richard J		Male	22	Black			1857			MD	W-3
Boon	Richmond		Male	22		8	Sept	1854	Norfolk	Norfolk	VA	
Booze	Jacob Mathias		Male	20		7	Feb	1855	Annapolis	Anne Arundel	MD	
Bowen	John		Male			17	Dec	1853				
Bow-Legs	Jim	Bill Paul	Male			25	Oct	1855	Lexington	Oglethorpe	GA	
Bowler	——							1858	Richmond	Henrico	VA	Q-4
Bowler	——							1858	Richmond	Henrico	VA	Q-4
Bowler	Nancy		Female					1858	Richmond	Henrico	VA	Q-4
Bowler	William		Male	41	Black			1858	Richmond	Henrico	VA	Q-4
Bowles	Reuben	Reuben Cunnigan	Male			12	Apr	1854	Hedgesville		VA	H-7
Bowser	Nathaniel		Male				July	1856	Portsmouth	Norfolk	VA	C-3
Boyce	Andrew Jackson		Male	26	Black			1858	Lewes	Sussex	DE	J-5
Boyer	Jacob Matthas		Male	20	Black			1855	Annapolis	Anne Arundel	MD	
Bradley	Richard		Male	27		1	June	1855	Richmond	Henrico	VA	W-2
Branson	Randolph		Male	31	Black			1857	Wasington		DC	V-3
Brister	Nancy		Female		Black			1856	Richmond	Henrico	VA	O-3
Briston	John	Charles Stewart	Male	34		25	Oct	1853	Richmond	Henrico	VA	

'Child	Literate	Station Master/ Conductor	Armed	Violence	Transportation	Owner	$ Reward	$ Value	Source
		Captain Alfred Fountain			Schooner	Miss Ann Blunte			343
						James Taylor			266, 318
X						George Carter	1200 in state		266, 318
X						George Carter			266, 318
						Mary C. Gibson			Journal C
						George Carter			266, 318
						William Campbell			447
			X	X	Horseback	David Claggart			223
		Captain "B"			Schooner				585-588
						Campbell			459
X						William H. Hyson			404
X						William H. Hyson			404
						William H. Hyson			404
						Charles Wright			237
	X					Jesse W. Paten			510, 512
					Steamer	Widow Peters			46-48
		Captain Alfred Fountain			Schooner	Samuel Simmons			325-329
						John Emie		550	230-231
									275
					Skiff	David Henry Houston			504
						Hezekiah Masten			452, 453
									494
						Dr. Hughes		1600	408-409
						John Bodun			Journal C
						Richard Carmen			Journal C
									Journal C
					Foot	Dr. Thomas Stephens	500 in state		245-247
X						Alexander Royster			469
X						Alexander Royster			469
						Alexander Royster			469
						Alexander Royster			469
					Foot	John Sabbard			233
		Captain Alfred Fountain			Schooner				325-329
						Dr. David Houston			518
						Richard Carman			323
		Captain "B"			Schooner	Samuel Ball			316-317
						Richard Reed		1700	406-407
					Boat	William Bears			391-394
									Journal C

L. Name	First / Middle	Alias	Gender	Age	Color	Day	Month	Year	City	County	State	Group
Brooks	Adam	William Smith	Male		Black	20	Jan	1855	Hardtown	Montgomery	MD	
Brooks	Susan		Female	40	Black	23	Apr	1854	Norfolk	Norfolk	VA	B-2
Brown	Albert		Male		Mulatto	3	June	1856	Hagarstown	Washington	MD	F-2
Brown	Albert		Male	27		7	Sept	1855	Tanners Creek	Norfolk	VA	T-2
Brown	Angeline		Female		Mulatto	3	June	1856	Hagarstown	Washington	MD	F-2
Brown	Anthony		Male	29		7	Sept	1855	Tanners Creek	Norfolk	VA	T-2
Brown	Charles		Male	25	Black				Sandy Hook	Harford	MD	Q-1
Brown	Charles		Male			3	June	1856	Hagarstown	Washington	MD	F-2
Brown	Charles Henry		Male	27		5	Feb	1856	Cambridge	Dorchester	MD	
Brown	Chaskey		Male	24	Black				Chestertown	Kent	MD	P-1
Brown	George W.	James White	Male	17		8	Sept	1854			MD	
Brown	Harriet	Jane Wooton	Female			3	Apr	1853	Baltimore	Baltimore	MD	N-1
Brown	Jacob		Male	20	Black			1856			NC	
Brown	James		Male					1859	North Point	Baltimore	MD	
Brown	John		Male			20	Nov	1855	Norfolk	Norfolk	VA	W-1
Brown	John	Jacob Williams	Male			3	Apr	1854	Frederickstown		MD	
Brown	John		Male					1859				
Brown	John		Male					1859	Frederick Mills	Montgomery	MD	
Brown	John W.		Male			10	Sept	1853	Baltimore	Baltimore	MD	
Brown	Louisa		Female	16	Mulatto				Baltimore	Baltimore	MD	
Brown	Rebecca	Helen Parker	Female			6	Apr	1853	Annapolis	Anne Arundel	MD	F-6
Brown	Robert	Thomas Jones	Male	25	Mulatto	25*	Dec	1856	Martinsburg	Henry	VA	
Brown	Solomon		Male	22	Black	13	Feb	1854	Norfolk	Norfolk	VA	
Brown	Stepney		Male	34	Black			1859	Richmond	Henrico	VA	
Brown	William		Male		Black	20	Dec	1855		Prince Georges	MD	
Brown	William		Male	36				1860	Baltimore	Baltimore	MD	W-5
Buchanan	Jenny		Female	45	Mulatto			1860	Rockbridge		VA	
Burkett	Elizabeth		Female					1860	Kunkletown	Worcester	MD	A-6
Burkett	Henry		Male					1860	Kunkletown	Worcester	MD	A-6
Burrell	James	W. Boural	Male	32	Mulatto	11	Mar	1853	Williamsburg	James City	VA	
Burrell	Lewis		Male			21	Apr	1856	Alexandria	Fairfax	VA	S-3
Burrell	Peter		Male			21	Apr	1856	Alexandria	Fairfax	VA	S-3
Burton	Hale		Male					1860	Kunkletown	Worcester	MD	A-6
Burton	Handy		Male					1858			DE	J-5
Burton	Perry		Male	27	Black			1857	Indian River			
Bush	Samuel	William Olebee	Male	33	Mulatto	16	Nov	1853			VA	
Butcher	William	William T. Mitchell	Male	28	Black	29	Nov	1854	Georgetown		MD	
Butler	James		Male	21	Black	4	June	1857	Abingdon PO	Harford	MD	D-1

Child	Literate	Station Master/ Conductor	Armed	Violence	Transportation	Owner	$ Reward	$ Value	Source
						John Phillips			322
					Steamer	Thomas Eckels, Esq			214-215
			X	X	Horseback	George Shaffer			223-224
	X				Boat	John & Henry Holland			300-301
					Horseback	George Shaffer			223-224
	X				Boat	John & Henry Holland			300-301
					Foot	William Wheeling			132-133
			X	X	Horseback	George Shaffer			223-224
						Dr. Richard Dorsey			354
					Foot	Major James H. Gales	1200 in state		131-132
						James Kinny			Journal C
					Foot	George Stewart			129-130
					Boat	Lewis Brown			539
						Henry Jones			524-525
		Captain Alfred Fountain			Schooner				165
						Joseph Postly			231
						Benjamin Thorn			527- 528
						James Edward Stevens			538
									Journal C
					Foot				128
						T.C. Howard			Journal C
	X				Horseback	Col. John F. Fraic			111-113
	X				Steamer	Mary A. Ely			159
	X					Julia A. Mitchell			518-521
						William Elliott			353-354
						Lynchum			546
						John Bower			544-546
					Boat				552-554
					Boat				552-554
	X								227-228
	X					Edward M. Clark			399-400
						Benjamin Johnson Hall			399-400
					Boat				552-554
						Shepherd Burton			518
					Foot	John R. Burton			95
						William Hoyle			206-207
						William Boyer			309-310
						Thomas Johnson	500 in state	1400	56-57

L. Name	First / Middle	Alias	Gender	Age	Color	Day	Month	Year	City	County	State	Group
Butler	John Alexander		Male	29	Black			1857	Arlington		MD	H-4
Butler	Stephen		Male	22	Black	4	June	1857	Abingdon PO	Harford	MD	D-1
Cain	James		Male	35	Black			1857	Hoopesville	Dorchester	MD	S-4
Cale	——		Female			25	Mar	1856				S-6
Cale	David		Male			25	Mar	1856				S-6
Cale	Ellen	Sarah Johnson	Female	18		15	Nov	1854	Baltimore	Baltimore	MD	K-6
Cale	Mary	Jane Johnson	Female	16		15	Nov	1854	Baltimore	Baltimore	MD	K-6
Camp	——		Female					1853	Richmond	Henrico	VA	
Camp	Joseph H.		Male	20		16	Nov	1853	Richmond	Henrico	VA	
Campbell	Frank		Male		Black			1858				
Camper	James		Male	24	Black	24	Oct	1857	Cambridge	Dorchester	MD	H-1
Cannon	Ansel		Male	25	Black			1859	New Market	Dorchester	MD	M-5
Cannon	Plymouth		Male	42	Mulatto	2	Feb	1858				V-4
Carlisle	William		Male		Black	4	July	1859			MD	K-5
Carney	William		Male	51	Black			1857	Norfolk	Norfolk	VA	R-4
Carpenter	William		Male					1858			VA	
Carr	Daniel		Male	38	Mulatto	20	Nov	1855	Norfolk	Norfolk	VA	W-1
Carr	John Thompson		Male					1858	Richmond	Henrico	VA	
Carr	Robert		Male			26*	Dec	1857	West River	Anne Arundel	MD	
Carroll	Edward		· Male	21				1858		Sussex	MD	
Carroll	George		Male	24	Black			1857	Washington		DC	V-3
Carter	Charles		Male	30	Mulatto	10	Apr	1856	Richmond	Henrico	VA	R-3
Cary	Harrison		Male	28	Mulatto				Washington		DC	
Casting	Edward		Male	17				1860	Duck Creek		MD	Y-5
Chambers	Henry	James Green	Male	24	Black	30	Jan	1856	Sassafras Neck		MD	K-3
Chambers	John	David Green	Male	26	Black	30	Jan	1856			MD	K-3
Chapman	Emeline		Female	25	Black	30*	Aug	1856	Washington		DC	I-2
Chapman	John Henry		Male	7 mos.	Mulatto	30*	Aug	1856	Washington		DC	I-2
Chapman	Margaret Ann		Female	2	Black	30*	Aug	1856	Washington		DC	I-2
Chase	John	Daniel Floyd	Male	20	Black	29	Dec	1854	Cambridge	Dorchester	MD	V-2
Chiles	Lewis		Male			2	June	1855	Richmond	Henrico	VA	
Chion	Emma		Female					1860		Dorchester	MD	V-5
Chion	William		Male	27	Black			1860		Dorchester	MD	V-5
Christian	James H.		Male		Mulatto				Richmond	Henrico	VA	
Christy	Jack		Male					1858	Belleair		MD	W-4
Clagart	John		Male	22	Mulatto			1857	Fairfax		VA	V-3

Child	Literate	Station Master/ Conductor	Armed	Violence	Transportation	Owner	$ Reward	$ Value	Source
						William Ford			433
						Thomas Johnson	500 in state	1400	56-57
						John Burnham			456
									Journal C
									Journal C
									Journal C
									Journal C
						Dr. K. Clark			52-53
		Robert Parrett			Steamer	Dr. K. Clark			52
						Henry Campbell			499
			X			Henry Hooper			85
						Kitty Cannon			524
						Nat Horsey			464
						Aquila Cain			521-522
						Mrs Sarah Twyne			453-455
						Senator Mason			484
		Captain Alfred Fountain			Schooner	John C. McBole			165-166
						Albert Lewis			468
	X					Thomas J. Richardson	125 in state / 300 out		463
			X	X		John Lewis			461-462
						C.C. Hirara		1300	406
						Daniel Delaplain			398
	X					Jane E. Ashley			423-425
						Robert Moore			550
					Foot	William Rybold			349-350
					Foot	Thomas Murphy			349-350
					Foot	Mrs. Emily Thompson	300 in state		148, 152–53
X					Foot	Mrs. Emily Thompson			148
X					Foot	Mrs. Emily Thompson			148
		Tubman-Garrett				John Campbell Henry			306
						Lewis Hill			Journal C
						Bushong Blake			543
						Mr. Tubman			543
X						William H. Christian, Esq.			54–56
									473-474
						George Coleman		1500	407

L. Name	First / Middle	Alias	Gender	Age	Color	Day	Month	Year	City	County	State	Group
Clark	Emily		Female			1	Oct	1855			MD	
Clayton	John		Male	20	Mulatto	26	Feb	1854	Richmond	Henrico	VA	C-1
Clayton	Levinia		Female			12	June	1854	Petersburg	Dinwiddie	VA	
Clexton	Perry		Male	25	Black			1858	Georgetown		DC	F-5
Clinton	Thomas		Male	21	Black			1856	Baltimore	Baltimore	MD	Q-3
Cobb	Lewis		Male		Mulatto			1856	Richmond	Henrico	VA	O-3
Colburn	Jeremiah	William Cooper	Male		Mulatto			1857	Charleston	Charleston	SC	
Cole	——		Female			23	Mar	1856				H-3
Cole	Bill		Male	37	Black	5*	Sept	1857		Howard	MD	J-4
Collins	Mary Ellen		Female	20	Black			1857	Cambridge	Dorchester	MD	F-6
Collins	Nathan		Male	25	Black			1857	Cambridge	Dorchester	MD	F-6
Collins	Theophilus		Male	24	Black			1858	Lewes	Sussex	DE	J-5
Combash	John Wesley		Male	32	Black	11	April	1858			MD	X-4
Congo	Charles		Male	28	Black						MD	O-1
Congo	Margaret		Female	28	Black						MD	O-1
Conner	——		Female					1859	Laurel	Sussex	DE	H-5
Conner	——							1859	Laurel	Sussex	DE	H-5
Conner	Charles		Male	27				1857		Sussex	DE	Z-3
Conner	Dennis B.		Male					1859	Laurel	Sussex	DE	H-5
Conner	James		Male	43		27	July	1857	New Orleans		LA	
Conner	Major Lewis		Male					1859	Laurel	Sussex	DE	H-5
Conner	Peter		Male					1859	Laurel	Sussex	DE	H-5
Conner	William J.		Male					1859	Laurel	Sussex	DE	H-5
Cooper	Charles Henry		Male	22		4	Aug	1856	Middletown	New Castle	DE	F-3
Cooper	Mary		Female	20	Black			1857			DE	
Cooper	Thomas		Male				July	1856	Portsmouth	Norfolk	VA	C-3
Cope	William Thomas		Male	24	Mulatto		Jan	1858	Lewes	Sussex	DE	C-5
Cornish	——					24	Oct	1857	Cambridge	Dorchester	MD	H-1
Cornish	Aaron		Male	38	Black	24	Oct	1857	Cambridge	Dorchester	MD	H-1
Cornish	Daffney		Female			24	Oct	1857	Cambridge	Dorchester	MD	H-1
Cornish	Delia		Female			11	Dec	1855	Eastern Shore		MD	Y-2
Cornish	Edward J.		Male			24	Oct	1857	Cambridge	Dorchester	MD	H-1
Cornish	George A.		Male			24	Oct	1857	Cambridge	Dorchester	MD	H-1
Cornish	Henrietta		Female			11	Dec	1855	Eastern Shore		MD	Y-2
Cornish	Joseph		Male	40	Black	25	Dec	1855		Dorchester	MD	
Cornish	Joseph		Male			24	Oct	1857	Cambridge	Dorchester	MD	H-1
Cornish	Perry L.		Male			24	Oct	1857	Cambridge	Dorchester	MD	H-1

Child	Literate	Station Master/ Conductor	Armed	Violence	Transportation	Owner	$ Reward	$ Value	Source
									Journal C
	X				Steamer	Mrs Clayton			38-44
									Journal C
						John M. Williams			508-509
						Benjamin Walmsly			396
	X				Boat	Samuel Myers			391-394
	X				Railroad	Mrs. E. Williamson			98
		Captain Alfred Fountain			Schooner				336
						W. Baker & Hammond Dorsey	200 in state / 300 out		436-437
					Foot	Abram Wilson			98-99
					Foot	Josiah Wilson			98-99
						Shepherd P. Houston			516-517
						Mr. Johnson			474-476
					Foot	David Stewart	1200 in state		131
					Foot	David Stewart	500 in state		131-132
						Kendall Major Llewis			513-514
	X					Kendall Major Llewis			513-514
						John Chipman		1200	414
						Kendall Major Llewis			514
						Charles Parlange	100 in/ out state		419-423
						Kendall Major Llewis			514
						Kendall Major Llewis			514
						Kendall Major Llewis			513-514
						Catherine Mendine			330
						Nathaniel Herne			448
		Captain Alfred Fountain			Schooner				325-329
					Skiff	Shepherd P. Houston			502-506
X					Foot	Reuben E. Phillips			87
			X		Foot	Rev. Levi D. Traverse	200 in state / 300 out		87-89
			X		Foot	Reuben E. Phillips	200 in state / 300 out		87
									Journal C
X					Foot	Reuben E. Phillips			87
X					Foot	Reuben E. Phillips			87
									Journal C
						Capt. Samuel Lecount			346
X					Foot	Reuben E. Phillips			87
X					Foot	Reuben E. Phillips			87

L. Name	First / Middle	Alias	Gender	Age	Color	Day	Month	Year	City	County	State	Group
Cornish	Solomon		Male			24	Oct	1857	Cambridge	Dorchester	MD	H-1
Cornish	William		Male			5	Sept	1856	Cambridge	Dorchester	MD	
Cotton	Henry		Male	24				1860	Newtown	Somerset	MD	
Cromwell	Henry		Male	25	Black		June	1855	Baltimore	Baltimore	MD	
Crummell	Henry		Male	25		18	July	1855	Goughingstown	Baltimore	MD	
Crummill	James		Male			1	June	1855	Ladies Manor	Haverford	MD	X-2
Curtis	Mary		Female	19	Black	10	Dec	1855	Baltimore	Baltimore	MD	
Dade	Henry		Male	25				1857	Washington	Washington	DC	Y-4
Dade	Jack		Male	22	Black			1857	Washington	Washington	VA	Y-4
Dade	John		Male	20				1857	Washington	Washington	DC	Y-4
Dade	Mary Ann		Female					1857	Washington	Washington	VA	Y-4
Dalton	Charles	William Robinson	Male	22		28	Sept	1854	Cambridge	Dorchester	MD	
Dauphus	Etna Elizabeth		Female	20	Black			1858		Queen Annes	MD	T-4
David	Cole		Male			23	Mar	1856				H-3
Davis	Clarissa	Mary D. Armstead	Female	20	Black	22	May	1854	Portsmouth	Norfolk	VA	
Davis	Daniel	David Smith	Male	20	Black	12	Apr	1854	Hedgesville		VA	H-7
Davis	Edward		Male			12	March	1854	Savannah		GA	
Davis	Enoch		Male					1859	Baltimore	Baltimore	MD	
Davis	Gordon	John Canon	Male	21		2	Nov	1854	Cedar Neck		MD	
Davis	Isaac D.		Male			1	Feb	1855			MD	
Davis	Jane		Female	60-70				1857	Eastern Shore		MD	
Davis	John	Adams	Male			14	Sept	1854	Baltimore	Baltimore	MD	
Davis	Samuel		Male	30	Black	14	May	1856	Norfolk	Norfolk	VA	U-3
Davis	Samuel	Benjamin Johnson	Male	35		21	Nov	1854	Fairfax	Fairfax	VA	
Davis	Singleton	William Snowden	Male	38		4	May	1853	Columbia			
Davis	William		Male	31	Mulatto	13	Dec	1853	Portsmouth	Norfolk	VA	
Davis	William		Male	32	Black	29	Mar	1854	Emmitsburg		MD	
Delaney	James Henry		Male	26		25	May	1854	Seaford	Sussex	DE	I-7
Derrickson	Peter		Male	24		1	Jan	1855	Berlin	Worcester	MD	Z-2
Derrix	——		Female					1857	Alexandria	Fairfax	VA	N-4
Derrix	Townsend		Male					1857	Alexandria	Fairfax	VA	N-4
Dickerson	Benjamin		Male	28		25	Mar	1856	Eatontown		NC	
Dickson	John		Male	30		7	Oct	1854	Dawson		MD	
Diggs	David		Male	37	Black			1857	Rockville	Montgomery	MD	Y-4
Dixon	Thomas Edward		Male	18	Black			1859	The Trap		DE	
Dobson	Henrietta		Female			17	Oct	1857	Cambridge	Dorchester	MD	I-1
Dorsey	Anna		Female	22	Mulatto	4	Aug	1856	Howard		MD	

Child	Literate	Station Master/Conductor	Armed	Violence	Transportation	Owner	$ Reward	$ Value	Source
X					Foot	Reuben E. Phillips			87
						William B. Dale			Journal C
						Nathaniel Dixon			556-557
						William Roberts			275
						William Roberts			Journal C
						William Hutchins			317
									353
									489
						Benjamin B. Chambers			488-489
	X								489
						Elias Rhoads			489
						Mrs. Mary Hurley			Journal C
						Joshua Duvall			458
		Captain Alfred Fountain			Schooner				336
	X	Wm. Bagnall			Steamer	Mrs. Brown & Mrs.Burkley	1000 in state		44-46
					Foot	Hon. Charles J. Fortner			232-233
					Steamship				247-251
						James Armstrong			538
						William Watson			Journal C
						Jesse Clark			323
		Thomas Garrett			Foot	Roger McZant			410
									Journal C
		Tubman/Garrett				James Hurst			401-402
						John Reed			Journal C
						Augustus Riggs			Journal C
						Joseph Reynolds			51
						Dr. James Shoul			230
						Captain Martin			237
						John Derrickson			319
									461
						Gallipappick			460-461
						Miss Anna Blunt			Journal C
						Richard Kaigh			Journal C
						Dr. Josiah Harding			487
						Thomas W.M. McCracken			538
					Foot				92
						Eli Molesworth			330

L. Name	First / Middle	Alias	Gender	Age	Color	Day	Month	Year	City	County	State	Group
Dorsey	George		Male		Mulatto	3	June	1856	Hagarstown	Washington	MD	F-2
Dorsey	Luther		Male	19	Black				Sairsville Mills	Frederick	MD	Q-1
Dorsey	Maria		Female	40	Black		Sept	1856	Washington		DC	G-1
Dotson	Isaac		Male	19	Mulatto	20*	Sept	1856	Mount Airy	Carroll	MD	A-2
Douglass	Thomas		Male	25	Black						MD	O-7
Dowling	Carter		Male					1858	Alexandria	Fairfax	VA	A-5
Ducket	Benjamin		Male	23	Black			1856	Bell Mountain	Prince Georges	MD	Q-3
Dulton	Charles	William Robinson	Male	22		28	Sept	1856			MD	S-2
Dunagan	Sarah	Anna Elizabeth Kingslow	Female	18	Mulatto	30	Jan	1855	Wilmington	New Castle	DE	
Duncans	Benjamin	George Scott	Male	25	Black	27	Apr	1854				
Dungy	John William		Male	27	Black		Feb	1860	Richmond	Henrico	VA	
Dunmore	Henry		Male	35	Black			1860	Elkton	Cecil	MD	
Dutton	Marshall		Male			24	Oct	1857	Cambridge	Dorchester	MD	H-1
Eden	Richard		Male	25					Wilmington	New Hanover	NC	T-1
Edmonds	David		Male	30		15	Jan	1855	Petersburg	Dinwiddie	VA	
Edwards	Alfred		Male	22	Black			1859	Tapps' Neck		MD	U-5
Edwards	David		Male	24	Black			1860	Patapsco River		MD	P-7
Edwards	David		Male	30	Black		Jan	1855	Petersburg	Dinwiddie	VA	
Edwards	William		Male	22		31	Oct	1855	Alexandria	Fairfax	VA	
Eglin	Harriet		Female	29		31	May	1856	Baltimore	Baltimore	MD	C-2
Elliot	Thomas		Male	23	Black		Mar	1857	Bucktown	Dorchester	MD	E-1
Ellis	Joe		Male	23	Black			1857	Cabin Point	Surrey	VA	
Ellis	Mary	Mary Jones	Female			6	Oct	1853			NC	E-6
Ellis	William	John Jones	Male			6	Oct	1853			NC	E-6
Emerson	Robert		Male	19	Mulatto	24	Oct	1857	Portsmouth	Norfolk	VA	Q-7
Emory	Robert	William Kemp	Male			1	June	1855		Talbot	MD	
Ennells	Noah		Male	19	Black	24	Oct	1857	Cambridge	Dorchester	MD	H-1
Ennets	——			3 mos.				1860		Dorchester	MD	B-6
Ennets	Amanda		Female	4				1860		Dorchester	MD	B-6
Ennets	Harriet		Female	6				1860		Dorchester	MD	B-6
Ennets	Maria		Female					1860		Dorchester	MD	B-6
Ennets	Stephen		Male					1860		Dorchester	MD	B-6
Ennis	Ephraim		Male					1858		Kent	MD	D-5
Ennis	Louisa Caroline	Louisia Hemmin	Female	3		10	Mar	1854	Georgetown	Sussex	DE	J-6
Ennis	Lydia Ann	Lydia Ann Hemmin	Female	7		10	Mar	1854	Georgetown	Sussex	DE	J-6
Ennis	Mary	Licia Hemmin	Female	33		10	Mar	1854	Georgetown	Sussex	DE	J-6
Epps	Mary	Emma Brown	Female	45	Black	1	Mar	1855	Petersburg	Dinwiddie	VA	F-1

Child	Literate	Station Master/ Conductor	Armed	Violence	Transportation	Owner	$ Reward	$ Value	Source
			X	X	Horseback	George Shaffer			223-224
					Foot	Edward Schriner			134
						George Parker	200 in state		65-67
						Thomas B. Owings	500 in state		211-213
						Mary Howard			548
			X			Miss Maria FitzHugh			500
						Sicke Perry			397
		Thomas Garrett				Mrs. Mary Hurley			294-295
						George Churchman			322-323
						Thomas Jeffries			234
						Governor Gregory			566-572
						John Maldon			551
					Foot				87-89
					Schooner	Mrs Mary Loren			144-147
						John J. Slater			Journal C
						John Bryant			534
						Joseph Bryant			550
						John Slater		1000	320
									Journal C
	X				Railroad	John Delahay			218-219
					Foot	Richard Meredith			59-60
						Bolling Ellis			425
									Journal C
									Journal C
	X	Captain Robert Lee			Skiff	William H. Wilson			87
						Edward Lloyd			315
			X			Black Head Bill LeCount			85
X		Tubman/Garrett			Foot	Algier Pearcy			554-555
X		Tubman/Garrett			Foot	Algier Pearcy			554-555
X		Tubman/Garrett			Foot	Algier Pearcy			554-555
		Tubman/Garrett			Foot	Algier Pearcy			554-555
		Tubman/Garrett			Foot	John Kaiger			554-555
						Michael Newbold			507
X						John Ennis			210
X						John Ennis			210
						John Ennis			210
	X	Captain "B"			Schooner	Mrs. Littleton Reeves			60-65

L. Name	First / Middle	Alias	Gender	Age	Color	Day	Month	Year	City	County	State	Group
Fall	Samuel	John Henry	Male	21	Black		Jan	1856			MD	K-3
Fidget	Isaac		Male	30	Black	17	Nov	1855	Berlin	Worcester	MD	N-3
Fields	Henry		Male	18	Mulatto				Port Deposit			
Fineer	Abe		Male	23	Black	14	May	1856	Norfolk	Norfolk	VA	U-3
Fisher	Jonathan		Male	19			Jan	1856			MD	K-3
Fisher	Robert		Male	30	Black	28*	Dec	1854		Anne Arundel	MD	Z-1
Fletcher	Benjamin R.		Male	27	Black		Sept	1856	Washington		DC	G-1
Ford	Sheridan		Male	28		29	Jan	1855	Portsmouth	Norfolk	VA	
Forman	Ellen	Elizabeth Young	Female	30	Black	16	May	1854	Baltimore	Baltimore	MD	
Forman	Isaac		Male	23	Mulatto		Dec	1853	Norfolk	Norfolk	VA	
Forman	Isaac		Male	50	Black	4	July	1856	Norfolk	Norfolk	VA	D-6
Forman	James H.		Male	23	Mulatto		June	1855	Norfolk	Norfolk	VA	O-2
Foster	Emily	Ann Wood	Female	22		24	Dec	1855	Alder	Loudon	VA	K-1
Foster	Henry		Male			27	July	1853	Richmond	Henrico	VA	
Foster	James		Male			20	Nov	1855	Norfolk	Norfolk	VA	W-1
Foster	Turner		Male	21				1859	Richmond	Henrico	VA	R-5
Fowler	Arthur	Benjamin Johnson	Male	30	Black	29	Dec	1854	Spring Hill		MD	
Francis	Elizabeth	Ellen Saunders	Female	22	Mulatto		Oct	1854	Norfolk	Norfolk	VA	Q-2
Francis	Lewis	Lewis Johnson	Male	27		30	Dec	1855	Abingdon	Harford	MD	
Freeland	George W.		Male	25	Black	5	June	1854	Petersburg	Dinwiddie	VA	
Freeman	Mary Jane		Female			1	Oct	1855			MD	
Freeman	Thomas		Male			20	Nov	1855	Norfolk	Norfolk	VA	W-1
Freeman	William Thomas	Ezekiel Chambers	Male	16	Black	2	Dec	1855	Chestertown	Kent	MD	L-3
Frisley	James Alfred		Male	24	Black							P-1
Fuller	Cornelius		Male					1859		Kent	MD	L-5
Fuller	Harriet		Female					1859	Chestertown	Kent	MD	L-5
Galloway	Abram		Male	21	Mulatto				Wilmington	New Hanover	NC	T-1
Gardener	Nathaniel		Male			20	Nov	1855	Norfolk	Norfolk	VA	W-1
Gardener	Priscilla		Female	30	Black			1858	Richmond	Henrico	VA	
Garrett	Lucy	Julia Wood	Female	19		12	May	1854	Western Shore		VA	
Garrison	Thomas		Male	9		20	July	1853	Wilmington	New Castle	DE	X-6
Garrison	William H.		Male			20	July	1853	Wilmington	New Castle	DE	X-6
Gaskins	Madison		Male						Middleburg	Louden	VA	
Gassway	Caroline		Female	27	Black			1859	Mount Airy	Carroll	MD	
Gault	Phyllis		Female	30	Mulatto	20	Nov	1855	Norfolk	Norfolk	VA	W-1
Gibbs	——		Male			31	Mar	1853	Greensbury		MD	G-6
Gibbs	——		Male			31	Mar	1853	Greensbury		MD	G-6
Gibbs	James		Male			31	Mar	1853	Greensbury		MD	G-6
Gibson	John Wesley		Male	28	Mulatto	22	Nov	1854	Taylor's Mount		MD	

Child	Literate	Station Master/Conductor	Armed	Violence	Transportation	Owner	$ Reward	$ Value	Source
					Foot	William Rybold			349-350
						Henry Fidget			354
						Washington Glasby			532
		Tubman/Garrett				George Spencer			401
						A. Rybold			349-350
						John Edward Jackson			208-209
		Rev. Hiram Wilson			Foot	Henry Martin			65-67
					Steamer	Miss Elizabeth Brown			52-53
						Mrs. Johnson			236
	X				Steamer	Mrs. Sanders			49-50
		Captain "B"			Schooner	George Brown			588
	X					James Saunders, Esq.			276-277
			X	X	Horse & Carriage	Townsend McVee			116-119
									Journal C
		Captain Alfred Fountain			Schooner				165
						A. A. Mosen, Esq.			529
						Edward Fowler			314
	X					Sarah Shepperd			282-284
						Mrs. Delinas			346-347
	X				Steamer	Capt. John Pollard	1500		237-238
									Journal C
		Captain Alfred Fountain			Schooner				165
		Elijah Pennypacker			Railroad	John Dwa			350-351
					Foot				132
						Diden			523-524
						Judge Chambers			523-524
					Schooner	Milton Hawkins			144-147
		Captain Alfred Fountain			Schooner				165
						Benjamin Hilliard			492
						John Williams			236
X									Journal C
									Journal C
						William Burns	300 in state		Journal C
						Summersett Walters			513
		Captain Alfred Fountain			Schooner				168-169
X									Journal C
X									Journal C
									Journal C
					Foot	William Y. Day			311-313

L. Name	First / Middle	Alias	Gender	Age	Color	Day	Month	Year	City	County	State	Group
Gilbert	Charles		Male		Mulatto	11	Nov	1854	Richmond	Henrico	VA	
Giles	Charlotte		Female	23		31	May	1856	Baltimore	Baltimore	MD	C-2
Giles	Lewis		Male			2	June	1855	Richmond	Henrico	VA	
Gilliam	William H.		Male	20	Black	26	Feb	1854	Richmond	Henrico	VA	C-1
Goins	Luke		Male					1860	Harpers Ferry		VA	
Good	Beverly		Male	24		18	Jan	1855	Petersburg	Dinwiddie	VA	B-3
Gooseberry	George W.	Isaac Stout	Male	23		19	Jan	1856		New Castle	DE	
Gooseberry	Thomas Jervis	Ezekial Chambers	Male	17	Black	2	Dec	1855	Chestertown	Kent	MD	L-3
Gorham	Henry		Male	34	Black		Nov	1856			NC	P-3
Goulden	Alfred		Male	23	Black							M-1
Govan	William		Male	33	Black		Aug	1855	Petersburg	Dinwiddie	VA	
Graff	Evan		Male	25	Black			1860		Frederick	MD	N-7
Graham	George	Henry Washington	Male	24	Black	16	Jan	1856	Alexandria	Fairfax	VA	J-3
Graham	Jane	Eliza Washington	Female	24		16	Jan	1856	Alexandria	Fairfax	VA	J-3
Graham	Montgomery		Male		Mulatto	13		1857	Alexandria	Fairfax	VA	A-4
Grant	Joseph		Male	27	Black	22*	Feb	1857	Eastern Shore		MD	F-7
Grantham	Nancy		Female	19	Mulatto			1858	Richmond	Henrico	VA	
Graves	Caroline	Julia Little	Female	40		16	Jan	1856			MD	
Gray	Henry		Male	12	Mulatto	4	July	1856	Portsmouth	Norfolk	VA	D-6
Gray	Mary		Female	14	Mulatto	4	July	1856	Portsmouth	Norfolk	VA	D-6
Gray	Sophia		Female	33	Mulatto	4	July	1856	Portsmouth	Norfolk	VA	D-6
Green	Anna Maria		Female	37				1857	Baltimore	Baltimore	MD	C-4
Green	Christopher		Male		Black			1857	Baltimore	Baltimore	MD	C-4
Green	David	George Taylor	Male			28	July	1856	Leesburg	Loudon	VA	
Green	George		Male	23	Black	29	June	1855	Baltimore	Baltimore	MD	N-2
Green	Lear		Female	18	Black	27			Baltimore	Baltimore	MD	
Green	Murdock		Male			20	Sept	1856	Mount Airy	Carroll	MD	A-2
Green	Nathan		Male	20				1857	Baltimore	Baltimore	MD	C-4
Green	Richard	William Smith	Male	25	Black	29	June	1855	Baltimore	Baltimore	MD	N-2
Green	Samuel	Wesley Kinnard	Male	25		28	Aug	1854	Indian Creek	Chester	MD	
Green	Samuel		Male			11	Dec	1855				
Green	Zebulon	Samuel Hill	Male	18	Black	18	Apr	1856	Duck Creek		MD	
Grey	John Boice		Male	19	Black		Jan	1858	Lewes	Sussex	DE	C-5
Griffen	William		Male	34		24	Oct	1857	Cambridge	Dorchester	MD	H-1
Griffin	James	Thomas Brown	Male	31	Black	20	Dec	1855	Baltimore	Baltimore	MD	
Grigby	Barnaby	John Boyer	Male	26	Mulatto	24	Dec	1855	Alder	Loudon	VA	K-1
Grigby	Mary Elizabeth	Elizabeth Boyer	Female	24	Black	24	Dec	1855	Alder	Loudon	VA	K-1

Child	Literate	Station Master/Conductor	Armed	Violence	Transportation	Owner	$ Reward	$ Value	Source
					Steamer	Benjamin Davis	550 in state		240-245
					Railroad	Capt. William Applegarth			218-219
						Mr. Lewis Hill		1200	317-318
	X				Steamer	Mrs. T.E. White			38-44
						Mrs. Carroll			544
					Steamer	Richard Perry			321
						Anthony Ryebold		1000	348
		Elijah Pennypacker			Railroad	Sarah Maria Perkins			350-351
		Fountain/Garrett			Schooner				395-396
					Foot	Fletcher Jackson			129
		Captain "B"			Schooner	Mark Davis, Esq			301-302
						Henry Heart			543
					Foot	Widow Beverly			349
					Foot				349
						Elizabeth Gordon	100 in state / 200 out		414-415
		English Sailors			Foot & Boat	Mary Gibson & others			124-127
					Boat	Dr. Christian			478-480
	X								348-349
X		Captain "B"			Schooner				590
X		Captain "B"			Schooner				590
		Captain "B"			Schooner				590
						James Pipper			425-426
						Clayton Wright			425-426
						Elliott Curlett			329-330
						George Chambers			273-275
					Chest	James Noble	50 in state / 150 out		289-292
						William Dorsey			212
						James Pipper			425-426
						George Chambers			273-275
	X	Harriet Tubman				Dr. James Muse			247-255
									Journal C
						John Appleton			399
					Skiff	David Henry Houston			504
			X			James Waters, Esq.			85
						Joshua Hitch			324-325
			X	X	Horse & Carriage	William Rogers			116-122
			X	X	Horse & Carriage	Townsend McVee			116-122

L. Name	First / Middle	Alias	Gender	Age	Color	Day	Month	Year	City	County	State	Group
Grimes	Harry		Male	46		7*	Nov	1857				K-4
Grinage	John		Male	20	Black			1859	Middle Neck	Cecil	MD	O-5
Gross	Albert		Male	20				1859		Cecil	MD	O-5
Gross	Charles Henry		Male					1859	Baltimore	Baltimore	MD	
Gross	Peter		Male	39	Black	10	Sept	1858		Culbert	MD	Z-4
Gross	Sam		Male	40		10	Sept	1858	George Island	Port Republc	MD	Z-4
Hackett	Lloyd	Perry Watkins	Male	55	Mulatto	1	Jan	1855			MD	A-3
Haines	Edward		Male	44	Black	7	Sept	1857			VA	G-4
Haines	Francis		Male			20	Nov	1855	Norfolk	Norfolk	VA	W-1
Haines	Joseph		Male	20	Mulatto	7	Sept	1857			VA	G-4
Haley	Elizabeth	Sarah Richardson	Female	21		26	Apr	1854	Havre de Grace	Harford	MD	J-2
Haley	Harriet	Ann Richardson	Female	19		26	Apr	1854	Havre de Grace	Harford	MD	J-2
Hall	— —		Male			8	Dec	1855	Ladies Manor	Haverford	MD	M-3
Hall	Charles		Male			8	Apr	1856	Baltimore	Baltimore	MD	
Hall	Charles		Male					1859			DE	N-5
Hall	Edward		Male	20				1859			DE	N-5
Hall	Henrietta		Female			8	Dec	1855	Ladies Manor	Haverford	MD	M-3
Hall	Jacob	Henry Thomas	Male	20		8	Dec	1855	Ladies Manor	Haverford	MD	M-3
Hall	John		Male					1859			DE	N-5
Hall	John		Male	31	Mulatto	27	Apr	1855	Richmond	Henrico	VA	
Hall	John	John Simpson	Male	32		12	July	1854	Charleston	Charleston	SC	
Hall, Jr	Joseph		Male				Jan	1855	Norfolk	Norfolk	VA	
Hall	Rebecca		Female	17		4	Aug	1855	Baltimore	Baltimore	MD	
Hall	Romulus	George Weems	Male				Mar	1857	Benedict	Charles	MD	B-1
Hamlet	Mark	Thomas Goff	Male			27	Oct	1853	Retirement		MD	
Handay	Joshua	Hamilton Hamby	Male	27		28	Sept	1856	Eastern Shore		MD	S-2
Handy	James Edward	Daniel Canon	Male	26		25	May	1854	Seaford	Sussex	DE	I-7
Harding	Louisa	Rebecca Hall	Female	17	Mulatto	1	Aug	1855	Baltimore	Baltimore	MD	
Harper	Ruth		Female					1858	Frederick	Frederick	MD	
Harper	Thomas		Male					1857	Alexandria	Fairfax	VA	E-4
Harris	Abram		Male	18			Mar	1857	Benedict	Charles	MD	B-1
Harris	Benjamin F.	Benjamin Franklin	Male	30		24	Aug	1854	Baltimore	Baltimore	MD	I-6
Harris	Charlotte		Female			20	July	1853	Wilmington	New Castle	DE	
Harris	Darius		Male	21				1858	Dunwoody	Dinwiddie	VA	
Harris	Franklin		Female	6		24	Aug	1854	Baltimore	Baltimore	MD	I-6
Harris	James		Male		Mulatto		Nov	1856	Middletown	New Castle	DE	
Harris	Joseph		Male	23			June	1855	Plymouth		NC	O-2

Child	Literate	Station Master/ Conductor	Armed	Violence	Transportation	Owner	$ Reward	$ Value	Source
		Fountain/Garrett				Jesse Moore			439-443
						William Flintham			526
						William Price			526
						Henry Slaughter			527
		Thomas Garrett				Joseph Griffiss	200 in state / 100 out		495
		Thomas Garrett				Joseph Griffiss	200 in state / 100 out		495-496
					Foot	John Griffin			319-320
	X					Tabby & Eliza Fortlock	50 in state		431-432
		Captain Alfred Fountain			Schooner				165
						Tabby & Eliza Fortlock			432
						George C. Davis			234
						George C. Davis			234
X					Horseback	Sarah Ann McGough			352
						Atwood Blunt			397-398
						James Rogers, Sr.			525
						Booth			525
					Horseback	Sarah Ann McGough			352
					Horseback	Major William Hutchins			352
						James B. Rodgers			525
	X	Captain "B"			Schooner	James Dunlap		1000	256-260
					Foot & Boat	Dr. Philip Mazyk			238-240
									323
						Lawyer Magill			Journal C
					Foot	John Henry Suthern			34-38
									Journal C
		Thomas Garrett				Isaac Harris			294-295
						Samuel Lewis			237
						Mcgill, Esq.			297
						John McPherson			492
						John Cowling			427-428
	X				Foot	John Henry Southern			34-38
						Richard Farmer			Journal C
									Journal C
					Boat	Thomas H. Hamlin			460-461
X						Richard Farmer			Journal C
						Catharine Odine			539-540
						David Morris			277

L. Name	First / Middle	Alias	Gender	Age	Color	Day	Month	Year	City	County	State	Group
Harris	Nathan		Male	21		28*	Dec	1854		Anne Arundel	MD	Z-1
Harris	Nelson	Charles Wilson	Male	27		25	Oct	1853	Richmond	Henrico	VA	
Harris	Thomas		Male	27		7	Sept	1857			VA	G-4
Harris	Wesley	Robert Jackson	Male	22	Black	2	Nov	1853	Martinsburg	Henry	VA	A-1
Heath	Charles		Male	25	Black	4	July	1859			MD	K-5
Heines	Peter		Male	21	Mulatto		July	1856	Eatontown		NC	C-3
Henderson	Eliza		Female	28	Black			1858	Richmond	Henrico	VA	
Henry	James		Male	32				1857		Kent		M-4
Henry	John	Samuel Full?	Male	21		30	Jan	1856	Sassafras Neck		MD	K-3
Henry	Joseph		Male	17				1860		Queen Annes	MD	Y-5
Henry	Thomas		Male	26	Black			1857	Cambridge	Dorchester	MD	F-6
Henson	James	David Caldwell	Male	32			Aug	1855	Elkton	Cecil	MD	
Henson	James		Male					1860	Baltimore	Baltimore	MD	W-5
Hickman	Charles	Charles Robinson	Male			7	Aug	1855	Indian River		DE	
Hill	——		Female			24	Oct	1857	Cambridge	Dorchester	MD	H-1
Hill	Alice		Female		Mulatto	24	Oct	1857	Cambridge	Dorchester	MD	H-1
Hill	George		Male	24	Black			1857	Arlington		MD	H-4
Hill	Henry		Male			24	Oct	1857	Cambridge	Dorchester	MD	H-1
Hill	Hezekiah		Male	30		1*	Dec	1854	Petersburg	Dinwiddie	VA	J-6
Hill	James		Male	21				1861	Richmond	Henrico	VA	
Hill	Joe		Male		Black	24	Oct	1857	Cambridge	Dorchester	MD	H-1
Hill	John Henry		Male	25	Black	1*	Jan	1853	Richmond	Henrico	VA	
Hill	Joseph Henry		Male	28				1859	Richmond	Henrico	VA	
Hill	Simon		Male	25	Black	29	Aug	1855			VA	
Hilliard	Frances		Female	29	Mulatto	30	Aug	1855	Richmond	Henrico	VA	
Hillis	John		Male					1859	New Market	Dorchester	MD	
Hilton	Elijah		Male	27	Mulatto	14*	July	1857	——	Chesterfield	VA	
Hines	Peter		Male	21		21	July	1856	Eastontown		NC	
Hinson	James	David Coldwell	Male	32		15	Aug	1855		Cecil	MD	
Hipkins	William Henry		Male	23	Mulatto			1857	Arlington		MD	H-4
Hitchens	C.		Male	22				1857	Milford		DE	
Hodges	Henry		Male	23			June	1855	Plymouth	Washington	NC	O-2
Hodges	Henry		Male	25		1	Aug	1855	Norfork	Norfolk	VA	
Hogg	William	John Smith	Male	25		26	Apr	1854	Baltimore	Baltimore	MD	
Holden	Levin		Male					1859	Laurel	Sussex	DE	
Holladay	Charles		Male	28		31	Aug	1855	Baltimore	Baltimore	MD	U-2
Hollis	Charles Henry		Male	20					Sandy Hook	Harford	MD	Q-1

Child	Literate	Station Master/ Conductor	Armed	Violence	Transportation	Owner	$ Reward	$ Value	Source
						John Edward Jackson			208-209
						William B. Beale			Journal C
						John Hatten, Esq			432
			X	X	Foot & Carriage	Phillip Pendelton			30-34
						Aquila Cain			521
		Captain Alfred Fountain			Schooner	Elias Heines, Esq.			325-329
						William Waverton			478
									447
						Anthony Ryebold			Journal C
						Greenberry Parker			550
					Foot	Josiah Wilson			98
						Jacob Johnson			299
						Mrs. Maria Thomas			547
						Charles Henry Hickman			Journal C
					Foot				87-89
					Foot				87-89
						Dr. Savington			434-435
X					Foot				87-89
					Steamer				202-204
					Steamer				204-205
			X		Foot			1000 in state / 2000 out	87
	X				Steamer	James Mitchell			189-192
						James Thomas, Jr			514
									300
	X	Colored Boatman			Steamer	Beverly Blair			295-297
					Schooner	Mrs. Louisa Lecount			522-523
	X				Foot	Major Edward Johnson	500 in state		157-158
		Captain Alfred Fountain			Schooner	Elias Hines			Journal C
						Jacob Johnson			Journal C
						Ephraim Swart			433-434
					Foot	William Hill			94
						Samuel Simmons			277-278
									Journal C
					Foot	Lewis Roberts			159-160
						Jonathan Bailey			513
						F. Smith			301-302
					Foot	John Webster			132-134

L. Name	First / Middle	Alias	Gender	Age	Color	Day	Month	Year	City	County	State	Group
Hollon	Alfred		Male	28	Black			1857	Baltimore	Baltimore	MD	L-4
Homer	Alfred		Male	22	Black	16	June	1856	Rockville	Montgomery	MD	
Hooper	Henry		Male	19		6	Dec	1855			MD	
Hooper	Miles		Male	23			Aug	1855	Federal Mills		NC	
Hopkins	Sidney		Male					1859	Havre de Grace	Harford	MD	I-5
Houston	George	Charles Robinson	Male			7	Aug	1855	Indian River		DE	
Houston	Maria Jane		Female	21	Black		Aug	1855	Cantwell's Bridge		DE	
Howard	Henry		Male	27		1	June	1855	Ladies Manor	Haverford	MD	X-2
Hubert	Alfred		Male	28	Black			1857			VA	
Hudson	Ephraim	John Spry	Male	22		28	Sept	1856	Cambridge	Dorchester	MD	S-2
Hughes	Daniel		Male		Black		Mar	1857	Bucktown	Dorchester	MD	E-1
Hughes	William		Male	22		29	Dec	1856	Eastern Shore		MD	
Hunt	Orlando J.		Male	29	Black			1858	Richmond	Henrico	VA	
Irwin	Asbury		Male	40	Black			1858		Kent	MD	D-5
Jackson	——		Female					1858	Georgetown		DC	Y-6
Jackson	Andrew	Henry Johnson	Male	23		29	Dec	1856	Cecil		DE	
Jackson	Anna Maria		Female	40	Black		Nov	1858	Milford	Sussex	DE	Z-6
Jackson	Ebenezer T.		Male				Nov	1858	Milford	Sussex	DE	Z-6
Jackson	Frances		Female				Nov	1858	Milford	Sussex	DE	Z-6
Jackson	General Andrew		Male	27	Black			1857	Lerwistown		DE	S-4
Jackson	James Henry		Male	17		10	Sept	1858	Frederica		DE	Z-4
Jackson	John E.		Male				Nov	1858	Milford	Sussex	DE	Z-6
Jackson	Mary Ann		Female				Nov	1858	Milford	Sussex	DE	Z-6
Jackson	Peter	Staunch Tilghman	Male			29	Dec	1854	Bucktown	Dorchester	MD	V-2
Jackson	Rebecca		Female	37	Mulatto			1858	Georgetown		DC	Y-6
Jackson	Robert		Male					1858			DE	J-5
Jackson	Wilhelmina		Female				Nov	1858	Milford	Sussex	DE	Z-6
Jackson	William		Male	50				1857	Alexandria	Fairfax	VA	
Jackson	William Albert		Male				Nov	1858	Milford	Sussex	DE	Z-6
Jackson	William Henry		Male				Nov	1858	Milford	Sussex	DE	Z-6
Janney	John		Male	22		10	Sept	1858		Culbert	MD	Z-4
Jasper	Elias		Male	32	Black	22	June	1855	Norfolk	Norfolk	VA	M-2
Jeffries	Mary		Female			29	Jan	1856				
Jenkins	——			35		13	Mar	1855	Norfolk	Norfolk	VA	
Johns	Lydia Ann		Female	22	Black			1858		Kent	MD	D-5
Johns	Robert		Male		Black			1858		Cecil	MD	E-5
Johns	Sue Ann		Female	23	Black			1858		Cecil	MD	E-5

Child	Literate	Station Master/ Conductor	Armed	Violence	Transportation	Owner	$ Reward	$ Value	Source
						Elijah J. Johnson			445
						John W. Anderson	50 in state / 100 out		403
									352
						George Montigue			298
						Jacob Hoag			514
						Isaac Houston			Journal C
									297-298
						Phillip Garrison			317
					Foot	Matilda Niles			95
		Thomas Garrett				John Campbell Henry			294-295
					Foot	Richard Meredith			58-59
						Daniel Cox			541
						High Holser			480-481
						Michael Newbold			506-507
X						Mrs. Margaret Dick			498-499
						Thomas Palmer			541
		Thomas Garrett				Joseph Brown			535-537
	x	Thomas Garrett				Joseph Brown			535-537
	x	Thomas Garrett				Joseph Brown			535-537
						Shepherd Houston			456
		Thomas Garrett				Joseph Brown	200 in state / 100 out		496
	x	Thomas Garrett				Joseph Brown			535-537
	x	Thomas Garrett				Joseph Brown			535-537
		Tubman-Garrett				George Wenthrop			307
						Mrs. Margaret Dick			498-499
						Mrs. Mary Hickman			518
	x	Thomas Garrett				Joseph Brown			535-537
						Daniel Minne			411-412
	x	Thomas Garrett				Joseph Brown			535-537
	x	Thomas Garrett				Joseph Brown			535-537
		Thomas Garrett				Joseph Griffiss	200 in state / 100 out		495
		Captain "B"			Schooner	Bayham		1200	271-272
									Journal C
									Journal C
						Michael Newbold			507
						William Casey			508
						Susan Flinthrew			508

L. Name	First / Middle	Alias	Gender	Age	Color	Day	Month	Year	City	County	State	Group
Johnson	——		Male	7			July	1855			NC	A-7
Johnson	——		Male	11			July	1855			NC	A-7
Johnson	Ann		Female	24	Black			1857	Cambridge	Dorchester	MD	V-1
Johnson	Cornelius Henry		Male	36	Black			1859	Richmond	Henrico	VA	
Johnson	David		Male			20	Nov	1855	Norfolk	Norfolk	VA	W-1
Johnson	Eliza Jane		Female	23	Black			1857	Georgetown	Sussex	DE	
Johnson	George		Male	25	Black	22*	Aug	1857	Washington	DC	DC	F-4
Johnson	Harriet	Harriet Gilbert	Female	25		28	July	1856		Prince Georges	MD	R-6
Johnson	Helen		Female			2	Sept	1853				
Johnson	Henry		Male	19	Black	4	June	1857	Abingdon	Harford	MD	D-1
Johnson	James	William Gilbert	Male	35		28	July	1856		Prince Georges	MD	R-6
Johnson	James		Male			9	Apr	1856	Deer Creek	Harford	MD	
Johnson	Jane		Female		Black		July	1855			NC	A-7
Johnson	John		Male	27	Mulatto			1857	Washington	Washington	DC	O-4
Johnson	Joseph G.		Male	23	Black			1860	Baltimore	Baltimore	MD	
Johnson	Nelson	Jackson Hall	Male	25		17	July	1854	Deer Creek		MD	
Johnson	Perry		Male	28		21	Nov	1853	Elkton	Cecil	MD	
Johnson	Roseanna	Catherine Brice	Female		Black	11	Jan	1857	Deer Creek	Harford	MD	
Johnson	Samuel W.		Male	27		6	Mar	1854	Richmond	Henrico	VA	
Johnson	Sarah		Female			19	June	1854	Norfolk	Norfolk	VA	
Johnson	Talbot		Male	35	Black	10	Sept	1858			MD	Z-4
Johnson	William		Male			29	July	1855		Dorchester	MD	
Johnson	William		Male	19	Black			1859	Gun Powder Neck		MD	
Johnson	William H.	John Wesley	Male	24	Mulatto	1	Jan	1855			MD	A-3
Joiner	Maria		Female	33	Mulatto	23	June	1855	Norfolk	Norfolk	VA	
Jones	Alice		Female			20	Nov	1855	Norfolk	Norfolk	VA	W-1
Jones	Arthur		Male	41	Black		June	1855	Norfolk	Norfolk	VA	O-2
Jones	Catharine		Female	24	Black			1858		Queen Annes	MD	T-4
Jones	Eliza		Female	40	Black	2	Aug	1855	Petersburg	Dinwiddie	VA	N-6
Jones	Fenton		Male			10	Dec	1855	Frederick	Frederick	MD	
Jones	Henry		Male	19		12	Nov	1855			MD	
Jones	Henry		Male	41	Black			1859	Richmond	Henrico	VA	R-5
Jones	Hill		Male	19	Black			1856	Middletown	New Castle	DE	Q-2
Jones	James	Henry Rider	Male	32	Mulatto	4	Apr	1856	King Georges		MD	
Jones	John	Henry Clark	Male	25		2	Sept	1854	Middletown	New Castle	DE	
Jones	Lewis		Male	52	Mulatto			1857			VA	Y-4
Jones	Margaret		Female			31	Oct	1855	Baltimore	Baltimore	MD	
Jones	Mary		Female			23	Mar	1856	Norfolk	Norfolk	VA	H-3

Child	Literate	Station Master/Conductor	Armed	Violence	Transportation	Owner	$ Reward	$ Value	Source
X					Carriage	Col. John H. Wheeler			73-84
X					Carriage	Col. John H. Wheeler			73-84
					Foot	Samuel Harrington			160-161
						Mrs. Mary F. Price			515-516
		Captain Alfred Fountain			Schooner				165
						Sally Spiser			435
						Miss Eleanor J. Conway	100 in state / 300 out		430
						William T. Wood			329-330
									Journal C
						Mrs Elizabeth Brown	500 in state	1700	56-57
						Thomas Wallace			329-330
						William Raulty			398
					Carriage	Col. John H. Wheeler			73-84
						William Stone			448
						William Jones			550-551
						Isaac Stansberry			Journal C
						Charles Johnson			48-49
	X					Dr. Abraham Street			542
	X				Steamer	James B. Foster			154-156
									Journal C
		Thomas Garrett				Duke Bond	200 in state / 100 out		495
						Samuel Harrington			Journal C
						John Bosley			523
					Foot	John Hall			320
		Captain Alfred Fountain			Schooner	Catharine Gordon		800	272-273
		Captain Alfred Fountain			Schooner				165
						John Jones			277
						Joshua Duvall			458
						Eliza H. Riche			278-279
									353
									Journal C
						Elizabeth Mann			529
						John Cochran			397
						Dr. William Stewart			335
						Amos Lynch			Journal C
						Thomas Sydan			485-486
									Journal C
X		Captain Alfred Fountain			Schooner	W.W. Davidson			336-337

L. Name	First / Middle	Alias	Gender	Age	Color	Day	Month	Year	City	County	State	Group
Jones	Mary		Female					1858	Washington		DC	L-7
Jones	Rebecca		Female	28	Mulatto	23	Mar	1856	Norfolk	Norfolk	VA	H-3
Jones	Rebecca		Female			23	Mar	1856	Norfolk	Norfolk	VA	H-3
Jones	Robert		Male	35	Black	2	Aug	1855	Petersburg	Dinwiddie	VA	N-6
Jones	Samuel		Male			1	June	1855	Ladies Manor	Haverford	MD	X-2
Jones	Sarah Frances		Female			23	Mar	1856	Norfolk	Norfolk	VA	H-3
Jones	Tolbert		Male			1	June	1855	Ladies Manor	Haverford	MD	X-2
Jones	William		Male			14	Feb	1854				
Jones	William Henry		Male	2				1858		Queen Annes	MD	T-4
Jordan	William	William Price	Male			25*	Dec	1854	Bertie		NC	
Judah	John		Male	32	Mulatto	1	June	1855	Petersburg	Dinwiddie	VA	W-2
Kane	Jane	Catherine Kane	Female	22		29	Dec	1854		Dorchester	MD	V-2
Kell	James		Male	24	Black	4	July	1859	Eastern Shore		MD	K-5
Kelley	Henson		Male					1860	Baltimore	Baltimore	MD	
Kelly	Mary	Charlotte Spriggs	Female			7	Apr	1853	Baltimore	Baltimore	MD	
King	Charles		Male	23		25	Sept	1854	Norfork	Norfolk	VA	
Knight	Mary		Female	26	Black	4	July	1856	Norfolk	Norfolk	VA	D-6
Kneeland	Joeseph	Joseph Hudson	Male	26	Black	14	Nov	1853				
Lambert	Elizabeth		Female					1856	Middletown	New Castle	DE	Q-2
Lambert	Horace		Male					1856	Middletown	New Castle	DE	Q-2
Lambert	Mary		Female					1856	Middletown	New Castle	DE	Q-2
Lambert	William Henry		Male					1856	Middletown	New Castle	DE	Q-2
Laminson	William H.		Male	21				1855		New Castle	DE	
Langhorn	Henry	William Scott	Male		Mulatto		Dec	1858	Richmond	Henrico	VA	
Latham	Major		Male	44	Mulatto		Nov	1856			NC	P-3
Laws	George		Male		Black			1858		Kent	DE	M-7
Lazarus	James		Male					1859	Laurel	Sussex	DE	H-5
Lee	Charles	Thomas Bushier	Male			3	Apr	1853	Baltimore	Baltimore	MD	N-1
Lee	John		Male			10	Aug	1854	Fayetteville		NC	
Lee	John Edward		Male					1859		Harford	MD	
Lee	Lewis		Male	25	Mulatto			1859	Fairfax	Fairfax	VA	
Lee	Ordee		Female	35	Black			1857			MD	W-3
Lee	William		Male	27	Mulatto			1857			MD	
Levinson	William Henry		Male	21		15	Jan	1856	Newcastle		DE	
Lewey	Rebecca		Female	28		4	July	1856	Norfolk	Norfolk	VA	D-6
Lewis	David		Male	27		3	June	1856	Leesburg		VA	
Lewis	Edward	William Brady	Male	36	Black	7*	Nov	1857		Franklin	NC	K-4
Lewis	George		Male	40				1858		Sussex	DE	G-5

Child	Literate	Station Master/Conductor	Armed	Violence	Transportation	Owner	$ Reward	$ Value	Source
						Mrs. Henry Harding			483
	X	Captain Alfred Fountain			Schooner	W.W. Davidson	150 in state		337-338
X		Captain Alfred Fountain			Schooner	W.W. Davidson			336-337
	X					Thomas N. Lee			278-279
						William Hutchins			317
X		Captain Alfred Fountain			Schooner	W.W. Davidson			336-337
						William Hutchins			317
									Journal C
X						Joshua Duvall			458-459
		Thomas Garrett			Foot	Governor Badger of N. Carolina			122-124
		Captain "B"			Schooner	Miss Eliza Lambert			316
		Tubman-Garrett				Rash Jones			307
						Thomas Murphy			521
						Reason Hastell			544
						William Watkins			Journal C
						Martha M. Hope			Journal C
		Captain "B"			Schooner				589-590
						Jacob Kneeland			54-56
						Andrew Peterson			397
X						Andrew Peterson			397
X						Andrew Peterson			397
X						Andrew Peterson			397
						Francis Haskins			348
	X				Steamer	Charles L. Hobson			560-563
		Fountain/Garrett			Schooner	John Latham			394-395
						Denny			490-491
						Kendall Major Llewis			514
					Foot	George Stewart			129
						Luke Gaines			Journal C
						John B. Slade			522
						William Watkins			537-538
						Elijah Thompson		1500	408
						Zechariah Merica			452-453
						Frances Hawkins			Journal C
		Captain "B"			Schooner				589
		Emily Ann Mah				Joshua Pussey			Journal C
	X	Fountain/Garrett				Carter Gay	100 in/out state		443-444
						Samuel Laws			511

L. Name	First / Middle	Alias	Gender	Age	Color	Day	Month	Year	City	County	State	Group
Lewis	Laura		Female	25	Mulatto	16	Aug	1855	Louisville	Jefferson	KY	
Light	George		Male			24	Oct	1857	Cambridge	Dorchester	MD	H-1
Light	Solomon		Male	23				1857	Cambridge	Dorchester	MD	X-3
Little	Nancy		Female			20	Nov	1855	Norfolk	Norfolk	VA	W-1
Logan`	George		Male	23	Black	10	Apr	1856	Georgetown		VA	R-3
Logan`	John W.		Male			10	Apr	1856	Little Georgetown	Berkeley	VA	R-3
Loney	Anthony	William Armstead	Male	25	Black		May	1857	Richmond	Henrico	VA	
Loney	Cordelia		Female	57	Mulatto	30*	Mar	1859	Fredericksburg	Spotsylvania	VA	
Long	Silas		Male	27	Black			1857	Cambridge	Dorchester	MD	X-3
Mackintosh	John		Male	44		4	Aug	1855	Darien	McIntosh	GA	
Mackey	William		Male					1858	Norfolk	Norfolk	VA	
Madden	Thomas		Male	22		9	Oct	1854	Easton	Talbot	MD	
Maddison	Wiley		Male	19			Nov	1856	Petersburg	Norfolk	VA	P-3
Mahoney	Matilda		Female	21		24	May	1854	Frederick	Frederick	MD	
Malary	John		Male			21	Oct	1854	Norfolk	Norfolk	VA	
Mason	James		Male	24				1858	Petersburg	Dinwiddie	VA	
Massey	James		Male	25	Black		Apr	1857		Queen Annes	MD	S-1
Matterson	——		Male			2	Nov	1853	Martinsburg	Henry	VA	A-1
Matterson	——		Male			2	Nov	1853	Martinsburg	Henry	VA	A-1
Matterson	——		Male			2	Nov	1853	Martinsburg	Henry	VA	A-1
Matthews	Peter	Samuel Sparrows	Male	35	Black	7	Oct	1855	Oak Hall		VA	
Matthews	Tom		Male	25	Black	4	Apr	1856	Bladensburg	Prince Georges	MD	
Maxwell	Thomas		Male	21	Black	4	July	1859	Eastern Shore		MD	K-5
Mayo	Harriet		Female	22		1	June	1855	Petersburg	Dinwiddie	VA	W-2
M'Coy	Eliza	Ellen Saunders	Female	38	Mulatto	1	Nov	1854	Norfolk	Norfolk	VA	
M'Coy	Robert	William Donar	Male	32	Mulatto	1	Oct	1854	Norfolk	Norfolk	VA	
Mead	Zechariah	John Williams	Male	20		25	Feb	1855			MD	
Melvin	Mary Frances		Female	23	Mulatto			1858	Norfolk	Norfolk	VA	
Menia	Jane Matilda	Mary Parker	Female			6	Apr	1853	Annapolis	Anne Arundel	MD	F-6
Mercer	James		Male	19	Black	26	Feb	1854	Richmond	Henrico	VA	C-1
Mercer	Verenea		Female	41	Black	1	Jan	1855	Richmond	Henrico	VA	
Miles	Samuel	Robert King	Male	31		15	Aug	1855	Revel's Neck	Somerset	MD	
Millburn	Mary	Louisa F. Jones	Female				May	1858	Norfolk	Norfolk	VA	
Mills	Cornelius		Male	27				1860			MD	C-6
Mills	Diana		Female	57				1860			MD	C-6
Mills	Jerry		Male	65				1860			MD	C-6
Mills	Margaret		Female	17				1860			MD	C-6
Mills	Sarah Ann		Female	16				1859	Haggerstown	Washington	MD	
Mills	Susan		Female	15				1860			MD	C-6

Child	Literate	Station Master/ Conductor	Armed	Violence	Transportation	Owner	$ Reward	$ Value	Source
						Widow Lewis			299
					Foot				87
						Willis Branick		1500	409
		Captain Alfred Fountain			Schooner				165
						Mrs. Jane Coultson			398-399
						Miss Cox			399
					Foot	Warring Talvert			114
					Foot	Mrs. Joseph Cahell			102-107
			X			Sheriff Robert Bell			409
						Thomas MacIntosh			297
						Mrs. Tunis			481-482
						Ed Ray		1000	302-303
		Fountain/Garrett			Schooner				396
						William Reigard			169-170
						Eliza Ann Anderson			Journal C
	X					Judith Burton			462
	X		X		Foot	James Pittman		1600	136-140
		Friends	X	X	Foot & Carriage	Phillip Pendelton			30-34
		Friends	X	X	Foot & Carriage	Phillip Pendelton			30-34
		Friends	X	X	Foot & Carriage	Phillip Pendelton			30-34
			X			William S. Matthews			303-305
						E. A. Jones	300 in state		335
						Aquila Cain			522
		Captain "B"			Schooner	James Cuthbert			316
	X				Steamer	Andrew Ligany			283-285
	X					The Trader Hall			281-283
						Charles C. Owens			323-324
						Widow Chapman			478
						Richard Ducke			Journal C
	X				Steamer	Mrs. T.E. White			38-44
						Thomas W. Quales			318-319
	X					Henry Miles			298-299
	X					Mrs. Chapman			583-585
						David Snively			556
						David Snively			556
						David Snively			556
						David Snively			556
						Joseph O'Neil			512-513
						David Snively			556

L. Name	First / Middle	Alias	Gender	Age	Color	Day	Month	Year	City	County	State	Group
Mitchell	Cyrus	John Steel	Male	26	Black	28	Sept	1856	Cambridge	Dorchester	MD	S-2
Mitchell	John		Male	24	Black	2	Feb	1858	Viana			V-4
Mitchell	Josiah		Male	23		2	Feb	1858				V-4
Mitchell	Lemuel		Male	35	Black	2	Feb	1858				V-4
Moduck	Green		Male			20*	Sept	1856	Mount Airy	Carroll	MD	A-2
Molock	Francis	Thomas Jackson	Male	21	Black	28	Sept	1856	Cambridge	Dorchester	MD	S-2
Monroe	James		Male			21	July	1856	South End		NC	C-3
Moody	William Henry		Male	20	Black			1857				W-6
Moor	Henry		Male	30	Black	24	Oct	1857	Cambridge	Dorchester	MD	H-1
Moore	George		Male			1	Mar	1853	Cantwells Bridge		DE	
Moore	Hannah	Aunt Hannah	Female	57				1854			MO	
Moore	John Henry		Male	24	Black			1857	Arlington		MD	H-4
Morgan	Edward		Male	21	Black	4	June	1857	Abingdon PO	Harford	MD	D-1
Morris	James		Male	27			July	1856	South End		NC	C-3
Morris	John		Male	21	Black		June	1855	Norfolk	Norfolk	VA	O-2
Mountain	——			1				1858			DE	B-7
Mountain	Ann		Female	22				1858			DE	B-7
Munson	Alexander	Samuel Garrett	Male	18	Black		Dec	1855	Martinsburg		VA	
Murray	Gracie	Sophia Sims	Female			3	Apr	1853	Baltimore	Baltimore	MD	N-1
Murray	Robert		Male							Loudon	VA	
Myers	John		Male					1857		Harford	MD	
Naylor	William		Male			6	June	1857	Richmond	Henrico	VA	H-6
Neall	Daniel		Male	23	Mulatto		Sept	1856	Washington		DC	G-1
Nelson	Peter		Male	29	Mulatto			1858		Stafford	VA	
Nelson	Susan	Susan Bell	Female	30	Black	22	June	1855	Norfolk	Norfolk	VA	M-2
Nelson	William	Thomas Russell	Male	40	Black	22	June	1855	Norfolk	Norfolk	VA	M-2
Nelson	William Thomas		Male			22	June	1855	Norfolk	Norfolk	VA	M-2
Newton	Isaac		Male	30					Richmond	Henrico	VA	
Nichols	Randolph		Male	20							MD	O-7
Nicholson	Adam	John Wynkoop	Male		Black	12	Apr	1854	Hedgesville		VA	H-7
Nickless	Kit		Male	45		21	Dec	1854	King Georges		VA	R-2
Nixon	Frederick		Male	35		20	Nov	1855	Norfolk	Norfolk	VA	W-1
Nixon	Isaiah		Male	22	Black		June	1855	Plymouth	Washington	NC	O-2
Nixon	Samuel	Dr. Thomas Bayne	Male	31	Black	13	Mar	1855	Norfolk	Norfolk	VA	
Nixon	Thomas		Male	19	Black	20	Nov	1855	Norfolk	Norfolk	VA	W-1
Nokey	Eliza		Female			15*	Nov	1856	Easton	Talbot	MD	P-2
Nole	Charles		Male		Mulatto		Oct	1858		Culpepper	VA	F-5
North	——					22	Mar	1856				C-7

Child	Literate	Station Master/Conductor	Armed	Violence	Transportation	Owner	$ Reward	$ Value	Source
		Thomas Garrett			Foot	James K. Lewis			294-295
						Miss Catharine Cornwell			465-466
						Thomas J. Hodgson			466
						James R. Lewis			465
						William Dorsey			212
		Thomas Garrett				James A. Waddell			294-295
		Captain Alfred Fountain			Schooner				325-329
					Horse & Carriage	William Henry Hyson			403-404
			X		Foot	Levin Dale			85
									Journal C
						Mary Moore			572-576
						David Mitchell			434
						Mrs Elizabeth Brown	500 in state		56-57
	X	Captain Alfred Fountain			Schooner	Ann McCourt			Journal C
						Edward Bloomer			278
X									468
									468
									347
					Foot	George Stewart			129-130
						Eliza Brooks			531
						Dr. Joshua R. Nelson			452
					Steamer				405
		Rev. Hiram Wilson			Foot	George Parker	200 in state		65-67
						James Ford			482-483
		Captain "B"			Schooner	Thomas Baltimore			268-270
		Captain "B"			Schooner	Turner & White			268-269
	X	Captain "B"			Schooner	Thomas Baltimore			268-269
									533
						Mrs. Caroline Brang			547-548
					Foot	Alexander Hill			233
					Foot	General Washington			293-294
		Captain Alfred Fountain			Schooner	Mr. Bockover			161-169
						Samuel Simmons			277
	X				Schooner	Dr. C.F. Martin	1000 in state		260-265
		Captain Alfred Fountain			Schooner	Mr. Bockover			167
									280
						Blooker W. Hansborough			509
X						Edward C. Dyer			Journal C

L. Name	First / Middle	Alias	Gender	Age	Color	Day	Month	Year	City	County	State	Group
North	Harry	Lanney	Male	12		22	Mar	1856				C-7
Oberne	Henry		Male	21	Black			1857	Seaford	Sussex	DE	
Oliver	William		Male	26	Black			1859		Prince Georges	MD	
Paeden	Celia		Female			27	Mar	1853	Norfolk	Norfolk	VA	G-2
Paeden	Edward		Male	44	Black	27	Mar	1853	Norfolk	Norfolk	VA	G-2
Paeden	Harriet		Female			27	Mar	1853	Norfolk	Norfolk	VA	G-2
Page	Thomas		Male	18		23	Mar	1856				H-3
Parker	Ann		Female			14	Nov	1856		Dorchester	MD	T-6
Parker	Henry		Male			14	Nov	1856		Dorchester	MD	T-6
Parker	Levin		Male	22	Black	24	Oct	1857	Cambridge	Dorchester	MD	
Parker	Lydia		Female			14	Nov	1856		Dorchester	MD	T-6
Parker	Thomas		Male			14	May	1856	Norfolk	Norfolk	VA	U-3
Patty	Elizabeth		Female			16	May	1856	Norfolk	Norfolk	VA	D-7
Patty	Winnie		Female	22	Black	16	May	1856	Norfolk	Norfolk	VA	D-7
Payne	Daniel		Male			1	June	1855	Richmond	Henrico	VA	
Payne	David		Male			24	May	1854	Richmond	Henrico	VA	
Payne	Oscar		Male	30	Mulatto			1857	Alexandria	Fairfax	VA	Y-4
Peaker	Thomas		Male			14	May	1856	Georget'n Crossroads	Kent	MD	
Peck	Lewis		Male		Black			1860	Patapsco River		MD	P-7
Peel	William	William "Box" Jones	Male	23	Black		Apr	1859	Baltimore	Baltimore	MD	
Pembrooke	Jacob		Male	19		24	May	1854	Sharpsburg		VA	M-6
Pembrooke	Robert		Male	17		24	May	1854	Sharpsburg		VA	M-6
Pembrooke	Stephen		Male	45		24	May	1854	Sharpsburg		VA	M-6
Pennington	Bob		Male				May	1854	Washington	DC	DC	
Pennington	Jake		Male				May	1854	Washington	DC	DC	
Pennington	Peter		Male	25	Black	15*	Nov	1856	Easton	Talbot	MD	P-2
Pennington	Stephen		Male				May	1854	Washington	DC	DC	
Pennington	Tom		Male	25	Black			1857		Cecil	MD	P-4
Penwell	Elizabeth		Female	22		20	July	1854	Little Caroline		MD	
Perry	Anna		Female	19	Black			1857	Hoopesville	Dorchester	MD	S-4
Peters	Hannah		Female			17	Oct	1857	Cambridge	Dorchester	MD	I-1
Pettifoot	John Henry	Sydney	Male	26	Mulatto			1858	Richmond	Henrico	VA	
Petty	Peter		Male	24		20	Nov	1855	Norfolk	Norfolk	VA	W-1
Pierce	William		Male	23	Black						MD	
Piner	Abe		Male	23		14	May	1856	Georget'n Crossroads	Kent	MD	

Child	Literate	Station Master/ Conductor	Armed	Violence	Transportation	Owner	$ Reward	$ Value	Source
						Edward C. Dyer	100 in state		Journal C
					Foot				94
						Mrs. Marshall			539
					Boat	David Baines			230
					Boat	Dr. Price			230
					Boat	David Baines			230
	X	Captain Alfred Fountain			Schooner				343-344
						Edward Wiley			Journal C
						Edward Wiley			Journal C
						Lawrence G. Colson			85
						Edward Wiley			Journal C
		Tubman/Garrett							402
X		Thomas Garrett				Jacob Shuster			402
		Thomas Garrett				Jacob Shuster			402-403
						M.M. Morris			316
									Journal C
						Mary Dade	150 in state / 200 out	1800	486
									Journal C
						Joseph Bryant			550
					Steamer	Robert Carr			28-30
									Journal C
									Journal C
									Journal C
						David Smith & Jacob Grove			170-174
		James Jefferson				Wm Rigard			159-170
						Wright	800 in state		280-281
						David Smith & Jacob Grove			169-170
						Hon. L. McLane			449-450
						Dr. Clift			Journal C
									456-457
					Foot				92
	X				Steamer	McHenry & McCulloch	100 in state		147-149
		Captain Alfred Fountain			Schooner	Joseph Boukley			167-168
						John Hickol			557-558
						George Spencer			Journal C

L. Name	First / Middle	Alias	Gender	Age	Color	Day	Month	Year	City	County	State	Group
Piney	Benjamin		Male	20	Black			1856	Baltimore	Baltimore	MD	
Pinket	John		Male	27	Black			1859	New Market	Dorchester	MD	M-5
Pipkins	Jefferson	David Jones	Male			3	Apr	1853	Baltimore	Baltimore	MD	N-1
Pipkins	Louisa	Elizabeth Brit	Female			3	Apr	1853	Baltimore	Baltimore	MD	N-1
Pitts	Catherine		Female			15	Nov	1855	Boslier?		MD	
Predo	Henry		Male	27	Black		Mar	1857	Bucktown	Dorchester	MD	E-1
Pry	Sauney		Male	27	Black			1856		Loudon	VA	Q-3
Pugh	Anthony		Male			24	Oct	1857	Portsmouth	Norfolk	VA	Q-7
Pugh	Isabella		Female			24	Oct	1857	Portsmouth	Norfolk	VA	Q-7
Purnell	Charles		Male	26		1	Jan	1855	Berlin	Worcester	MD	Z-2
Purnell	Irvin		Male			31	Jan	1853	Eastern Shore		MD	
Purnell	John		Male					1860	Kunkletown	Worcester	MD	A-6
Purnell	Oliver		Male	26	Black	17	Nov	1855	Berlin	Worcester	MD	N-3
Quantence	Pascal		Male		Mulatto			1857		Rappahannock	VA	
Quinn	William		Male	22	Black			1859	Tapps' Neck		MD	U-5
Redden	Mary		Female			29	Jan	1856				U-6
Redden	Sarah		Female			29	Jan	1856				U-6
Redick	Willis		Male	32	Black	13	Dec	1853	Portsmouth	Norfolk	VA	
Reed	Isaac	James Reed	Male			28	July	1856	Eastern Shore		MD	D-3
Rhoads	——			8 mos.				1857	Perryville	Caroline	MD	S-1
Rhoads	George		Male	25	Black			1857	Perryville	Caroline	MD	S-1
Rhoads	James		Male	23	Black			1857	Perryville	Caroline	MD	S-1
Rhoads	Sarah Elizabeth		Female	17	Black			1857	Perryville	Caroline	MD	S-1
Richards	John Henry		Male	24		31	May	1856	Baltimore	Baltimore	MD	E-2
Rickets	John H.	Ed Henry Waples	Male	22		8	Sept	1854	Lewistown		DE	
Ringgold	Charles		Male	18	Black	4	July	1859	Eastern Shore		MD	K-5
Ringgold	Charles		Male	19					Perrymanville		MD	
Ringold	Charles H.		Male			31	May	1856	Baltimore	Baltimore	MD	E-2
Ringgold	William		Male						Baltimore	Baltimore	MD	
Rister	Amarian Lucretia		Female	21	Mulatto			1857	Westminster	Carroll	MD	
Roach	John		Male	33				1859	Seaford	Sussex	DE	Q-5
Roach	Lamby		Female					1859	Seaford	Sussex	DE	Q-5
Roberts	Emory	William Kemp	Male			1	June	1855	Prest Rock	Talbot	MD	
Robinson	Daniel		Male			23	Mar	1856	Petersburg	Norfolk	VA	H-3
Robinson	George		Male	21	Black			1858	Elkton	Cecil	MD	
Robinson	Isaiah		Male	23	Mulatto	23	Mar	1856	Norfolk	Norfolk	VA	H-3
Robinson	John		Male			1	Jan	1855	Black Bird, Newcastle		MD	O-6
Robinson	Joseph		Male	30	Black	1	Mar	1855	Richmond	Henrico	VA	F-1

Child	Literate	Station Master/Conductor	Armed	Violence	Transportation	Owner	$ Reward	$ Value	Source
						Mary Hawkins			540-541
						Mary Brown			524
	X				Foot	Widow Pipkins			129-130
					Foot	George Stewart			129-130
						John Pitts			Journal C
					Foot		3000 in state		57-58
						Nathan Clapton			396-397
		Captain Robert Lee			Skiff				87
		Captain Robert Lee			Skiff				87
						John Derrickson			319
									Journal C
					Boat				552-554
						Moses Purnell			354
						John Quantence	100 in state		438-439
									534
									Journal C
									Journal C
						S.J. Wilson			51
						Benjamin Franklin Houston			329
X					Foot	John P. Dellum			139
					Foot	John P. Dellum		1400	138-139
					Foot	John P. Dellum		1700	139
					Foot	John P. Dellum			139-140
					Railroad	James Hodges	1300 in state		221
						Stephen Houston			Journal C
						Dr. Jacob Preston			522
									532
					Railroad	James Hodges			221
					Foot	Henry Wallace			532-533
						Mr. Boile			453
					Foot	Joshua O'Bear			528
					Foot	Dr. Shipley			528
						Edward Lloyd			315
		Captain Alfred Fountain			Schooner				340-342
						Samuel Smith			492
		Captain Alfred Fountain			Schooner		250 in state		338-339
						William Wilson			Journal C
	X	Captain "B"			Schooner	George E. Sadler		1000	60-65

L. Name	First / Middle	Alias	Gender	Age	Color	Day	Month	Year	City	County	State	Group
Robinson	Josephine		Female					1858	Washington		DC	
Robinson	Mary Ann		Female	19		1	Jan	1855	Black Bird, Newcastle		MD	O-6
Robinson	Miles		Male	22				1859	Richmond	Henrico	VA	
Robinson	Robert N.		Male	22		1	Mar	1855	Richmond	Henrico	VA	F-1
Robinson	William	Thomas Harred	Male	28		19	Mar	1853		Fauquer	VA	
Rodgers	Charles		Male					1857	Baltimore	Baltimore	MD	L-4
Rodgers	George		Male	26	Black			1857	Baltimore	Baltimore	MD	L-4
Ross	Benjamin	James Stewart	Male	28	Black	29	Dec	1854	Bucktown	Dorchester	MD	V-2
Ross	Benjamin		Male				June	1857	Eastern Shore	Caroline	MD	Y-3
Ross	Charles		Male	23				1859	Greensborough	Caroline	MD	
Ross	George	John Brown	Male	26		29	Dec	1854	Horses Crossroads		DE	
Ross	Harriet		Female				June	1857	Eastern Shore	Caroline	MD	Y-3
Ross	Henry	Levin Stewart	Male	22		29	Dec	1854	Bucktown	Dorchester	MD	V-2
Ross	Major		Male					1857	Havre de Grace	Harford	MD	
Ross	Robert	John Stewart	Male	35	Black	29	Dec	1854	Bucktown	Dorchester	MD	V-2
Royan	William		Male	35				1857	Washington		DC	V-3
Russell	George		Male		Black			1858	Baltimore	Baltimore	MD	
Salter	Charles Henry		Male	30					Baltimore	Baltimore	MD	P-1
Saunders	Henry		Male			14	May	1856	Georget'n Crossroads	Kent	MD	
Saunders	Sarah		Female			4	July	1856	Norfolk	Norfolk	VA	D-6
Scott	—-					25	Nov	1853	Havana		MD	Y-1
Scott	—-					25	Nov	1853	Havana		MD	Y-1
Scott	Anna		Female				Dec	1855	Cecil Cross Roads		MD	I-3
Scott	Bill		Male	21				1857		Cecil	MD	P-4
Scott	Cornelius		Male	23	Mulatto		Mar	1857	Salvington	Stafford	VA	
Scott	Godfrey		Male			20	Nov	1855	Norfolk	Norfolk	VA	W-1
Scott	Hetty	Margaret Duncans	Female			25	Nov	1853	Havana		MD	Y-1
Scott	Jack		Male	36	Black	3	Nov	1857	Richmond	Henrico	VA	
Scott	Jane		Female	14	Black	3	June	1856	Hagarstown	Washington	MD	F-2
Scott	Jim		Male	19	Black			1857		Cecil	MD	P-4
Scott	John	Levis Duncans	Male	22		3	Oct	1853		Haverford	MD	
Scott	John		Male			17	Oct	1857	Cambridge	Dorchester	MD	I-1
Scott	Priscilla	Priscilla Duncans	Female			25	Nov	1853	Havana		MD	Y-1
Scott	Sam		Male	22				1857		Cecil	MD	P-4
Scott	Samuel		Male				Dec	1855	Cecil Cross Roads		MD	I-3

Child	Literate	Station Master/ Conductor	Armed	Violence	Transportation	Owner	$ Reward	$ Value	Source
						Eliza Hambleton			507
									Journal C
						Mrs. Roberts			563-566
		Captain "B"			Schooner	Robert Slater			60-65
						John G. Beal, Esq.			229-230
			X			Elijah J. Johnson			446-447
			X			Elijah J. Johnson			445-446
		Tubman-Garrett				Eliza Ann Brodins			306-307
						Dr. Anthony Thompson			411
						Rodgers			523
						Lewis N. Wright			Journal C
						Dr. Amthony Thompson			411
		Tubman-Garrett				Eliza Ann Brodins			307
					Foot	John Jay			94
		Tubman-Garrett				Eliza Ann Brodins			307-308
						Captain Cunningham			407
						Henry Harris			457
					Foot	Doctor B. Crain			132
									Journal C
		Captain "B"			Schooner	Richard Gatewood			589-590
X		Henry Franklin				Daniel Coolby			207-208
X		Henry Franklin				Daniel Coolby			207-208
						Mrs. Ann Elizabeth Lushy			347-348
						Hon. L. McLane			450
					Foot	Henry L. Brooke	500	114	
		Captain Alfred Fountain			Schooner			165	
		Henry Franklin				Daniel Coolby			207-208
					Foot	David B. Turner, Esq.	94		
					Horseback	George Shaffer		225	
						Hon. L. McLane			449
									Journal C
					Foot			92	
X						Daniel Coobly			207-208
						Hon. L. McLane			450
									347-348

L. Name	First / Middle	Alias	Gender	Age	Color	Day	Month	Year	City	County	State	Group
Scott	William		Male	24				1857	Stafford		MD	
Scott	Winfield		Male			4	July	1856	Norfolk	Norfolk	VA	D-6
Seymour	William		Male	34	Black	4	July	1856	Norfolk	Norfolk	VA	D-6
Shaw	Elijah		Male	23	Mulatto			1858	Baltimore	Baltimore	MD	
Shaw	Nace		Male	45	Black	11*	Sept	1858	Marlboro	Prince Georges	MD	B-5
Sheldon	James		Male			7	Sept	1857	Norfolk	Norfolk	VA	G-4
Shepherd	Andrew		Male	26			Nov	1856	South End	Camden	NC	P-3
Shepherd	Anna Maria		Female			8	Nov	1855	Chestertown	Kent	MD	P-6
Shepherd	Edwin		Male			8	Nov	1855	Chestertown	Kent	MD	P-6
Shepherd	Eliza Jane		Female			8	Nov	1855	Chestertown	Kent	MD	P-6
Shepherd	Harriet		Female			8	Nov	1855	Chestertown	Kent	MD	P-6
Shepherd	John Henry		Male			8	Nov	1855	Chestertown	Kent	MD	P-6
Shepherd	Mary Ann		Female			8	Nov	1855	Chestertown	Kent	MD	P-6
Shephard	Perry	Richard Reed	Male			28	July	1856	Eastern Shore		MD	D-3
Shidon	James		Male			10	Jan	1854	Georgetown		DC	
Sims	Samuel		Male	30	Black	20*	Sept	1856	Mount Airy	Carroll	MD	A-2
Sipple	Mary Ann		Female					1860	Kunkletown	Worcester	MD	A-6
Sipple	Thomas		Male					1860	Kunkletown	Worcester	MD	A-6
Skinner	Thomas Edward		Male	18	Mulatto	11*	Apr	1858	Baltimore	Baltimore	MD	X-4
Slater	Samuel	Patterson Smith	Male	30	Black	3	Apr	1854	Power Bridge		MD	
Slycum	Jesse		Male	24		16	May	1856		Dorchester	MD	
Smallwood	Henry		Male	36	Black			1859			MD	
Smallwood	John		Male			9	Feb	1857	Ellicott's Mills		MD	
Smith	Adam		Male	30	Black	22*	Aug	1857	Beltsville	Prince Georges	MD	F-4
Smith	Betsy	Fanny Jackson	Female	27	Black	18	Aug	1856	Alder	Loudon	VA	L-1
Smith	Daniel M.		Male		Mulatto	11*	Sept	1858	Alexandria	Fairfax	VA	B-5
Smith	Edward		Male	17				1858	Belleair		MD	W-4
Smith	Henry		Male	23	Black			1858	Belleair		MD	W-4
Smith	James		Male					1858	Belleair		MD	W-4
Smith	Jesse		Male	34		12	Dec	1854	Norfolk	Norfolk	VA	
Smith	Jeremiah		Male	26	Black	29	Jan	1854	Richmond	Henrico	VA	R-1
Smith	John		Male	19	Mulatto			1856	Marshall District	Harford	MD	
Smith	John		Male			20	Nov	1855	Norfolk	Norfolk	VA	W-1
Smith	John		Male	20	Black			1857	Hoopesville	Dorchester	MD	S-4
Smith	John Wesley		Male	26					Cambridge	Dorchester	MD	
Smith	Josephine		Female						Washington		DC	T-5
Smith	Julia		Female	30	Black	29	Jan	1854	Richmond	Henrico	VA	R-1

Child	Literate	Station Master/ Conductor	Armed	Violence	Transportation	Owner	$ Reward	$ Value	Source
					Foot	Susan Fox	200 in state / 500 out	1000	405-406
		Captain "B"			Schooner	William Taylor			585
		Captain "B"			Schooner	William Taylor			588-589
						Dr. Ephraim Bell			477-478
						Sarah Ann Talburtt	100 in/out state		501-502
	X					Mrs. Maria Hansford			432-433
		Fountain/Garrett			Schooner				396
X		Thomas Garrett			Horse & Carriage				311-313
X		Thomas Garrett			Horse & Carriage				311-313
X		Thomas Garrett			Horse & Carriage				311-313
		Thomas Garrett			Horse & Carriage				311-313
X		Thomas Garrett			Horse & Carriage				311-313
X		Thomas Garrett			Horse & Carriage				311-313
						Sarah Ann Burgess			329
						Thomas Young			Journal C
						Thomas B. Owings	500 in state		211-213
					Boat				552-554
					Boat				552-554
						George H. Carman	20 in state		477
	X					William Martin			231-232
									Journal C
						Washington Bonafont			528
						Samuel Simons			542
						Isaac Scaggs	50 in state / 100 out		431
		Frank Wanzer	X		Foot	Widow Hutchinson's daughter			121-122
						James Garnett			502
						Robert Hollan			473-474
						Robert Hollan			473-474
	X					Robert Hollan			473-474
						Cornelius Herman			Journal C
					Steamer	James Kinard			134-136
						Dr. Abraham Street			541
		Captain Alfred Fountain			Schooner				165
						George Morgan			457
						Daniel Hubert			531
						Anna Maria Warren			532
					Steamer	A. Judson Crane			134-136

L. Name	First / Middle	Alias	Gender	Age	Color	Day	Month	Year	City	County	State	Group
Smith	Julius		Male	25	Black			1858	Belleair		MD	W-4
Smith	Mary		Female					1858	Belleair		MD	W-4
Smith	Nathaniel	John Hutchins	Male	24		15	Nov	1854	Baltimore	Baltimore	MD	
Smith	Page		Female	9		10	May	1854	Wilmington	New Castle	DE	L-6
Smith	Robert		Male	24		31	May	1856	Baltimore	Baltimore	MD	E-2
Smith	Samuel		Male			4	July	1859	Eastern Shore		MD	K-5
Smith	Sarah	Mildred Page	Female	30	Black	10	May	1854	Wilmington	New Castle	DE	L-6
Smith	Stafford		Male					1860		Westmoreland	VA	
Smith	Thomas		Male			22*	Aug	1857	Washington	DC	DC	F-4
Smith	Vincent	John Jackson	Male	23	Black	18	Aug	1856	Alder	Loudon	VA	L-1
Smith	William Israel		Male	21		4	Aug	1856	Middletown	New Castle	DE	F-3
Snively	David		Male	26	Black			1860	Frederick	Frederick	MD	
Snowden	Lewis	Lewis Williams	Male	28		20	June	1854	Washington		DC	
Solomon	George		Male	33	Mulatto		Sept	1856	Washington	DC	DC	G-1
Somlor	Washington	James Moore	Male	32				1855	Norfolk	Norfolk	VA	
Sparks	John		Male			22*	Feb	1857	Eastern Shore		MD	F-7
Spence	Arthur		Male	24		23	Mar	1856			NC	H-3
Spencer	John		Male					1853	Eastern Shore		MD	X-1
Spencer	William		Male					1853	Eastern Shore		MD	X-1
Sperryman	George	Thomas Johnson	Male			28	July	1856	Richmond	Henrico	VA	E-3
Spires	Valentine	Jonathan Wesley	Male			28	July	1856	Petersburg	Norfolk	VA	E-3
Stanly	——		Female			17	Oct	1857	Cambridge	Dorchester	MD	I-1
Stanly	Caroline		Female			17	Oct	1857	Cambridge	Dorchester	MD	I-1
Stanly	Daniel		Male	35		17	Oct	1857	Cambridge	Dorchester	MD	I-1
Stanly	Daniel, Jr.		Male			17	Oct	1857	Cambridge	Dorchester	MD	I-1
Stanly	John		Male			17	Oct	1857	Cambridge	Dorchester	MD	I-1
Stanly	Josiah		Male			17	Oct	1857	Cambridge	Dorchester	MD	I-1
Stanly	Miller		Male			17	Oct	1857	Cambridge	Dorchester	MD	I-1
Stanton	Philip		Male	22							MD	O-7
Stephenson	Mary		Female	20	Black			1857		Caroline	MD	S-1
Stewart	Harriet		Female	29	Black			1857	Washington		DC	I-4
Stewart	Henry		Male	23		19	June	1855	Plymouth	Washington	NC	L-2
Stewart	James	William Jackson	Male	21		26	Apr	1854		Fauquer	VA	
Stewart	Mary Eliza		Female	8				1857	Washington		DC	I-4
Stewart	Robert	Gasberry Robinson	Male	30	Black	18	Aug	1856	Alder	Loudon	VA	L-1
Stewart	Susan		Female		Black				Washington		DC	T-5
Stinger	John		Male	40	Mulatto	24	Oct	1857	Portsmouth	Norfolk	VA	Q-7
Swan	Stebney		Male	34	Mulatto	24	Oct	1857	Portsmouth	Norfolk	VA	Q-7
Tatum	Alan		Male	30	Black	20	Nov	1855	Norfolk	Norfolk	VA	W-1

Child	Literate	Station Master/Conductor	Armed	Violence	Transportation	Owner	$ Reward	$ Value	Source
						Robert Hollan			473-474
						Robert Hollan			473-474
									Journal C
	X					Rev. A.D. Pollock			Journal C
					Railroad	William H. Normis			221
						Aquila Cain			521-522
						Rev. A.D. Pollock			235-236
						Harriet Parker			544
						William Rowe	100 in state		430-431
		Frank Wanzer	X		Foot	Nathan Skinner			121-122
						John P. Cather			330
						Charles Preston			551
		James Massey				A. Nayton			Journal C
					Foot	Daniel Minor			65-67
			X	X	Steamer	Smith			313-314
		English sailors			Foot & Boat	Mary Gibson & others			122-124
		Captain Alfred Fountain			Schooner				343
					Foot				207
					Foot				207
						Nicholas Templeman			329
						Dr. Jesse Squires			329-330
					Foot	Samuel Count			92
X					Foot	Samuel Count			92
					Foot	Robert Calender			92
X					Foot	Robert Calender			92
X					Foot	Samuel Count			92
X					Foot	Samuel Count			92
X					Foot	Samuel Count			92
						John Smith			547
								1100	139-140
					Foot	William A. Linton			435
						James Monroe Woodhouse			268
						William Rose			233-234
X					Foot	William A. Linton			435-436
		Frank Wanzer	X		Foot	Widow Hutchinson			121
						Henry Harley			531-532
		Captain Robert Lee			Skiff	Joseph Carter			86-87
		Captain Robert Lee	X		Skiff	Joseph Carter			85-86
		Captain Alfred Fountain			Schooner	Lovey White			165

L. Name	First / Middle	Alias	Gender	Age	Color	Day	Month	Year	City	County	State	Group
Taylor	——		Female				Mar	1856	Haggerstown	Washington	MD	G-3
Taylor	——		Female				Mar	1856	Haggerstown	Washington	MD	G-3
Taylor	——		Female				Mar	1856	Haggerstown	Washington	MD	G-3
Taylor	Benjamin		Male	20				1858	Alexandria	Fairfax	VA	A-5
Taylor	Benjamin		Male				Mar	1856	Haggerstown	Washington	MD	G-3
Taylor	Caroline		Female		Mulatto	23	Mar	1856	Norfolk	Norfolk	VA	H-3
Taylor	Edward		Male				Mar	1856	Haggerstown	Washington	MD	G-3
Taylor	Harriet		Female			4	July	1856	Norfolk	Norfolk	VA	D-6
Taylor	Jacob		Male	20	Black	11*	Apr	1858	Baltimore	Baltimore	MD	X-4
Taylor	James		Male	20	Mulatto			1859	Fredericksburg	Spotsylvania	VA	O-5
Taylor	Mary		Female	9		23	Mar	1856	Norfolk	Norfolk	VA	H-3
Taylor	Mary Ann		Female				Mar	1856	Haggerstown	Washington	MD	G-3
Taylor	Nancy		Female	11		23	Mar	1856	Norfolk	Norfolk	VA	H-3
Taylor	Otho		Male				Mar	1856	Haggerstown	Washington	MD	G-3
Taylor	Owen		Male	31			Mar	1856	Haggerstown	Washington	MD	G-3
Taylor	Roberta		Female	23	Mulatto			1858	Baltimore	Baltimore	MD	
Taylor	Stephen		Male	20					Sandy Hook	Harford	MD	Q-1
Taylor	William N.		Male	35	Black	2*	June	1857	Hanover	Hanover	VA	
Teamour	Thomas		Male			20	Nov	1855	Norfolk	Norfolk	VA	W-1
Thomas	Alice		Female			26	Mar	1853		Frederick	MD	
Thomas	Joseph		Male							Prince Georges	MD	
Thomas	William		Male			22	June	1855	Norfolk	Norfolk	VA	M-2
Thompson	——					22	July	1853	Baltimore	Baltimore	MD	H-6
Thompson	Charity		Female	12			July	1856	Portsmouth	Norfolk	VA	C-3
Thompson	Charles		Male	40		21	Oct	1854	Richmond	Henrico	VA	
Thompson	Charles		Male	25	Black			1857	Richmond	Henrico	MD	
Thompson	Charles		Male				July	1856	Portsmouth	Norfolk	VA	C-3
Thompson	Elizabeth		Female			22	July	1853	Baltimore	Baltimore	MD	H-6
Thompson	Hannah Jane		Female			12	Dec	1853		Sussex	DE	
Thompson	James Henry	Milton Brown	Male	28	Black			1858	Johnsonville		MD	
Thompson	John		Male	19	Mulatto			1857	Huntsville	Madison	AL	
Thompson	Robert		Male	39				1858	Hightstown			
Thompson	William		Male			29	Dec	1854	Horses Crossroads		DE	
Thompson	William Henry		Male	24	Black	14	May	1856	Norfolk	Norfolk	VA	U-3
Thornton	Alfred S.		Male	22	Black			1858			VA	
Thornton	Lawrence		Male	23	Black			1857	Alexandria	Fairfax	VA	O-4
Tilison	Abram		Male					1857	Georget'n Crossroads	Kent	MD	D-4

Child	Literate	Station Master/ Conductor	Armed	Violence	Transportation	Owner	$ Reward	$ Value	Source
					Horse & Carriage				331-335
X					Horse & Carriage				331-335
X					Horse & Carriage				331-335
			X			Meed			500
					Horse & Carriage	Henry Fiery			331-335
		Captain Alfred Fountain			Schooner	Peter March, Esq.	250		339-340
X					Horse & Carriage				331-335
		Captain "B"			Schooner				585
						William J.B. Parlett	50 in state / 200 out		476
						George Ailer			526
X		Captain Alfred Fountain			Schooner	Peter March Esq.			Journal C
					Horse & Carriage				331-335
X		Captain Alfred Fountain			Schooner	Peter March Esq.			Journal C
					Horse & Carriage	Henry Fiery			331-335
					Horse & Carriage	Henry Fiery		500	331-335
	X					Mr. & Mrs. McCoy			469-470
					Foot	James Smithen			132-133
					Foot	Walter H. Tyler	100 in state		127-128
		Captain Alfred Fountain			Schooner				Journal C
						James Short			Journal C
									533
		Captain "B"			Schooner				270
	X								Journal C
		Captain Alfred Fountain			Schooner				325-329
						Widow Thornton			Journal C
					Foot	Fleming Bibbs			140-144
		Captain Alfred Fountain			Schooner				325-329
									Journal C
		Jacob Parsons							Journal C
						Dennis Mannard			457-458
	x				Railroad	Hezekiah Thompson			95-97
						John R. Laten			470-471
						Lewis N. Wright			Journal C
		Tubman/Garrett							402
						C.E Shinn			471-473
						Dr. Isaac Winslow			448
						Samuel Jarman			427

L. Name	First / Middle	Alias	Gender	Age	Color	Day	Month	Year	City	County	State	Group
Todd	——		Female					1857	Unionville	Frederick	MD	K-7
Todd	Isaac		Male	23	Mulatto			1857	Unionville	Frederick	MD	K-7
Tonnell	——		Male	7			Dec	1853	Georgetown	Sussex	DE	K-6
Tonnell	Rose Anna	Maria Hide	Female				Dec	1853	Georgetown	Sussex	DE	K-6
Townsend	Henry		Male	21	Black	17	Feb	1857	Purnell P.O. Box	Caroline	MD	
Triplett	William		Male	23	Black			1857	Alexandria	Fairfax	VA	E-4
Trusty	Perry Henry		Male	31	Black			1857		Caroline		S-1
Tubman	Harriet		Female			13	May	1856			MD	V-6
Tucker	Henry		Male		Black			1858	Arabella Creek Place	Baltimore	MD	
Tudle	Henry		Male					1860	Fredricksburg	Spotsylvania	VA	X-5
Turner	Edmundson		Male	25	Black		Dec	1857	Petersburg	Dinwiddie	VA	J-1
Turner	Isaac		Male	28	Black		Dec	1857	Petersburg	Dinwiddie	VA	J-1
Turner	Jackson		Male	27	Black		May	1857	Petersburg	Dinwiddie	VA	
Turner	Samuel		Male					1857				M-4
Unidentified			Male	17		16	Aug	1853	Eastern Shore		MD	
Unidentified			Male			6	Jan	1853			MD	
Unidentified			Male			6	Jan	1853			MD	
Unidentified			Male			25	Nov	1853	Havana		MD	Y-1
Unidentified			Female			25	Nov	1853	Havana		MD	Y-1
Unidentified			Female			14	Aug	1854			DE	
Unidentified			Female			24	Aug	1854	Baltimore	Baltimore	MD	
Unidentified			Female			3	Mar	1854	Georgetown	Sussex	DE	
Unidentified			Male			3	Mar	1854	Georgetown	Sussex	DE	
Unidentified			Male	7		1*	Dec	1854	Richmond	Henrico	VA	J-6
Unidentified			Male			10	Dec	1855	Chestertown	Kent	MD	Q-6
Unidentified			Male			10	Dec	1855	Chestertown	Kent	MD	Q-6
Unidentified			Male			1	Nov	1855				G-6
Unidentified			Male			1	Nov	1855				G-6
Unidentified			Female			1	Nov	1855				G-6
Unidentified			Female			1	Nov	1855				G-6
Unidentified			Female			1	Nov	1855				G-6
Unidentified			Male			13	May	1856			MD	V-6
Unidentified			Male			13	May	1856			MD	V-6
Unidentified			Male			13	May	1856			MD	V-6
Unidentified			Male			13	May	1856			MD	V-6
Unidentified			Female			31	May	1856	Leesburg	Loudon	VA	D-2
Unidentified			Female	10		31	May	1856	Leesburg	Loudon	VA	D-2

Child	Literate	Station Master/ Conductor	Armed	Violence	Transportation	Owner	$ Reward	$ Value	Source
						Thornton Pool			407
						Dr. Greenberry Sappington		1500	407
X						Isaac Tom			210
						Isaac Tom			210
						E. Townsend			543
						Mrs. A.B. Fairfax	50 in state / 150 out		427-428
	X				Foot	James Pittman		1200	138
		Mrs. Buchannan							Journal C
						Elias Sneveley			482
						Ezra Houpt			549
	X				Foot	Ann Coley			109-111
					Foot	Ann Coley			107-109
					Foot	Ann Coley	25 in state / 50 out		107-108
									447
									Journal C
		A.D. Shadd; Sam'l Williams							Journal C
		A.D. Shadd; Sam'l Williams							Journal C
		Henry Franklin				Daniel Coolby			207-208
		Henry Franklin				Daniel Coolby			207-208
						Rebecca Johnson			Journal C
									Journal C
						Isaac Tom			Journal C
						Issac Tom			Journal C
X					Steamer				203
		Thomas Garrett			Horse & Wagon				353
		Thomas Garrett			Horse & Wagon				353
									311-314
									311-314
									311-314
									31`-314
									313-314
		Mrs. Buchannan							Journal C
		Mrs. Buchannan							Journal C
		Mrs. Buchannan							Journal C
		Mrs. Buchannan							Journal C
					Horse & Carriage				219-221
X					Horse & Carriage				219-221

L. Name	First / Middle	Alias	Gender	Age	Color	Day	Month	Year	City	County	State	Group
Unidentified							April	1856			MD	J-7
Unidentified							April	1856			MD	J-7
Unidentified							April	1856			MD	J-7
Unidentified							April	1856			MD	J-7
Unidentified								1857				W-6
Unidentified								1857				W-6
Unidentified								1857				W-6
Unidentified			Male		Black			1858		Kent	DE	M-7
Unidentified								1859	Washington		DC	E-7
Unidentified				2				1859	Washington		DC	E-7
Unidentified								1860		Frederick	MD	N-7
Unidentified								1860		Frederick	MD	N-7
Unidentified								1860		Frederick	MD	N-7
Unidentified								1860		Frederick	MD	N-7
Upsher	George		Male			7*	Nov	1857	Richmond	Henrico	VA	K-4
Vaughn	Michael	William Brown	Male	31	Black	20	Nov	1855	Norfolk	Norfolk	VA	W-1
Viney	——		Male	9 mos.		24	Oct	1857	Cambridge	Dorchester	MD	H-1
Viney	——		Male	8		24	Oct	1857	Cambridge	Dorchester	MD	H-1
Viney	——		Male			24	Oct	1857	Cambridge	Dorchester	MD	H-1
Viney	——		Female			24	Oct	1857	Cambridge	Dorchester	MD	H-1
Viney	Joseph		Male	40	Black	24	Oct	1857	Alexandria	Fairfax	VA	
Viney	Susan		Female	35	Black	24	Oct	1857	Cambridge	Dorchester	MD	H-1
Walker	——		Female	38		4	July	1856	Norfolk	Norfolk	VA	D-6
Walker	George	Austin Valentine	Male	43		18	Jan	1855	Petersburg	Dinwiddie	VA	B-3
Walker	John		Male	25		13	Sept	1853	Clarksville		VA	
Walters	Mary		Female	18		26	July	1854			MD	
Wanzer	Frank	Robert Scott	Male	25	Mulatto	24	Dec	1855	Alder	Loudon	VA	K-1
Waples	Hansel		Male			30	Dec	1853	Hillsboro, Indian R.		DE	
Washington	George		Male	15	Black			1857	Perryville	Caroline	MD	S-1
Washington	George	James Williams	Male	19		5	Dec	1854	Bellair	Harford	MD	
Washington	George Nelson		Male	19				1858		Queen Annes	MD	T-4
Washington	Henry	Anthony Hanley	Male	50		19	June	1855	Norfolk	Norfolk	VA	L-2
Washington	Mark	William Wilson	Male	27		2	Sept	1854	Hall's Crossroads		MD	
Washington	Samuel	James Moore	Male	32		27	Feb	1855	Norfolk	Norfolk	VA	
Washington	William Henry		Male	20					Baltimore	Baltimore	MD	P-1
Waters	Jacob		Male	21	Black				Frederick	Frederick	MD	M-1
Waters	John		Male	40	Black			1859	Tapps' Neck		MD	U-5
Watson	James Henry		Male	20	Black	11	Apr	1856	Snowhill	Worcester	MD	

Child	Literate	Station Master/ Conductor	Armed	Violence	Transportation	Owner	$ Reward	$ Value	Source
		Harriet Tubman							401
		Harriet Tubman							401
		Harriet Tubman							401
		Harriet Tubman							401
						William H. Hyson			404
						William H. Hyson			404
						William H. Hyson			404
						Denny			491
X									527
X									527
									543
									543
									543
									543
	X	Fountain/Garrett				Dr. Thomas W. Upsher	100 in state		444-445
	X	Captain Alfred Fountain			Schooner				166-167
X					Foot				90
X					Foot				90
X					Foot				90
X					Foot				90
					Foot	Charles Bryant			89-92
					Foot	Samuel Pattison			90
		Captain "B"			Schooner				588-589
					Steamer	Eliza Jones			321-322
						Mr. Easley			Journal C
									Journal C
			X	X	Horse & Carriage	Luther Sullivan			116-122
						William E. Burton			209
					Foot	Benjmin Sylves			139
						William Fernandus			Journal C
						Joshua Duvall			459
						Seth March			266-267
						James Worthington			Journal C
						Benjamin Smith			Journal C
					Foot	Doctor B. Crain			132
					Foot	William Dorsey			128
						H. Lynch			534
						James Purnell			399

L. Name	First / Middle	Alias	Gender	Age	Color	Day	Month	Year	City	County	State	Group
Weems	——			1			July	1857	Washington		DC	G-7
Weems	Arrah		Female				July	1857	Washington		DC	G-7
Weems	John	Jack Herring	Male					1858			DE	
Weems	Maria	Joe Wright/ Ellen Capron	Female	15	Black	25	Nov	1855	Washington		DC	
Wellington	Jane	Jane Johnson	Female			12	June	1856	Hagarstown		MD	
Wells	Jack		Male		Black			1857		Cecil	MD	P-4
Wheeler	Henry		Male	21				1859	Havre de Grace	Harford	MD	I-5
White	Albert		Male					1860		Cecil	MD	Z-5
White	Emanuel T.		Male	25	Mulatto			1857	Norfolk	Norfolk	VA	
White	George		Male					1860		Cecil	MD	Z-5
White	Isaac		Male	22	Black		Jan	1858	Lewes	Sussex	DE	C-5
White	Miles		Male	21		12	June	1854	Elizabeth City	Pasquotan	NC	
White	Robert		Male	35		25	Sept	1854	Norfork	Norfolk	VA	
White	Tucker		Male				Dec	1854	Dinwiddie	Dinwiddie	VA	
White	William B.		Male	36	Black	23	Apr	1854	Richmond	Henrico	VA	B-2
White Lady	——		Female						Leesburg	Loudon	VA	D-2
Whiting	Ralph		Male	26	Black		June	1855	Norfolk	Norfolk	VA	O-2
Whitney	Israel		Male	36			Oct	1857	Alexandria	Fairfax	VA	
Wiggins	Daniel	Daniel Robinson	Male	29		16	Mar	1854	Norfolk	Norfolk	VA	
Wilkins	Charles		Male	3				1859	Cecil	Cecil	MD	P-5
Wilkins	James Andy		Male					1859	Cecil	Cecil	MD	P-5
Wilkins	Lucinda		Female	21	Black			1859	Cecil	Cecil	MD	P-5
Wilkinson	Horatio		Male	44	Mulatto	2	Feb	1858				V-4
William	Mary		Female					1860	Fredericksburg	Spotsylvania	VA	X-5
Williams	——		Female			30	Apr	1856	Haven Manor		MD	T-3
Williams	Edward	Henry Johnson	Male			3	Apr	1853	Baltimore	Baltimore	MD	N-1
Williams	Elizabeth		Female	20	Black			1857	Wrightstown	Baltimore	MD	
Williams	George		Male			31	Aug	1855	St. Louis		MO	U-2
Williams	Hanson		Male	40	Black	11*	Sept	1858	Washington		DC	B-5
Williams	Henderson		Male	32		4	July	1856	Norfolk	Norfolk	VA	D-6
Williams	Isaac		Male	26		21	Dec	1854	Hampsted	King Georges	VA	R-2
Williams	John		Male	25		6	Oct	1855			MD	
Williams	Richard		Male					1859	Richmond	Henrico	VA	
Williams	Samuel	John Williams	Male	32	Black		Mar	1857	Cumberland	Alleganey	MD	
Williams	Wesley		Male			3	Jan	1857	Warrick		MD	
Williams	William		Male			30	Apr	1856	Haven Manor		MD	T-3
Williamson	William		Male	24				1858	Perrymanville		MD	U-4
Wilmer	George		Male			5	Sept	1856	Georget'n Crossroads	Kent	MD	

Child	Literate	Station Master/ Conductor	Armed	Violence	Transportation	Owner	$ Reward	$ Value	Source
X									150-152
		E.L. Stevens							150-152
						Kendall B. Herring			491-492
X		Dr. H			Carriage	Charles M. Price	500 in state		174-188
						David Beiller			Journal C
						William Knight			452
						Amos Barnes			514
						William Parker			550
	X				Steamer	Edward H. Hubert			149
						William Parker			550
					Skiff	Thomas Carper			504
					Boat	Albert Kern	1500 in state		238
						Henry Handy			Journal C
						Major Isaac Rooney			580-583
					Steamer	H.B. Dickinson			213-214
						James Hodges			Journal C
						Geo. W. Kemp, Esq.			Journal C
					Foot	Elijah Money			Journal C
	X					Richard Scott			Journal C
X						George Ford			526-527
						George Biddle			526-527
						George Ford			526-527
						Thomas J. Hodgson			465
						Christian Thomas			549
						John Peak			400-401
					Foot	Charles Moondo			129
						Samuel Ward			447
						Isaac Hill			301-302
						Levi Pumphrey	100 in state		501
		Captain "B"			Schooner	A. Briggs		1200	588
					Foot	D. Fitchhugh			292-294
									Journal C
						John A. Smith			514
					Foot	Elvina Duncans			114-115
						Jack Jones			541
						John Peak			400-401
						Rebecca Davidge			459
						Eben Welch			Journal C

L. Name	First / Middle	Alias	Gender	Age	Color	Day	Month	Year	City	County	State	Group
Wilson	Franklin		Male	18		24	Oct	1855			DE	
Wilson	Lewis		Male	50				1859	Tapps' Neck		MD	U-5
Wilson	Ned		Male			20	Nov	1855	Norfolk	Norfolk	VA	W-1
Wilson	Perry	Henry Wilson	Male	22		10	Oct	1854	Baltimore	Baltimore	MD	
Wilson	Sarah E.		Female			20	Nov	1855	Norfolk	Norfolk	VA	W-1
Wilson	Thomas		Male			8	Feb	1853			MD	
Wilson	William		Male	42			Nov	1856			NC	P-3
Wilson	Willis		Male			20	Nov	1855	Norfolk	Norfolk	VA	W-1
Wines	Moses		Male		Black	6	May	1854	Portsmouth	Norfolk	VA	
Winston	Joe		Male	23	Black	6	June	1857	Richmond	Henrico	VA	H-6
Wise	Harry		Male	24	Black		Aug	1857		Harford	MD	
Wood	Edward		Male					1859	Drummerstown	Accomac	VA	
Wood	John		Male	28				1857	Unionville		MD	B-4
Wood	Mose		Male					1857	Georgetown		DC	Y-4
Wooden	William	William Nelson	Male	23	Black	21	May	1854	Georgetown	Sussex	DE	
Wooders	Abram		Male	35	Black			1857	Norfolk	Norfolk	VA	
Woolfley	Lavina		Female					1857	Cambridge	Dorchester	MD	V-1
Wright	Elizabeth		Female	32				1857	Laurel	Sussex	MD	Z-3
Wright	John		Male	30	Black			1857		Sussex	MD	Z-3
Wright Crossroads	Leeds		Male					1857	Georget'n Crossroads	Kent	MD	D-4
Young	Anna Elizabeth		Female	24	Black					Kent	MD	S-5
Young	Gusta		Male	21	Black	11*	Sept	1858	Washington		DC	B-5
Young	Murray		Male	21	Black					New Castle	DE	
Young	Sarah Catharine		Female	19 mos						Kent	MD	S-5

Child	Literate	Station Master/Conductor	Armed	Violence	Transportation	Owner	$ Reward	$ Value	Source
						Dr. William Daniels			Journal C
						H. Lynch			534
		Captain Alfred Fountain			Schooner				165
						John Talbot			Journal C
		Captain Alfred Fountain			Schooner				165
									Journal C
		Fountain/Garrett			Schooner	Dr. Thomas Warren			395
		Captain Alfred Fountain			Schooner				165
					Steamer	Abigail Wheeler			234-235
					Steamer	Samuel Ellis	200 in state / 500 out	1500	404-405
						Elliott Burwell	50 in state / 100 out		428-429
						James White			523
	X					Judge Birch			418-419
						General Briscoe			486-487
						Judge Wooden			236-237
						Taylor Sewell	50 in state	429	
					Foot				160-161
						Jane Cooper			412-413
						William S. Phillips			412-413
						Rev. John Wesley Pearson			426-427
						Massey			529-530
			X			Levi Pumphrey	100 in state		501
						Dr. Lober			493-494
X						Massey			530

ABBREVIATIONS

CBAAC Charles L. Blockson Afro-American Collection, Temple University Libraries, Philadelphia

CCA Chester County Archives, Chester County Historical Society, West Chester, PA

HCL Haverford College Library, Haverford, PA

HSP Historical Society of Pennsylvania, Philadelphia

LCP Library Company of Philadelphia

PYM Philadelphia Yearly Meeting

PYMPF Pennsylvania Yearly Meeting of Progressive Friends

QC Quaker Collection

WSC William Still Collection

WSP William Still Papers

NOTES

INTRODUCTION

1. William Still, *The Underground Railroad: A Record of Facts, Authentic Narratives, Letters, Etc.* (1872; repr., Chicago: Johnson, 1970), 1–2, 18–19. The complete story of Peter Freedman Still was first published in Kate E. R. Pickard, *The Kidnapped and the Ransomed: Being the Personal Recollections of Peter Still and His Wife "Vina," after Forty Years of Slavery* (Syracuse, NY: William T. Hamilton, 1856). Peter took the surname "Freedman" after Joseph Freedman, a Jewish friend who was entrusted with his earnings until he raised the $500 needed to purchase his freedom.

2. William Still to J. Miller McKim, *Pennsylvanian Freeman*, August 8, 1850.

3. Pickard, *Kidnapped and the Ransomed*, v; Fergus M. Bordewich, *Bound for Canaan: The Underground Railroad and the War for the Soul of America* (New York: Amistad, 2005), 357.

4. Benjamin Quarles, "Foreword to the 1970 Edition," in W. Still, *Underground Railroad* (1872/1970), vi.

5. According to Pennsylvania's Gradual Abolition Act of 1780, children of slaves born after November 1780 were to be freed upon their twenty-eighth birthday. Although these children were held in bondage for twenty-eight years, they were considered "servants." See "An Act for the Gradual Abolition of Slavery," transcription, CCA; and Gary B. Nash and Jean R. Soderlund, *Freedom by Degrees: Emancipation in Pennsylvania and Its Aftermath* (New York: Oxford University Press, 1991), 119.

6. Stanley W. Campbell, *The Slave Catchers: Enforcement of the Fugitive Slave Law, 1850–1860* (1968; repr., Chapel Hill: University of North Carolina Press, 1970). For text of the 1850 Fugitive Slave Act, see "The Fugitive Slave Bill of 1850: An Act Respecting Fugitives from Justice, and Persons Escaping from the Service of Their Masters," in W. Still, *Underground Railroad* (1872/1970), 355–60.

7.   John Hope Franklin and Evelyn Brooks Higginbotham, *From Slavery to Freedom: A History of Negro Americans*, 9th ed. (New York: McGraw-Hill, 2011), 199–203. *Agent* was a more generic term, referring to anyone who worked on the Underground Railroad.

8.   Quarles, "Foreword to the 1970 Edition," vi–vii.

9.   Benjamin Quarles, *Black Abolitionists* (New York: Oxford University Press, 1969), 154–55; Gary B. Nash, *Forging Freedom: The Formation of Philadelphia's Black Community, 1720–1840* (Cambridge, MA: Harvard University Press, 1988), 265–67. The predecessor of the Pennsylvania Anti-Slavery Society's General Vigilance Committee was the Vigilant Committee of Philadelphia, founded by the Vigilant Association of Philadelphia in 1837. Though it was interracial in membership, only two of the thirteen members of the standing committee were African American: Robert Purvis, the president; and Jacob C. White. After 1839, the white members stopped attending the monthly meetings of the committee and it became an exclusively black operation. Between 1839 and 1844, when the organization disbanded, the Vigilant Committee of Philadelphia assisted some three hundred fugitives each year. See Joseph A. Boromé, "The Vigilant Committee of Philadelphia," *Pennsylvania Magazine of History and Biography* 92 (July 1968): 320–51.

10.   James Oliver Horton and Lois E. Horton, *In Hope of Liberty: Culture, Community and Protest among Northern Free Blacks, 1700–1860* (New York: Oxford University Press, 1997), 230.

11.   Quarles, *Black Abolitionists*, 156.

12.   "William Still Dead," *New York Times*, July 15, 1902.

13.   See Eber Pettit, *Sketches in the History of the Underground Railroad* (1867; repr., Westfield, NY: Chautauqua Regional Press, 1999); Levi Coffin, *Reminiscences* (Cincinnati, OH: Western Tract Society, 1876); R. C. Smedley, *History of the Underground Railroad in Chester and Neighboring Counties* (1883; repr., Mechanicsburg, PA: Stackpole Books, 2005); Wilbur H. Siebert, *The Underground Railroad from Slavery to Freedom* (1898; repr., New York: Dover Publications, 2006); and William Cockrum, *History of the Underground Railroad as It Was Conducted by the Anti-Slavery League* (Oakland City, IN: J. W. Cockrum Printing, 1915). Two other books, published in the twentieth century, propagated the mythology of these earlier accounts: Henrietta Buckmaster, *Let My People Go: The Story of the Underground Railroad and the Growth of the Abolition Movement.* (New York: Harper and Brothers, 1941); and William A. Breyfogle, *Make Free: The Story of the Underground Railroad* (Philadelphia: J. B. Lippincott, 1958). Despite the historical inaccuracy of these works, some historians consider them useful. David Brion Davis, for example, argues that the "romanticizing" of the Underground Railroad recognizes the "humanity of the slaves and the dehumanizing effects permanently confining people in times and spaces chosen by white masters." See David Brion Davis, *The Problem of Slavery in the Age of Emancipation* (New York: Alfred A. Knopf, 2014), 232. Similarly, David Blight insists on the need to respect local lore and mythology as a way of understanding the "extraordinary hold of the Underground Railroad on Americans' historical imagi-

nation." See David Blight, "Why the Underground Railroad, and Why Now? A Long View," in *Passages to Freedom: The Underground Railroad in History and Memory*, ed. David W. Blight (Washington, DC: Smithsonian Books, 2004), 217.

14.   Some folklorists believe that quilt codes, done in geometric patterns and distinctive stitches, were used to aid slaves in memorizing certain directives before their escape. Specific names, which functioned as metaphors in the code, were assigned to various quilt patterns. If a "Monkey Wrench" quilt pattern was being displayed, for example, slaves knew that they were to gather all the "tools" they would need on an impending escape to the North. A "Wagon Wheel" pattern signified the method of transportation they would take. If a "Tumbling Bear" pattern appeared, slaves knew that the moment of escape had arrived. See Jacqueline L. Tobin and Raymond G. Dobard, *Hidden in Plain View: A Secret Story of Quilts and the Underground Railroad* (New York: Anchor, 2000), 69–71. For other works on quilt codes, see Roland L. Freeman, *A Communion of the Spirits: African-American Quilters, Preservers and Their Stories* (Nashville, TN: Rutledge Hill, 1996); and Glady-Marie Fry, *Stitched from the Soul: Slave Quilts from the Antebellum South* (New York: Dutton, 1990).

15.   For works on escape songs and spirituals, see Harold Courlander, *Negro Folk Music, U.S.A.* (1963; repr., New York: Dover, 1992); Miles M. Fisher, *Negro Slave Songs in the United States* (New York: Citadel, 1968); and Samuel A. Floyd Jr., *The Power of Black Music* (New York: Oxford University Press, 1995).

16.   For works on oral tradition and African American culture, see Linda Goss and Clay Goss, *Jump Up and Say: A Collection of Black Storytelling* (New York: Simon and Schuster, 1995); Virginia Hamilton, *The People Could Fly: American Black Folktales* (New York: Alfred Knopf, 1985); and Nancy Roan and Donald Roan, *Lest I Shall Be Forgotten: Anecdotes and Traditions of Quilts* (Green Lane, PA: Goschenhoppen Historians, 1993).

17.   See Larry Gara's *The Liberty Line: The Legend of the Underground Railroad* (Lexington: University of Kentucky Press, 1961), vii, 92–95.

18.   See Horatio T. Strother, *The Underground Railroad in Connecticut* (Middletown, CT: Wesleyan University Press, 1962).

19.   See Quarles, *Black Abolitionists*, 143–67.

20.   See James A. McGowan, *Station Master on the Underground Railroad: The Life and Letters of Thomas Garrett* (1977; repr., Jefferson, NC: McFarland, 2005).

21.   See Charles L. Blockson, *The Underground Railroad in Pennsylvania* (Jacksonville, NC: Flame International, 1981), "Escape from Slavery," *National Geographic*, July 1984, 3–39, *The Underground Railroad: Dramatic Firsthand Accounts of Daring Escapes to Freedom* (New York: Prentice Hall, 1987), and *Hippocrene Guide to the Underground Railroad* (New York: Hippocrene, 1994).

22.   See James Oliver Horton, *Free People of Color: Inside the African American Community* (Washington, DC: Smithsonian Institution Press, 1993); Horton and Horton, *In Hope of Liberty*, 231; and James Oliver Horton and Lois Horton, *Black Bostonians: Family Life and Community Struggle in the Antebellum North*, rev. ed. (New York: Homes and Meier, 1999).

23. See Thomas P. Slaughter, *Bloody Dawn: The Christiana Riot and Racial Violence in the Antebellum North* (New York: Oxford University Press, 1991); James F. Caccamo, *Hudson, Ohio, and the Underground Railroad* (Hudson, OH: Friends of the Hudson Library, 1992); Daniel G. Hill, *The Freedom Seekers: Blacks in Early Canada* (Toronto: Stoddart, 1992); Carole C. Marks, ed., *A History of African Americans of Delaware and Maryland's Eastern Shore* (Wilmington: Delaware Heritage Commission, 1998); Raymond P. Zirblis, *Friends of Freedom: The Vermont Underground Railroad Survey Report* (Montpelier: State of Vermont Department of State Buildings and Division for Historic Preservation, 1996); Ella Forbes, *But We Have No Country: The 1851 Christiana Resistance* (Cherry Hill, NJ: Africana Homestead Legacy, 1998); Matthew Pinsker, *Vigilance in Pennsylvania: Underground Railroad Activities in the Keystone State, 1837–1861* (Harrisburg: Pennsylvania Historical and Museum Commission, 2000); Carol Pirtle, *Escape betwixt Two Suns: A True Tale of the Underground Railroad in Illinois* (Carbondale: Southern Illinois University Press, 2000); Maxine F. Brown, *The Role of Free Blacks in Indiana's Underground Railroad: The Case of Floyd, Harrison and Washington Counties* (Indianapolis: Indiana Department of Natural Resources, 2001); Kathryn Grover, *The Fugitive's Gibraltar: Escaping Slaves and Abolitionism in New Bedford, Massachusetts* (Amherst: University of Massachusetts Press, 2001); Pamela R. Peters, *The Underground Railroad in Floyd County, Indiana* (Jefferson, NC: McFarland, 2001); Hilary Russell, *The Operation of the Underground Railroad in Washington, D.C., 1800–1860* (Washington, DC: Historical Society of Washington and National Park Service, 2001); William J. Switala, *Underground Railroad in Pennsylvania* (Mechanicsburg, PA: Stackpole Books, 2001); J. Blaine Hudson, *Fugitive Slaves and the Underground Railroad in the Kentucky Borderland* (Jefferson, NC: McFarland, 2002); Ann Hagedorn, *Beyond the River: The Untold Story of the Heroes of the Underground Railroad* (New York: Simon and Schuster, 2002); William C. Kashatus, *Just over the Line: Chester County and the Underground Railroad* (University Park: Penn State University Press, 2002); Milton C. Sernett, *North Star Country: Upstate New York and the Crusade for African American Freedom* (Syracuse, NY: Syracuse University Press, 2002); and William J. Switala, *Underground Railroad in Delaware, Maryland and West Virginia* (Mechanicsburg, PA: Stackpole Books, 2004).

24. See John Hope Franklin and Loren Schweninger, *Runaway Slaves: Rebels on the Plantation* (New York: Oxford University Press, 1999), 209–33, 328–32.

25. See Stanley Harrold, *Subversives: Antislavery Community in Washington, D.C., 1828–1865* (Baton Rouge: Louisiana State University Press, 2003); James Oliver Horton and Lois E. Horton, *Slavery and the Making of America* (New York: Oxford University Press, 2005); Bordewich, *Bound for Canaan*; and Jacqueline L. Tobin, *From Midnight to Dawn: The Last Tracks of the Underground Railroad*, with Hettie Jones (New York: Doubleday, 2007).

26. Franklin and Schweninger, *Runaway Slaves*, 294–95.

27. William Switala's *Underground Railroad in Pennsylvania* relies heavily on Still's book in its interpretation of Pennsylvania's role on the Eastern Line. Switala retraces the

various routes of escape with detailed maps, discusses the large city networks, and identifies the stationmasters and sites where runaways found refuge. Kashatus's *Just over the Line* places Still's activities in the context of antebellum Chester County, Pennsylvania, a fierce battleground between proslavery and antislavery elements located just over the Mason-Dixon Line, which divided the free states of the North from the slaves states of the South. Other studies based on William Still's work are limited to published essays, journal articles, graduate theses, and unpublished papers, including Alberta Norwood, "Negro Welfare in Philadelphia as Illustrated by the Career of William Still" (MA thesis, University of Pennsylvania, 1931); Larry Gara, "William Still and the Underground Railroad," *Pennsylvania History* 28 (January 1961): 33–44; Boromé, "Vigilant Committee of Philadelphia"; Phil Lapsansky, "Aboard William Still's Underground Railroad: Celebrating the African-American Classic," unpublished paper presented at the Library Company of Philadelphia, February 9, 1993; Pinsker, *Vigilance in Pennsylvania*; William C. Kashatus, "Two Station Masters on the Underground Railroad: A Tale of Black and White," *Pennsylvania Heritage*, Fall 2001, 8–16; James Oliver Horton, "A Crusade for Freedom: William Still and the Real Underground Railroad," in Blight, *Passages to Freedom*, 175–94; and Sarah Smith Ducksworth, foreword to *Underground Railroad*, by William Still (1872; repr. Medford, NJ: Plexus, 2005), ix–xiv.

28. Charles Blockson estimated that the total was closer to four thousand over a thirty-three-year period, but this number is based on Blockson's belief that "Still and his assistant Miller McKim helped 300 fugitives a year" during those three decades. See Charles Blockson, "The Underground Railroad: The Quaker Connection," in *For Emancipation and Education: Some Black and Quaker Efforts, 1680–1900*, ed. Germantown Historical Society and Awbury Arboretum Association (Philadelphia: Germantown Historical Society and Awbury Arboretum Association, 1997), 38. This study, on the other hand, is limited to the cases Still identifies in his 1872 book and "Journal C" over an eight-year period, 1853–61, when Still was chairman of the acting committee of PASS's Vigilance Committee.

29. W. Still, *Underground Railroad* (1872/1970), 555.

30. Still recorded the backgrounds and circumstances of 847 runaways in *The Underground Railroad*, published in 1872. He also recorded the details of 446 runaways in a separate "Journal C," which can be found in manuscript form at the Historical Society of Pennsylvania in Philadelphia. Of the 446 runaways in Journal C, the data of 297 are repeated in Still's book, leaving just 149 *new* cases from Journal C. Thus the total number of runaways Still assisted is 996 (i.e., the 847 listed in his book, plus the 149 cases listed in Journal C).

31. Stephen G. Hall, "To Render the Private Public: William Still and the Selling of the Underground Rail Road," *Pennsylvania Magazine of History and Biography* 127, no. 1 (January 2003): 47, 54.

32. Among the popular treatments of Still's life are Lurey Khan Holmes, *One Day, Levin . . . He Be Free: William Still and the Underground Railroad* (1972; repr. Lincoln, NE:

iUniverse, 2002); Judith Bentley, *"Dear Friend": Thomas Garrett and William Still* (New York: Cobblehill Books / Dutton, 1997); and Kathleen Stevens, *William Still and the Underground Railroad* (West Berlin, NJ: Townsend Press, 2008).

33. Levi Coffin, a Quaker Underground Railroad agent from the Midwest, claimed to have helped three thousand fugitives escape. See Coffin, *Reminiscences*, 671. Similarly, Thomas Garrett, a Wilmington, Delaware, Quaker, and close associate of William Still's, claimed to have assisted 2,322 runaways. See Thomas Garrett to Samuel May Jr., November 24, 1863, in McGowan, *Station Master,* 189–90. Neither Coffin nor Garrett kept any detailed records of those they assisted, though. Still not only kept detailed records but guarded them carefully, going so far as to hide them in a cemetery building during the Civil War. On the other hand, Still did confess that his "notes were very brief" after John Brown's unsuccessful attempt to seize munitions at Harpers Ferry, Virginia, in 1859. "It was deemed prudent in those days, not to keep as full reports," he explained. "The capture of John Brown's papers and letters, with names and plans in full, admonished us that such papers and correspondence . . . concerning the Underground Railroad, might be captured by a pro-slavery mob." Consequently, Still, after 1859, "omitted some of the most important particulars in the escapes and narratives of fugitives." He also "sent books and papers away for a long time," and whatever notes he recorded on his Underground Railroad activities "were kept on loose slips of paper." See W. Still, *Underground Railroad* (1872/1970), 555.

CHAPTER ONE

1. Switala, *Underground Railroad in Delaware*, 61–64.

2. Clara L. Small, "Abolitionists, Free Blacks and Runaway Slaves: Surviving Slavery on Maryland's Eastern Shore," in *A History of African Americans of Delaware and Maryland's Eastern Shore*, ed. Carole C. Marks (Wilmington: Delaware Heritage Commission, 1998), 55–57; Switala, *Underground Railroad in Delaware*, 64–70.

3. Jeffery R. Brackett, *The Negro in Maryland: A Study of the Institution of Slavery* (Baltimore: John Murphy, 1889), 52–57.

4. Small, "Abolitionists, Free Blacks," 56–57; Switala, *Underground Railroad in Delaware*, 64–70; Blockson, *Hippocrene Guide*, 45.

5. James P. Boyd, preface to *The Underground Railroad*, by William Still (Philadelphia: William Still, 1886), iv; Lurey Khan, *One Day, Levin . . . He Be Free: William Still and the Underground Railroad* (1972; repr., Lincoln, NE: iUniverse, 2002), 1.

6. Levin Still Sr., quoted in Blockson, *The Underground Railroad: Dramatic First-Hand Accounts*, 6; Dennis B. Fradin, *My Family Shall Be Free* (New York: Harper Collins, 2001), 4.

7. George Fishman, *The African American Struggle for Freedom and Equality: The Development of a People's Identity, New Jersey, 1624–1850* (New York: Garland, 1997), 156.

8. Spencer R. Crew, "The Saga of Peter Still," paper presented as Twenty-Fourth Annual Louis Faugeres Bishop III Lecture, Alexander Library of Rutgers University, February 23, 2009, 63.

9. Boyd, preface to W. Still, *Underground Railroad* (1886), iv–v; Khan, *One Day, Levin*, 4–7; Crew, "Saga of Peter Still," 65.

10. Billy G. Smith and Richard Wojtowicz, *Blacks Who Stole Themselves: Advertisements for Runaways in the* Pennsylvania Gazette, *1728–1790* (Philadelphia: University of Pennsylvania Press, 1989), 7–13.

11. Boyd, preface to W. Still, *Underground Railroad* (1886), v–vi.

12. Pickard, *Kidnapped and the Ransomed*, 28–29, 36–38.

13. Ibid., 38–39.

14. Ibid., 56, 68, 79–80.

15. Ibid., 87–88, 112–13, 135–36.

16. Peter Kolchin, *American Slavery, 1619–1877* (New York: Hill and Wang, 2003), 99–100.

17. Horton and Horton, *Slavery and the Making*, 69.

18. Kolchin, *American Slavery*, 95.

19. Franklin and Higginbotham, *From Slavery to Freedom*, 140.

20. Horton, *Slavery and the Making*, 98–99.

21. Franklin and Higginbotham, *From Slavery to Freedom*, 135.

22. James Oliver Horton quoted in Laine Drewery, *Underground Railroad: The William Still Story*, DVD (Buffalo, NY/Toronto: WNEDO-TV, 2011).

23. Kolchin, *American Slavery*, 96–97.

24. See Eugene Genovese, *Roll, Jordan, Roll: The World the Slaves Made* (1972; repr., New York: Vintage, 1974); John W. Blassingame, *The Slave Community: Plantation Life in the Antebellum South.* (New York: Oxford University, 1972); and Leslie H. Owens, *This Species of Property: Slave Life and Culture in the Old South* (New York: Oxford University Press, 1976).

25. Blassingame, *Slave Community*, 78.

26. Kenneth M. Stampp, *The Peculiar Institution: Slavery in the Ante-Bellum South* (New York: Vintage Books, 1956), 171–77.

27. William Wells Brown, *Narrative of William W. Brown, a Fugitive Slave, Written by Himself* (1848), in *Puttin' on Ole Massa: The Slave Narratives of Henry Bibb, William Wells Brown, and Solomon Northup*, ed. Gilbert Osofsky (New York: Harper and Row, 1969).

28. Franklin and Higginbotham, *From Slavery to Freedom*, 153–54; Stampp, *Peculiar Institution*, 87–88, 97–109, 124–32; Genovese, *Roll, Jordan, Roll*, 597–98.

29. Stampp, *Peculiar Institution*, 109–24.

30. See Henry H. Bisbee, *Burlington Island: The Best and Largest on the South River, 1624–1972* (Burlington, NJ: Heidelberg Press, 1972); Fishman, *African American Struggle*.

31. Ernest Lyght, *Path of Freedom: The Black Presence in New Jersey's Burlington County, 1659–1900* (Cherry Hill, NJ: E & E Publishing House, 1978).

32. Ibid.

33. Giles R. Wright and Edward L. Wonkeryor, "*Steal Away, Steal Away . . .*": *A Guide to the Underground Railroad in New Jersey* (Trenton: New Jersey Historical Commission, 2002), 4–9. For more information on New Jersey's Underground Railroad history, see William J. Switala, *The Underground Railroad in New York and New Jersey* (Mechanicsburg, PA: Stackpole Books, 2006); Dennis Rizzo, *Parallel Communities: The Underground Railroad in South Jersey.* (New York: History Press, 2008); and James J. Gigantino Jr., *The Ragged Road to Abolition. Slavery and Freedom in New Jersey, 1775–1865* (Philadelphia: University of Pennsylvania Press, 2015).

34. Boyd, preface to W. Still, *Underground Railroad* (1886), v–vi; Khan, *One Day, Levin*, 8. William's birth is listed in these and other sources as October 7, 1821. But he gave the date of November 1819 in the 1900 Federal Census. Although many sources claim that William was the youngest of eighteen children born to Charity and Levin Still, only eleven have been identified: Levin Junior, Peter, Mahalah, Kitturah, Samuel, James, John, Mary, Charles, Joseph, and William.

35. Boyd, preface to W. Still, *Underground Railroad* (1886), vi, vi.

36. Ibid., viii–ix.

37. Ibid., ix–x, xiv.

38. Francis E. Still, "Recollections of the Still Family History," in *The Underground Railroad*, by William Still (Philadelphia: William Still, 1886), ix.

39. Khan, *One Day, Levin*, 10. The *Colored American* was owned and published by Charles B. Ray and Philip Bell of New York. The *Freedmen's Journal*, established in 1829, was the first antislavery newspaper in the United States.

40. Boyd, preface to W. Still, *Underground Railroad* (1886), vii–viii.

41. Ibid., x; Khan, *One Day, Levin*, 10.

42. Khan, *One Day, Levin*, 10–11.

43. William Still quoted in Boyd, preface to W. Still, *Underground Railroad* (1886), x–xi.

44. See Hugh Barbour and Arthur O. Roberts, *Early Quaker Writings, 1650–1700* (Grand Rapids, MI: William B. Eerdmans, 1973). Barbour and Roberts offer examples of seventeenth-century Quaker writing representing the variations of manners, styles, and beliefs of early Friends.

CHAPTER TWO

1. Boyd, preface to W. Still, *Underground Railroad* (1886), xi–xii.

2. Ibid., xiv–xviii; Khan, *One Day, Levin*, 12. Elizabeth Langdon Elwyn, a wealthy widow, hired Still in 1845 as an errand runner. She descended from a prominent family of shipbuilders from Portsmouth, NH. After her husband, Thomas Elwyn, died in 1816,

Elizabeth relocated to Philadelphia. She assigned Still a lengthy list of household duties as well as a code of conduct. But she also paid him handsomely at fourteen dollars per month and encouraged his education by selecting books for him from her large library. In 1847, the widow relocated to New York to live with a daughter, and Still was forced to look for employment again. He briefly worked for William Wurtz, a retired merchant, before accepting employment with the PASS. For biographical information on Elizabeth Langdon Elwin, see John Langdon, William Whipple and Elwin Family Papers, 1713–1965, Genealogical Collection, Portsmouth Athenaeum, Portsmouth, NH.

3. Boyd, preface to W. Still, *Underground Railroad* (1886), xviii; Horton, "Crusade for Freedom," 178.

4. Ira V. Brown, "Miller McKim and Pennsylvania Abolitionism," *Pennsylvania History* 20 (1963): 56–72.

5. Boyd, preface to W. Still, *Underground Railroad* (1886), xvii–xviii.

6. William Still to J. M. McKim, Esq., September 21, 1847, in William Still Letters, CBAAC.

7. Boyd, preface to W. Still, *Underground Railroad* (1886), xvii–xviii.

8. Howard Brinton, *The Religious Philosophy of Quakerism* (Wallingford, PA: Pendle Hill Press, 1969), 1–17; Hugh Barbour and J. William Frost, *The Quakers* (Westport, CT: Greenwood Press, 1988), 43.

9. Frances Daniel Pastorius, "Germantown Protest, 1688," quoted in Thomas E. Drake, *Quakers and Slavery in America* (1950; repr., Gloucester, MA: Peter Smith, 1965), 12. Original manuscript is in the Minutes of PYM (Orthodox), vol. N24, QC, HCL.

10. Hugh Thomas, *The Slave Trade: The Story of the Atlantic Slave Trade, 1440–1870* (New York: Simon and Schuster, 1997), 298. Among those early prominent Quakers engaged in slaveholding and slave trading were James Logan, William Penn's deputy governor; Isaac Norris, clerk of PYM; and Jonathan Dickinson, a member of the Second Continental Congress. See Jack Marietta, *The Reformation of American Quakerism, 1748–1783* (Philadelphia: University of Pennsylvania Press, 1984), 112.

11. Roberts Vaux, *Memoirs of the Lives of Benjamin Lay and Ralph Sandiford* (Philadelphia, 1815), 17, 25–28; Marcus Rediker, *The Fearless Benjamin Lay: The Quaker Dwarf Who Became the First Revolutionary Abolitionist* (Boston: Beacon Press, 2017), 1–2.

12. John Woolman, "Some Considerations on the Keeping of Negroes" (1754), in *The Journal and Major Essays of John Woolman*, ed. Philip Moulton (New York: Oxford University Press, 1971), 198–209; Thomas P. Slaughter, *The Beautiful Soul of John Woolman, Apostle of Abolition* (New York: Hill and Wang, 2008).

13. Maurice Jackson, *Let This Voice Be Heard: Anthony Benezet, Father of Atlantic Abolitionism* (Philadelphia: University of Pennsylvania Press, 2010).

14. Marietta, *Reformation of American Quakerism*, 46–72, 150–68.

15. PYM, Minutes: 1754, QC, HCL.

16. PYM, Minutes: 1758, QC, HCL.

17. Jean R. Soderlund, *Quakers and Slavery: A Divided Spirit* (Princeton, NJ: Princeton University Press, 1985), 98–100. For a more recent history of early Quaker

abolitionism, see Brycchan Carey, *From Peace to Freedom: Quaker Rhetoric and the Birth of American Anti-slavery, 1657–1761* (New Haven, CT: Yale University Press, 2012).

18. See Arthur J. Mekeel, *The Quakers and the American Revolution* (York: William Sessions, 1996), 232–310. Mekeel points out that the persecution of Quakers by the new American government and the Continental Army was widespread and included Quakers throughout the thirteen colonies. The most severe case was the forcible exile of a group of Philadelphia Quakers to Winchester, Virginia, in 1777, on the suspicion of loyalty to the British Crown.

19. Marietta, *Reformation of American Quakerism*, 267–79; Richard Bauman, *For the Reputation of Truth: Politics, Religion, and Conflict among the Pennsylvania Quakers, 1750–1800* (Baltimore: Johns Hopkins University Press, 1971), 227–29; Sydney V. James, *A People among Peoples: Quaker Benevolence in Eighteenth-Century America* (Cambridge, MA: Harvard University Press, 1963), 268–85.

20. Richard S. Newman, "The Pennsylvania Abolition Society: Restoring a Group to Glory," *Pennsylvania Legacies*, November 2005, 6–10; Margaret Hope Bacon, *History of the Pennsylvania Society for Promoting the Abolition of Slavery* (Philadelphia: Pennsylvania Abolition Society, 1959); Edward R. Turner, "The First Abolitionist Society in the United States," *Pennsylvania Magazine of History and Biography*, 36, no. 1 (1912): 94–95. In 1787, the PAS broadened its membership to include such prominent figures as Benjamin Franklin and Benjamin Rush. Its mission also changed from litigating on behalf of free blacks to corresponding with antislavery societies in other states and in England and petitioning the US Congress to ban the slave trade. For a list of PAS members, see "United States Abolitionist and Anti-Slavery Organizations," on the website "American Abolitionists and Antislavery Activists: Conscience of the Nation," ed. Eric Saul, 2016, retrieved November 29, 2017, www.americanabolitionists.com/american-anti-slavery-society .html.

21. Drake, *Quakers and Slavery*, 80–84. PYM was the first to disown slaveholding members in 1776, followed shortly thereafter by New York Yearly Meeting. Within the next eight years, all the yearly meetings in North America adopted the discipline in the following order: Baltimore Yearly Meeting (1778); North Carolina Yearly Meeting (1781); New England Yearly Meeting (1782); and Virginia Yearly Meeting (1784).

22. Henry J. Cadbury, "Negro Membership in the Society of Friends," *Journal of Negro History* 21 (1936): 151–213. Cadbury examines the late eighteenth- and early nineteenth-century minutes of PYM's monthly and quarterly constituent meetings, which reveal a conspicuous absence of African American members. Cadbury concludes that black membership was discouraged among Friends because of a fear of assimilation and/or miscegenation. More recently, Ryan P. Jordan identified the existence of segregated seating within many Quaker meetinghouses after 1776. He claimed that the so-called Negro pews were located "toward the back of the meetinghouse" and indicated that "large numbers within the Society of Friends were unable to imagine African Americans as equals within their spiritual fellowship." When a more radical minority of Quaker abolitionists began to raise arguments over ending the segregated seating in the early 1840s,

the Society of Friends ignored their pleas, choosing to "frame efforts at racial equality as a dangerous and public politicization of the Quakers' private anti-slavery testimony." See Ryan P. Jordan, *Slavery and the Meetinghouse: The Quakers and the Abolitionist Dilemma, 1820–1865* (Bloomington: Indiana University Press, 2007), 67, 72. Similarly, Donna Mc-Daniel and Vanessa Julye identify a pattern of racism among Friends that began in the seventeenth century and persists to the present day. See Donna McDaniel and Vanessa Julye, *Fit for Freedom, Not for Friendship: Quakers, African Americans, and the Myth of Racial Justice* (Philadelphia: Quaker Press, 2000).

23. For the most complete biography of Warner Mifflin, see Gary B. Nash, *Warner Mifflin: Unflinching Abolitionist* (Philadelphia: University of Pennsylvania Press, 2017).

24. Nash and Soderlund, *Freedom by Degrees*, xi–xv, 75.

25. "An Act for the Gradual Abolition of Slavery—Pennsylvania: March 1, 1780," The Avalon Project, Yale Law School, retrieved November 7, 2017, https://.avalon.law .yale.edu/subject_menus/18th.asp. The bill passed the Pennsylvania legislature by a vote of 34 to 21. The greatest opposition came from representatives of counties heavily populated by German settlers (Nash and Soderlund, *Freedom by Degrees*, 106–8).

26. Nash and Soderlund, *Freedom by Degrees*, 99–100.

27. Pennsylvania Historical and Museum Commission, "Editor's Note" to "An Act for the Gradual Abolition of Slavery, March 1, 1780," in *Documenting Pennsylvania's Past* (Harrisburg: Pennsylvania Historical and Museum Commission, 2003), 58–59.

28. For statistics on slave and free black populations, see Edward R. Turner, *The Negro in Pennsylvania: Slavery, Servitude and Freedom, 1639–1861* (New York: Negro Universities Press, 1910), 253.

29. The most serious schism in American Quakerism occurred in 1827–28, when younger and more progressive-thinking Friends, often living in large cities, were affected by the new and vibrant evangelical movement. They pressed for changes in PYM's religious discipline that complemented evangelical thought. But when they met with resistance from older members, some Quakers left the Society of Friends altogether to join other, more evangelical denominations. See Barbour and Frost, *Quakers*, 173. Frustrations over theology between older, more Quietist Friends and their younger evangelical opposition coalesced around the ministry of Elias Hicks, a traveling Quaker minister from Long Island, New York, who championed a more spiritualistic and less dogmatic approach. Although Hicks accepted the truth of scripture, the divinity of Christ, and the Resurrection, he emphasized that the Inner Light, or indwelling Christ, was the unerring source of divine revelation. Tensions between urban and rural Friends, issues of control, and personality conflicts compounded the difficulties. Matters came to a head in 1827 when PYM split into two yearly meetings. One group, the "Hicksites," followed the beliefs of Elias Hicks and retained the majority of members in Philadelphia Quakerdom. The other yearly meeting was established by the "Orthodox," the minority who embraced evangelical thought. Each faction consolidated their control of meeting houses, schools, graveyards, and trust funds. See Robert W. Doherty, *The Hicksite Separation: A Sociological Analysis of Religious Schism in Early Nineteenth Century America* (New Brunswick,

NJ: Rutgers University Press, 1967); and H. Larry Ingle, *Quakers in Conflict: The Hicksite Reformation* (Knoxville: University of Tennessee, 1986).

Between 1830 and 1860, the evangelical movement became stronger in the United States and Orthodox Friends felt pressured to conform to its principles. Joseph John Gurney, a wealthy British Quaker, attempted to strengthen evangelical thought among Orthodox Friends. Gurney's theology appealed to the authority of the Bible and to the human need for atonement. But he did not deny the importance of such Hicksite beliefs as silent worship, plain speech and dress, and pacifism. Nor did he deny the significance of the Inner Light, maintaining only that the Bible was the primary source of revelation (see Barbour and Frost, *Quakers*, 194). But Gurney's ministry served to divide Orthodox Friends. The conflict, known as the "Wilburite-Gurneyite controversy," pitted the followers of John Wilbur, a New England Friend who defended the authority of the Holy Spirit as primary and worked to prevent what he saw as the dilution of the Friends' tradition of Spirit-led ministry, against those of Gurney.

Despite their theological differences, Quakers shared a basic antipathy to slavery, believing that human bondage was a disgrace to the nation and must be abolished. That shared belief transcended theological differences between "Orthodox" and "Hicksite," "Wilburite" and "Gurneyite," "Conservative" and "Progressive" and even between those who were "Congregational" Friends and all other Friends. Thus *doctrine* was much less important than the *approach* used to eradicate human slavery (see Barbour and Frost, *Quakers*, 190–92).

30. S. James, *People among Peoples*, 291–99, 316–34; Marietta, *Reformation of American Quakerism,* 272–79; Drake, *Quakers and Slavery*, 167–85; Smedley, *History of the Underground Railroad*; Margaret H. Bacon, *The Quiet Rebels: The Story of Quakers in America* (New York: Basic Books, 1969), 94–121. It's important to note that Quaker historians Hugh Barbour and Jerry Frost contend that we lack "statistics of Friends from each branch of Quakerism to determine which Quakers embraced a particular approach to abolitionism" (see Barbour and Frost, *Quakers*, 192).

31. Drake, *Quakers and Slavery*, 166; Jordan, *Slavery and the Meetinghouse*, 6–10; Kashatus, *Just over the Line*, 35–67.

32. Henry Mayer, *All on Fire: William Lloyd Garrison and the Abolition of Slavery* (New York: St. Martin's Press, 1998), 224–26.

33. William Lloyd Garrison, "On Immediate Emancipation," *Liberator*, January 1, 1831.

34. William Lloyd Garrison, "On the Constitution and the Union," *Liberator*, December 29, 1832.

35. David Brion Davis, *Slavery and Human Progress* (New York: Oxford University Press, 1984), 137–38; Mayer, *All on Fire*, 413–14.

36. Aileen S. Kraditor, *Means and Ends in American Abolitionism: Garrison and His Critics on Strategy and Tactics, 1834–1850* (1967; repr., Vintage, 1970), 45–51.

37. Drake, *Quakers and Slavery*, 145–46, 154, 179–80; McDaniel and Julye, *Fit for Freedom*, 72–73.

38. Richard S. Newman, "Abolitionism," in *The Encyclopedia of Greater Philadelphia* (New Brunswick, NJ: Rutgers University, 2012), retrieved November 20, 2017, philadelphiaencyclopedia.org/archive/abolitionism/.

39. Edward Wagenknecht, *John Greenleaf Whittier: A Portrait in Paradox* (New York: Oxford University Press, 1967), 13.

40. *Abolitionist* 1, no. 12 (December 1833); Drake, *Quakers and Slavery*, 118, 130.

41. *Abolitionist* 1, no. 12 (December 1833); Smedley, *History of the Underground Railroad*, 260–74.

42. Drake, *Quakers and Slavery*, 118, 140, 154; Carleton Mabee, *Black Freedom: The Nonviolent Abolitionists from 1830 through the Civil War* (New York: Macmillan, 1970), 9, 131, 305, 345, 406n13; American Council of Learned Studies, *Dictionary of American Biography*, 20 vols. (New York: Charles Scribner's Sons, 1936), 7:288.

43. Margaret Hope Bacon, *Valiant Friend: The Life of Lucretia Mott* (New York: Walker, 1980); Jean R. Soderlund, "Priorities and Power: The Philadelphia Female Anti-Slavery Society," in *The Abolitionist Sisterhood: Women's Political Culture in Antebellum America,* ed. Jean Fagan Yellin and John C. Van Horne (Ithaca, NY: Cornell University Press, 1994), 18, 26, 43, 74, 159–62, 175–76, 286–87, 301–2, 327–28.

44. Drake, *Quakers and Slavery*, 145–46, 154, 179–80; McDaniel and Julye, *Fit for Freedom,* 72–73.

45. Julie Winch, *A Gentleman of Color: The Life of James Forten* (New York: Oxford University Press, 2002).

46. Margaret Hope Bacon, *But One Race: The Life of Robert Purvis* (Albany: State University of New York, 2007).

47. Mayer, *All on Fire*, 241–42; American Anti-Slavery Society, *Annual Reports,* vols. 1–6 (New York: William S. Dorr and Butterfield, 1834–39).

48. Julie Winch, *Philadelphia's Black Elite: Activism, Accommodation and the Struggle for Autonomy, 1787–1848* (Philadelphia: Temple University Press, 1988), 83.

49. Mayer, *All on Fire*, 174–77.

50. McDaniel and Julye, *Fit for Freedom*, 74–76; M. Bacon, *Valiant Friend*, 59–65; Carolyn Williams, "Religion, Race and Gender in Antebellum American Radicalism: The Philadelphia Female Anti-Slavery Society, 1833–1870" (PhD diss., UCLA, 1991).

51. I. Brown, "Miller McKim," 60. McKim married Sarah Allibone Speakman (1813–91), the daughter of Chester County Quakers Micajah and Phoebe Speakman.

52. Samuel Webb, *History of Pennsylvania Hall* (Philadelphia: Merrihew and Gunn, 1838), 3–6.

53. I. Brown, "Miller McKim," 57–58.

54. Mayer, *All on Fire*, 261–84.

55. The best treatment of the Pennsylvania's Yearly Meeting's founding is Christopher Densmore, "Be Ye Therefore Perfect: Anti-slavery and the Origins of the Yearly Meeting of Progressive Friends in Chester County, Pennsylvania," *Quaker History* 93, no. 2 (Fall 2004): 28– 46. See also Albert J. Wahl, "The Congregational or Progressive Friends in the Pre–Civil War Reform Movement," (PhD diss., Temple University, 1951).

56.　Albert J. Wahl, "The Progressive Friends of Longwood," *Friends Historical Society Bulletin* 42, no. 1 (Spring 1953): 14–16. For names of the founding members of the Longwood Progressive Friends Meeting, see Wahl, "Congregational or Progressive Friends," 344. Christopher Densmore argues that "because many active agents of the Underground Railroad were associated with Progressive Friends, some people have interpreted the 1852–1853 separation of activist, anti-slavery Friends from Kennett Monthly Meeting as connected with the question of involvement with the Underground Railroad. This was not the case." Densmore points out that both the main body of Kennett Monthly Meeting (Hicksite) as well as the separatists Progressive Friends submitted to the PYM (Hicksite) 1851 directive to resist complying with the 1850 Fugitive Slave Law and be willing to "suffer the penalties" rather than obey a law that was "so clearly unjust." See Christopher Densmore, introduction to Smedley, *History of the Underground Railroad*, xvi–xvii.

57.　PYMPF, *Proceedings* (1853): 5, CCA.

58.　Thomas Whitson, quoted in *Pennsylvania Freeman*, November 4, 1853.

59.　Lucretia Mott to Martha Wright, December 5, 1861, Lucretia Mott Papers, Friends Historical Library, Swarthmore College.

60.　Thomas Garrett to Samuel May Jr., Wilmington, DE, November 24, 1863, quoted in McGowan, *Station Master*, 189–90.

61.　Wahl, "Progressive Friends of Longwood," 287–89.

62.　PYMPF, "Slavery," *Proceedings* (1856): 43–44, CCA. Progressive Friends contributed to the flood of antislavery petitions descending upon Congress in the years before the Civil War. When the Kansas-Nebraska Bill was before Congress on February 7, 1854, the Kennett Monthly Meeting of Progressive Friends adopted a remonstrance against it, sending it to William Everhart, a member of the House from Chester County and a West Chester stationmaster himself (see *Jeffersonian and Democratic Herald*, March 25, 1854). Similar petitions were sent from the Kennett Quarterly Meeting of Progressive Friends and the PYMPF shortly after (see *Pennsylvania Freeman*, February 23, March 30, May 4, 1854). They also raised funds for antislavery societies across the North by holding and patronizing antislavery fairs. See Wahl, "Progressive Friends," 278–81.

63.　"Slavery," PYMPF, *Proceedings* (1857), 13–15, CCA.

64.　Mayer, *All on Fire*, 371–74, 428–33.

65.　"Caste," PYMPF, *Proceedings* (1858), 35, CCA.

66.　"Complexional Distinctions," PYMPF, *Proceedings* (1863), 16, CCA.

67.　Ibid., 16.

68.　Robert Purvis rebuts Reverend H. P. Crozier of Long Island, NY, quoted in "Caste," PYMPF, *Proceedings* (1858), 35.

69.　Purvis quoted in *Village Record*, October 30, 1860.

70.　Boyd, preface to W. Still, *Underground Railroad* (1886), xix; Gara, "William Still," 34; I. Brown, "Miller McKim," 59–60.

71.　Boyd, preface to W. Still, *Underground Railroad* (1886), xix, xlvi.

72.　Ibid., xx; Khan, *One Day, Levin*, 22.

CHAPTER THREE

1. W. Still, *Underground Railroad* (1872/1970), 67–68, 70.

2. Henry Brown, *Narrative of the Life of Henry Box Brown, Written by Himself* (Boston: Charles L. Stearns, 1849), 61–62.

3. Ibid., 40–41. Henry Brown was born enslaved in Louisa County, Virginia, in 1815. The precise date of his birth is unknown. At the age of fifteen he was sent to Richmond to work in a tobacco factory.

4. Ibid., 51–52.

5. Horton, "Crusade for Freedom," 179–80. McKim later discouraged Samuel Smith from shipping slaves to freedom in wooden crates, but Smith ignored his advice and aided at least two other fugitives in the same manner. Smith was eventually arrested and served an eight-year prison sentence. See Horton, "Crusade for Freedom," 182.

6. Ibid., 180.

7. H. Brown, *Narrative of the Life*, 60.

8. Ibid., 60–61.

9. W. Still, *Underground Railroad* (1872/1970), 71.

10. Ibid., 68, 70–71; Horton, "Crusade for Freedom," 182–83. Brown's last recorded performance took place in Ontario, Canada, on February 26, 1889. The date and location of his death are unknown.

11. McKim quoted in Horton, "Crusade for Freedom," 181.

12. George Washington to Robert Morris, April 12, 1786, in *The Writings of George Washington, 1745–1799*, ed. John C. Fitzpatrick, 39 vols. (Washington, DC: US Government Printing Office, 1931–44), 28:407–8.

13. Franklin and Higginbotham, *From Slavery to Freedom*, 199.

14. Gara, *Liberty Line*, 173–74.

15. Franklin and Higginbotham, *From Slavery to Freedom*, 200–201.

16. Switala, *Underground Railroad in Pennsylvania*, 26.

17. Franklin and Schweninger, *Runaway Slaves*, 328–32, 396. Franklin and Schweninger examine advertisements for runaways in twenty newspapers from North Carolina, South Carolina, Virginia, Tennessee, and Louisiana. They provide a "Runaway Slave Database" that covers an early period, 1790–1816, and a later period, 1838–60. The database consists of approximately 8,400 runaways, nearly half of whom were advertised during the two time periods.

18. William Craft, "Running a Thousand Miles for Freedom; or the Escape of William and Ellen Craft from Slavery, 1860," in *Slave Narratives*, ed. William L. Andrews and Henry Louis Gates Jr. (New York: Library of America, 2000), 681, 697–98.

19. Ibid., 682.

20. Ibid., 705–6.

21. Ibid., 707–8.

22. Ibid., 721–22.

23. W. Still, *Underground Railroad* (1872/1970), 382–84.

24. Ibid., 391; Marian Smith Holmes, "The Great Escape from Slavery of Ellen and William Craft," *Smithsonian Magazine*, June 16, 2010, www.smithsonianmag.com/history /the-great-escape-from-slavery-of-ellen-and-william-craft-497960/.

25. W. Still, *Underground Railroad* (1872/1970), 67–70, 382–91.

26. Switala, *Underground Railroad in Delaware*, 115–16.

27. Ibid., 99–107; Switala, *Underground Railroad in Pennsylvania*, 29–102.

28. Switala, *Underground Railroad in Pennsylvania*, 103–19.

29. Ibid., 121–39.

30. Ibid., 141–51.

31. Ibid., 152–54.

32. Switala, R. C. Smedley, Wilbur Siebert, and Charles Blockson identify an extensive network of secondary routes that branch from Pennsylvania's three major avenues of escape. Not all of these routes lead northward, either. Some are located due west or east of the major route, indicating that the UGRR maintained diversionary passageways as well. See Blockson, *Underground Railroad in Pennsylvania*; Siebert, *Underground Railroad*; and Smedley, *History of the Underground Railroad*.

33. Julie Winch, "Philadelphia and the Other Underground Railroad," *Pennsylvania Magazine of History and Biography* 61 (January 1987): 7, 23.

34. M. Bacon, *But One Race*; Joseph A. Boromé, "Robert Purvis and His Early Exposure to American Racism," *Negro History Bulletin* 30, no. 3 (1967): 8–10.

35. *National Enquirer*, September 7, 1837.

36. Boromé, "Vigilant Committee of Philadelphia," 323–24. See also Minute Book of the Vigilant Committee of Philadelphia, 1839–1844, kept by Jacob C. White, HSP.

37. Boromé, "Vigilant Committee of Philadelphia," 323.

38. Ibid., 324.

39. Ibid.

40. Ibid., 324–25.

41. Nicholas B. Wainwright, "The Age of Nicholas Biddle, 1825–1841," in *Philadelphia: A 300-Year History*, ed. Russell F. Weigley (New York: Norton, 1982), 294–95; Denis Clark, "Urban Blacks and Irishmen: Brothers in Prejudice," in *Black Politics in Philadelphia*, ed. Miriam Ershkowitz and Joseph Zikmund (New York: Basic Books, 1973), 15–16.

42. *Pennsylvania Register*, September 27, 1834.

43. Sam Bass Warner, *Philadelphia: The Private City*, rev. ed. (Philadelphia: University of Pennsylvania Press, 1987), 127; Wainwright, "Age of Nicholas Biddle," 294–95.

44. Bruce Laurie, *Working People of Philadelphia, 1800–1850* (Philadelphia: Temple University Press, 1980), 62–66; Wainwright, "Age of Nicholas Biddle," 295. Some historians argue that the 1844 riots were primarily motivated by nativist resentment toward the Catholic Church and the city's growing Irish immigrant population. See Michael Feldberg, *The Philadelphia Riots of 1844: A Study of Ethnic Conflict* (Westport, CT: Greenwood Press, 1975); and Zachary M. Schrag, "Nativist Riots of 1844," in *Encyclopedia of Greater Philadelphia*, ed. Mid-Atlantic Regional Center for the Humanities, n.d., re-

trieved November 15, 2017, www.philadelphiaencyclopedia.org/archives/nativist-riots
-of-1844.

45. *Register of Pennsylvania*, August 23, 1834.

46. Wainwright, "Age of Nicholas Biddle," 295–96; Mayer, *All on Fire*, 243–46.

47. Boromé, "Vigilant Committee of Philadelphia," 326–27.

48. Robert Purvis to Henry C. Wright, August 22, 1842, quoted in *A Documentary History of the Negro People in the United States*, ed. Herbert Aptheker (New York: Citadel Press, 1951), 220.

49. Boromé, "Vigilant Committee of Philadelphia," 327–28.

CHAPTER FOUR

1. Campbell, *Slave Catchers*, 23; Thomas D. Morris, *Free Men All: The Personal Liberty Laws of the North, 1780–1861* (Baltimore: Johns Hopkins University Press, 1974), 49. The 1793 Fugitive Slave Law enforced Article IV, Section 2, of the US Constitution in authorizing any federal district judge or circuit court judge, or any state magistrate, to decide finally and without a jury trial the status of an alleged fugitive slave.

2. *Liberator*, October 11, 1850.

3. *Liberator*, October 25, 1850.

4. Fred Landon, "The Negro Migration to Canada after the Passage of the Fugitive Slave Act," *Journal of Negro History* 5 (January 1920): 26–27.

5. W. Still, *Underground Railroad* (1872/1970), 592.

6. See David M. Potter, *The Impending Crisis: America before the Civil War, 1848–1861* (New York: Harper and Row, 1976), 26–42.

7. Campbell, *Slave Catchers*, 8–10; E. Turner, *Negro in Pennsylvania*, 233–34.

8. E. Turner, *Negro in Pennsylvania*, 235.

9. Ibid., 236.

10. Campbell, *Slave Catchers*, 10, 173; Blockson, *Underground Railroad in Pennsylvania*, 189.

11. Minutes: 1846, Philadelphia Meeting for Sufferings, Friends Historical Library, Swarthmore College, Swarthmore, PA.

12. Joseph J. Lewis, *A Memoir of Enoch Lewis* (West Chester, PA: Hickman, 1882), 90.

13. E. Turner, *Negro in Pennsylvania*, 237–39.

14. Ibid., 253.

15. See Bruce Levine, *Half Slave and Half Free: The Roots of the Civil War* (New York: Hill and Wang, 1992), 160–67.

16. Fugitive Slave Act of 1850, reprinted in W. Still, *Underground Railroad* (1872/1970), 355–60. For the most recent scholarship on the act, see R. J. M. Blackett, *The Captive's Quest for Freedom: Fugitive Slaves, the 1850 Fugitive Slave Law, and the Politics of Slavery* (Cambridge: Cambridge University Press, 2018).

17. Horton, *Slavery and the Making*, 148–49.

18. Matthew Pinsker, "After 1850: Reassessing the Impact of the Fugitive Slave Law," in *Fugitive Slaves and Spaces of Freedom in North America*, ed. Damian Alan Pargas (Gainesville: University of Florida Press, 2018), 94–95.

19. Pinsker, "After 1850," 94. For a detailed treatment of reception, see Eric Foner, *Gateway to Freedom: The Hidden History of the Underground Railroad* (New York: W. W. Norton, 2015), 32.

20. Pinsker, "After 1850," 94–95.

21. Drake, *Quakers and Slavery*, 185.

22. Ibid.

23. See Walter and Mary Dyson, "George Wall," unpublished manuscript, 1959, 19, Special Collections, Lincoln University, Jefferson City, MO. Wall descendants Hersey Gray, Brenda Boddy, and Ed Draper all confirm George Wall's kidnapping activity, pointing to his significant wealth, which came from an undisclosed source.

24. Robin W. Winks, *The Blacks in Canada* (New Haven, CT: Yale University Press, 1971), 233–40. Winks notes that the exact size of the Canadian black population is difficult to ascertain and that these particular figures were probably inflated for propaganda value.

25. Jane Rhodes, *Mary Ann Shadd Cary: The Black Press and Protest in the Nineteenth Century* (Bloomington: Indiana University Press, 1998), 29–32.

26. Mary Ann Shadd to Isaac Shadd, September 16, 1851, quoted in Rhodes, *Mary Ann Shadd Cary*, 34.

27. Rhodes, *Mary Ann Shadd Cary*, 47–134.

28. Winch, "Philadelphia and the Other Underground Railroad."

29. David Evans, Journal, December 1, 1850, Evans Family Papers, CCA.

30. Ibid.

31. The most comprehensive treatment of the Christiana Resistance is Slaughter, *Bloody Dawn*. For an African-centered perspective, see Forbes, *But We Have No Country*.

32. Slaughter, *Bloody Dawn*, 18–19.

33. Thomas Whitson, "Early Abolitionists of Lancaster County," *Historical Papers and Addresses of the Lancaster County Historical Society* 15 (1911): 69–86.

34. Parker quoted in Forbes, *But We Have No Country*, 37–38.

35. William Parker, "Freedman's Story," *Atlantic Monthly*, February 1866, 160.

36. Ibid., 160–61. In 1860, the *Philadelphia Inquirer* reported that "ever since the passage of the Fugitive Slave law, Lancaster County has been infested with a set of villains who steal and sell into slavery free negroes who they can either by force or some lying pretext decoy themselves." *Philadelphia Inquirer*, December 3, 1860.

37. Parker quoted in William U. Hensel, *The Christiana Riot and the Treason Trial of 1851* (Lancaster, PA: New Era Printing, 1911), 15.

38. Jonathan Katz, *Resistance at Christiana: A Documentary Account* (New York: Thomas Crowell, 1974), 27; Slaughter, *Bloody Dawn*, 4–5.

39. Slaughter, *Bloody Dawn*, 11–14.

40. Katz, *Resistance at Christiana*, 72–73; Slaughter, *Bloody Dawn*, 11–14.

41. W. Still, *Underground Railroad* (1872/1970), 361; Boyd, preface to W. Still, *Underground Railroad* (1886), xxi–xxii; Bordewich, *Bound for Canaan*, 356.

42. For details of the Christiana encounter, see Joshua Gorsuch, "The Christiana Tragedy," *Lancaster Intelligencer and Journal*, September 16 and 23, 1851; W. Still, *Underground Railroad* (1872/1970), 360–71.

43. James R. Robbins, *Report of the Trial of Castner Hanway for Treason* (Philadelphia, 1852), 243–44.

44. *American Republican*, December 16, 1851; Slaughter, *Bloody Dawn*, 112–38.

45. W. Still, *Underground Railroad* (1872/1970), 381.

46. Robert Purvis quoted in Blockson, *African Americans in Pennsylvania: Above Ground and Underground. An Illustrated Guide* (Harrisburg, PA: RB Books, 2001), 23.

47. Frederick Douglass, *My Bondage and My Freedom*, ed Philip S. Foner (1855; repr., New York: Dover Publications, 1969), 454–56.

CHAPTER FIVE

1. PASS, *Fifteenth Annual Report*, October 25, 1852, 3–4, HSP.

2. McKim quoted in *Pennsylvania Freeman*, December 9, 1852.

3. *Pennsylvania Freeman*, December 9, 1852.

4. Boromé, "Vigilant Committee of Philadelphia," 328–29; *Pennsylvania Freeman*, December 9, 1852.

5. Harry Silcox, "Philadelphia Negro Educator: Jacob C. White, Jr., 1837–1902," *Pennsylvania Magazine of History and Biography* 97, no. 1 (January 1973): 75–78.

6. *Colored American*, September 8, 1838; *Christian Recorder*, August 20, 1874.

7. Laurie Rofini, "Chester County's Passmore Williamson, Famed Abolitionist," *Daily Local News* (West Chester, PA), September 26, 2013. Williamson's involvement in radical abolitionism, along with his failure to attend Quaker meeting, led to his disownment by the Society of Friends in 1848. In spite of his disownment, he married Mercie Knowles Taylor in a Quaker ceremony later that same year. The couple would have four children, two girls and two boys.

8. Harry Silcox, "The Black 'Better Class' Political Dilemma: Philadelphia Prototype Isaiah C. Wears," *Pennsylvania Magazine of History and Biography* 113, no. 1 (January 1989): 45–47. See also *Christian Recorder*, February 24, 1866, January 12, 1867, December 4, 1869, August 18, 1874, and August 17, 1876; *Colored American*, August 5, 1837, May 23 and July 25, 1840, and April 24, 1841.

9. Bordewich, *Bound for Canaan*, 356.

10. *Pennsylvania Freeman*, December 30, 1852, and February 13, 1853.

11. William Still quoted in Horton, "Crusade for Freedom," 186.

12. William Henry Johnson, *Autobiography* (Albany, NY: Argus, 1900), 125–26.

13. Jacob C. White Jr., quoted in Daniel R. Biddle and Murray Dubin, *Tasting Freedom: Octavius Catto and the Battle for Equality in Civil War America* (Philadelphia: Temple University Press, 2010), 208.

14. According to federal census figures, the total population of Philadelphia would increase by 37 percent from 258,037 residents in 1840 to 408,762 a decade later. While the free black population declined slightly from 19,831 to 19,761 during the same period, free blacks still constituted between 5 and 7 percent of the city's total population.

15. Theodore Hershberg, *Philadelphia: Work, Space, Family and Group Experience in the 19th Century* (New York: Oxford University Press, 1981), 380. According to Hershberg, who completed a statistical study of Philadelphia's antebellum black community based on census data for 1838, 1847, and 1856, the total wealth (i.e., the combined value of real and personal property holdings) for three of every five black households in 1838 and in 1847 amounted to sixty dollars or less. See Theodore Hershberg, "Free Blacks in Antebellum Philadelphia: A Study of Ex-slaves, Freeborn, and Socioeconomic Decline," *Journal of Social History* 5 (December 1971): 183–209.

16. Wainwright, "Age of Nicholas Biddle," 293; Winch, *Philadelphia's Black Elite*, 185; and Emma Lapsansky, *"Making It Home": Black Presence in Pennsylvania* (University Park: Pennsylvania Historical Association, 1990), 18–19.

17. D. Davis, *Problem of Slavery*, xiii–xiv, 7–8.

18. Frederick Douglass to Harriet Beecher Stowe, March 8, 1853, quoted in *The Mind of the Negro as Reflected in Letters Written during the Crisis, 1800–1860*, ed. Carter G. Woodson (Westport, CT: Greenwood Press, 1969), 654.

19. Frederick Douglass, "Temperance and Anti-slavery: An Address Delivered in Paisley, Scotland, March 30, 1846," in *Frederick Douglass Papers: Speeches, Debates and Interviews*, ed. John W. Blassingame, vol. 1, *1841–1846* (New Haven, CT: Yale University Press, 1979), 206.

20. Elizabeth Varon, "'Beautiful Providences': William Still, the Vigilance Committee and Abolitionists in the Age of Sectionalism," in *Antislavery and Abolition in Philadelphia*, ed. Richard Newman and James Mueller (Baton Rouge: Louisiana State University Press, 2011), 232; W. Still, *Underground Railroad* (1872/1970), 740–61; *Provincial Freeman*, March 7, 1857.

21. Wainwright, "Age of Nicholas Biddle," 293; Winch, *Philadelphia's Black Elite*, 185; and E. Lapsansky, *"Making It Home,"* 18–19.

22. Miriam Ershkowitz and Joseph Zikmund, eds., *Black Politics in Philadelphia* (New York: Basic Books, 1973), 8–9; E. Lapsansky, *"Making It Home,"* 14–15; Hershberg, *Work, Space, Family*, 379–80.

23. Horton, *Free People of Color*, 55, 58.

24. Horton and Horton, *Hard Road to Freedom*, 143.

25. Horton and Horton, *In Hope of Liberty*, 230.

26. Phil Lapsansky, "Notes of Philadelphia's Underground Railroad," Philip Lapsansky Papers, LCP.

27. W. Still, preface to Still, *Underground Railroad* (1872; repr., Chicago: Johnson, 1970), xiii–xiv.

28. Franklin and Higginbotham, *From Slavery to Freedom*, 203–6; Tobin, *From Midnight to Dawn*, 47–48; William C. Kashatus, "In Immortal Splendor: Wilkes-Barre's Fugitive Slave Case of 1853," *Pennsylvania Heritage*, Spring 2008, 24–31.

29. Harriet Tubman, a slave of Edward Brodess of Dorchester County, Maryland, escaped on the Underground Railroad in 1849. Between 1849 and 1860, she returned to the Eastern Shore of Maryland thirteen times to guide family and friends to freedom. See Kate Clifford Larson, *Bound for the Promised Land: Harriet Tubman, Portrait of an American Hero* (New York: Ballantine Books, 2004), xvii. During the period 1852 to 1860, Tubman regularly made at least one trip a year—and often two trips—into the South to serve as a conductor. She usually moved fugitives through the Wilmington, Delaware, station of Quaker Thomas Garrett, or to William Still in Philadelphia. See Catherine Clinton, *Harriet Tubman: The Road to Freedom* (Boston: Little, Brown, 2004), 85. This time period coincides with the proliferation or reconstitution of vigilance committees in populous cities like New York, Philadelphia, and Boston, as well as in smaller communities like Syracuse, New York, and Springfield, Massachusetts. See Boromé, "Vigilant Committee of Philadelphia," 104–9.

30. Franklin and Higginbotham, *From Slavery to Freedom*, 201; C. Peter Ripley, *The Underground Railroad* (Washington, DC: US Department of the Interior /National Park Service, 1998), 52; Pinsker, *Vigilance in Pennsylvania*, 54–95. Only Larry Gara emphasizes the significant role of water transportation on the Underground Railroad, pointing out that "steamships running from southern ports provided excellent opportunities for escaping slaves." Light-colored slaves could often pass for white passengers, while others stowed away in the holds of the ships. He concludes that of the slaves who fled North, "probably the greatest number used water transportation." Gara, *Liberty Line*, 50–51.

31. W. Still, *Underground Railroad* (1872/1970), 28–30.

32. Ibid., 214–15.

33. Ibid., 552–53.

34. Ibid., 247–51.

35. Ibid., 566–67.

36. Ibid., 585–88.

37. Ibid., 74–75, 166, 263.

38. Ibid., 289–92.

39. Ibid., 632–35.

40. Horton and Horton, *In Hope of Liberty,* 235.

41. Varon, "'Beautiful Providences,'" 233.

42. *Pennsylvania Freeman*, December 8, 1853.

43. E. Foner, *Gateway to Freedom*, 163.

44. *National Anti-Slavery Standard*, November 4, 1854.

45. *Provincial Freeman*, May 5, 1855.
46. *National Anti-Slavery Standard*, August 18, 1860.
47. Varon, "'Beautiful Providences,'" 233–37.

CHAPTER SIX

1. W. Still, *Underground Railroad* (1872/1970), 73–84. See also Arthur Cannon, *The Case of Passmore Williamson* (Philadelphia: Uriah Hunt and Son, 1856). For alternative descriptions of the Jane Johnson rescue, see Philip S. Foner, *History of Black Americans: From the Compromise of 1850 to the End of the Civil War* (Westport, CT: Greenwood Press, 1983), 3:83; and James Oliver Horton, "Crusade for Freedom," 186–87.

2. Pennsylvania Anti-Slavery Society (PASS), *Narrative of Facts in the Case of Passmore Williamson* (Philadelphia: PASS, 1855), 16.

3. Ibid., 9; Richard Hildreth, *Atrocious Judges* (New York: Miller, Orton and Mulligan, 1856), 422.

4. Laurie Rofini, "Chester County's Passmore Williamson, Famed Abolitionist," *Daily Local News* (West Chester, PA), September 26, 2013.

5. Thomas Curtis, "Passmore Williamson, In Moyamensing Prison for Alleged Contempt of Court," lithograph accession #1990.2436, CCA.

6. Still quoted in *Pennsylvania Freeman*, August 22, 1855, and in *National Anti-Slavery Standard*, September 29, 1855. See also Varon, "'Beautiful Providences,'" 234.

7. Charles Sumner to Passmore Williamson, August 11, 1855, undated note signed by John Greenleaf Whittier, hand-carried by Sarah Lloyd, 1855, Alanson Work to Passmore Williamson, October 13, 1855, and C. G. Henessey to Passmore Williamson, September 6, 1855, all in Passmore Williamson Letters, CCA.

8. Lucretia Mott quoted in Rofini, "Chester County's Passmore Williamson."

9. PASS, *Narrative Facts*, 16; Pamela Powell, "The Case of Passmore Williamson," unpublished manuscript, CCA, 1998. Williamson would later bring suit against Judge Kane for unlawfully detaining him. The suit ended when Kane died in 1858. Williamson later suffered financial difficulties, and in ailing health from his imprisonment he died at the age of seventy-three, on February 28, 1895. He is buried next to his wife, Mercie, who died in 1878, and his father in a Friends cemetery in Upper Darby. See Rofini, "Chester County's Passmore Williamson."

10. *Philadelphia Daily Sun* quoted in Horton, "Crusade for Freedom," 187.

11. The Jane Johnson case was made popular by Lorene Cary's novel *The Price of a Child* (New York: Vintage, 1996) and Henry Louis Gates's discovery of the "Bondswoman's Narrative." See Hannah Crafts, *The Bondswoman's Narrative*, ed. Henry Louis Gates (New York: Warner Books, 2002).

12. E. Foner, *Gateway to Freedom*, 195, 205; Franklin and Higginbotham, *From Slavery to Freedom*, 201; Horton and Horton, *Slavery and the Making*, 129; Franklin and

Schweninger, *Runaway Slaves*, 210; Genovese, *Roll, Jordan, Roll*, 648; and Stampp, *Peculiar Institution*, 110–11.

13. W. Still, *Underground Railroad* (1872/1970), 174–88.

14. Ibid., 289–92.

15. Ibid., 410; Cannon, *Case of Passmore Williamson*, 14.

16. W. Still, *Underground Railroad* (1872/1970), 311–13, 529–32, 535–37; William Still, "Journal C," HSP.

17. W. Still, *Underground Railroad* (1872/1970), 73–84.

18. Ibid., 436.

19. Ibid., 318.

20. Ibid., 556.

21. Ibid., 410.

22. See Stampp, *Peculiar Institution*, 193–96; Blassingame, *Slave Community*, 155–58; Joel Williamson, *New People: Miscegenation and Mulattoes in the United States* (New York: Free Press, 1980); P. Foner, *History of Black Americans*, 102; Horton, *Hard Road to Freedom*, 241–42; Franklin and Schweninger, *Runaway Slaves*, 213–15.

23. W. Still, *Underground Railroad* (1872/1970), 78.

24. Crafts, *Bondswoman's Narrative*; Henry Louis Gates, "The Fugitive," *New Yorker*, February 18–25, 2002, 104–8, 113–15; and Henry Louis Gates, "Slave's Story May Be Earliest Novel by Black Woman," *New York Times*, November 11, 2001.

25. Henry Louis Gates, introduction to Crafts, *Bondswoman's Narrative*, xxxi.

26. Henry Louis Gates, "A Note on Crafts' Literary Influences," in Crafts, *Bondswoman's Narrative*, 331–32.

27. Katherine E. Flynn, "Jane Johnson, Found! But Is She 'Hannah Crafts'? The Search for the Author of 'The Bondswoman's Narrative,'" *National Geographic Society Quarterly* 90 (September 2002): 165–90. Phil Lapsansky, curator of African American history at the Library Company of Philadelphia, adds an interesting twist to the story. Lapsansky believes that Mattie Griffith Browne, a white antislavery novelist and American suffragist, discovered *The Bondswoman's Narrative,* copied the manuscript, and published it under her own name in 1857. See Mattie Griffith Browne, *Autobiography of a Female Slave* (New York: Redfield, 1857)]. Because Browne acknowledged that she was a white woman shortly after publication, the book was considered a "fictional novel" rather than a true autobiography. Lapsansky points out that Browne's work "mimics the *Bondswoman's Narrative* word-for-word." Nor are there many corrections. "It's as if someone had written the book before," he concludes. Phil Lapsansky, interview by author, January 25, 2016.

28. F. James Davis, *Who Is Black? One Nation's Definition* (University Park: Penn State University Press, 1991).

29. Ibid.

30. W. Still, *Underground Railroad* (1872/1970), 162.

31. See US Department of State, *Sixth Census* (Washington, DC, 1841).

32. See Ira Berlin, "The Structure of the Free Negro Caste in the Antebellum United States," *Journal of Social History* 9 (Spring 1976): 305–11; Willard B. Gatewood, *Aristocrats of Color: The Black Elite, 1880–1920* (Bloomington: Indiana University Press, 1990), 7–29; Horton, *Free People of Color*, 122–44. It is also important to note that at least one historian refutes the theory that mulattoes were considered superior to black slaves or that they constituted a separate caste. See Genovese, *Roll, Jordan, Roll*, 429.

33. Franklin and Higginbotham, *From Slavery to Freedom*, 150.

34. Franklin and Schweninger, *Runaway Slaves*, 213–16.

35. W. Still, *Underground Railroad* (1872/1970), 537–38.

36. Ibid., 256–57.

37. Ibid., 257.

38. Ibid., 329.

39. Michael Coffey, ed., *The Irish in America* (New York: Hyperion, 1997), 35, 67, 143.

40. John Thompson quoted in W. Still, *Underground Railroad* (1872/1970), 26.

41. Mary Epps quoted in W. Still, *Underground Railroad* (1872/1970), 61–62.

42. See Kolchin, *American Slavery*, 141–42.

43. W. Still, *Underground Railroad* (1872/1970), 260–61.

44. Drake, *Quakers and Slavery*, 185.

CHAPTER SEVEN

1. W. Still, *Underground Railroad* (1872/1970), 646; Garrett quoted in McGowan, *Station Master*, 134–53. Garrett destroyed all of Still's letters to avoid incriminating himself and his friend. But Still saved most if not all of Garrett's letters to him, and they were republished in Jim McGowen's book *Station Master on the Underground Railroad*. In 1997, Judith Bentley authored a moving and eloquent children's book on Still and Garrett's friendship. Generously illustrated, the book is based, in part, on the correspondence of the two Underground Railroad agents. See Judith Bentley, *"Dear Friend": Thomas Garrett and William Still: Collaborators on the Underground Railroad* (New York: Cobblehill Books / Dutton, 1997). Similarly, in 2001, Teleduction, an award-winning, Delaware-based documentary film company, produced *Whispers of Angels*, which also detailed the close partnership of Garrett (portrayed by Ed Asner) and Still (Blair Underwood). See Sharon Kelly Baker, dir., *Whispers of Angels: A Story of the Underground Railroad* (Wilmington, DE: Teleduction, 2001).

2. John Hunn, "An Account of the Escape from Slavery of Samuel Hawkins and Family on the Underground Railroad," in W. Still, *Underground Railroad* (1872/1970), 551–60. In December 1845, Garrett harbored Samuel Hawkins, a free man from Queen Anne's County, Maryland, his wife, Emeline, and their six children, ranging in age from eighteen months to sixteen years. The two eldest sons were slaves, but the other four children were born free. Had Garrett provided transportation only for the younger children

and not for the two boys he knew to be slaves, he would have avoided a lawsuit for "knowingly harboring" fugitives. Instead, he was sued by the slave owner for helping fugitives escape. Thomas Garrett to the *Blue Hen's Chicken*, June 9, 1848, in McGowan, *Station Master*, 60–61.

3. Thomas Garrett to Eliza Wigham, August 8, 1854, Thomas P. Cope Family Papers: Letters of Thomas Garrett, 1854–57, QC, HCL; McGowan, *Station Master*, 60–61.

4. W. Still, *Underground Railroad* (1872/1970), 741–44.

5. McGowan, *Station Master*, 32–38.

6. Thomas Garrett to Aaron Powell, April 5, 1870, quoted in the *Liberator*, April 1870.

7. Garrett kept meticulous records of the numbers of fugitives he assisted, who by November 24, 1863, totaled 2,322. See Garrett to Samuel May Jr., November 24, 1863, Anti-Slavery Collection, Boston Public Library.

8. McGowen, *Station Master*, 53–54; William H. Williams, *Slavery and Freedom in Delaware, 1639–1865* (Wilmington, DE: Scholarly Resources, 2001), 167.

9. Smedley, *History of the Underground Railroad.* Chaps. 10–17 deal exclusively with Chester County.

10. McGowan, *Station Master*, 46–47, 198. See also *Daily Local News* (West Chester, PA), December 30, 1882.

11. Dr. Bartholomew Fussell quoted in W. Still, *Underground Railroad* (1872/1970), 720–21.

12. *Journal of Friends Historical Society* 20, no. 3 (1923): 126; *Friends Intelligencer* 28 (1871–72): 104.

13. *Pennsylvania Freeman*, October 9, 1845.

14. David Evans Diary, November 26, 1848, CCA.

15. Biographical sketches of Dr. Bartholomew Fussell can be found in Smedley, *History of the Underground Railroad*, 260–73, and in W. Still, *Underground Railroad* (1872/1970), 720–23.

16. *Daily Local*, September 15, 1873.

17. *Philadelphia Public Ledger*, September 25, 1935. Biographical sketches of John and Hannah Cox can be found in Smedley, *History of the Underground Railroad*, 273–81.

18. Lewis, *Memoir of Enoch Lewis*, 33.

19. Enoch Lewis quoted in ibid., 79–80.

20. *Friend* (Philadelphia) 24 (1851): 21, and 68 (1895): 116; Francis C. Taylor, *The Trackless Trail Leads On* (Kennett Square, PA: KNA Press, 1995), 31–33.

21. *Friend* (Philadelphia) 64 (1891): 256; *Friends Review* 45 (1891): 526.

22. George W. Taylor, *The Autobiography and Writings of George W. Taylor* (Philadelphia, 1891), 40–45.

23. Barnard Family Papers, CCA.

24. *Daily Republican*, February 23, 1887.

25. Smedley, *History of the Underground Railroad*, 290.

26. See John Sheppard, "Train to the North Star," *Chester County Town and Country*, Spring 1999, 70; Constance Garcia-Barrio, "Underground Railroad Station: Reminders of Perilous Journeys," *Philadelphia Inquirer*, February 4, 1994; F. Taylor, *Trackless Trail Leads On*, 66–67.

27. Arthur E. James, *The Potters and Potteries of Chester County, Pennsylvania* (West Chester, PA: D. Edwards Biehn, 1945), 9.

28. A biographical sketch of John Vickers can be found in Smedley, *History of the Underground Railroad*, 143–63.

29. Samuel W. Pennypacker, *Annals of Phoenixville and Its Vicinity: From the Settlement to the Year 1871* (Philadelphia: Bavis and Pennypacker, 1872), 214.

30. Biographical sketches of Elijah Pennypacker can be found in Smedley, *History of the Underground Railroad*, 206–15; and W. Still, *Underground Railroad* (1872/1970), 712–15.

31. W. Still, *Underground Railroad* (1872/1970), 713.

32. Frederick Tolles, in his seminal work *Meeting House and Counting House: The Quaker Merchants of Colonial Philadelphia, 1682–1763* (Chapel Hill: University of North Carolina Press, 1948), was the first to examine, in depth, the intimate network that bound Friends together in business, humanitarian, social, and to a lesser degree political realms. Although he focuses on eighteenth-century Philadelphia Quaker merchants, this "peculiar" relationship continued among Friends throughout the nineteenth century, though it did not preclude their involvement with non-Quakers in reform activities.

33. For statistical data on Chester County's Quaker Underground Railroad agents, see Kashatus, *Just over the Line*, 92–96.

34. For a complete treatment of the reciprocal influence between abolitionism and women's rights, see Julie Roy Jeffrey, *The Great Silent Army of Abolitionism: Ordinary Women in the Anti-slavery Movement* (Chapel Hill: University of North Carolina Press, 1998); Aileen S. Kraditor, *Means and Ends in American Abolitionism: Garrison and His Critics on Strategy and Tactics, 1834–1850* (1967; repr., New York: Vintage, 1970), chap. 2.

35. *Philadelphia Bulletin*, November 7, 1868.

36. W. Still, *Underground Railroad* (1872/1970), 775–76.

37. Ibid., 778.

38. Lucretia Mott and Elizabeth Cady Stanton, "Declaration of Sentiments" (1848), in *History of Woman Suffrage*, ed. E. C. Stanton (New York, 1881), 1:70–71.

39. *Proceedings of the Woman's Rights Convention Held at West Chester, PA* (Philadelphia: Merrihew and Thompson, 1852), 3, 15–16.

40. *Pennsylvania Freeman*, June 12, 1852.

41. *Jeffersonian*, June 8, 1852.

42. M. Bacon, *Valiant Friend*, 59–61.

43. Blockson, "Escape from Slavery," 23.

44. *Jeffersonian*, November 7, 1868. For more information on the theological differences that influenced Quaker involvement and noninvolvement with non-Quaker re-

formers, see Doherty, *Hicksite Separation*; Barbour and Frost, *Quakers*; and William C. Kashatus, *A Virtuous Education: William Penn's Vision for Philadelphia Schools* (Wallingford, PA: Pendle Hill, 1997).

45. See Larson, *Bound for the Promised Land*; Jean M. Humez, *Harriet Tubman: The Life and the Life Stories* (Madison: University of Wisconsin Press, 2003); and Milton C. Sernett, *Harriet Tubman: Myth, Memory, and History* (Durham, NC: Duke University Press, 2007).

46. Thomas Garrett to Sarah Bradford, June 1866, QC, HCL.

47. Thomas Garrett to William Still, March 27, 1857, and December 1, 1860, in McGowan, *Station Master*, 142–43, 152–53; W. Still, *Underground Railroad* (1872/1970), 305–8, 554–55; Larson, *Bound for Promised Land*, 130–31, 137–38.

48. Thomas Garrett to Eliza Wigham, December 27, 1856, QC, HCL.

49. Thomas Garrett to Eliza Wigham, December 27, 1856, and Garrett to Wigham, October 24, 1856, QC, HCL.

50. W. Still, *Underground Railroad* (1872/1970), 305–6.

51. J. Smith Futhey and Gilbert Cope, *History of Chester County* (Philadelphia: Lippincott, 1881); Margaret L. Wolf, *A History of West Whiteland* (Exton, PA: West Whiteland Historical Commission, 1982), 42–43.

52. *Jeffersonian*, November 7, 1868.

53. *Oxford Press* (Oxford, PA), April 7, 1898.

54. *Village Record* (West Chester, PA), August 9, 1850.

55. *Daily Local* (West Chester, PA), May 31, 1893.

56. Switala, *Underground Railroad in Pennsylvania*, 165–75. See also Jordan, *Slavery and the Meetinghouse*, 81–103; McDaniel and Julye, *Fit for Freedom*, 96–106; William W. Sweet, *The Story of Religion in America* (New York: Harper and Row, 1930), 170–80; David Christy, *Pulpit Politics, or Ecclesiastical Legislation on Slavery in Its Disturbing Influences on the American Union* (New York: Farran and McLean, 1862).

57. W. Still, *Underground Railroad* (1872/1970), 637–812. Still published these pages after the passage of the Thirteenth Amendment abolishing slavery in 1865. Thus there would be no legal recriminations against the agents after the book's publication in 1872.

58. Ibid., 114–22, 136–40, 305–8, 554–55.

59. For "Colored Boatmen," see ibid. For Abraham Shadd, see William Still, Journal C, HSP; Smedley, *History of the Underground Railroad*, 33, 323, 337; and Rhodes, *Mary Ann Shadd Cary*, 14.

60. Thomas Garrett to William Still, March 27, 1857, and December 1, 1860, in McGowan, *Station Master*, 142–43, 152–53. For free black agents who assisted Garrett, see McGowan, *Station Master*, 122–28.

61. W. Still, *Underground Railroad* (1872/1970), xiii.

62. Ibid., 63, 162.

63. Ibid., 161–64.

64. E. Foner, *Gateway to Freedom*, 153.

65. W. Still, *Underground Railroad* (1872/1970), 63.

66. Ibid., 162.

67. Ibid., 256–57.

68. John T. Kneebone, "A Breakdown on the Underground Railroad: Captain B. and the Capture of Keziah, 1858," *Virginia Cavalcade* 48, no. 2 (Spring 1999): 74–83.

CHAPTER EIGHT

1. Popular accounts of Canada West's fugitive slave population claim that there were approximately forty thousand blacks in the province in 1860 and that the large majority of these were runaway slaves and their children who came from the United States. See Winks, *Blacks in Canada*, 233–40, Appendix; C. Peter Ripley, ed., *The Black Abolitionist Papers*, vol. 2, *Canada 1830–1865* (Chapel Hill: University of North Carolina Press, 1986); Jason Silverman, *Unwelcome Guests: American Fugitive Slaves in Canada, 1830–1860* (Millwood, NY: Associated Faculty Press, 1985); and William H. Pease and Jane Pease, *Black Utopia: Negro Communal Experiments in America* (Madison: Wisconsin State Historical Society, 1963). But Michael Wayne argues that "enumerators' schedules from the 1861 census for Canada West . . . suggest that historians have exaggerated the size of the black population in general, [and] significantly overstated the proportion who were fugitives from slavery." He claims that the numbers of fugitive slaves were considerable lower, since the total black population of Canada West was only 17,053 in 1861. See Michael Wayne, "The Black Population of Canada West on the Eve of the American Civil War: A Reassessment Based on the Manuscript Census of 1861," *Histoire Sociale / Social History* 56 (November 1995): 466–67.

2. William R. Riddell, "The Slave in Upper Canada," *Journal of Criminal Law and Criminology* 14, no. 2 (1923): 256–58; Winks, *Blacks in Canada*, 149, 170–73; Silverman, *Unwelcome Guests*, 37–40.

3. Fred Landon, "Henry Bibb, a Colonizer," *Journal of Negro History* 5, no. 4 (1920): 447, 442–43.

4. Benjamin Drew, *A North-Side View of Slavery. The Refugee, or The Narratives of Fugitive Slaves in Canada, Related by Themselves: With an Account of the History and Condition of the Colored Population of Upper Canada* (1856; repr., New York: Negro Universities Press, 1968), v.

5. Bordewich, *Bound for Canaan*, 324.

6. Drew, *North-Side View of Slavery*, v; Boulou Ebanda de B'beri et al., *The Promised Land: History and Historiography of the Black Experience in Chatham-Kent's Settlements and Beyond* (Toronto: University of Toronto Press, 2014), 22; Tobin, *From Midnight to Dawn*, 16. The largest concentration of black immigrants and refugees was in the Chatham-Kent region of Canada West, and the most popular destinations for runaway slaves were the black settlements of Wilberforce and Dawn.

7. Natasha L. Henry, "The Underground Railroad in Canada," in *The Canadian Encyclopedia*, online ed., edited by Bronwen Graves, retrieved January 12, 2018, www.the canadianencyclopedia.ca/en/article/underground-railroad/.

8. Hill, *Freedom Seekers*, 118–21; Winks, *Blacks in Canada*, 151–52; Bordewich, *Bound for Canaan*, 247.

9. John Henry Hill to William Still, January 19, 1854, reprinted in Still, *Underground Railroad* (1872/1970), 199–200.

10. Rosemary Sadler quoted in Laine Drewery, dir., *Underground Railroad: The William Still Story*, DVD, PBS Home Video, 2012.

11. Rhodes, *Mary Ann Shadd Cary*, 44–48; Henry Bibb, *Voice of the Fugitive*, February 12, 1851. Other prominent black abolitionists who supported emigration to Canada were Henry Bibb, editor of the antislavery newspaper, *Voice of the Fugitive*; Reverend Samuel Ringgold Ward, editor of the antislavery newspaper the *Impartial Citizen* and an agent for the Anti-Slavery Society of Canada; and Lewis Woodson, an early leader of the AME Church and a founding member of Wilberforce College.

12. Rhodes, *Mary Ann Shadd Cary*, 13–14; Manisha Sinha, *The Slave's Cause: A History of Abolition* (New Haven, CT: Yale University Press, 2016), 332. Abraham Shadd, a mulatto shoemaker, is mentioned as an important stationmaster in several accounts, including Smedley, *History of the Underground Railroad*, 33, 337; and E. Turner, *Negro in Pennsylvania*, 240. He was also an ambitious man, who gradually amassed land holdings in Chester County, Pennsylvania, that resulted, by 1850, in an estate valued at $3,000, ensuring him and his thirteen children a comfortable existence See Chester County Tax Lists, 1836, 1850, and Chester County Septennial Census, 1835, 1842, microfilm copies, CCA. One of six African Americans named to the American Anti-Slavery Society, founded in 1833 by William Lloyd Garrison, Shadd, along with Philadelphia blacks William Whipper and Robert Purvis, called on the state legislature to repeal a portion of the Pennsylvania Constitution, ratified a decade earlier, that limited the franchise to white men. See "Minutes of the State Convention of the Coloured Citizens of Pennsylvania, Convened at Harrisburg, December 13–14, 1848," in *Proceedings of the Black State Conventions, 1840–1865*, ed. Philip S. Foner and George S. Walker (Philadelphia: Temple University Press, 1979), 119–35; and Rhodes, *Mary Ann Shadd Cary*, 16–20.

13. Rhodes, *Mary Ann Shadd Cary*, 17–21.

14. Mary Ann Shadd quoted in *North Star*, March 23, 1849.

15. Mary Ann Shadd, *A Plea for Emigration or, Notes of Canada West, in Its Moral, Social and Political Aspect: With Suggestions Respecting Mexico, West Indies, and Vancouver's Island, for the Information of Colored Emigrants* (Detroit, MI: George W. Pattison, 1852).

16. Rhodes, *Mary Ann Shadd Cary*, 74–77.

17. *Voice of the Fugitive*, February 26, 1852. Bibb's newspaper was the official organ of the Refugee Home Society Project, which encouraged segregated black settlements, schools, and churches.

18.   Rhodes, *Mary Ann Shadd Cary*, 42. Ironically, Bibbs, who advocated return-ing to the United States, lived out his life in Canada, and Mary Ann Shadd, who sought Canada as a permanent refuge, returned to her native America.

19.   Ibid., 85–91. Despite Shadd's best efforts to raise funds, the *Provincial Freeman* had only a seven-year run.

20.   Ibid., 93–97. Mary Ann Shadd Cary's lecture tours were both well received and disrupted by anti-abolitionist heckling. They also provided her with information on Af-rican Americans' living conditions in Canada and the United States, which she then pub-lished in the *Provincial Freeman*. At an 1855 convention of African Americans in Philadelphia, Mary Ann Shadd became the first black woman to be admitted as a corre-sponding member because of her prominent work as a lecturer.

21.   Ibid., 127–28.

22.   William Still quoted in Tobin, *From Midnight to Dawn*, 69; Horton, "Crusade for Freedom," 185. For Still's essay contributions, see *Provincial Freeman*, March 24 and December 1, 1855.

23.   William Still to Henry Bibb, quoted in *Voice of the Fugitive*, April 9, 1851.

24.   *Provincial Freeman*, December 22, 1855.

25.   Shadd, *Plea for Emigration*.

26.   *Pennsylvania Freeman*, September 29, 1853.

27.   James and Lucretia Mott to the "Lovers of Liberty and Friends of Humanity in Canada," September 5, 1855, quoted in W. Still, *Underground Railroad* (1886), xxi.

28.   J. Miller McKim to Thomas Henning, Esq., September 10, 1855, quoted in W. Still, *Underground Railroad* (1886), xxv.

29.   Population figures for Chatham vary, but Jaqueline Tobin estimates that the black population was approximately one-third of the total population (*From Dawn to Midnight*, 40). If that estimation is accurate, the 1,252 black residents Michael Wayne cal-culated in his 1995 study would make the total population of Chatham 3,756 by 1861. See Wayne, "Black Population," 483.

30.   Drew, *North-Side View of Slavery*.

31.   William Wells Brown, *The Travels of William Wells Brown* (1848; repr., New York: Marcus Weiner, 1991).

32.   Tobin, *From Dawn to Midnight*, 41.

33.   Ibid., 41.

34.   William Wells Brown, "The Colored People of Canada," *Pine and Palm*, Octo-ber 19, 1861, in "*Weekly Anglo-African* and *Pine and Palm*: Excerpts from 1861–62," ed. Brigitte Fielder, Cassander Smith, and Derrick R. Spires, Just Teach One, http://jtoaa .common-place.org/wp-content/uploads/sites/3/2018/08/PineandPalm.pdf.

35.   Mary Ann Shadd Cary quoted in *Provincial Freeman*, November 3, 1855.

36.   Tobin, *From Dawn to Midnight*, 151.

37.   William Still, *Underground Railroad* (1872/1970), 279–80; Kate Larson, *Bound for the Promised Land*, 133–36, 159; and Sarah Bradford, *Scenes in the Life of Harriet Tub-man* (Auburn: W. J. Moses, 1869), 27–35.

38. Boyd, preface to W. Still, *Underground Railroad* (1886), xxvi.

39. *Philadelphia Public Ledger*, January 21, 1860.

40. *North American*, February 1, 1860.

CHAPTER NINE

1. Historians differ significantly on their estimates of the number of runaway slaves who escaped via the Underground Railroad. Wilbur Siebert gave the highest estimate, at one hundred thousand between 1810 and 1850 (Siebert, *Underground Railroad*, 341), and Larry Gara the lowest, at eleven thousand (Gara, *Liberty Line*, 37). But the report written for the Freedmen's Inquiry Commission in Washington, D.C., in 1864 estimated that between thirty thousand and forty thousand fugitives reached Canada using the Underground Railroad between 1800 and 1864 (S. G. Howe, *Report to the Freedmen's Inquiry Commission, 1864: The Refugees from Slavery in Canada West* [1864; repr., Arno Press and New York Times, 1969], 15). Samuel Ringgold Ward, a fugitive himself, corroborated the report's finding in his 1855 autobiography, stating that there were between thirty-five thousand and forty-thousand "coloured people" in Canada. Of these, Ward claimed that about three thousand were free-born and the rest were fugitives. See Samuel Ringgold Ward, *Autobiography of a Fugitive Negro: His Anti-slavery Labors in the United States, Canada and England* (1855; repr., Arno Press and New York Times, 1969), 154.

2. *Pennsylvania Freeman*, August 22, 1850.

3. *National Anti-Slavery Standard*, February 3, 1855.

4. For the best biographical account of Seth Concklin, see William Furness, "Seth Concklin," in Pickard, *Kidnapped and the Ransomed*, 377–409.

5. Sinha, *Slave's Cause*, 447.

6. Seth Concklin to William Still, February 18, 1851, in W. Still, *Underground Railroad* (1872/1970), 7–8.

7. Ibid., 8–9.

8. N. R. Johnston to William Still, March 31, 1851, in W. Still, *Underground Railroad* (1872/1970), 9–11.

9. Ibid.

10. Still, *Underground Railroad* (1872/1970), 11.

11. Bernard McKiernan to William Still, August 6, 1851, in W. Still, *Underground Railroad* (1872/1970), 14–15.

12. Levi Coffin to William Still, Cincinnati, May 11, 1851, quoted in W. Still, *Underground Railroad* (1872/1970), 13–14.

13. McKiernan to Still, August 6, 1851.

14. Sinha, *Slave's Cause*, 446–47.

15. W. Still, *Underground Railroad* (1872/1970), 19.

16. D. Davis, *Problem of Slavery*, 237.

17. Ibid., 237.

18. Kolchin, *American Slavery*, 100–102.

19. W. Still, *Underground Railroad* (1872/1970), 536–37.

20. Ibid., 87, 207–8, 513–14.

21. Ibid., 403–4.

22. See Stampp, *Peculiar Institution*; Franklin and Schweninger, *Runaway Slaves*, 285; and Thomas, *Slave Trade*, 807–8.

23. Franklin and Schweninger, *Runaway Slaves*, 176–78.

24. W. Still, *Underground Railroad* (1872/1970), 245–47.

25. Ibid., 279–80.

CHAPTER TEN

1. W. Still, *Underground Railroad* (1872/1970), 84–91.

2. Perhaps the largest escape in the history of the Underground Railroad occurred in 1848, when seventy-seven slaves from Washington, D.C., attempted to flee from bondage down the Potomac River in a schooner called the *Pearl*. They were caught, however, and the captain spent more than four years in jail before being pardoned by President Millard Fillmore. See Mary Kay Ricks, *Escape on the Pearl: The Heroic Bid for Freedom on the Underground Railroad* (New York: Harper, 2008); and Stanley Harrold, "The Pearl Affair: The Washington Riot of 1848," *Records of the Columbia Historical Society* 50 (1980): 140–60.

3. W. Still, *Underground Railroad* (1872/1970), 94–95, 165, 325–29, 336–46, 585–88.

4. See Stampp, *Peculiar Institution*, 340–49; Blassingame, *Slave Community*, 77–103; Genovese, *Roll, Jordan, Roll*, 450–518; and Horton, *Slavery and the Making*, 106–8, 129.

5. W. Still, *Underground Railroad* (1872/1970), 417–18.

6. Ibid., 412–14.

7. Ibid., 423–25.

8. See Campbell, *Slave Catchers*, 199–207. Campbell argues that there was a significant increase in the number of fugitives arrested in 1851, with the vast majority being returned to slavery. He found twenty-one cases of arrest in 1850, with nineteen returned. The following year, however, he found sixty-six cases of arrest, with fifty-eight returned. In addition, Campbell found that Pennsylvania, a free state located just over the border from slavery, witnessed the arrest of eighty-six fugitives between 1850 and 1860, compared to only seventeen in New York and seven in Massachusetts.

9. W. Still, *Underground Railroad* (1872/1970), 588.

10. Ibid., 339.

11. Franklin and Schweninger, *Runaway Slaves*, 4, 98.

12. Ripley, *Underground Railroad*, 48, 54; E. Turner, *Negro in Pennsylvania*, 253. In 1850, Philadelphia's 19,761 free blacks constituted one of the largest free black popula-

tions in the United States. That number represented 5 percent of the city's total population of 408,762 residents. By 1860, the city's free black population increased to 22,185, or 4 percent of the total population of 565,529.

13. Switala, *Underground Railroad in Delaware*, 28–33, 62–71, 109–10, 114–15; W. Williams, *Slavery and Freedom in Delaware*, 31–34.

14. Switala, *Underground Railroad in Delaware*, 33–34.

15. Ibid., 31–33; Blockson, *Hippocrene Guide*, 23–31.

16. Switala, *Underground Railroad in Delaware*, 72–76.

17. Small, "Abolitionists, Free Blacks," 55–72; Switala, *Underground Railroad in Delaware*, 63–71.

18. Lewis Burrell to William Still, February 2, 1859, quoted in W. Still, *Underground Railroad* (1872/1970), 400.

19. W. Still, *Underground Railroad* (1872/1970), 400.

20. W. Still, Journal C, entries for 1857, HSP.

21. W. Still, Journal C, entries for 1854, HSP. Still resumed sending fugitives to New York City in August 1855, but not under the care of the city's vigilance committee, which was in disarray. Instead, he worked with Sydney H. Gay, the editor of the *National Anti-Slavery Standard*, who assumed leadership of the city's UGRR network and operated out of the American Anti-Slavery Society's office. See E. Foner, *Gateway to Freedom*, 171.

CHAPTER ELEVEN

1. Potter, *Impending Crisis*, 18–32; Kenneth M. Stampp, *The Imperiled Union: Essays on the Background of the Civil War* (New York: Oxford University Press, 1981), 198–208; Edward L. Ayers, *What Caused the Civil War? Reflections on the South and Southern History* (New York: W. W. Norton, 2005), 131–44.

2. James M. McPherson, *This Mighty Scourge: Perspectives on the Civil War* (New York: Oxford University Press, 2007), 3–16.

3. Don E. Fehrenbacher, *The Dred Scott Case: Its Significance in American Law and Politics* (New York: Oxford University Press, 1978), 239–48.

4. Judgment in the US Supreme Court Case Dred Scott v. John F. A. Sanford, March 6, 1857, Case Files 1792–1995, Record Group 267, Records of the Supreme Court of the United States, National Archives, www.ourdocuments.gov/doc.php?flash=true&doc=29; John S. Vishneski, "What the Court Decided in *Dred Scott v. Sandford*," *American Journal of Legal History* 32, no. 4 (October 1988): 373–90; Paul Finkelman, "*Scott v. Sanford*: The Court's Most Dreadful Case and How It Changed History," *Chicago-Kent Law Review* 82 (December 2006): 3–48.

5. Robert Purvis quoted in Horton, "Crusade for Freedom," 191.

6. Charles Lenox Redmond quoted in *Liberator*, April 10, 1857.

7. Biddle and Dubin, *Tasting Freedom*, 195–97.

8. For the best biographies of John Brown, see W. E. B. Du Bois, *John Brown* (1909; repr., International Publishers, 1972); Stephen B. Oates, *To Purge This Land with Blood: A Biography of John Brown* (Amherst: University of Massachusetts Press, 1984); and David S. Reynolds, *John Brown, Abolitionist: The Man Who Killed Slavery, Sparked the Civil War and Seeded Civil Rights* (New York: Vintage, 2006).

9. Du Bois, *John Brown*, 132–33.

10. Nicole Etcheson, *Bleeding Kansas: Contested Liberty in the Civil War Era* (Lawrence: University of Kansas Press, 2006), chap. 1; Potter, *Impending Crisis*, 146–55.

11. Etcheson, *Bleeding Kansas*, 89–95.

12. Potter, *Impending Crisis*, 199–220; and Dale E. Watts, "How Bloody Was Bleeding Kansas? Political Killings in Kansas Territory, 1854–1861," *Kansas History* 18, no. 2 (Summer 1995): 116–29.

13. John Brown quoted in Du Bois, *John Brown*, 158–59.

14. Du Bois, *John Brown*, 199–202.

15. Oates, *To Purge This Land*, 241–42.

16. Bordewich, *Bound for Canaan*, 417: Larson, *Bound for the Promised Land*, 156–57.

17. Douglass, *My Bondage*, 454–56.

18. Edward J. Renehan Jr., *The Secret Six: The True Tale of the Men Who Conspired with John Brown* (New York: Crown, 1995), 118–20; Bordewich, *Bound for Canaan*, 417.

19. Oates, *To Purge This Land*, 240–42; Bordewich, *Bound for Canaan*, 417.

20. Sernett, *North Star Country*, 78.

21. Bordewich, *Bound for Canaan*, 418.

22. John Brown to John Brown Jr., April 8, 1858, quoted in Frederick Sanborn, ed., *The Life and Letters of John Brown* (New York: Negro Universities Press, 1885), 452.

23. Sernett, *North Star Country*, 79.

24. Brown to Brown Junior, April 8, 1858.

25. Osborne Perry Anderson, *A Voice from Harper's Ferry* (Washington, DC: J. D. Enos, 1878), 5.

26. *National Era*, December 15, 1859; Oates, *To Purge This Land*, 248; Benjamin Quarles, *Allies for Freedom: Blacks and John Brown* (New York: Oxford University Press, 1974), 45–51.

27. Boyd, preface to W. Still, *Underground Railroad* (1886), xxii. When Frederick Douglass learned that authorities had confiscated Brown's carpetbag containing letters linking him to the radical abolitionist, he wired his son, Lewis, requesting that he "secure" any incriminating evidence. Also found among the letters was a canceled check for $100 from Gerrit Smith, one of the "Secret Six" abolitionists who funded the raid. See William S. McFeely, *Frederick Douglass* (New York: W. W. Norton, 1991), 199.

28. Oates, *To Purge This Land*, 290–302; *New York Herald*, October 17, 1859.

29. Boyd, preface to W. Still, *Underground Railroad* (1886), xxiii.

30. Ibid., xxiii–xxiv.

31. Ibid., xxiii–xxiv; Tobin, *From Midnight to Dawn*, 53; Bordewich, *Bound for Canaan*, 425.

32. Boyd, preface to W. Still, *Underground Railroad* (1886), xxxiv.

33. See *New York Herald*, October 17, 1859; *National Era*, October 20, 1859.

34. Boyd, preface to W. Still, *Underground Railroad* (1886), xxii; W. Still, *Underground Railroad* (1886), 531.

35. Thomas Garrett to Sarah Bradford, June 1868, in McGowan, *Station Master*, 97–98.

36. John Brown, "Address of John Brown to the Virginia Court," December 1859, Gilder Lehrman Institute of American History Collection, retrieved March 4, 2018, www .gilderlehrman.org.

37. Boyd, preface to W. Still, *Underground Railroad* (1886), xxiii. See also M. Bacon, *But One Race*, 135; Gary Nash, *First City: Philadelphia and the Forging of Historical Memory* (Philadelphia: University of Pennsylvania Press, 2002), 196–97. After John Brown's burial, his daughter, Annie, sent William Still a lock of her father's hair, along with a note that read: "Mother sends a lock of father's hair which she promised you. She also sends her love to you and your family." The note, the clip of hair, and the gold locket in which it was sent are now in the HSP's collections in Philadelphia.

38. Quarles, *Allies for Freedom*, 128.

39. Reynolds, *John Brown, Abolitionist*, 6.

40. Renehan, *Secret Six*, 3–4.

41. Russell F. Weigley, "The Border City in Civil War, 1854–1865," in Weigley, *Philadelphia*, 390–91.

42. Ibid., 389–93; M. Bacon, *But One Race*, 135; Varon, "'Beautiful Providences,'" 240.

43. Nash, *First City*, 197.

44. Abraham Lincoln, "Speech at New Haven, Connecticut," March 6, 1860, in *The Collected Works of Abraham Lincoln*, ed. Roy P. Basler, 9 vols. (New Brunswick, NJ: Rutgers University Press, 1953–55), 4:16.

45. James McPherson, *Ordeal by Fire: The Civil War and Reconstruction*, 3rd ed. (New York: McGraw-Hill, 2001), 164–72.

46. Ibid., 163.

47. J. Miller McKim to William Still, June 1, 1861, quoted in W. Still, *Underground Railroad* (1886), xxx.

48. Boyd, preface to W. Still, *Underground Railroad* (1886), xxix.

49. Ibid., xxx.

50. Larry Gara, "William Still and the Underground Railroad," *Pennsylvania History* 28 (January 1961): 37–38.

51. Boyd, preface to W. Still, *Underground Railroad* (1886), xlvii.

52. *National Anti-Slavery Standard*, May 16, 1863; Philadelphia City Directory, 1862, LCP.

53. Boyd, preface to W. Still, *Underground Railroad* (1886), xlix.

54. Ibid., xlviii.

55. *Anglo-African* (New York), March 23, 1861. The SCSA anticipated a similar effort by W. E. B. Du Bois, the first African American to earn a doctorate at Harvard University. Du Bois was hired by the University of Pennsylvania in 1896 to collect data to prove that the black residents of Philadelphia's Seventh Ward were responsible for the rise in crime and disorder in the city. What he discovered, however, was that the problems confronting Philadelphia's blacks had nothing to do with their supposed racial proclivities but derived from the discriminatory way they had been treated in the past and their relegation in the present to the most menial and lowest-paying jobs. The final product, *The Philadelphia Negro: A Social Study* (1899), proved to be the first great empirical study on blacks in American society. See W. E. B. Du Bois, *The Philadelphia Negro: A Social Study* (1899; repr., Philadelphia: University of Pennsylvania Press, 1996).

56. McPherson, *Ordeal by Fire*, 378.

57. James M. McPherson, *Battle Cry of Freedom: The Civil War Era* (New York: Oxford University Press, 1989), 563–64.

58. The most authentic account of the Fifty-Fourth Massachusetts's assault on Fort Wagner was written by a member of that regiment, Luis F. Emilio, *A Brave Black Regiment: History of the Fifty-Fourth Regiment of Massachusetts Volunteer Infantry, 1863–1865* (Boston: Boston Book, 1894).

59. Russell Duncan, ed., *Blue-Eyed Child of Fortune: The Civil War Letters of Colonel Robert Gould Shaw* (Athens: University of Georgia Press, 1992), 52.

60. James M. McPherson, *The Negro's Civil War: How American Blacks Felt and Acted during the War for the Union*, 3rd ed. (New York: Ballantine Books, 1991), 241.

61. James Elton Johnson, "A History of Camp William Penn and Its Black Troops in the Civil War, 1863–1865" (PhD diss., University of Pennsylvania, 1999), 41.

62. Donald Scott, *Camp William Penn, 1863–1865* (Atglen, PA: Schiffer Books, 2012), 78. Despite her pacifist convictions, Lucretia Mott was impressed by the black regiments as they drilled within sight of her parlor window. On July 12, 1863, she even accepted an invitation to preach to the Eleventh Black Regiment—some six hundred soldiers—at the camp.

63. Ibid., 78.

64. Boyd, preface to W. Still, *Underground Railroad* (1886), xlix.

65. *Christian Recorder*, January 30, 1864.

66. Lew Foster, Assistant Adjutant General, to Lieutenant Colonel Louis Wagner, December 21, 1863, quoted in Scott, *Camp William Penn*, 19.

67. Bordewich, *Bound for Canaan*, 431; Boyd, preface to W. Still, *Underground Railroad* (1886), xlix.

68. Mayer, *All on Fire*, 569.

69. Boyd, preface to W. Still, *Underground Railroad* (1886), xlix–l.

70. Ibid.

71. Scott, *Camp William Penn*, 19.

72. Ibid., 45. Among the ICY students who joined the Union Army were Lombard L. Nickens, William T. Jones, Martin M. White, Joseph White, Joseph B. Adger, Andrew Glasgow, Henry Boyer Jr., and Jacob R. Ballard. Together with Catto, these new recruits paraded off to the train station in West Philadelphia, where a train would carry them to Harrisburg and they would be mustered into the Union Army. But Major General Darius N. Couch, who was in charge of recruits from the Susquehanna region, refused to induct them because of his own racial prejudice. When Secretary of War Edwin Stanton learned of the incident, he sent Couch a caustic telegram ordering him to "authorize and receive into service any volunteer troops that may be offered without regard to color" (46–47).

CHAPTER TWELVE

1. Roger Lane, *William Dorsey's Philadelphia and Ours: On the Past and Future of the Black City in America* (New York: Oxford University Press, 1991), 105–6; Bordewich, *Bound for Canaan*, 411–12. Other abolitionists of Still's generation included Henry Bibb, George DeBaptiste, Lewis Hayden, William Lambert, and Rev. William Monroe.

2. For Still's reform involvements, see William Still to Charity Still, July 27, 1865, WSC, CBAAC; Charles H. Wesley, *The Quest for Equality* (Washington, DC: United Publishing, 1968), 67–73; and Diane Turner, "William Still's National Significance," n.d., William Still Online Collection, Temple University Libraries, Philadelphia, PA, retrieved February 10, 2018, http://stillfamily.library.temple.edu/exhibits/show/william-still /historical-perspective/william-still---s-national-sig.

3. William Still, *A Brief Narrative of the Struggle for the Rights of the Colored People of Philadelphia in the Railway Cars; and a Defense of William Still Relating to His Agency Touching the Passage of the Late Bill* (Philadelphia: Merrihew and Son, 1867), 23–24.

4. Philip Foner, "The Battle to End Discrimination against Negroes on the Philadelphia Streetcars: (Part I): Background and the Beginnings of the Battle," *Pennsylvania History* 40 (April 1973): 275–80.

5. William Still, "Colored People and the Cars," *North American and United States Gazette*, August 31, 1859.

6. Still, *Brief Narrative*, 4.

7. Weigley, "Border City," 415.

8. William Still et al., "Petition for the Colored People of Philadelphia to Ride in the Railway Cars," Miscellaneous Collection, HSP.

9. W. Still, *Brief Narrative*, 7; *Philadelphia Bulletin*, June 12, 1862; *Christian Recorder*, June 14, 1862.

10. W. Still, *Brief Narrative*, 9–10.

11. Ibid., 11–12.

12. Biddle and Dubin, *Tasting Freedom*, 323–25.

13. Alston quoted in *Philadelphia Press*, July 21, 1864.

14. Hugh Davis, "The Pennsylvania State Equal Rights League and the Northern Black Struggle for Equality: 1864–1877," *Pennsylvania Magazine of History and Biography* 126, no. 4 (October 2002): 611–34.

15. Silcox, "Black 'Better Class' Political Dilemma," 47–48; Silcox, "Negro Educator," 86–87.

16. Biddle and Dubin, *Tasting Freedom*, 77–78, 97.

17. Harry Silcox, "Nineteenth Century Philadelphia Black Militant: Octavius Catto, 1839–1871," Pennsylvania History 44 (1977): 53–76, republished in *African Americans in Pennsylvania: Shifting Historical Perspectives*, ed. Joe William Trotter Jr. and Eric Ledell Smith (University Park: Penn State University Press, 1997), 201.

18. Biddle and Dubin, *Tasting Freedom*, 292. In June 1863, Pennsylvania's governor Andrew Curtin declared martial law and requested short-term soldiers for the state militia to protect Harrisburg from the encroaching Confederate Army. Catto and his ninety recruits had answered the governor's call for this emergency. When they arrived at Harrisburg on June 17, Catto's troops were given weapons and mustered into the army. But Major General Darius N. Couch, commander of the Department of the Susquehanna, who was responsible for the state's defense, barred Catto's company from serving in the emergency volunteer militia. Couch insisted that Congress allowed blacks to serve only a three-year enlistment in the army, not a limited term. Catto and his soldier were sent back to Philadelphia because of institutional racism. See Silcox, "Black Militant Octavius Catto," 203–4.

19. H. Davis, "Pennsylvania State Equal Rights League," 613–15.

20. Biddle and Dubin, *Tasting Freedom*, 3.

21. P. Foner, "Battle to End Discrimination (I)," 272–73, 282–84; Biddle and Dubin, *Tasting Freedom*, 329–34.

22. Still quoted in *North American and United States Gazette*, December 8, 1864. Satterlee General Hospital was located in West Philadelphia and Summit Hospital at Sixty-Ninth and Woodland in Paschallville.

23. William Still and J. Miller McKim, "Resolutions Presented at Public Meeting on Passenger Cars," January 13, 1865, quoted in Still, *Brief Narrative*, 12.

24. Weigley, "Border City," 415–16.

25. Biddle and Dubin, *Tasting Freedom*, 339–41.

26. Silcox, "Black Militant Octavius Catto," 207, 218n39; Biddle and Dubin, *Tasting Freedom*, 391. Forney was also the first editor of a major American newspaper to hire a black Civil War correspondent, Thomas M. Chester.

27. Philip Foner, "The Battle to End Discrimination against Negroes on the Philadelphia Streetcars: (Part II): The Victory," *Pennsylvania History* 40 (October 1973): 355–79.

28. Ibid., 376.

29. H. Davis, "Pennsylvania State Equal Rights League," 616–18. Although the Social, Civic, and Statistical Association of the Colored People of Pennsylvania refused to

become an auxiliary of the Pennsylvania Equal Rights League and rejected its request for a financial contribution, members of PERL and SCSA often attended each other's lectures and public meetings.

30. Pennsylvania Equal Rights League, "Minutes of Annual Convention, 1865," quoted in H. Davis, "Pennsylvania State Equal Rights League," 618–19.

31. *Christian Recorder*, November 25, 1865, February 23, 1867.

32. Boyd, preface to W. Still, *Underground Railroad* (1886), xlix.

33. Still, *Brief Narrative*, 12–15, 23–24. Still identifies the following black-owned and -operated businesses: W. C. Banton and W. H. Hunter's Publishing House of the AME Church at 631 Pine Street; Warley Bascom's upholstery business at 261 South Eighth Street; J. F. Wallace's grocery store at 618 South Eleventh Street; and Craven's China store at 1107 South Street.

34. W. Still, *Brief Narrative*, 1–2, 17–21.

35. Ibid., 21–22.

36. Ibid., 1–2.

37. Ibid., 11.

CHAPTER THIRTEEN

1. Silcox, "Black 'Better Class' Political Dilemma," 47.

2. Lane, *William Dorsey's Philadelphia*, 305. According to Lane, Catto, at the time of his death in 1871, was earning "some $1,400 a year" as a teacher at the Institute for Colored Youth.

3. Biddle and Dubin. *Tasting Freedom*, 2; Lane, *William Dorsey's Philadelphia*, 305–6.

4. Michael E. Lomax, *Black Baseball Entrepreneurs, 1860–1901* (New York: Syracuse University Press, 2003), 18–19; Biddle and Dubin, *Tasting Freedom*, 361–64.

5. Silcox, "Negro Educator," 86–87.

6. William Still to Pythian Baseball Club, January 30, 1869, Pythian Baseball Club Papers, HSP.

7. Jacob C. White Jr. to William Still, March 1, 1869, Pythian Baseball Club Papers, HSP.

8. William Gillette, *The Right to Vote: Politics and Passage of the Fifteenth Amendment* (Baltimore: Johns Hopkins University Press, 1965), 42–43, 50–52, 56–57; Edward Price, "The Black Voting Rights Issue in Pennsylvania, 1780–1900," *Pennsylvania Magazine of History and Biography* 100, no. 3 (July 1976): 356–73.

9. Walter Licht, "Civil Wars: 1850–1900," in *Pennsylvania: A History of the Commonwealth*, ed. Randall M. Miller and William Pencak (University Park: Penn State University Press, 2002), 253–54.

10. Philip S. Klein and Ari Hooganboom, *A History of Pennsylvania*, 2nd ed. (University Park: Penn State University Press, 1980), 357.

11. Dorothy G. Beers, "The Centennial City, 1865–1876," in Weigley, *Philadelphia*, 438–39.

12. Klein and Hooganboom, *History of Pennsylvania*, 357.

13. Gillette, *Right to Vote*, 56–57; Price, "Black Voting Rights Issue," 370–73.

14. *Philadelphia Public Ledger*, April 1 and 4, 1870.

15. *Philadelphia Public Ledger*, April 27, 1870; *Philadelphia Inquirer*, April 27, 1870; *Patriot-Union* (Harrisburg, PA), April 27, 1870; *New National Era* (Washington, PA), May 5, 1870.

16. Silcox, "Black Militant Octavius Catto," 212–15.

17. Silcox, "Black 'Better Class' Political Dilemma," 49. For the complete public debate between Douglass and Wears, see *Philadelphia Press*, May 30 and June 2, 5, 9, 20, and 27, 1870.

18. *Philadelphia Public Ledger*, April 27, 1870; *Patriot-Union* (Harrisburg, PA), April 26, 1870; Silcox, "Black 'Better Class' Political Dilemma," 48–49; and Price, "Black Voting Rights Issue," 368.

19. Silcox, "Black 'Better Class' Political Dilemma," 50.

20. Thomas A. Sanelli, "The Struggle for Black Suffrage in Pennsylvania, 1838–1870" (PhD diss., Temple University, 1977), 232, 240–42; Clark, "Urban Blacks and Irishmen," 15–30; Beers, "Centennial City."

21. Du Bois, *Philadelphia Negro*, 373.

22. Price, "Black Voting Rights Issue," 370. For primary source accounts of the rioting, see *Philadelphia Public Ledger*, October 11 and 14, 1871; and *Philadelphia Inquirer*, October 11, 1971.

23. Biddle and Dubin, *Tasting Freedom*, 427.

24. Catto quoted in Klein and Hooganboom, *History of Pennsylvania*, 352.

25. Biddle and Dubin, *Tasting Freedom*, xix–x, 427.

26. Ershkowitz and Zikmund, *Black Politics in Philadelphia*, 9; Biddle and Dubin, *Tasting Freedom*, 428–29, 436–38, 468; Phil Lansansky, "Notes," WSP, LCP.

27. Silcox, "Negro Educator," 95–96. Silcox points out that a careful review of the *Christian Recorder* during the period 1870 to 1890 reveals that White's name appears on just a few occasions.

28. Klein and Hooganboom, *History of Pennsylvania*, 358–59.

29. Ibid., 356, 359–60.

30. Harry C. Silcox, "William McManus, Nineteenth Century Political Boss," *Pennsylvania Magazine of History and Biography* 110, no. 3 (July 1986): 406; Silcox, "Black 'Better Class' Political Dilemma," 51–52.

31. William Still, *Address on Voting and Laboring, March 10, 1874* (Philadelphia: Jason B. Rodgers, 1874), 8–9.

32. *Philadelphia Press*, January 20, 1874, and February 4, 1874,; Khan, *One Day, Levin*, 215–17; Albert S. Norwood, "Negro Welfare Work in Philadelphia, especially as illustrated by the Career of William Still, 1875–1900" (MA thesis, University of Pennsylvania, 1931), 104–5.

33. Reverend Theodore Gould et al. to William Still, March 2, 1874; and William Still to Rev. Gould et al., March 5, 1874, William Still, Letterbook, 1873–74, HSP. Among the individuals who signed the letter to Still were W. C. Banton, Rev. R. B. Johns, David Rosell, MD, Rev. John E. Price, William Crawford, A. R. Bascom, Rev. H. Mode, John F. Brown, William H. Scott, Chaplain W. H. Hunter, F. P. Main, Rev. B. T. Tanner, Warley Bascom, Robert Adger, Rev. John F. Thomas, Samuel Bevans, James W. Brown, Rev. M. F. Sluby, and James Fells. All of these men were active civil rights reformers, many of whom belonged to the Pennsylvania Equal Rights League.

34. *Philadelphia Press*, March 11, 1874.

35. W. Still, *Address on Voting*, 1–4.

36. Ibid., 6–7.

37. Ibid., 8–9.

38. Ibid., 15–16.

39. Licht, "Civil Wars," 253–55.

40. Price, "Black Voting Rights Issue," 371.

41. Du Bois, *Philadelphia Negro*, 23.

42. Ibid., 34.

43. Ibid., 35, 38–39.

CHAPTER FOURTEEN

1. Nathaniel Burt and Wallace Davis, "The Iron Age, 1876–1905," in Weigley, *Philadelphia*, 492–93; Lane, *William Dorsey's Philadelphia*, 256–57, 266–67; E. Lapsansky, *"Making It Home,"* 22.

2. Bordewich, *Bound for Canaan*, 435; Horton, "Crusade for Freedom," 192; Margaret Hope Bacon, "'One Great Bundle of Humanity': Frances Ellen Watkins Harper," *Pennsylvania Magazine of History and Biography* 113, no. 1 (January 1989): 25.

3. Du Bois, *Philadelphia Negro*, 50, 53.

4. Burt and Davis, "Iron Age," 492–43.

5. W. E. B. Du Bois, *Dusk of Dawn: An Essay toward an Autobiography of a Race Concept* (1940; repr., New York: Schocken, 1968), 58–59.

6. Du Bois, *Philadelphia Negro*, 58.

7. Ibid., 385–97.

8. Ibid., 392, 397.

9. Ibid., 35–36.

10. William Still to Caroline Still, April 30, 1866; Caroline Still to William Still, January 28, 1867; William Still to Caroline Still, August 13, 1867; William Still to Caroline Still, March 5, 1868; Caroline Still to Edward Wiley, February 17, 1869; Caroline Still to Edward Wiley, May 10, 1869; Edward Wiley to "Carrie" [Still], August 2, 1869; Caroline Still to Edward Wiley, June 18, 1873, all in WSC, CBAAC. Caroline Still was married twice. She married her first husband, Edward Wiley, in 1869 at age twenty-one. In the four years

they were married, the couple had two children, Letitia and William. Wiley died suddenly in 1873. In 1880 Caroline married again, to Reverend Matthew Anderson, a Presbyterian minister. The Andersons had five children together, three of whom survived to adulthood: Helen, Maude, and Margaret.

11. William Wilberforce Still to Caroline Ridgeway, March 29, 1873, WSC, CBAAC; Horton, "Crusade for Freedom," 193.

12. Horton, "Crusade for Freedom," 193.

13. W. Still, preface to *Underground Railroad* (1872/1970), xiii–xiv; Roger Lane, *William Dorsey's Philadelphia*, 105–6; Benjamin Quarles, "Foreword to the 1970 Edition," in W. Still, *Underground Railroad* (1872/1970), vii.

14. W. Still, preface to *Underground Railroad* (1872/1970), xii.

15. William Still to Dr. Henry Charles, June 6, 1873, and Still to J. W. Jones, November 4, 1873, both in WSP, HSP.

16. Hall, "To Render the Private Public," 39–40; Phillip Lapsansky, "Aboard William Still's Underground Railroad: Celebrating an African-American Classic," unpublished paper presented at the Library Company of Philadelphia, February 9, 1993. For other nineteenth-century accounts of the Underground Railroad, see Coffin, *Reminiscences*; Smedley, *History of the Underground Railroad*; and Siebert, *Underground Railroad*.

17. Lane, *William Dorsey's Philadelphia*, 260–62. Turner, Cain, and Porter founded the Liberian Exodus Association, bought a ship, and proposed to transport several hundred blacks to Africa for just thirty-five dollars each.

18. William Still, *The Underground Railroad* (Philadelphia: William Still, 1883), front matter. Still also claimed that he wrote the book to promote the "self-elevation of the colored man." William Still to J. C. Price, June 3, 1873, WSP, HSP.

19. Hall, "To Render the Private Public," 35–36.

20. Boyd, preface to W. Still, *Underground Railroad* (1886), ii–iii.

21. For the PASS resolution, see W. Still, "Author's Preface," in W. Still, *Underground Railroad* (1872/1970), xi.

22. Boyd, preface to W. Still, *Underground Railroad* (1886), xxxv–xxxvi.

23. Ibid., xxxv.

24. Tobin, *From Midnight to Dawn*, 74. Still asked Mary Ann Shadd Cary to contribute to the chapter of the Christiana Riot because he assumed that she had interviewed William Parker, one of the free black principals, before he fled to Canada. Although Cary did not reply to his request, she did return the favor of selling subscriptions to his published book, just as he had sold subscriptions to her antislavery newspaper two decades earlier. Still also encouraged Cary to write her own account of the Underground Railroad, though she was already considering a book on John Brown. Unfortunately, neither work ever came to fruition. Instead, Shadd turned her attentions to women's suffrage and became one of the first black students to enroll in Howard University's School of Law, completing her degree in 1883 at age sixty.

25. William Still to J. Miller McKim, November 10, 1871, quoted in Gara, "William Still and the Underground Railroad," 40.

26. Frederick Douglass to Wilbur H. Siebert, March 27, 1893, quoted in Gara, "William Still and the Underground Railroad," 40.

27. Boyd, preface to W. Still, *Underground Railroad* (1886), xxxv–xxxvi.

28. Hall, "To Render the Private Public," 43; Ronald J. Zboray, "Antebellum Reading and the Ironies of Technological Innovation," in *Reading in America: Literature and Social History*, ed. Cathy Davidson (Baltimore: Johns Hopkins University Press, 1989), 180–200.

29. "Agreement with Porter & Coates, Publishers," January 1, 1872, and "Supplemental Agreement," March 5, 1872, WSP, HSP.

30. Hall, "To Render the Private Public," 43–44; J. M. McKim to William Still, Lewellyn Park, PA, March 15, 1872, in Boyd, preface to W. Still, *Underground Railroad* (1886), xliii–xliv; Horace Greeley to William Still, February 22, 1872, in Boyd, preface to W. Still, *Underground Railroad* (1886), xiv; and Hon. Charles Sumner to William Still, March 3, 1872, in Boyd, preface to W. Still, *Underground Railroad* (1886), xxxviii–xl.

31. William Lloyd Garrison to William Still, April 7, 1872, in Boyd, preface to W. Still, *Underground Railroad* (1886), xliii.

32. Boyd, preface to W. Still, *Underground Railroad* (1886), xxxvi–xxxvii.

33. Salmon P. Chase to William Still, March 1, 1872, quoted in Boyd, preface to W. Still, *Underground Railroad* (1886), xxxvii.

34. Lapsansky, "Aboard William Still's Underground Railroad"; *Christian Recorder*, April 3 and 10, 1873; June 5, 12, 19, and 26, 1873; July 3, 10, 17, 24, and 31, 1873; and August 7, 14, 21, and 28, 1873.

35. "Underground Railroad stationery," WSP, HSP.

36. P. Lapsansky, "Aboard William Still's Underground Railroad"; Hall, "To Render the Private Public," 53. Two of the most highly publicized cases of fraud involved Felton Jones and William Perry, both agents in Delaware. When they refused to pay for book shipments, Still fired them and threatened to take legal action.

37. Hall, "To Render the Private Public," 50–51.

38. Ibid., 51; P. Lapsansky, "Aboard William Still's Underground Railroad." See also William Still to T. L. W. Titus, January 7, 1874, to W. D. Teiser, June 10, 1873, to Robert Furnas, June 18, 1873, to James E. Thompson, July 9, 1873, and to J. C. Proce, June 23, 1873, all in WSP, HSP.

39. Edward Wiley to Caroline Still Wiley, July 18, 1872. WSC, CBAAC.

40. Hall, "To Render the Private Public," 52.

41. Edward Wiley to Caroline Still Wiley, April 26, 1873, WSC, CBAAC.

42. William Still to Edward Wiley, May 22, 1873, WSC, CBAAC.

43. Hall, "To Render the Private Public," 52.

44. William Still to Edward Wiley, August 11, 1873, WSC, CBAAC.

45. Caroline Still Wiley to Edward Wiley, August 22, 1873, WSC, CBAAC.

46. William Still to Edward Wiley, September 27, 1873, WSC, CBAAC.

47. Edward Wiley to Caroline Still Wiley, October 2, 1873, WSC, CBAAC.

48. Caroline Still Wiley to Edward Wiley, November 19, 1873, WSC, CBAAC.

49. William Still to John Green, January 15, 1974, in W. Still, Letterbook, WSP, HSP.

50. M. Anderson to Caroline Still Wiley, May 5, 1874, WSC, CBAAC.

51. P. Lapsansky, "Aboard William Still's Underground Railroad."

52. Hall, "To Render the Private Public," 53–54.

53. "William Still Dead," *New York Times*, July 15, 1902.

54. Booker T. Washington, *Up from Slavery: An Autobiography* (Garden City, NY: Doubleday, 1900), 63–67.

55. Booker T. Washington, "Atlanta Exposition Speech" (1895), quoted in Franklin and Higginbotham, *From Slavery to Freedom*, 296.

56. Franklin and Higginbotham, *From Slavery to Freedom*, 297–98.

57. W. E. B. Du Bois, "Of Mr. Booker T. Washington and Others," in *The Souls of Black Folk* (New York: New America Library, 1969), 87. Du Bois failed to realize that Washington anticipated a future where full integration of the races would be achieved. He advocated vocational education only as the means by which blacks would achieve that integration.

58. W. E. B. Du Bois, "The Talented Tenth," in *The Negro Problem*, ed. Booker T. Washington (New York: James Potts, 1903), 31–32.

59. Franklin and Higginbotham, *From Slavery to Freedom*, 300–303. As the twentieth century unfolded, Washington became regarded by blacks as an Uncle Tom for his accommodationist philosophy. Du Bois, on the other hand, lost faith in integration and by the 1940s began to advocate a form of black self-segregation that led to his dismissal from the NAACP. Increasingly disillusioned with American society, he joined the Communist Party, renounced his US citizenship, and joined the African nationalist leader Kwame Nkrumah in Ghana. For a more complete account of Du Bois's life, see David Levering Lewis, *W.E.B. Du Bois: Biography of a Race, 1868–1919* (New York: Henry Holt, 1994), and *W.E.B. Du Bois: The Fight for Equality and the American Century, 1919–1963* (New York: Henry Holt, 2000).

BIBLIOGRAPHY

PRIMARY SOURCES

Special Collections

Anti-Slavery Collection, Boston Public Library

Charles L. Blockson Afro-American Collection, Temple University Libraries, Philadelphia, PA
 William Still Collection

Chester County Archives, Chester County Historical Society, West Chester, PA
 David Evans Journal, 1850–58, Evans Family Papers
 Passmore Williamson Letters, August-October, 1855
 Pennsylvania Yearly Meeting of Progressive Friends, *Proceedings*, 1853–60
 William Still, *The Underground Railroad* (Philadelphia: William Still, 1883).

Friends Historical Library, Swarthmore College, Swarthmore, PA
 Lucretia Mott Papers
 Philadelphia Meeting for Sufferings Minutes, 1830–60
 Philadelphia Yearly Meeting (Hicksite) Minutes, 1827–60

Genealogical Collection, Portsmouth Athenaeum, Portsmouth, NH
 John Langdon, William Whipple and Elwin Family Papers, 1713–1965

Gilder Lehrman Institute of American History Collection, www.gilderlehrman.org.
 "Address of John Brown to the Virginia Court," December 1859

Historical Society of Pennsylvania, Philadelphia
 Minute Book of the Vigilant Committee of Philadelphia, 1839–44, kept by Jacob C. White

Pennsylvania Anti-Slavery Society Records, 1852–70
William Still, "Address on Voting and Laboring," March 10, 1874
William Still, Journal C, interviews of runaways, 1853–61
William Still, Letterbook, 1873–74
William Still, *The Underground Railroad* (Philadelphia: Porter and Coates, 1872)
Library Company of Philadelphia
William Still, *The Underground Railroad* (Philadelphia: William Still, 1886), with life sketch by James P. Boyd
William Still's contract for publishing 1872 edition of *Underground Railroad*
Philip Lapsansky Papers
Quaker Collection, Haverford College Library, Haverford, PA
Philadelphia Yearly Meeting Minutes, 1688–26
Philadelphia Yearly Meeting (Orthodox) Minutes, 1827–60
Thomas P. Cope Family Papers: Letters of Thomas Garrett, 1854–57
Special Collections, Lincoln University, Jefferson City, MO

Newspapers

Anglo-African (New York)
Blue Hen's Chicken (Wilmington, DE)
Christian Recorder (Philadelphia)
Colored American (New York)
Daily Local News (West Chester, PA)
Friend (Philadelphia)
Friends' Review (Philadelphia)
Jeffersonian and Democratic Herald (West Chester, PA)
Lancaster Intelligencer and Journal (Lancaster, PA)
Liberator (Boston)
National Anti-Slavery Standard (Philadelphia and New York)
National Era (Washington. DC)
New York Herald
North American and United States Gazette (Philadelphia)
Oxford Press (Oxford, PA)
Pennsylvania Freeman (Philadelphia)
Philadelphia Bulletin
Philadelphia Press
Philadelphia Public Ledger
Provincial Freeman (Chatham and Toronto, Canada West)
Village Record (West Chester, PA)
Voice of the Fugitive (Sandwich, Canada West)

Books, Pamphlets, and Articles

American Anti-Slavery Society. *Annual Reports*. Vols. 1–6. New York: William S. Dorr and Butterfield, 1834–39.

Anderson, Osborne Perry. *A Voice from Harper's Ferry*. Washington, DC: J. D. Enos, 1878.

Aptheker, Herbert, ed. *A Documentary History of the Negro People in the United States*. New York: Citadel Press, 1951.

Bacon, Benjamin C. *Statistics of Colored People of Philadelphia*. Philadelphia: T. Ellwood Chapman, 1856. www.librarycompany.org/JaneJohnson/facsimiles/statistics01 .html.

Barbour, Hugh, and Arthur O. Roberts, eds. *Early Quaker Writings, 1650–1700*. Grand Rapids, MI: William B. Eerdmans, 1973.

Basler, Roy P., ed. *The Collected Works of Abraham Lincoln*. 9 vols. New Brunswick, NJ: Rutgers University Press, 1953–55.

Boyd, James P. Preface to *The Underground Railroad*, by William Still. Philadelphia: William Still, 1886.

Brackett, Jeffrey R. *The Negro in Maryland: A Study of the Institution of Slavery*. Baltimore: John Murphy, 1889.

Bradford, Sarah. *Scenes in the Life of Harriet Tubman*. Auburn, NY: W. J. Moses, 1869.

Brown, Henry. *Narrative of the Life of Henry Box Brown, Written by Himself*. Boston: Charles L. Stearns, 1849.

Brown, William Wells. "The Colored People of Canada." *Pine and Palm*, October 19, 1861. In "*Weekly Anglo-African* and *Pine and Palm*: Excerpts from 1861–62," edited by Brigitte Fielder, Cassander Smith, and Derrick R. Spires. Just Teach One. http:/ /jtoaa.common-place.org/wp-content/uploads/sites/3/2018/08/PineandPalm.pdf.

———. *Narrative of William W. Brown, a Fugitive Slave, Written by Himself* (1848). In *Puttin' on Ole Massa*, edited by Gilbert Osofsky. New York: Harper and Row, 1969.

———. *The Travels of William Wells Brown*. 1848. Reprint, New York: Marcus Weiner, 1991.

Browne, Mattie Griffith. *Autobiography of a Female Slave*. New York: Redfield, 1857.

Cannon, Arthur. *The Case of Passmore Williamson*. Philadelphia: Uriah Hunt and Son, 1856.

Cockrum, William. *History of the Underground Railroad as It Was Conducted by the Anti-Slavery League*. Oakland City, IN: J. W. Cockrum Printing, 1915.

Coffin, Levi. *Reminiscences*. Cincinnati, OH: Western Tract Society, 1876.

Craft, William. "Running a Thousand Miles for Freedom; or the Escape of William and Ellen Craft from Slavery, 1860." In *Slave Narratives*, edited by William L. Andrews and Henry Louis Gates Jr., 681–742. New York: Library of America, 2000.

Crafts, Hannah. *The Bondswoman's Narrative*. Edited by Henry Louis Gates. New York: Warner Books, 2002.

Douglass, Frederick. *My Bondage and My Freedom.* Edited by Philip S. Foner. 1855. Reprint, New York: Dover Publications, 1969.

———. "Temperance and Anti-slavery: An Address Delivered in Paisley, Scotland, March 30, 1846." In *Frederick Douglass Papers: Speeches, Debates and Interviews,* edited by John W. Blassingame, vol. 1, *1841–1846,* 200–208. New Haven, CT: Yale University Press, 1979.

Drew, Benjamin, ed. *The Narratives of Fugitive Slaves.* 1856. Reprint, Toronto: Prospero Books, 2000.

———. *A North-Side View of Slavery. The Refugee, or The Narratives of Fugitive Slaves in Canada, Related by Themselves: With an Account of the History and Condition of the Colored Population of Upper Canada.* 1856. Reprint, New York: Negro Universities Press, 1968.

Du Bois, W. E. B. *Dusk of Dawn: An Essay toward an Autobiography of a Race Concept.* 1940. Reprint, New York: Schocken, 1968.

———. *John Brown.* 1909. Reprint, New York: International Publishers, 1972.

———. "Of Mr. Booker T. Washington and Others." In *The Souls of Black Folk.* 1903. Reprint, New York: New American Library, 1969.

———. *The Philadelphia Negro: A Social Study.* 1899. Reprint, Philadelphia: University of Pennsylvania Press, 1996.

———. "The Talented Tenth." In *The Negro Problem,* edited by Booker T. Washington. New York: James Potts, 1903.

Duncan, Russell, ed. *Blue-Eyed Child of Fortune: The Civil War Letters of Colonel Robert Gould Shaw.* Athens: University of Georgia Press, 1992.

Emilio, Luis F. *A Brave Black Regiment: History of the Fifty-Fourth Regiment of Massachusetts Volunteer Infantry, 1863–1865.* Boston: Boston Book, 1894.

Foner, Philip S., and George S. Walker, eds. *Proceedings of the Black State Conventions, 1840–1865.* Philadelphia: Temple University Press, 1979.

Furness, William. "Seth Concklin." In *The Kidnapped and the Ransomed: Being the Personal Recollections of Peter Still and His Wife "Vina," after Forty Years of Slavery,* 3rd ed., by Kate E. R. Pickard, 377–409. Syracuse, NY: William T. Hamilton, 1856.

Futhey, J. Smith, and Gilbert Cope. *History of Chester County.* Philadelphia: Lippincott, 1881.

Hildreth, Richard. *Atrocious Judges.* New York: Miller, Orton and Mulligan, 1856.

Howe, S. G. *Report to the Freedmen's Inquiry Commission, 1864: The Refugees from Slavery in Canada West.* 1864. Reprint, Arno Press and New York Times, 1969.

Hunn, John. "An Account of the Escape from Slavery of Samuel Hawkins and Family on the Underground Railroad." In *The Underground Railroad,* by William Still, 551–60. Philadelphia: William Still, 1886.

Johnson, William Henry. *Autobiography.* Albany, NY: Argus, 1900.

Lewis, Joseph J. *A Memoir of Enoch Lewis.* West Chester, PA: Hickman, 1882.

Mott, Lucretia, and Elizabeth Cady Stanton. "Declaration of Sentiments" (1848). In *History of Woman Suffrage*, edited by Elizabeth Cady Stanton, 1:70–71. New York, 1881.

Parker, William. "Freedman's Story." *Atlantic Monthly*, February 1866.

Pennsylvania Anti-Slavery Society. *Narrative of Facts in the Case of Passmore Williamson*. Philadelphia: Pennsylvania Anti-Slavery Society, 1855.

Pennypacker, Samuel W. *Annals of Phoenixville and Its Vicinity: From the Settlement to the Year 1871*. Philadelphia: Bavis and Pennypacker, 1872.

Pettit, Eber. *Sketches in the History of the Underground Railroad*. 1867. Reprint, Westfield, NY: Chautauqua Regional Press, 1999.

Pickard, Kate E. R. *The Kidnapped and the Ransomed: Being the Personal Recollections of Peter Still and His Wife "Vina," after Forty Years of Slavery*. 3rd ed. Syracuse, NY: William T. Hamilton, 1856.

Proceedings of the Woman's Rights Convention Held at West Chester, PA. Philadelphia: Merrihew and Thompson, 1852.

Ripley, Peter, ed. *The Black Abolitionist Papers*. Vol. 2. *Canada, 1830–1865*. Chapel Hill: University of North Carolina Press, 1986.

Robbins, James R. *Report of the Trial of Castner Hanway for Treason*. Philadelphia, 1852.

Sanborn, Frederick, ed. *The Life and Letters of John Brown*. New York: Negro Universities Press, 1885.

Shadd, Mary Ann. *A Plea for Emigration or, Notes of Canada West, in Its Moral, Social and Political Aspect: With Suggestions Respecting Mexico, West Indies, and Vancouver's Island, for the Information of Colored Emigrants*. Detroit, MI: George W. Pattison, 1852.

Siebert, Wilbur H. *The Underground Railroad: From Slavery to Freedom*. 1898. Reprint, New York: Dover Publications, 2006.

Smedley, R. C. *History of the Underground Railroad in Chester and Neighboring Counties*. 1883. Reprint, Mechanicsburg, PA: Stackpole Books, 2005.

Still, Francis E. "Recollections of the Still Family History." In *The Underground Railroad*, by William Still. Philadelphia: William Still, 1886.

Still, William. *Address on Voting and Laboring, March 10, 1874*. Philadelphia: Jason B. Rodgers, 1874.

———. *A Brief Narrative of the Struggle for the Rights of the Colored People of Philadelphia in the Railway Cars; and a Defense of William Still Relating to His Agency Touching the Passage of the Late Bill*. Philadelphia: Merrihew and Son, 1867.

———. *The Underground Railroad*. 1872. Reprint, Chicago: Johnson, 1970.

———. *The Underground Railroad*. Philadelphia: William Still, 1883.

———. *The Underground Railroad*. Philadelphia: Porter and Coates, 1872.

———. *The Underground Railroad*. Philadelphia: William Still, 1886.

Taylor, George W. *The Autobiography and Writings of George W. Taylor*. Philadelphia, 1891.

US Department of State, *Sixth Census*. Washington, DC, 1841.

Vaux, Roberts. *Memoirs of the Lives of Benjamin Lay and Ralph Sandiford*. Philadelphia, 1815.

Ward, Samuel Ringgold. *Autobiography of a Fugitive Negro: His Anti-slavery Labors in the United States, Canada and England*. 1855. Reprint, Arno Press and New York Times, 1969.

Washington, Booker T., ed. *The Negro Problem*. New York: James Potts, 1903.

———. *Up from Slavery: An Autobiography*. Garden City, NY: Doubleday, 1900.

Washington, George. *The Writings of George Washington, 1745–1799*. Edited by John C. Fitzpatrick. 39 vols. Washington, DC: US Government Printing Office, 1931–44.

Woodson, Carter G., ed. *The Mind of the Negro as Reflected in Letters Written during the Crisis, 1800–1860*. Westport, CT: Greenwood Press, 1969.

Woolman, John. "Some Considerations on the Keeping of Negroes" (1754). In *The Journal and Major Essays of John Woolman*, edited by Philip Moulton, 198–209. New York: Oxford University Press, 1971.

SECONDARY SOURCES

American Council of Learned Studies. *Dictionary of American Biography*. 20 vols. New York: Charles Scribner's Sons, 1936.

Ayers, Edward L. *What Caused the Civil War? Reflections on the South and Southern History*. New York: W. W. Norton, 2005.

Bacon, Margaret H. *But One Race: The Life of Robert Purvis*. Albany: State University of New York Press, 2007.

———. *History of the Pennsylvania Society for Promoting the Abolition of Slavery*. Philadelphia: Pennsylvania Abolition Society, 1959.

———. *The Quiet Rebels: The Story of Quakers in America*. New York: Basic Books, 1969.

———. *Valiant Friend: The Life of Lucretia Mott*. New York: Walker, 1980.

Barbour, Hugh, and J. William Frost. *The Quakers*. Westport, CT: Greenwood Press, 1988.

Bauman, Richard. *For the Reputation of Truth: Politics, Religion, and Conflict among the Pennsylvania Quakers, 1750–1800*. Baltimore: Johns Hopkins University Press, 1971.

Bentley, Judith. *"Dear Friend": Thomas Garrett and William Still*. New York: Cobblehill Books / Dutton, 1997.

Berlin, Ira. "The Structure of the Free Negro Caste in the Antebellum United States." *Journal of Social History* 9 (Spring 1976): 305–11.

Biddle, Daniel R., and Murray Dubin. *Tasting Freedom: Octavius Catto and the Battle for Equality in Civil War America*. Philadelphia: Temple University Press, 2010.

Bisbee, Henry H. *Burlington Island: The Best and Largest on the South River, 1624–1972.* Burlington, NJ: Heidelberg Press, 1972.

Blackett, R. J. M. *The Captive's Quest for Freedom: Fugitive Slaves, the 1850 Fugitive Slave Law, and the Politics of Slavery.* Cambridge: Cambridge University Press, 2018.

Blassingame, John W. *The Slave Community: Plantation Life in the Antebellum South.* New York: Oxford University Press, 1972.

Blight, David W., ed. *Passages to Freedom; The Underground Railroad in History and Memory.* Washington, DC: Smithsonian Books, 2004.

———. "Why the Underground Railroad, and Why Now? A Long View." In Blight, *Passages to Freedom,* 233–47.

Blockson, Charles L. *African Americans in Pennsylvania: Above Ground and Underground. An Illustrated Guide.* Harrisburg, PA: RB Books, 2001.

———. "Escape from Slavery: The Underground Railroad." *National Geographic,* July 1984, 3–39.

———. *Hippocrene Guide to the Underground Railroad.* New York: Hippocrene, 1994.

———. *The Underground Railroad: Dramatic Firsthand Accounts of Daring Escapes to Freedom.* New York: Prentice Hall, 1987.

———. "The Underground Railroad: The Quaker Connection." In *For Emancipation and Education: Some Black and Quaker Efforts, 1680–1900,* edited by Germantown Historical Society and Awbury Arboretum Association. Philadelphia: Germantown Historical Society and Awbury Arboretum Association, 1997.

———. *The Underground Railroad in Pennsylvania.* Jacksonville, NC: Flame International, 1981.

Bordewich, Fergus M. *Bound for Canaan: The Underground Railroad and the War for the Soul of America.* New York: Amistad, 2005.

Boromé, Joseph A. "Robert Purvis and His Early Exposure to American Racism." *Negro History Bulletin* 30, no. 3 (1967): 8–10.

———. "The Vigilant Committee of Philadelphia." *Pennsylvania Magazine of History and Biography* 92 (July 1968): 320–51.

Breyfogle, William A. *Make Free: The Story of the Underground Railroad.* Philadelphia: J. B. Lippincott, 1958.

Brinton, Howard. *The Religious Philosophy of Quakerism.* Wallingford, PA: Pendle Hill Press, 1969.

Brown, Ira V. "Miller McKim and Pennsylvania Abolitionism." *Pennsylvania History* 20 (1963): 56–72.

Brown, Maxine F. *The Role of Free Blacks in Indiana's Underground Railroad: The Case of Floyd, Harrison and Washington Counties.* Indianapolis: Indiana Department of Natural Resources, 2001.

Buckmaster, Henrietta. *Let My People Go: The Story of the Underground Railroad and the Growth of the Abolition Movement.* New York: Harper and Brothers, 1941.

Caccamo, James F. *Hudson, Ohio, and the Underground Railroad.* Hudson, OH: Friends of the Hudson Library, 1992.

Cadbury, Henry J. "Negro Membership in the Society of Friends." *Journal of Negro History* 21 (1936): 151–213.

Campbell, Stanley W. *The Slave Catchers: Enforcement of the Fugitive Slave Law, 1850–1860.* Chapel Hill: University of North Carolina Press, 1968.

Carey, Brycchan. *From Peace to Freedom: Quaker Rhetoric and the Birth of American Anti-slavery, 1657–1761.* New Haven, CT: Yale University Press, 2012.

Christy, David. *Pulpit Politics, or Ecclesiastical Legislation on Slavery in Its Disturbing Influences on the American Union.* New York: Farran and McLean, 1862.

Clark, Denis. "Urban Blacks and Irishmen: Brothers in Prejudice." In *Black Politics in Philadelphia,* edited by Miriam Ershkowitz and Joseph Zikmund, 15–30. New York: Basic Books, 1973.

Clinton, Catherine. *Harriet Tubman: The Road to Freedom.* Boston: Little, Brown, 2004.

Coffey, Michael, ed. *The Irish in America.* New York: Hyperion, 1997.

Courlander, Harold. *Negro Folk Music, U.S.A.* 1963. Reprint, New York: Dover, 1992.

Crew, Spencer R. "The Saga of Peter Still." Paper presented as Twenty-Fourth Annual Louis Faugeres Bishop III Lecture, Alexander Library of Rutgers University, February 23, 2009.

Davis, David Brion. *The Problem of Slavery in the Age of Emancipation.* New York: Alfred A. Knopf, 2014.

———. *Slavery and Human Progress.* New York: Oxford University Press, 1984.

Davis, F. James. *Who Is Black? One Nation's Definition.* University Park: Penn State University Press, 1991.

Davis, Hugh. "The Pennsylvania State Equal Rights League and the Northern Black Struggle for Equality: 1864–1877." *Pennsylvania Magazine of History and Biography* 126, no. 4 (October 2002): 611–34.

de B'beri, Boulou Ebanda, et al. *The Promised Land: History and Historiography of the Black Experience in Chatham-Kent's Settlements and Beyond.* Toronto: University of Toronto Press, 2014.

Densmore, Christopher. "Be Ye Therefore Perfect: Anti-slavery and the Origins of the Yearly Meeting of Progressive Friends in Chester County, Pennsylvania." *Quaker History* 93, no. 2 (Fall 2004): 28–46.

———. Introduction to *History of the Underground Railroad in Chester and Neighboring Counties,* by R. C. Smedley. 1883. Reprint, Mechanicsburg, PA: Stackpole Books, 2005.

Doherty, Robert W. *The Hicksite Separation: A Sociological Analysis of Religious Schism in Early Nineteenth Century America.* New Brunswick, NJ: Rutgers University Press, 1967.

Drake, Thomas E. *Quakers and Slavery in America.* 1950. Reprint, Gloucester, MA: Peter Smith, 1965.

Ducksworth, Sarah Smith. Foreword to *Underground Railroad*, by William Still. 1872. Reprint, Medford, NJ: Plexus, 2005.

Ershkowitz, Miriam, and Joseph Zikmund II, eds. Introduction to *Black Politics in Philadelphia*. New York: Basic Books, 1973.

Etcheson, Nicole. *Bleeding Kansas: Contested Liberty in the Civil War Era*. Lawrence: University of Kansas Press, 2006.

Fehrenbacher, Don E. *The Dred Scott Case: Its Significance in American Law and Politics* New York: Oxford University Press, 1978.

Feldberg, Michael. *The Philadelphia Riots of 1844: A Study of Ethnic Conflict*. Westport, CT: Greenwood Press, 1975.

Finkelman, Paul. "Scott v. Sanford: The Court's Most Dreadful Case and How It Changed History." *Chicago-Kent Law Review* 82 (December 2006): 3–48.

Fisher, Miles M. *Negro Slave Songs in the United States*. New York: Citadel, 1968.

Fishman, George. *The African American Struggle for Freedom and Equality The Development of a People's Identity, New Jersey, 1624–1850*. New York: Garland, 1997.

Floyd, Samuel A., Jr. *The Power of Black Music*. New York: Oxford University Press, 1995.

Flynn, Katherine E. "Jane Johnson, Found! But Is She 'Hannah Crafts'? The Search for the Author of *The Bondswoman's Narrative*." *National Geographic Society Quarterly* 90 (September 2002): 165–90.

Foner, Eric. *Gateway to Freedom: The Hidden History of the Underground Railroad*. New York: W. W. Norton, 2015.

Foner, Philip S. "The Battle to End Discrimination against Negroes on Philadelphia Streetcars: (Part I): Background and the Beginnings of the Battle." *Pennsylvania History* 40 (April 1973): 261–92.

———. "The Battle to End Discrimination against Negroes on Philadelphia Streetcars: (Part II): The Victory." *Pennsylvania History* 40 (October 1973): 355–79.

———. *History of Black Americans: From the Emergence of the Cotton Kingdom to the Eve of the Compromise of 1850*. Westport, CT: Greenwood Press, 1983.

Forbes, Ella. *But We Have No Country: The 1851 Christiana Resistance*. Cherry Hill, NJ: Africana Homestead Legacy, 1998.

Fradin, Dennis B. *My Family Shall Be Free*. New York: Harper Collins, 2001.

Franklin, John Hope, and Evelyn Brooks Higginbotham. *From Slavery to Freedom: A History of Negro Americans*. 9th ed. New York: McGraw-Hill, 2011.

Franklin, John Hope, and Loren Schweninger. *Runaway Slaves: Rebels on the Plantation*. New York: Oxford University Press, 1999.

Freeman, Roland L. *A Communion of the Spirits: African-American Quilters, Preservers and Their Stories*. Nashville, TN: Rutledge Hill, 1996.

Fry, Gladys-Marie. *Stitched from the Soul: Slave Quilts from the Antebellum South*. New York: Dutton, 1990.

Gara, Larry. *The Liberty Line: The Legend of the Underground Railroad*. 1961. Reprint, Lexington: University of Kentucky Press, 1996.

———. "William Still and the Underground Railroad." *Pennsylvania History* 28 (January 1961): 33–44.

Gates, Henry Louis. "The Fugitive." *New Yorker*, February 18–25, 2002, 104–8, 113–15.

———. Introduction to Crafts, *Bondswoman's Narrative*.

———. "A Note on Crafts' Literary Influences." In Crafts, *Bondswoman's Narrative*, 331–32.

Gatewood, Willard B. *Aristocrats of Color: The Black Elite, 1880–1920*. Bloomington: Indiana University Press, 1990.

Genovese, Eugene D. *Roll, Jordan, Roll: The World the Slaves Made*. 1972. Reprint, New York: Vintage, 1974.

———. *The World the Slaveholders Made*. New York: Pantheon, 1969.

Gigantino, James J., Jr. *The Ragged Road to Abolition: Slavery and Freedom in New Jersey, 1775–1865*. Philadelphia: University of Pennsylvania Press, 2015.

Goss, Linda, and Clay Goss. *Jump Up and Say: A Collection of Black Storytelling*. New York: Simon and Schuster, 1995.

Grover, Kathryn. *The Fugitive's Gibraltar: Escaping Slaves and Abolitionism in New Bedford, Massachusetts*. Amherst: University of Massachusetts Press, 2001.

Hagedorn, Ann. *Beyond the River: The Untold Story of the Heroes of the Underground Railroad*. New York: Simon and Schuster, 2002.

Hall, Stephen G. "To Render the Private Public: William Still and the Selling of the Underground Rail Road." *Pennsylvania Magazine of History and Biography* 127, no. 1 (January 2003): 35–55.

Hamilton, Virginia. *The People Could Fly: American Black Folktales*. New York: Alfred Knopf, 1985.

Harrold, Stanley. "The Pearl Affair: The Washington Riot of 1848." *Records of the Columbia Historical Society* 50 (1980): 140–60.

———. *Subversives: Antislavery Community in Washington, D.C., 1828–1865*. Baton Rouge: Louisiana State University Press, 2003.

Henry, Natasha L. "The Underground Railroad in Canada." In *The Canadian Encyclopedia*, online ed., edited by Bronwen Graves. Retrieved January 12, 2018. www.the canadianencyclopedia.ca/en/article/underground-railroad/.

Hensel, William U. *The Christiana Riot and the Treason Trial of 1851*. Lancaster, PA: New Era Printing, 1911.

Hershberg, Theodore. "Free Blacks in Antebellum Philadelphia: A Study of Ex-slaves, Freeborn, and Socioeconomic Decline." *Journal of Social History* 5 (December 1971): 183–209.

———. *Philadelphia: Work, Space, Family and Group Experience in the 19th Century*. New York: Oxford University, 1981.

Hill, Daniel G. *The Freedom Seekers: Blacks in Early Canada*. Toronto: Stoddart, 1992.

Holmes, Marian Smith. "The Great Escape from Slavery of Ellen and William Craft." *Smithsonian Magazine*, June 16, 2010. www.smithsonianmag.com/history/the -great-escape-from-slavery-of-ellen-and-william-craft-497960/.

Horton, James Oliver. "A Crusade for Freedom: William Still and the Real Underground Railroad." In Blight, *Passages to Freedom*, 175–94.

———. *Free People of Color: Inside the African American Community*. Washington, DC: Smithsonian Institution Press, 1993.

Horton, James Oliver, and Lois E. Horton. *Black Bostonians: Family Life and Community Struggle in the Antebellum North*. Rev. ed. New York: Homes and Meier, 1999.

———. *Hard Road to Freedom: The Story of African America*. New Brunswick, NJ: Rutgers University Press, 2001.

———. *In Hope of Liberty: Culture, Community and Protest among Northern Free Blacks, 1700–1860*. New York: Oxford University Press, 1997.

———. *Slavery and the Making of America*. New York: Oxford University Press, 2005.

Hudson, J. Blaine. *Fugitive Slaves and the Underground Railroad in the Kentucky Borderland*. Jefferson, NC: McFarland, 2002.

Humez, Jean M. *Harriet Tubman: The Life and the Life Stories*. Madison: University of Wisconsin Press, 2003.

Ingle, H. Larry. *Quakers in Conflict: The Hicksite Reformation*. Knoxville: University of Tennessee, 1986.

Jackson, Maurice. *Let This Voice Be Heard: Anthony Benezet, Father of Atlantic Abolitionism*. Philadelphia: University of Pennsylvania Press, 2010.

James, Arthur E. *The Potters and Potteries of Chester County, Pennsylvania*. West Chester, PA: D. Edwards Biehn, 1945.

James, Sydney V. *A People among Peoples: Quaker Benevolence in Eighteenth-Century America*. Cambridge, MA: Harvard University Press, 1963.

Jeffrey, Julie R. *The Great Silent Army of Abolitionism: Ordinary Women in the Antislavery Movement*. Chapel Hill: University of North Carolina Press, 1998.

Johnson, James E. "A History of Camp William Penn and Its Black Troops in the Civil War, 1863–1865." PhD diss., University of Pennsylvania, 1999.

Jordan, Ryan P. *Slavery and the Meetinghouse: The Quakers and the Abolitionist Dilemma, 1820–1865*. Bloomington: Indiana University Press, 2007.

Kashatus, William C. "In Immortal Splendor: Wilkes-Barre's Fugitive Slave Case of 1853." *Pennsylvania Heritage*, Spring 2008, 24–31.

———. *Just over the Line: Chester County and the Underground Railroad*. University Park: Penn State University Press, 2002.

———. "Two Station Masters on the Underground Railroad: A Tale of Black and White." *Pennsylvania Heritage*, Fall 2001, 8–16.

———. *A Virtuous Education: William Penn's Vision for Philadelphia Schools*. Wallingford, PA: Pendle Hill, 1997.

Katz, Jonathan. *Resistance at Christiana: A Documentary Account*. New York: Thomas Crowell, 1974.

Khan, Lurey. *One Day, Levin . . . He Be Free: William Still and the Underground Railroad*. Lincoln, NE: iUniverse, Inc., 2002.

Klein, Philip S., and Ari Hooganboom. *A History of Pennsylvania.* 2nd ed. University Park: Penn State University Press, 1980.

Kneebone, John T. "A Breakdown on the Underground Railroad: Captain B. and the Capture of Keziah, 1858." *Virginia Cavalcade* 48, no. 2 (Spring 1999): 74–83.

Kolchin, Peter. *American Slavery, 1619–1877.* New York: Hill and Wang, 1993.

Kraditor, Aileen S. *Means and Ends in American Abolitionism: Garrison and His Critics on Strategy and Tactics, 1834–1850.* 1967. Reprint, Vintage, 1970.

Landon, Fred. "Henry Bibb, a Colonizer." *Journal of Negro History* 5, no. 4 (1920): 442–47.

———. "The Negro Migration to Canada after the Passage of the Fugitive Slave Act." *Journal of Negro History* 5 (January 1920): 22–28.

Lane, Roger. *William Dorsey's Philadelphia and Ours: On the Past and Future of the Black City in America.* New York: Oxford University Press, 1991.

Lapsansky, Emma. *"Making It Home": Black Presence in Pennsylvania.* University Park: Pennsylvania Historical Association, 1990.

Lapsansky, Phillip. "Aboard William Still's Underground Railroad: Celebrating the African-American Classic." Paper presented at the Library Company of Philadelphia, February 9, 1993.

Larson, Kate Clifford. *Bound for the Promised Land: Harriet Tubman, Portrait of an American Hero.* New York: Ballantine Books, 2004.

Laurie, Bruce. *Working People of Philadelphia, 1800–1850.* Philadelphia: Temple University Press, 1980.

Levine, Bruce. *Half Slave and Half Free: The Roots of the Civil War.* New York: Hill and Wang, 1992.

Lewis, David Levering. *W.E.B. Du Bois: Biography of a Race, 1868–1919.* New York: Henry Holt, 1994.

———. *W.E.B. Du Bois: The Fight for Equality and the American Century, 1919–1963.* New York: Henry Holt, 2000.

Lomax, Michael E. *Black Baseball Entrepreneurs, 1860–1901.* Syracuse, NY: Syracuse University Press, 2003.

Lyght, Ernest. *Path of Freedom: The Black Presence in New Jersey's Burlington County, 1659–1900.* Cherry Hill, NJ: E & E Publishing House, 1978.

Mabee, Carleton. *Black Freedom: The Nonviolent Abolitionists from 1830 through the Civil War.* New York: Macmillan, 1970.

Maddox, Lucy. *The Parker Sisters: A Border Kidnapping.* Philadelphia: Temple University Press, 2016.

Marietta, Jack. *The Reformation of American Quakerism, 1748–1783.* Philadelphia: University of Pennsylvania Press, 1984.

Marks, Carole C., ed. *A History of African Americans of Delaware and Maryland's Eastern Shore.* Wilmington: Delaware Heritage Commission, 1998.

Mayer, Henry. *All on Fire: William Lloyd Garrison and the Abolition of Slavery.* New York: St. Martin's Press, 1998.

McDaniel, Donna, and Vanessa Julye. *Fit for Freedom, Not for Friendship: Quakers, African Americans and the Myth of Racial Justice.* Philadelphia: Quaker Press, 2009.

McFeely, William S. *Frederick Douglass.* New York: W. W. Norton, 1991.

McGowan, James A. *Station Master on the Underground Railroad: The Life and Letters of Thomas Garrett.* Rev. ed. Jefferson, NC: McFarland, 2005.

McPherson, James M. *Battle Cry of Freedom: The Civil War Era.* 1988. Reprint, New York: Oxford University Press, 1989.

———. *The Negro's Civil War: How American Blacks Felt and Acted during the War for the Union.* 3rd ed. New York: Ballantine Books, 1991.

———. *Ordeal by Fire: The Civil War and Reconstruction.* 3rd ed. New York: McGraw-Hill, 2001.

———. *This Mighty Scourge: Perspectives on the Civil War.* New York: Oxford University Press, 2007.

Mekeel, Arthur J. *The Quakers and the American Revolution.* York: William Sessions, 1996.

Miller, Randall M., and William Pencak, eds. *Pennsylvania: A History of the Commonwealth.* University Park: Penn State University Press, 2002.

Morris, Thomas D. *Free Men All: The Personal Liberty Laws of the North, 1780–1861.* Baltimore: Johns Hopkins University Press, 1974.

Nash, Gary B. *First City: Philadelphia and the Forging of Historical Memory.* Philadelphia: University of Pennsylvania Press, 2002.

———. *Forging Freedom: The Formation of Philadelphia's Black Community, 1720–1840.* Cambridge, MA: Harvard University Press, 1988.

———. *Warner Mifflin: Unflinching Quaker Abolitionist.* Philadelphia: University of Pennsylvania Press, 2017.

Nash, Gary B., and Jean R. Soderlund, *Freedom by Degrees: Emancipation in Pennsylvania and Its Aftermath.* New York: Oxford University Press, 1991.

Newman, Richard S. "Abolitionism." In *The Encyclopedia of Greater Philadelphia.* New Brunswick, NJ: Rutgers University, 2012. Retrieved November 20, 2017. philadelphiaencyclopedia.org/archive/abolitionism/.

———. "The Pennsylvania Abolition Society: Restoring a Group to Glory." *Pennsylvania Legacies*, November 2005, 6–10.

Newman, Richard S., and James Mueller, eds. *Anti-slavery and Abolition in Philadelphia.* Baton Rouge: Louisiana State University Press, 2011.

Norwood, Alberta. "Negro Welfare in Philadelphia as Illustrated by the Career of William Still." MA thesis, University of Pennsylvania, 1931.

Oates, Stephen B. *To Purge This Land with Blood: A Biography of John Brown.* Amherst: University of Massachusetts Press, 1984.

Owens, Leslie H. *This Species of Property: Slave Life and Culture in the Old South.* New York: Oxford University Press, 1976.

Pease, William H., and Jane Pease. *Black Utopia: Negro Communal Experiments in America*. Madison: Wisconsin State Historical Society, 1963.

Pennsylvania Historical and Museum Commission. "Editor's Note" to "An Act for the Gradual Abolition of Slavery, March 1, 1780." In *Documenting Pennsylvania's Past*, 58–59. Harrisburg: Pennsylvania Historical and Museum Commission, 2003.

Peters, Pamela R. *The Underground Railroad in Floyd County, Indiana*. Jefferson, NC: McFarland, 2001.

Pinsker, Matthew. "After 1850: Reassessing the Impact of the Fugitive Slave Law." In *Fugitive Slaves and Spaces of Freedom in North America*, edited by Damian Alan Pargas, 93–115. Gainesville: University of Florida Press, 2018.

———. *Vigilance in Pennsylvania: Underground Railroad Activities in the Keystone State, 1837–1861*. Harrisburg: Pennsylvania Historical and Museum Commission, 2000.

Pirtle, Carol. *Escape betwixt Two Suns: A True Tale of the Underground Railroad in Illinois*. Carbondale: Southern Illinois University Press, 2000.

Potter, David M. *The Impending Crisis: America before the Civil War, 1848–1861*. New York: Harper and Row, 1976.

Quarles, Benjamin. *Allies for Freedom: Blacks and John Brown*. New York: Oxford University Press, 1974.

———. *Black Abolitionists*. New York: Oxford University Press, 1969.

———. "Foreword to the 1970 Edition." In *The Underground Railroad*, by William Still. 1872. Reprint, Chicago: Johnson, 1970.

Rediker, Marcus. *The Fearless Benjamin Lay: The Quaker Dwarf Who Became the First Revolutionary Abolitionist*. Boston: Beacon Press, 2017.

Renehan, Edward J., Jr. *The Secret Six: The True Tale of the Men Who Conspired with John Brown*. New York: Crown, 1995.

Reynolds, David S. *John Brown, Abolitionist: The Man Who Killed Slavery, Sparked the Civil War and Seeded Civil Rights*. New York: Vintage, 2006.

Rhodes, Jane. *Mary Ann Shadd Cary: The Black Press and Protest in the Nineteenth Century*. Bloomington: Indiana University Press, 1998.

Ricks, Mary Kay. *Escape on the Pearl: The Heroic Bid for Freedom on the Underground Railroad*. New York: Harper, 2008.

Riddell, William R. "The Slave in Upper Canada." *Journal of Criminal Law and Criminology* 14, no. 2 (1923): 249–78.

Ripley, C. Peter. *The Underground Railroad*. Washington, DC: US Department of the Interior / National Park Service, 1998.

Rizzo, Dennis. *Parallel Communities: The Underground Railroad in South Jersey*. New York: History Press, 2008.

Roan, Nancy, and Donald Roan. *Lest I Shall Be Forgotten: Anecdotes and Traditions of Quilts*. Green Lane, PA: Goschenhoppen Historians, 1993.

Russell, Hilary. *The Operation of the Underground Railroad in Washington, D.C., 1800–1860*. Washington, DC: Historical Society of Washington and National Park Service, 2001.

Sanelli, Thomas A. "The Struggle for Black Suffrage in Pennsylvania, 1838–1870." PhD diss., Temple University Press, 1977.

Schrag, Zachary M. "Nativist Riots of 1844." In *Encyclopedia of Greater Philadelphia.*, edited by Mid-Atlantic Regional Center for the Humanities. n.d. Retrieved November 15, 2017, https://philadelphiaencyclopedia.org/archives/nativist-riots-of-1844.

Scott, Donald. *Camp William Penn, 1863–1865.* Atglen, PA: Schiffer Books, 2012.

Sernett, Milton C. *Harriet Tubman: Myth, Memory, and History.* Durham, NC: Duke University Press, 2007.

———. *North Star Country: Upstate New York and the Crusade for African American Freedom.* Syracuse, NY: Syracuse University Press, 2002.

Silcox, Harry C. "The Black 'Better Class' Political Dilemma: Philadelphia Prototype Isaiah C. Wears." *Pennsylvania Magazine of History and Biography* 113, no. 1 (January 1989): 45–66.

———. "Negro Educator: Jacob C. White, Jr." *Pennsylvania Magazine of History and Biography* 97, no. 1 (January 1973): 75–98.

———. "Nineteenth Century Philadelphia Black Militant: Octavius Catto, 1839–1871." *Pennsylvania History* 44 (1977): 53–76.

Silverman, Jason. *Unwelcome Guests: American Fugitive Slaves in Canada, 1830–1860.* Millwood, NY: Associated Faculty Press, 1985.

Sinha, Manisha. *The Slave's Cause: A History of Abolitionism.* New Haven, CT: Yale University Press, 2016.

Slaughter, Thomas P. *The Beautiful Soul of John Woolman, Apostle of Abolition.* New York: Hill and Wang, 2008.

———. *Bloody Dawn: The Christiana Riot and Racial Violence in the Antebellum North.* New York: Oxford University Press, 1991.

Small, Clara L. "Abolitionists, Free Blacks and Runaway Slaves: Surviving Slavery on Maryland's Eastern Shore." In *A History of African Americans of Delaware and Maryland's Eastern Shore*, edited by Carole C. Marks, 55–73. Wilmington: Delaware Heritage Commission, 1998.

Smith, Billy G., and Richard Wojtowicz. *Blacks Who Stole Themselves: Advertisements for Runaways in the* Pennsylvania Gazette, *1728–1790.* Philadelphia: University of Pennsylvania Press, 1989.

Soderlund, Jean R. "Priorities and Power: The Philadelphia Female Anti-Slavery Society." In *The Abolitionist Sisterhood: Women's Political Culture in Antebellum America*, edited by Jean Fagan Yellin and John C. Van Horne, 67–88. Ithaca, NY: Cornell University Press, 1994.

———. *Quakers and Slavery: A Divided Spirit.* Princeton, NJ: Princeton University Press, 1985.

Stampp, Kenneth M. *The Imperiled Union: Essays on the Background of the Civil War.* New York: Oxford University Press, 1981.

———. *The Peculiar Institution: Slavery in the Ante-Bellum South.* New York: Vintage, 1956.

Stevens, Kathleen. *William Still and the Underground Railroad*. West Berlin, NJ: Townsend Press, 2008.

Strother, Horatio T. *The Underground Railroad in Connecticut*. Middletown, CT: Wesleyan University Press, 1962.

Sweet, William W. *The Story of Religion in America*. New York: Harper and Row, 1930.

Switala, William J. *Underground Railroad in Delaware, Maryland and West Virginia*. Mechanicsburg, PA: Stackpole Books, 2004.

———. *The Underground Railroad in New York and New Jersey*. Mechanicsburg, PA: Stackpole Books, 2006.

———. *Underground Railroad in Pennsylvania*. Mechanicsburg, PA: Stackpole Books, 2001.

Taylor, Francis C. *The Trackless Trail Leads On*. Kennett Square, PA: KNA Press, 1995.

Thomas, Hugh. *The Slave Trade: The Story of the Atlantic Slave Trade, 1440–1870*. New York: Simon and Schuster, 1997.

Tobin, Jacqueline L. *From Midnight to Dawn: The Last Tracks of the Underground Railroad*. With Hettie Jones. New York: Doubleday, 2007.

Tobin, Jacqueline L., and Raymond G. Dobard. *Hidden in Plain View: A Secret Story of Quilts and the Underground Railroad*. New York: Anchor, 2000.

Tolles, Frederick. *Meeting House and Counting House: The Quaker Merchants of Colonial Philadelphia, 1682–1763*. Chapel Hill: University of North Carolina Press, 1948.

Turner, Diane. "William Still's National Significance." n.d. William Still Online Collection, Temple University Libraries, Philadelphia. Retrieved February 10, 2018. http://stillfamily.library.temple.edu/exhibits/show/william-still/historical-perspective/william-still---s-national-sig.

Turner, Edward R. "The First Abolitionist Society in the United States." *Pennsylvania Magazine of History and Biography* 36, no. 1 (1912): 94–95.

———. *The Negro in Pennsylvania: Slavery, Servitude, Freedom, 1639–1861*. New York: Negro Universities Press, 1910.

Varon, Elizabeth. "'Beautiful Providences': William Still, the Vigilance Committee and Abolitionists in the Age of Sectionalism." In *Antislavery and Abolition in Philadelphia: Emancipation and the Long Struggle for Racial Justice in the City of Brotherly Love*, edited by Richard Newman and James Mueller, 229–46. Baton Rouge: Louisiana State University Press, 2011.

Vishneski, John S. "What the Court Decided in *Dred Scott v. Sandford*." *American Journal of Legal History* 32, no. 4 (October 1988): 373–90.

Wagenknecht, Edward. *John Greenleaf Whittier: A Portrait in Paradox*. New York: Oxford University Press, 1967.

Wahl, Albert J. "The Congregational or Progressive Friends in the Pre–Civil War Reform Movement." PhD diss., Temple University, 1951.

———. "The Progressive Friends of Longwood." *Friends Historical Society Bulletin* 42, no. 1 (Spring 1953): 14–16.

Wainwright, Nicholas B. "The Age of Nicholas Biddle, 1825–1841." In Weigley, *Philadelphia*, 258–306.

Warner, Sam Bass. *Philadelphia: The Private City*. Rev. ed. Philadelphia: University of Pennsylvania Press, 1987.

Watts, Dale E. "How Bloody Was Bleeding Kansas? Political Killings in Kansas Territory, 1854–1861," *Kansas History* 18, no. 2 (Summer 1995): 116–29.

Wayne, Michael. "The Black Population of Canada West on the Eve of the American Civil War: A Reassessment Based on the Manuscript Census of 1861." *Histoire Sociale / Social History* 56 (November 1995): 465–85.

Webb, Samuel *History of Pennsylvania Hall*. Philadelphia: Merrihew and Gunn, 1838.

Weigley, Russell F. "The Border City in Civil War, 1854–1865." In Weigley, *Philadelphia*, 363–416.

———, ed. *Philadelphia: A 300-Year History*. New York: W. W. Norton, 1982.

Whitson, Thomas. "The Early Abolitionists of Lancaster County." *Historical Papers and Addresses of the Lancaster County Historical Society* 15, no. 3 (1911): 69–86.

Williams, Carolyn. "Religion, Race and Gender in Antebellum American Radicalism: The Philadelphia Female Anti-Slavery Society, 1833–1870." PhD diss., UCLA, 1991.

Williams, William H. *Slavery and Freedom in Delaware, 1639–1865*. Wilmington, DE: Scholarly Resources, 2001.

Williamson, Joel. *New People: Miscegenation and Mulattoes in the United States*. New York: Free Press, 1980.

Winch, Julie. *A Gentleman of Color: The Life of James Forten*. New York: Oxford University Press, 2002.

———. "Philadelphia and the Other Underground Railroad." *Pennsylvania Magazine of History and Biography* 61 (January 1987): 3–25.

———. *Philadelphia's Black Elite: Activism, Accommodation and the Struggle for Autonomy, 1787–1848*. Philadelphia: Temple University Press, 1988.

Winks, Robin. *Blacks in Canada: A History*. New Haven, CT: Yale University Press, 1971.

Wolf, Margaret L. *A History of West Whiteland*. Exton, PA: West Whiteland Historical Commission, 1982.

Wright, Giles R., and Edward L. Wonkeryor. *"Steal Away, Steal Away . . .": A Guide to the Underground Railroad in New Jersey*. Trenton: New Jersey Historical Commission, 2002.

Yellin, Jean F., and John C. Van Horne, eds. *The Abolitionist Sisterhood: Women's Political Culture in Antebellum America*. Ithaca, NY: Cornell University Press, 1994.

Zboray, Ronald J. "Antebellum Reading and the Ironies of Technological Innovation." In *Reading in America: Literature and Social History*, edited by Cathy Davidson, 180–200. Baltimore: Johns Hopkins University Press, 1989.

Zirblis, Raymond P. *Friends of Freedom: The Vermont Underground Railroad Survey Report*. Montpelier: State of Vermont Department of State Buildings and Division for Historic Preservation, 1996.

INDEX

Page numbers in italics refer to figures.

WILLIAM C. KASHATUS

holds a doctorate in history education from the University of Pennsylvania.

He curated *Just Over the Line: Chester County and the Underground Railroad*,

recognized by *The Journal of American History* as a

"first rate exhibit and model of outreach to the local community"

and winner of the American Association of Historical Societies

and Museums Award of Merit.

He is the author or co-author of thirty books, including

Harriet Tubman: A Biography and *In Pursuit of Freedom:*

Teaching the Underground Railroad.